Shojo Beat

ORESAMA
TEACHER

Vol. 13

Story & Art by
Izumi Tsubaki

ORESAMA TEACHER

Volume 13
CONTENTS

ORESAMA TEACHER

CHARACTERS AND THE STORY THUS FAR

PUBLIC MORALS CLUB

Mafuyu Kurosaki

THE FORMER BANCHO OF SAITAMA EAST HIGH. SHE ALSO PLAYS THE PARTS OF NATSUO AND SUPER BUN. SHE IS CONCERNED BY THE FACT THAT SHE HAS NO FEMALE FRIENDS.

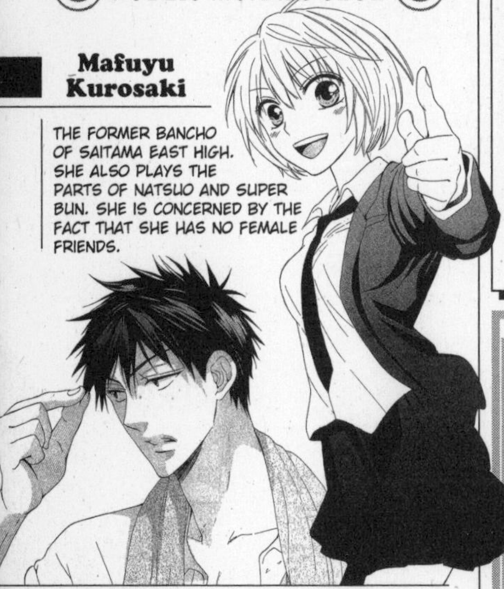

Takaomi Saeki

THE ONE RESPONSIBLE FOR TURNING MAFUYU INTO A TERRIFYING PERSON. HE'S NOW MAFUYU'S HOMEROOM TEACHER AND THE ADVISOR OF THE PUBLIC MORALS CLUB.

Public Morals Club

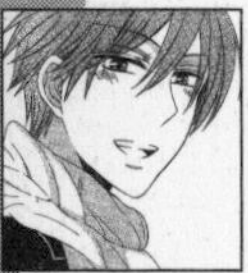

HAYASAKA

MAFUYU'S CLASSMATE. HE ADMIRES SUPER BUN. HE IS A PLAIN AND SIMPLE DELINQUENT.

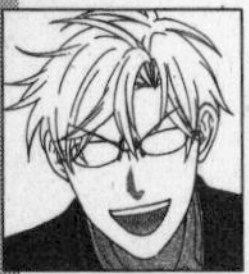

SHINOBU YUI

A FORMER MEMBER OF THE STUDENT COUNCIL AND A SELF PROCLAIMED NINJA. HE JOINED THE PUBLIC MORALS CLUB TO SPY ON THEM.

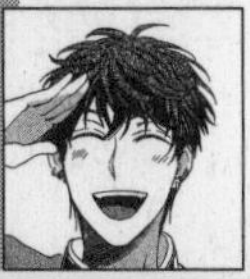

AKI SHIBUYA

A TALKATIVE AND WOMANIZING UNDERCLASSMAN. HIS NICKNAME IS AKKI. HE JOINED BECAUSE HE TOOK A LIKING TO MAFUYU.

★ FOR MORE DETAILS, CHECK OUT THE CHARACTER RELATIONSHIP CHART AT THE END OF THE VOLUME!

STORY

★ MAFUYU KUROSAKI WAS ONCE THE BANCHO WHO CONTROLLED ALL OF SAITAMA, BUT WHEN SHE WAS TRANSFERRED TO MIDORIGAOKA ACADEMY, SHE CHANGED COMPLETELY AND BECAME A NORMAL (BUT SPIRITED) HIGH SCHOOL GIRL...OR AT LEAST SHE WAS SUPPOSED TO! TAKAOMI SAEKI, MAFUYU'S CHILDHOOD FRIEND AND HOMEROOM TEACHER, FORCED HER TO JOIN THE PUBLIC MORALS CLUB, THUS MAKING SURE HER LIFE CONTINUED TO BE FAR FROM AVERAGE.

★ THE PUBLIC MORALS CLUB IS FIGHTING THE STUDENT COUNCIL FOR CONTROL OF MIDORIGAOKA ACADEMY, AND ALREADY BESTED STUDENT COUNCIL MEMBERS KOSAKA AND AYABE. THEY NOW HAVE A NEW MEMBER NAMED SHIBUYA.

WHO WILL THE STUDENT COUNCIL SEND TO FIGHT THEM NEXT?

STUDENT COUNCIL

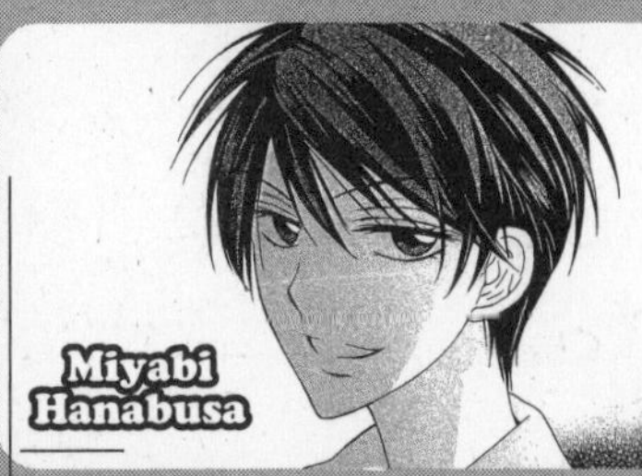

Miyabi Hanabusa

THE SCHOOL DIRECTOR'S SON AND THE PRESIDENT OF THE STUDENT COUNCIL. HE HAS THE POWER TO CAPTIVATE ANYONE WHO LOOKS AT HIM.

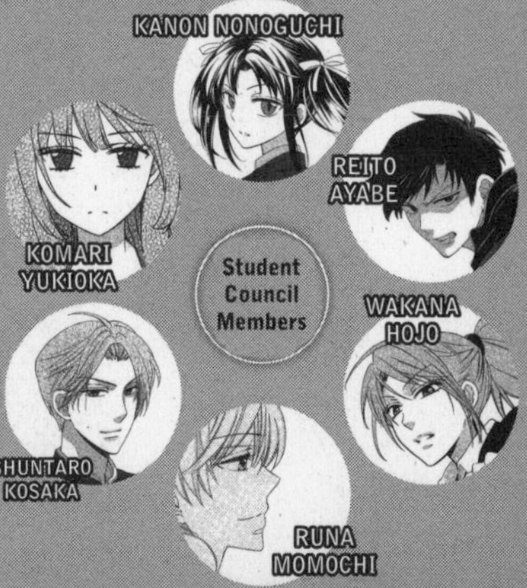
KANON NONOGUCHI
REITO AYABE
KOMARI YUKIOKA
Student Council Members
WAKANA HOJO
SHUNTARO KOSAKA
RUNA MOMOCHI

PRETEND KARAOKE, PART 1

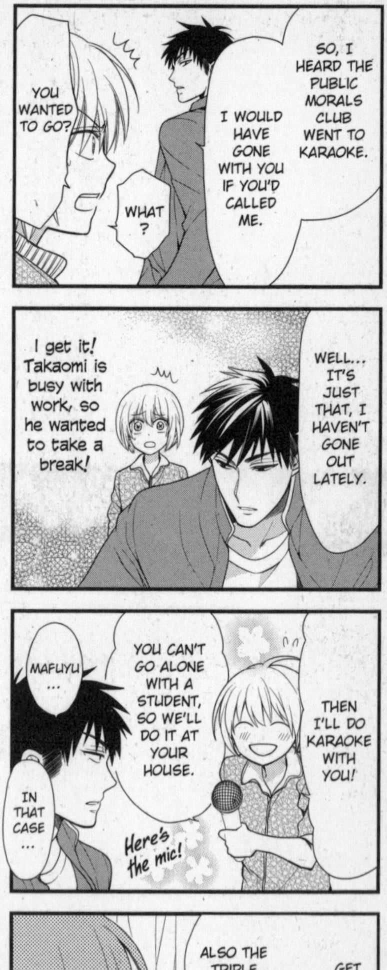
SO, I HEARD THE PUBLIC MORALS CLUB WENT TO KARAOKE.
I WOULD HAVE GONE WITH YOU IF YOU'D CALLED ME.
WHAT ?
YOU WANTED TO GO?
WELL... IT'S JUST THAT, I HAVEN'T GONE OUT LATELY.
I get it! Takaomi is busy with work, so he wanted to take a break!
THEN I'LL DO KARAOKE WITH YOU!
YOU CAN'T GO ALONE WITH A STUDENT, SO WE'LL DO IT AT YOUR HOUSE.
MAFUYU ...
Here's the mic!
IN THAT CASE ...
...GET ME POPCORN AND A COLA.
ALSO THE TRIPLE SAMPLER.
Bring it quickly.
What? I'm playing the part of an employee?

PRETEND KARAOKE, PART 2

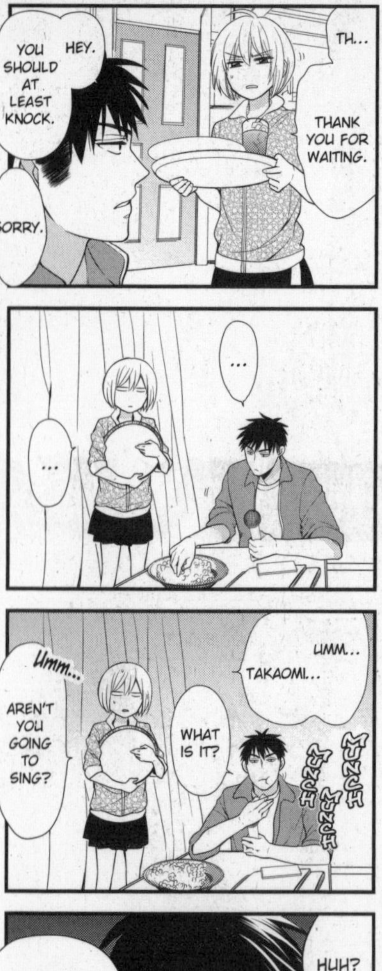
TH...
THANK YOU FOR WAITING.
HEY.
YOU SHOULD AT LEAST KNOCK.
SORRY.
...
...
UMM... TAKAOMI...
WHAT IS IT?
MUNCH MUNCH
Umm...
AREN'T YOU GOING TO SING?
HUH?
I'M GOING TO ONCE THE EMPLOYEE LEAVES, OF COURSE.

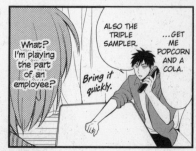

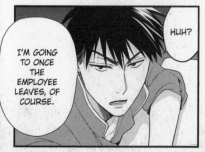

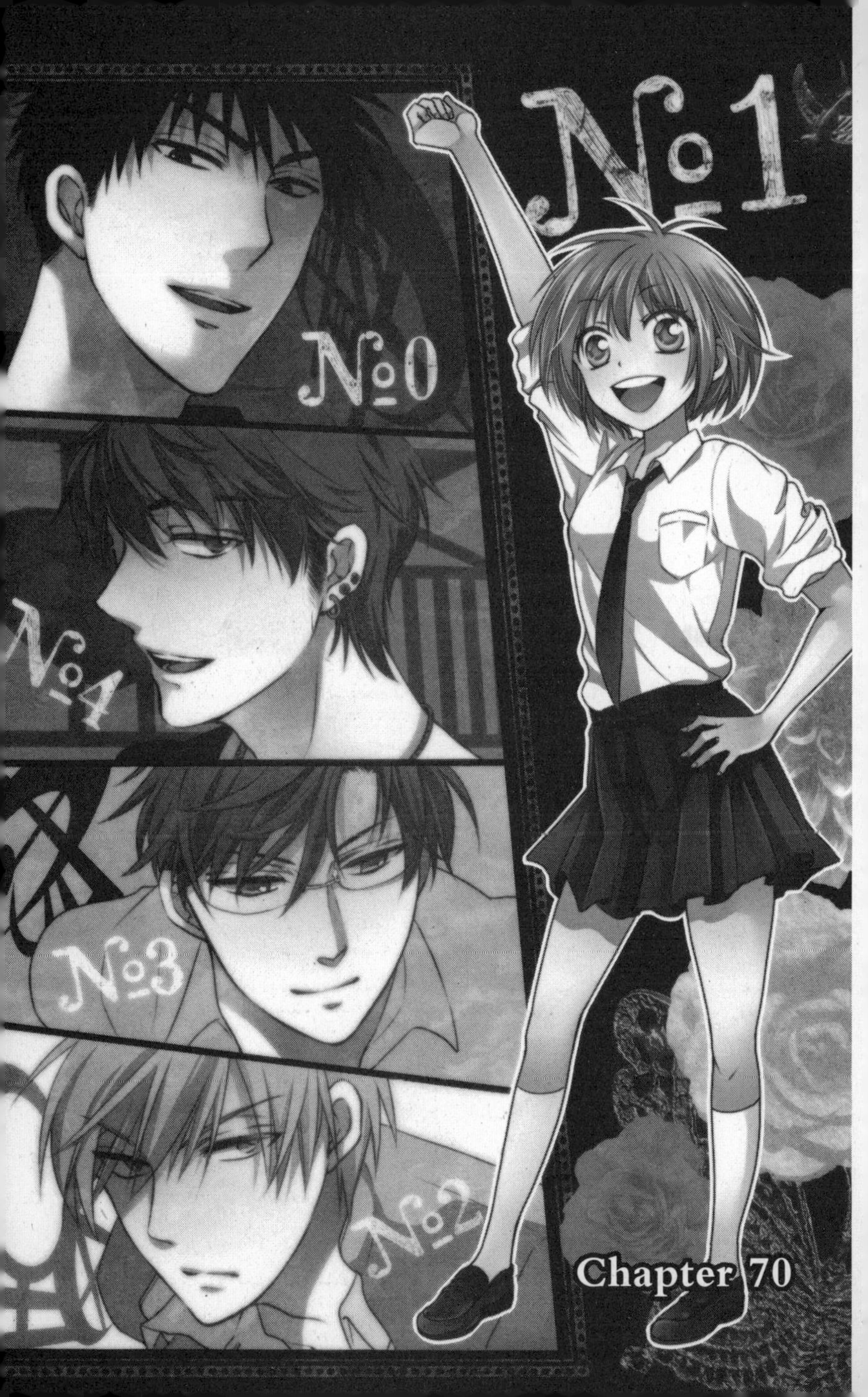

Chapter 70

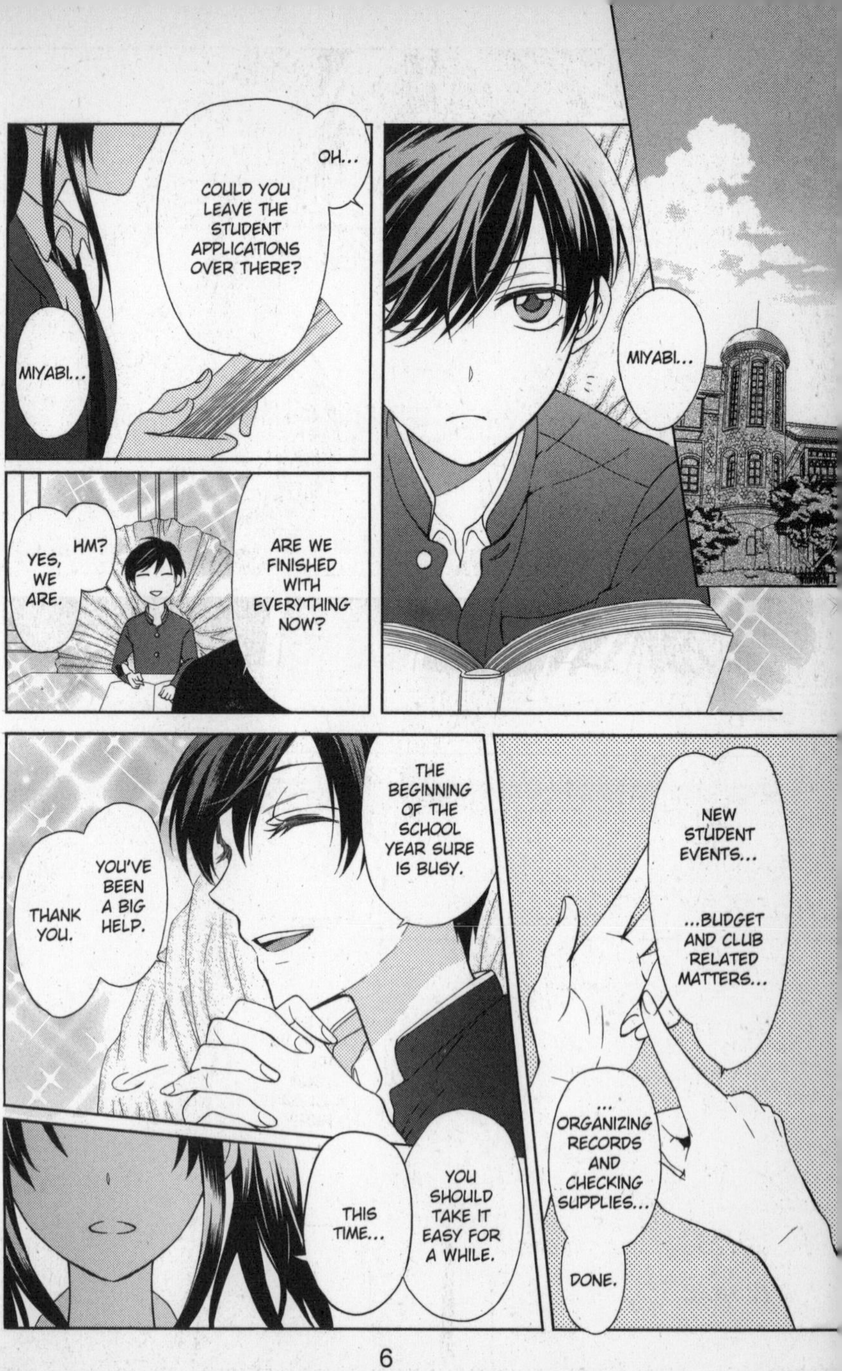
MIYABI...
OH...
COULD YOU LEAVE THE STUDENT APPLICATIONS OVER THERE?
MIYABI...
ARE WE FINISHED WITH EVERYTHING NOW?
HM?
YES, WE ARE.
NEW STUDENT EVENTS...
...BUDGET AND CLUB RELATED MATTERS...
...ORGANIZING RECORDS AND CHECKING SUPPLIES...
DONE.
THE BEGINNING OF THE SCHOOL YEAR SURE IS BUSY.
YOU'VE BEEN A BIG HELP.
THANK YOU.
YOU SHOULD TAKE IT EASY FOR A WHILE.
THIS TIME...

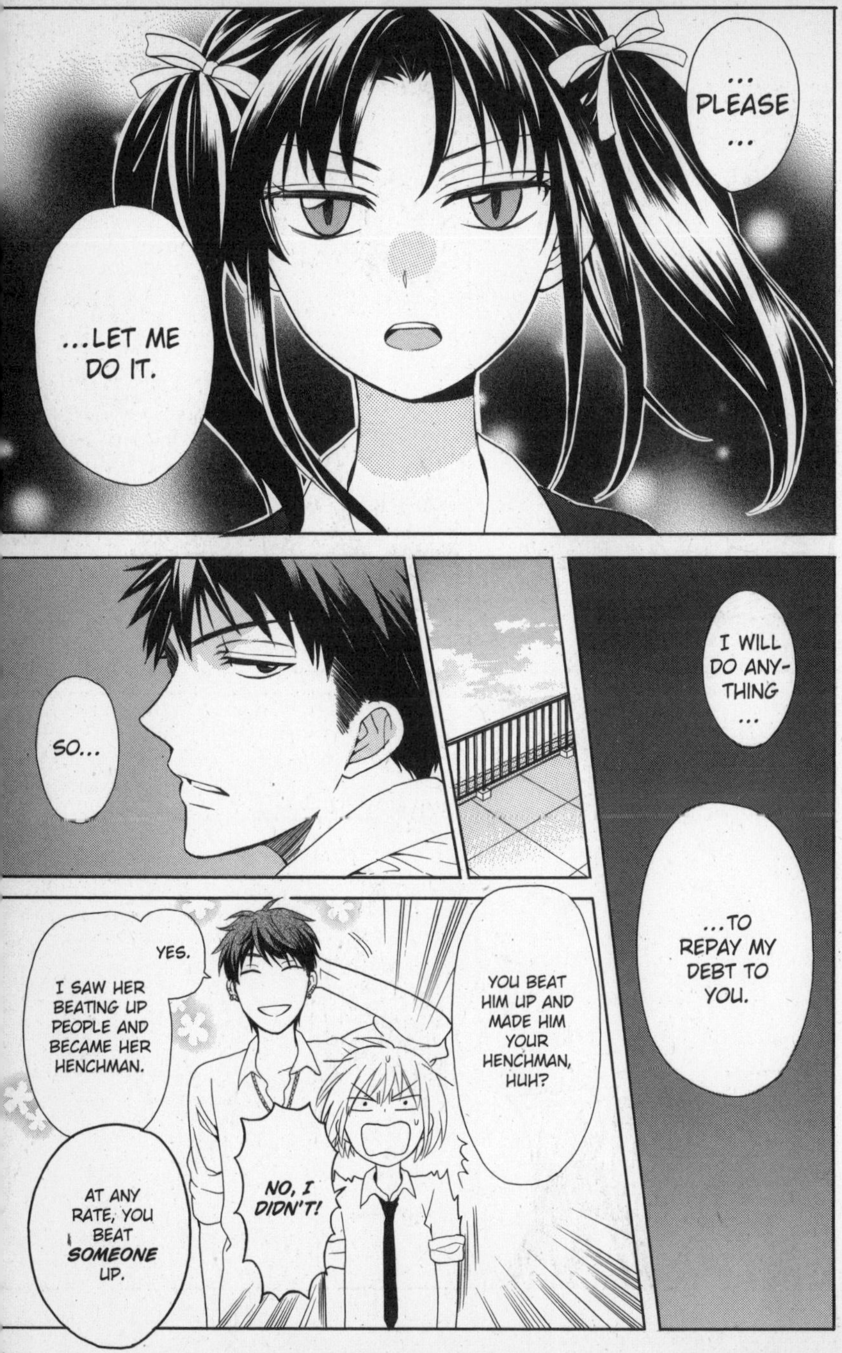
...PLEASE...
...LET ME DO IT.
I WILL DO ANYTHING...
...TO REPAY MY DEBT TO YOU.
SO...
YOU BEAT HIM UP AND MADE HIM YOUR HENCHMAN, HUH?
YES.
I SAW HER BEATING UP PEOPLE AND BECAME HER HENCHMAN.
NO, I DIDN'T!
AT ANY RATE, YOU BEAT SOMEONE UP.

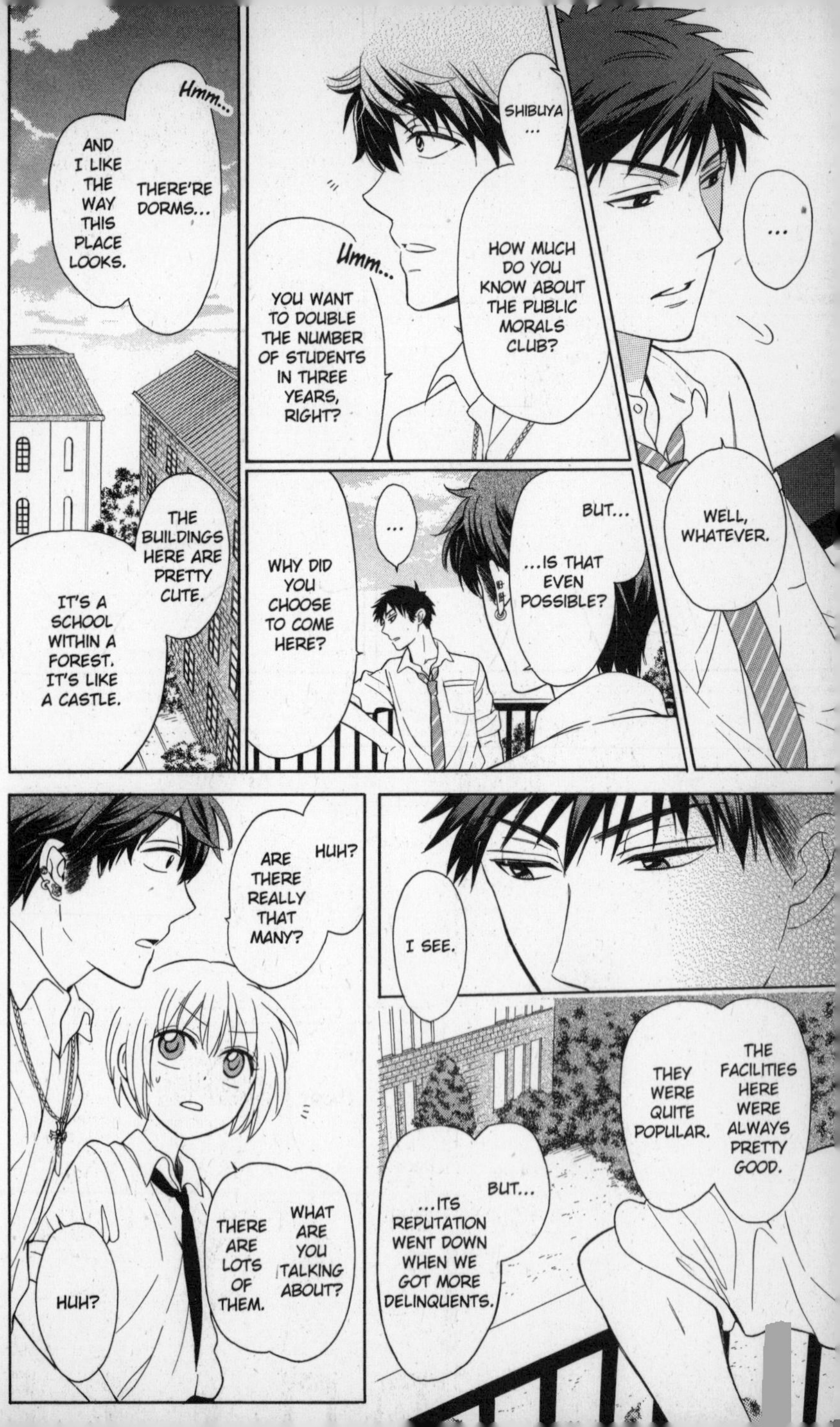
...
SHIBUYA...
HOW MUCH DO YOU KNOW ABOUT THE PUBLIC MORALS CLUB?
Umm...
YOU WANT TO DOUBLE THE NUMBER OF STUDENTS IN THREE YEARS, RIGHT?
WELL, WHATEVER.
BUT...
...IS THAT EVEN POSSIBLE?
...
WHY DID YOU CHOOSE TO COME HERE?
Hmm...
THERE'RE DORMS...
AND I LIKE THE WAY THIS PLACE LOOKS.
THE BUILDINGS HERE ARE PRETTY CUTE.
IT'S A SCHOOL WITHIN A FOREST. IT'S LIKE A CASTLE.
I SEE.
THE FACILITIES HERE WERE ALWAYS PRETTY GOOD.
THEY WERE QUITE POPULAR.
BUT...
...ITS REPUTATION WENT DOWN WHEN WE GOT MORE DELINQUENTS.
HUH?
ARE THERE REALLY THAT MANY?
WHAT ARE YOU TALKING ABOUT?
THERE ARE LOTS OF THEM.
HUH?

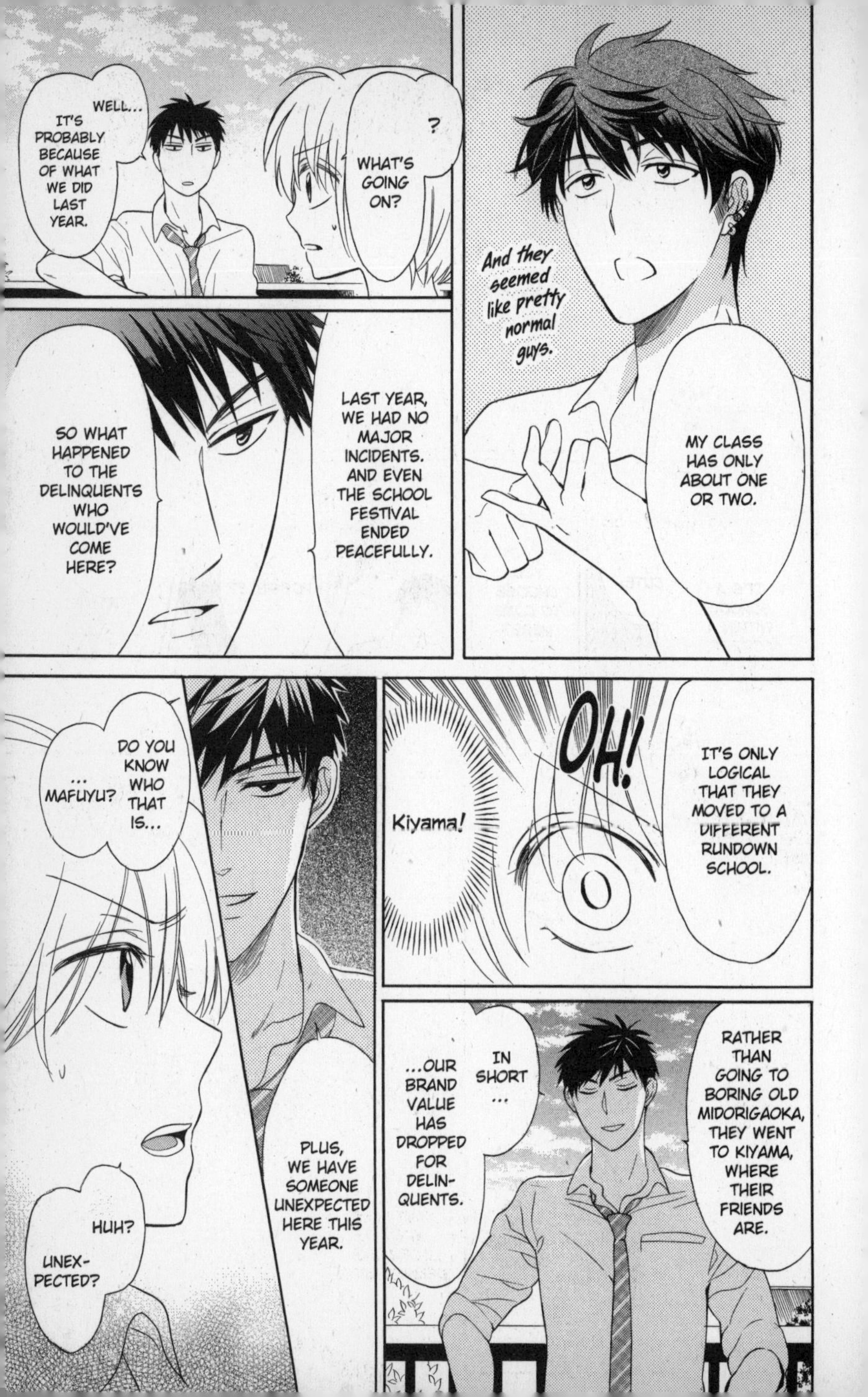
MY CLASS HAS ONLY ABOUT ONE OR TWO.
And they seemed like pretty normal guys.
?
WHAT'S GOING ON?
WELL... IT'S PROBABLY BECAUSE OF WHAT WE DID LAST YEAR.
LAST YEAR, WE HAD NO MAJOR INCIDENTS. AND EVEN THE SCHOOL FESTIVAL ENDED PEACEFULLY.
SO WHAT HAPPENED TO THE DELINQUENTS WHO WOULD'VE COME HERE?
IT'S ONLY LOGICAL THAT THEY MOVED TO A DIFFERENT RUNDOWN SCHOOL.
OH!
Kiyama!
RATHER THAN GOING TO BORING OLD MIDORIGAOKA, THEY WENT TO KIYAMA, WHERE THEIR FRIENDS ARE.
IN SHORT...
...OUR BRAND VALUE HAS DROPPED FOR DELIN-QUENTS.
PLUS, WE HAVE SOMEONE UNEXPECTED HERE THIS YEAR.
HUH? UNEX-PECTED?
DO YOU KNOW WHO THAT IS... ...MAFUYU?

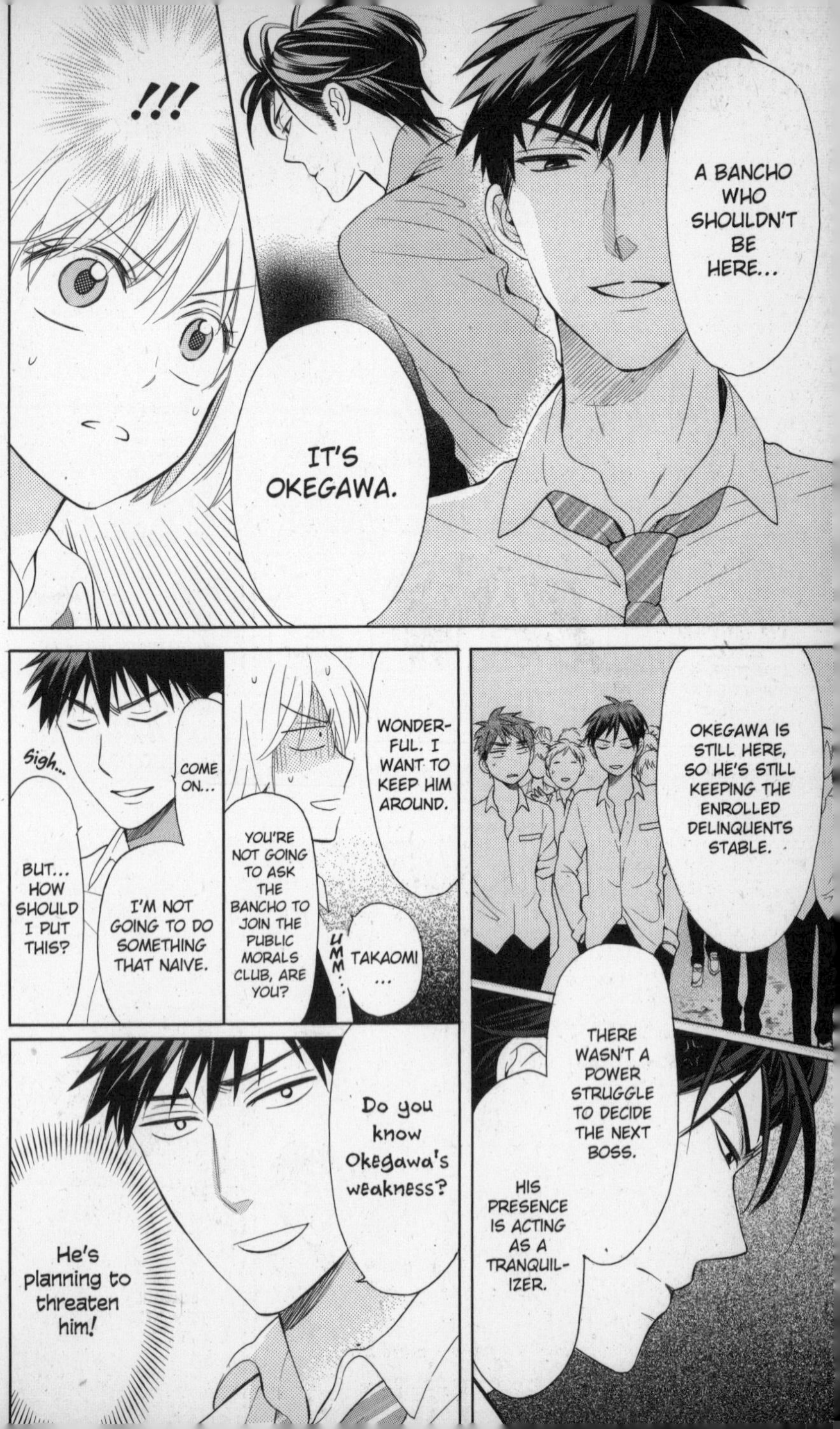
A BANCHO WHO SHOULDN'T BE HERE...
IT'S OKEGAWA.
!!!
OKEGAWA IS STILL HERE, SO HE'S STILL KEEPING THE ENROLLED DELINQUENTS STABLE.
THERE WASN'T A POWER STRUGGLE TO DECIDE THE NEXT BOSS.
HIS PRESENCE IS ACTING AS A TRANQUIL-IZER.
WONDER-FUL. I WANT TO KEEP HIM AROUND.
YOU'RE NOT GOING TO ASK THE BANCHO TO JOIN THE PUBLIC MORALS CLUB, ARE YOU?
UMM...
TAKAOMI ...
COME ON...
Sigh...
I'M NOT GOING TO DO SOMETHING THAT NAIVE.
BUT... HOW SHOULD I PUT THIS?
Do you know Okegawa's weakness?
He's planning to threaten him!

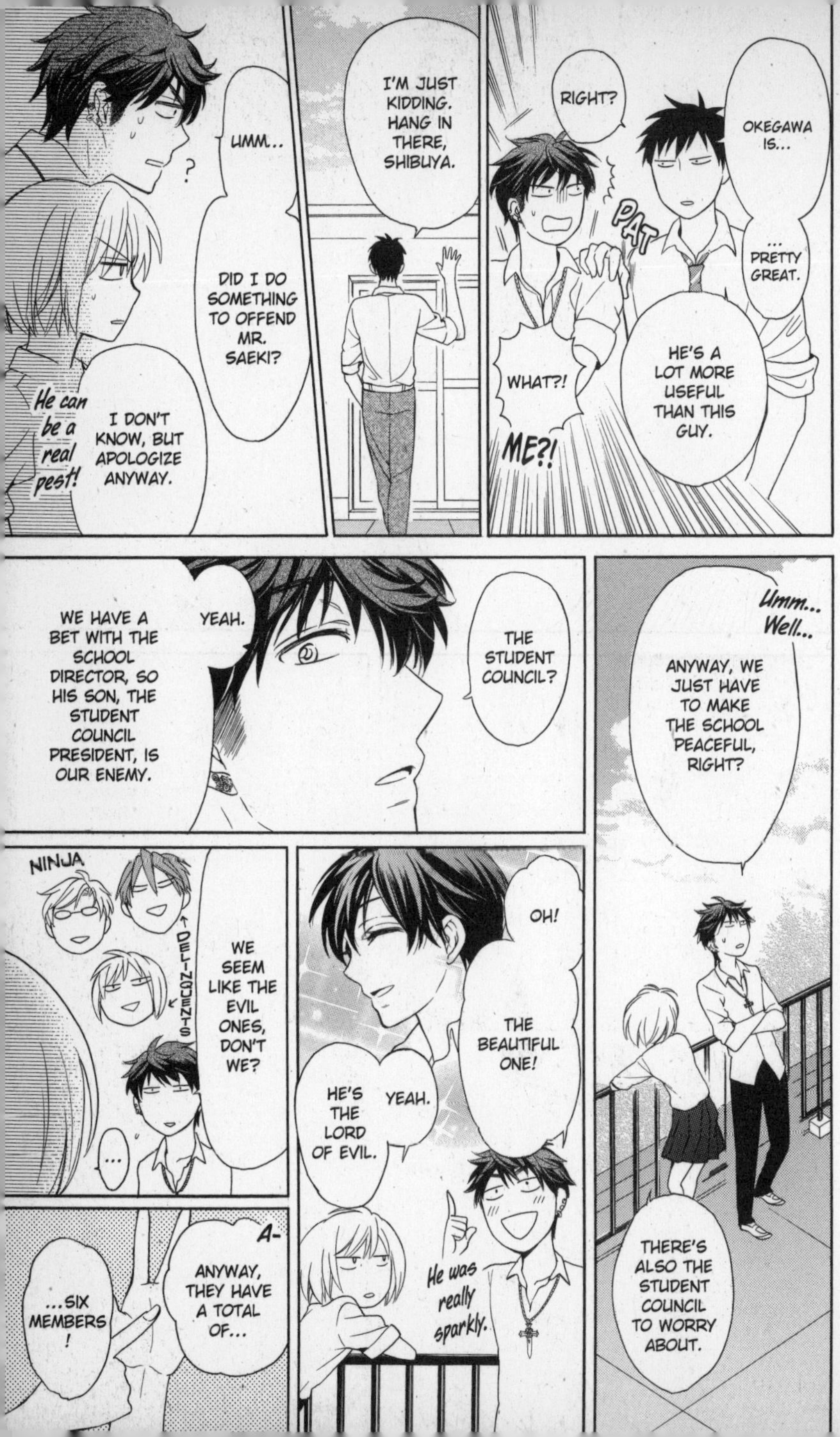
OKEGAWA IS...
... PRETTY GREAT.
HE'S A LOT MORE USEFUL THAN THIS GUY.
RIGHT?
PAT
WHAT?!
ME?!
I'M JUST KIDDING. HANG IN THERE, SHIBUYA.
UMM...
?
DID I DO SOMETHING TO OFFEND MR. SAEKI?
I DON'T KNOW, BUT APOLOGIZE ANYWAY.
He can be a real pest!
Umm... Well...
ANYWAY, WE JUST HAVE TO MAKE THE SCHOOL PEACEFUL, RIGHT?
THERE'S ALSO THE STUDENT COUNCIL TO WORRY ABOUT.
THE STUDENT COUNCIL?
YEAH.
WE HAVE A BET WITH THE SCHOOL DIRECTOR, SO HIS SON, THE STUDENT COUNCIL PRESIDENT, IS OUR ENEMY.
OH!
THE BEAUTIFUL ONE!
YEAH.
HE'S THE LORD OF EVIL.
He was really sparkly.
WE SEEM LIKE THE EVIL ONES, DON'T WE?
NINJA
DELINQUENTS
...
A-
ANYWAY, THEY HAVE A TOTAL OF...
...SIX MEMBERS!

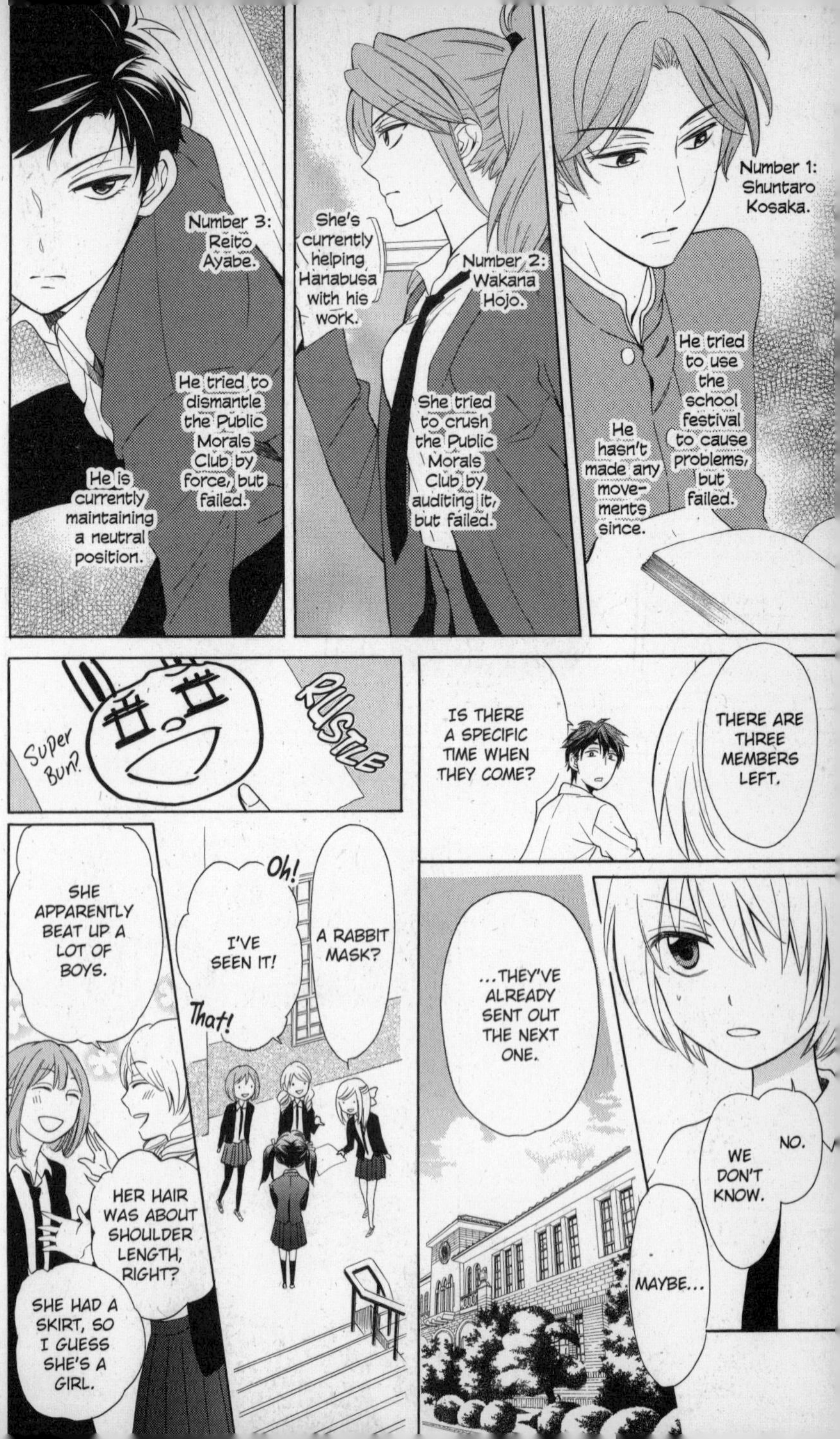

Number 1: Shuntaro Kosaka.
He tried to use the school festival to cause problems, but failed.
He hasn't made any movements since.
Number 2: Wakana Hojo.
She tried to crush the Public Morals Club by auditing it, but failed.
She's currently helping Hanabusa with his work.
Number 3: Reito Ayabe.
He tried to dismantle the Public Morals Club by force, but failed.
He is currently maintaining a neutral position.
THERE ARE THREE MEMBERS LEFT.
IS THERE A SPECIFIC TIME WHEN THEY COME?
RUSTLE
Super Bun?
NO.
WE DON'T KNOW.
MAYBE...
...THEY'VE ALREADY SENT OUT THE NEXT ONE.
A RABBIT MASK?
Oh!
I'VE SEEN IT!
That!
SHE APPARENTLY BEAT UP A LOT OF BOYS.
HER HAIR WAS ABOUT SHOULDER LENGTH, RIGHT?
SHE HAD A SKIRT, SO I GUESS SHE'S A GIRL.

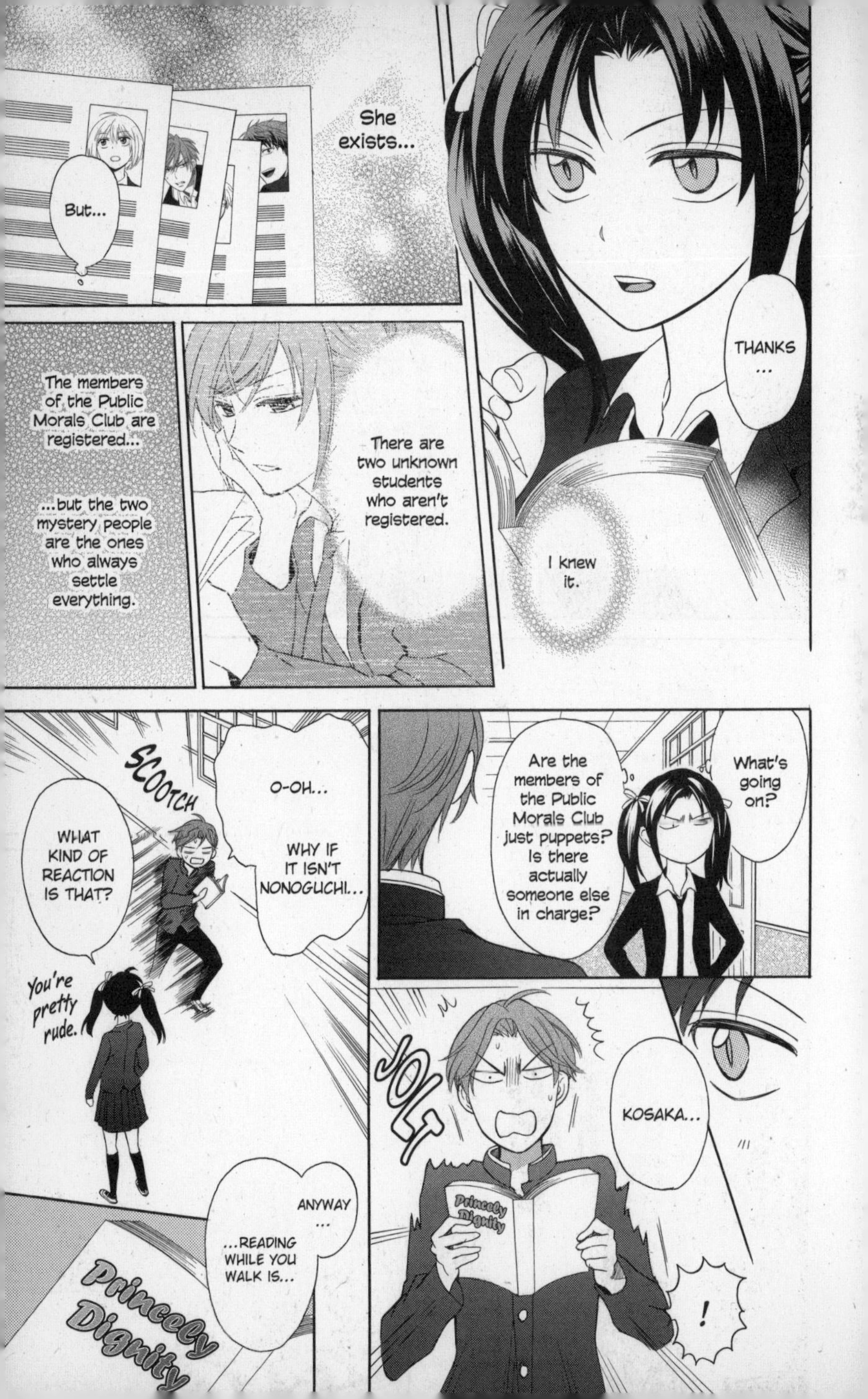
THANKS ...
I knew it.
She exists...
But...
There are two unknown students who aren't registered.
The members of the Public Morals Club are registered...
...but the two mystery people are the ones who always settle everything.
What's going on?
Are the members of the Public Morals Club just puppets? Is there actually someone else in charge?
KOSAKA...
!
JOLT
Princely Dignity
O-OH...
WHY IF IT ISN'T NONOGUCHI...
SCOOTCH
WHAT KIND OF REACTION IS THAT?
You're pretty rude.
ANYWAY ...
...READING WHILE YOU WALK IS...
Princely Dignity

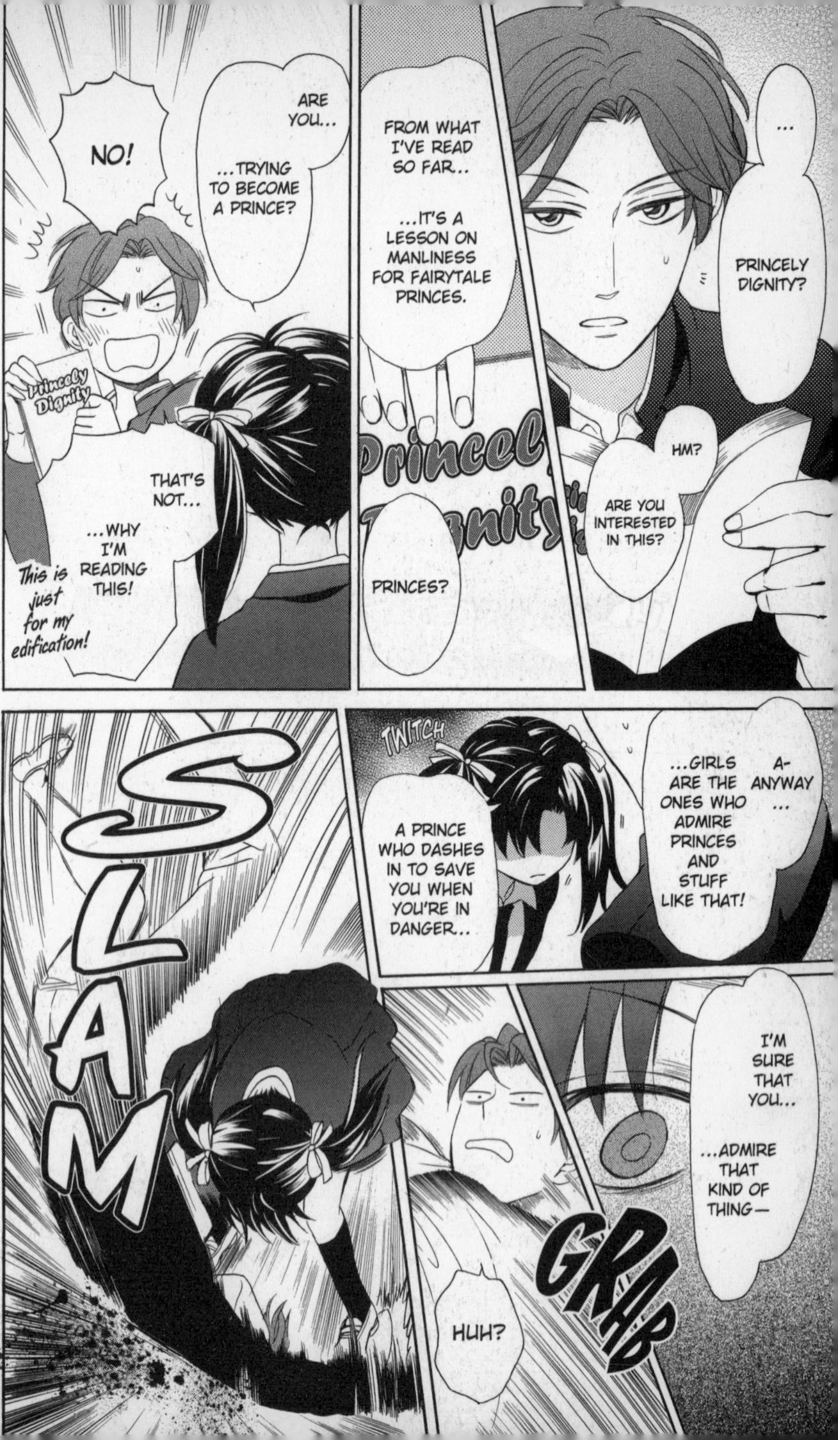
...
PRINCELY DIGNITY?
HM?
ARE YOU INTERESTED IN THIS?
FROM WHAT I'VE READ SO FAR...
...IT'S A LESSON ON MANLINESS FOR FAIRYTALE PRINCES.
Princely Dignity
PRINCES?
ARE YOU...
...TRYING TO BECOME A PRINCE?
NO!
Princely Dignity
THAT'S NOT...
...WHY I'M READING THIS!
This is just for my edification!
A-ANYWAY...
...GIRLS ARE THE ONES WHO ADMIRE PRINCES AND STUFF LIKE THAT!
TWITCH
A PRINCE WHO DASHES IN TO SAVE YOU WHEN YOU'RE IN DANGER...
I'M SURE THAT YOU...
...ADMIRE THAT KIND OF THING—
GRAB
HUH?
SLAM

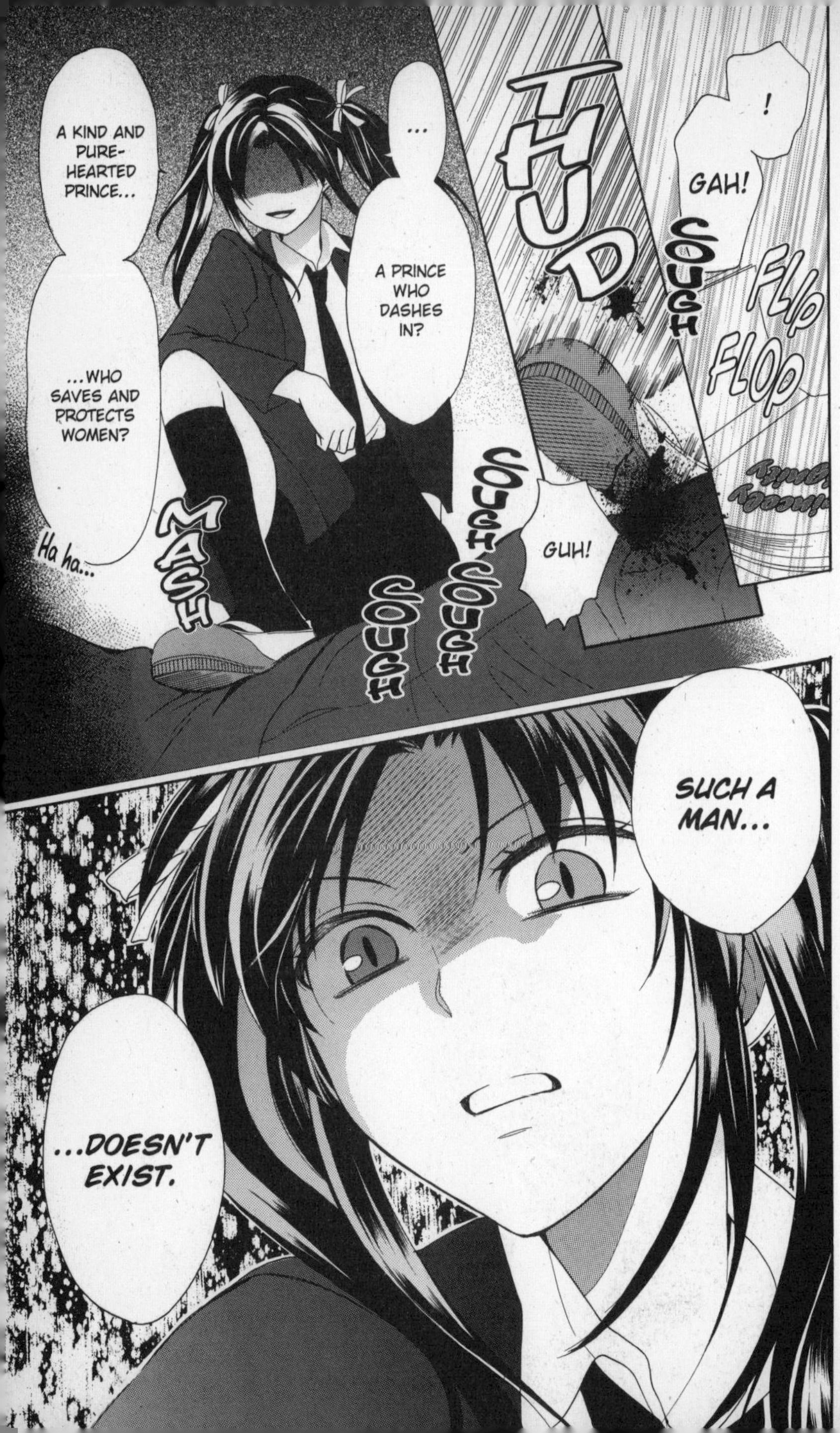
!
GAH!
THUD
COUGH
FLIP FLOP
...
A PRINCE WHO DASHES IN?
A KIND AND PURE-HEARTED PRINCE...
...WHO SAVES AND PROTECTS WOMEN?
GUH!
COUGH COUGH
COUGH
MASH
Ha ha...
SUCH A MAN...
...DOESN'T EXIST.

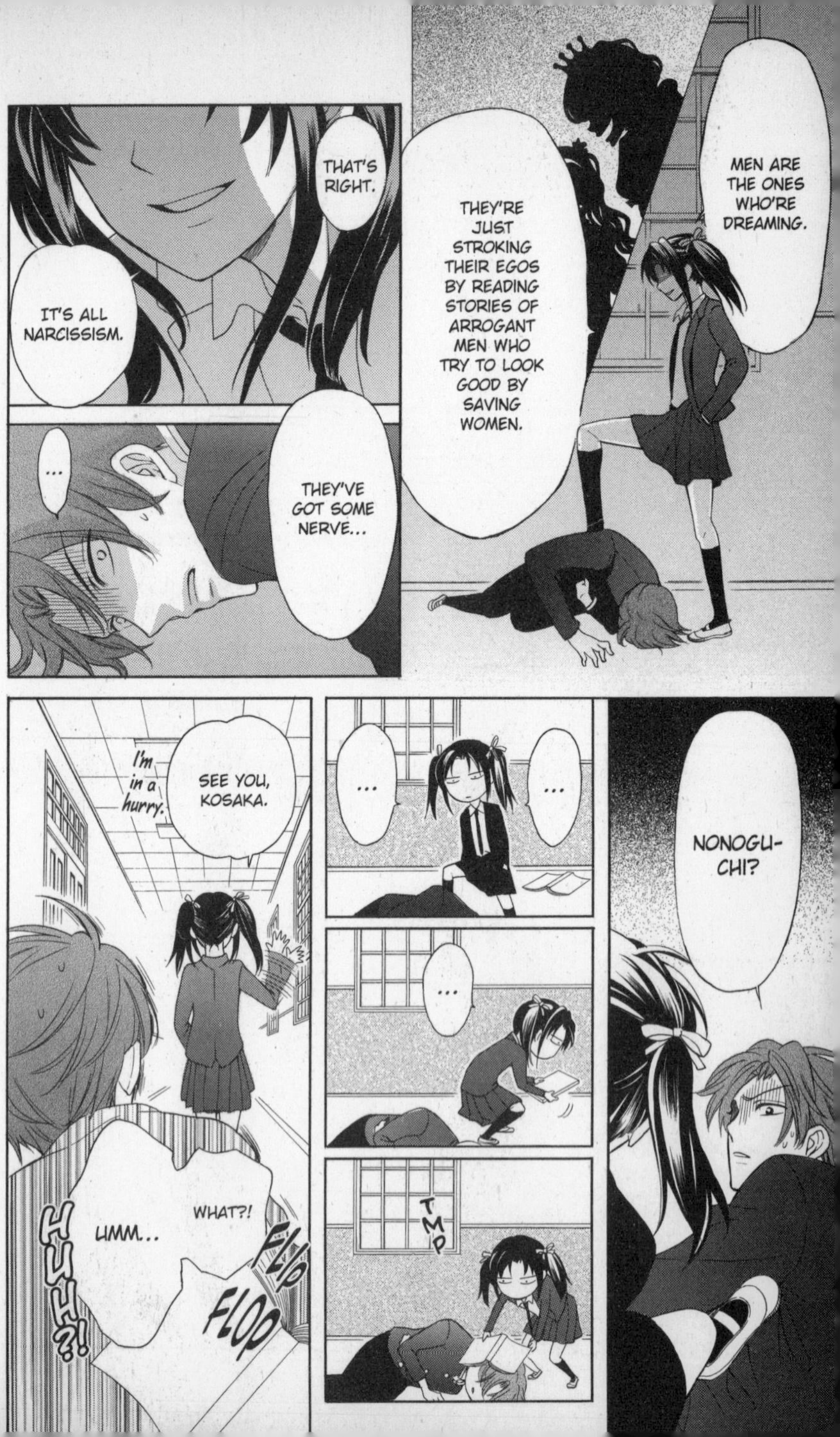
MEN ARE THE ONES WHO'RE DREAMING.
THEY'RE JUST STROKING THEIR EGOS BY READING STORIES OF ARROGANT MEN WHO TRY TO LOOK GOOD BY SAVING WOMEN.
THAT'S RIGHT.
IT'S ALL NARCISSISM.
THEY'VE GOT SOME NERVE...
...
NONOGU-CHI?
...
...
...
TMP
SEE YOU, KOSAKA.
I'm in a hurry.
WHAT?!
FLIP
UMM...
FLOP
HUH?!

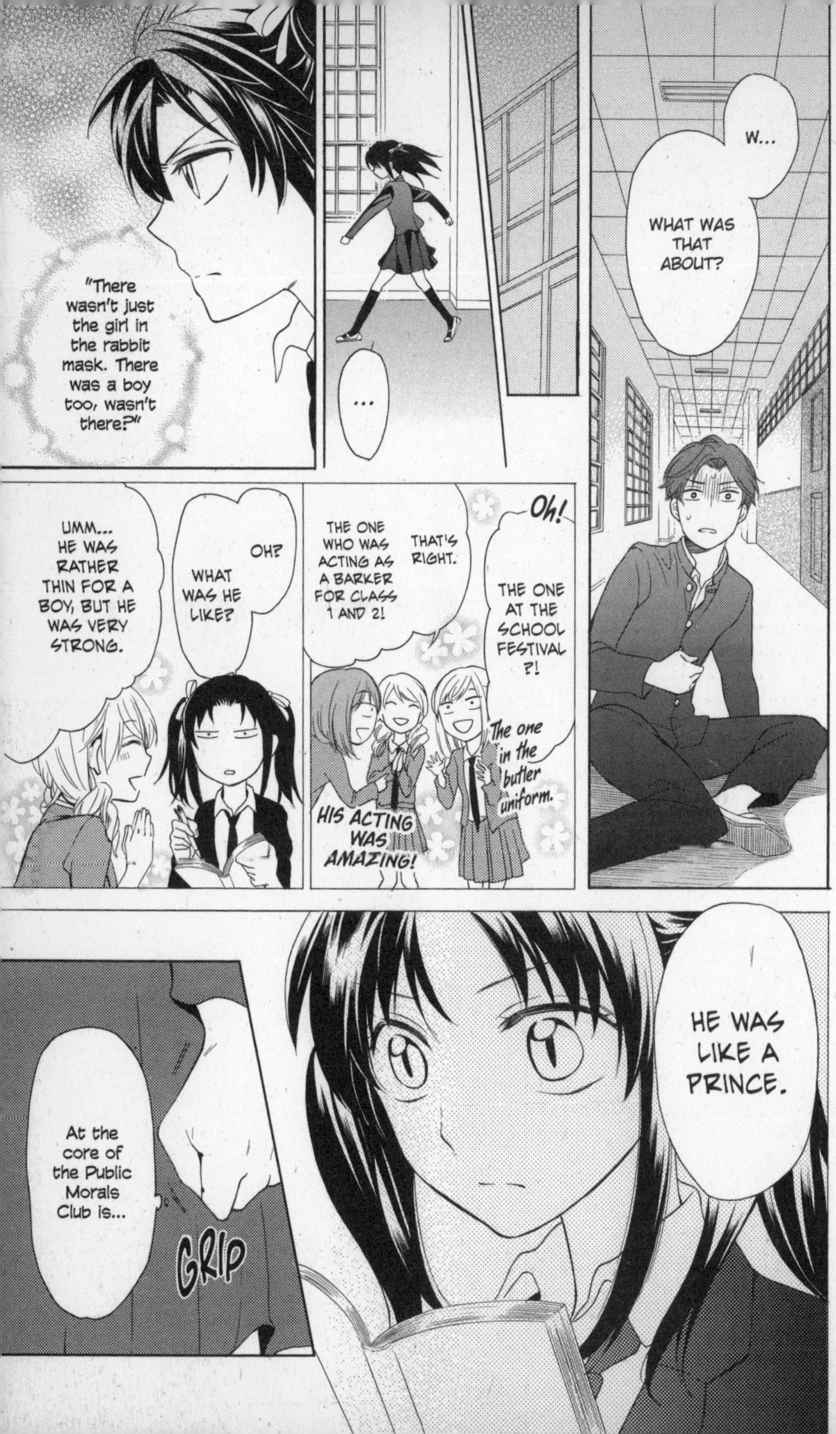
W...
WHAT WAS THAT ABOUT?
...
"There wasn't just the girl in the rabbit mask. There was a boy too, wasn't there?"
Oh!
THE ONE AT THE SCHOOL FESTIVAL ?!
The one in the butler uniform.
THAT'S RIGHT.
THE ONE WHO WAS ACTING AS A BARKER FOR CLASS 1 AND 2!
HIS ACTING WAS AMAZING!
OH?
WHAT WAS HE LIKE?
UMM... HE WAS RATHER THIN FOR A BOY, BUT HE WAS VERY STRONG.
HE WAS LIKE A PRINCE.
At the core of the Public Morals Club is...
GRIP

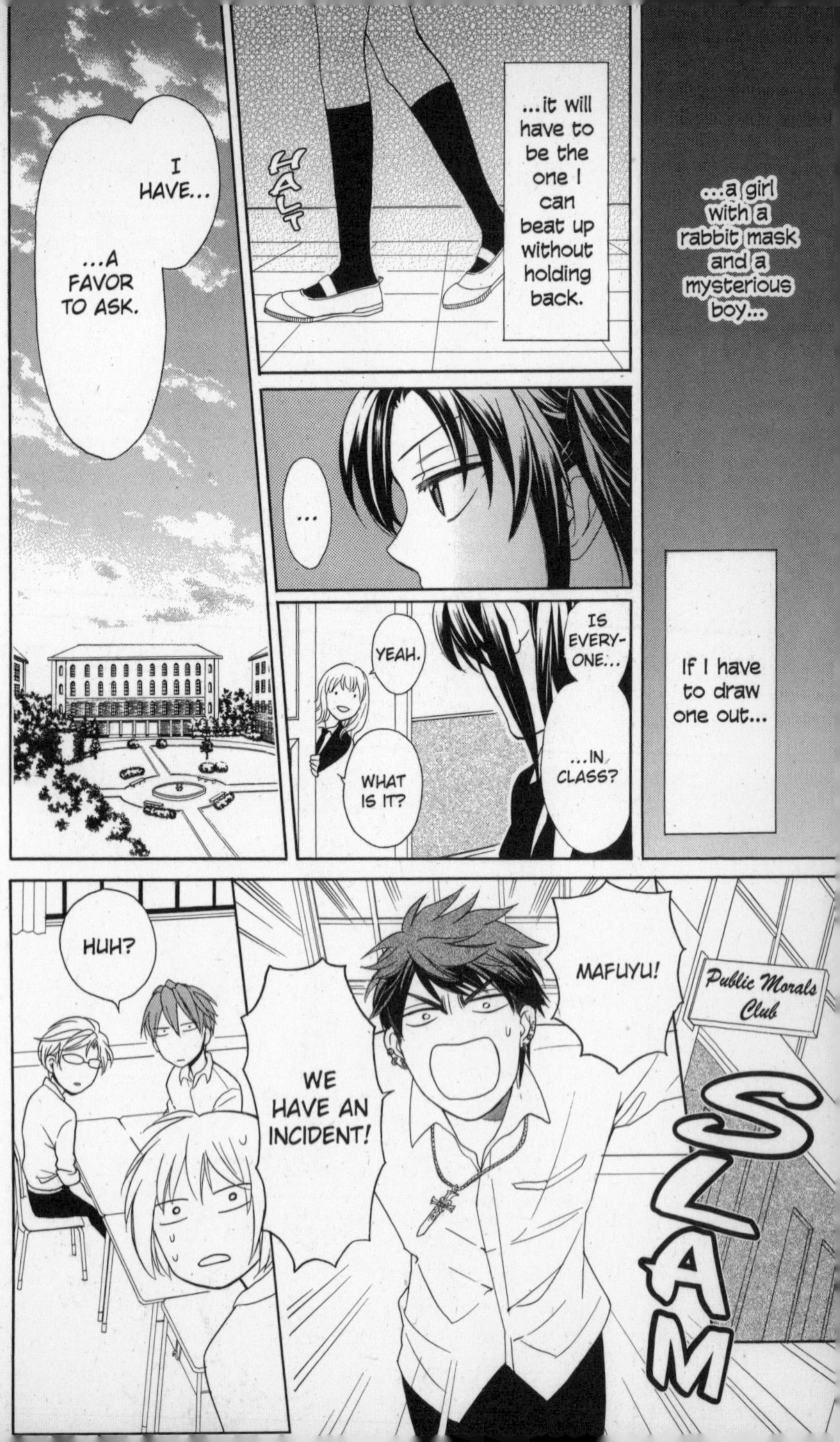
...a girl with a rabbit mask and a mysterious boy...
If I have to draw one out...
...it will have to be the one I can beat up without holding back.
HALT
...
IS EVERYONE...
...IN CLASS?
YEAH.
WHAT IS IT?
I HAVE...
...A FAVOR TO ASK.
SLAM
Public Morals Club
MAFUYU!
WE HAVE AN INCIDENT!
HUH?

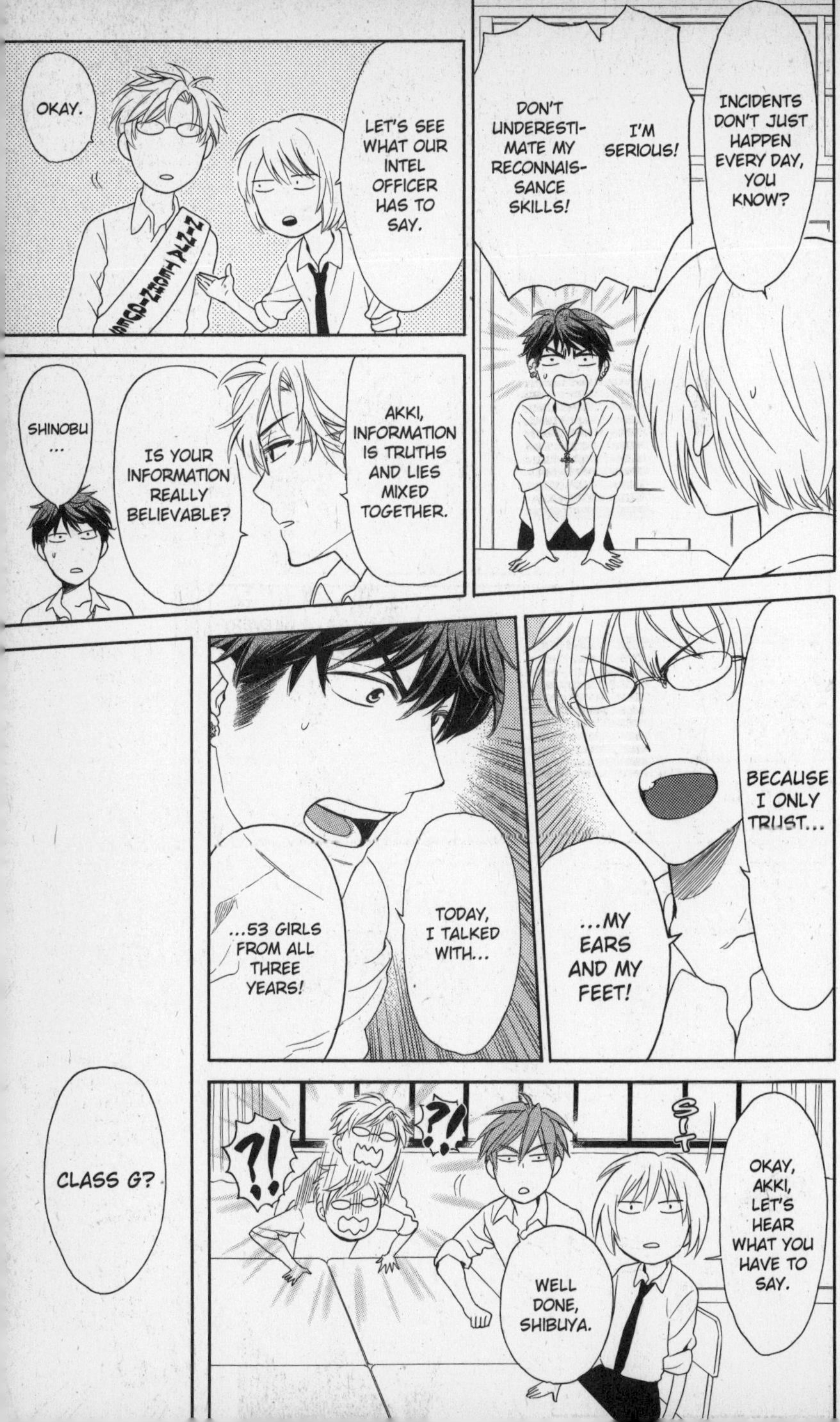
INCIDENTS DON'T JUST HAPPEN EVERY DAY, YOU KNOW?
I'M SERIOUS!
DON'T UNDERESTI-MATE MY RECONNAIS-SANCE SKILLS!
LET'S SEE WHAT OUR INTEL OFFICER HAS TO SAY.
OKAY.
AKKI, INFORMATION IS TRUTHS AND LIES MIXED TOGETHER.
IS YOUR INFORMATION REALLY BELIEVABLE?
SHINOBU...
BECAUSE I ONLY TRUST...
...MY EARS AND MY FEET!
TODAY, I TALKED WITH...
...53 GIRLS FROM ALL THREE YEARS!
SIT
OKAY, AKKI, LET'S HEAR WHAT YOU HAVE TO SAY.
WELL DONE, SHIBUYA.
?!
?!
CLASS G?

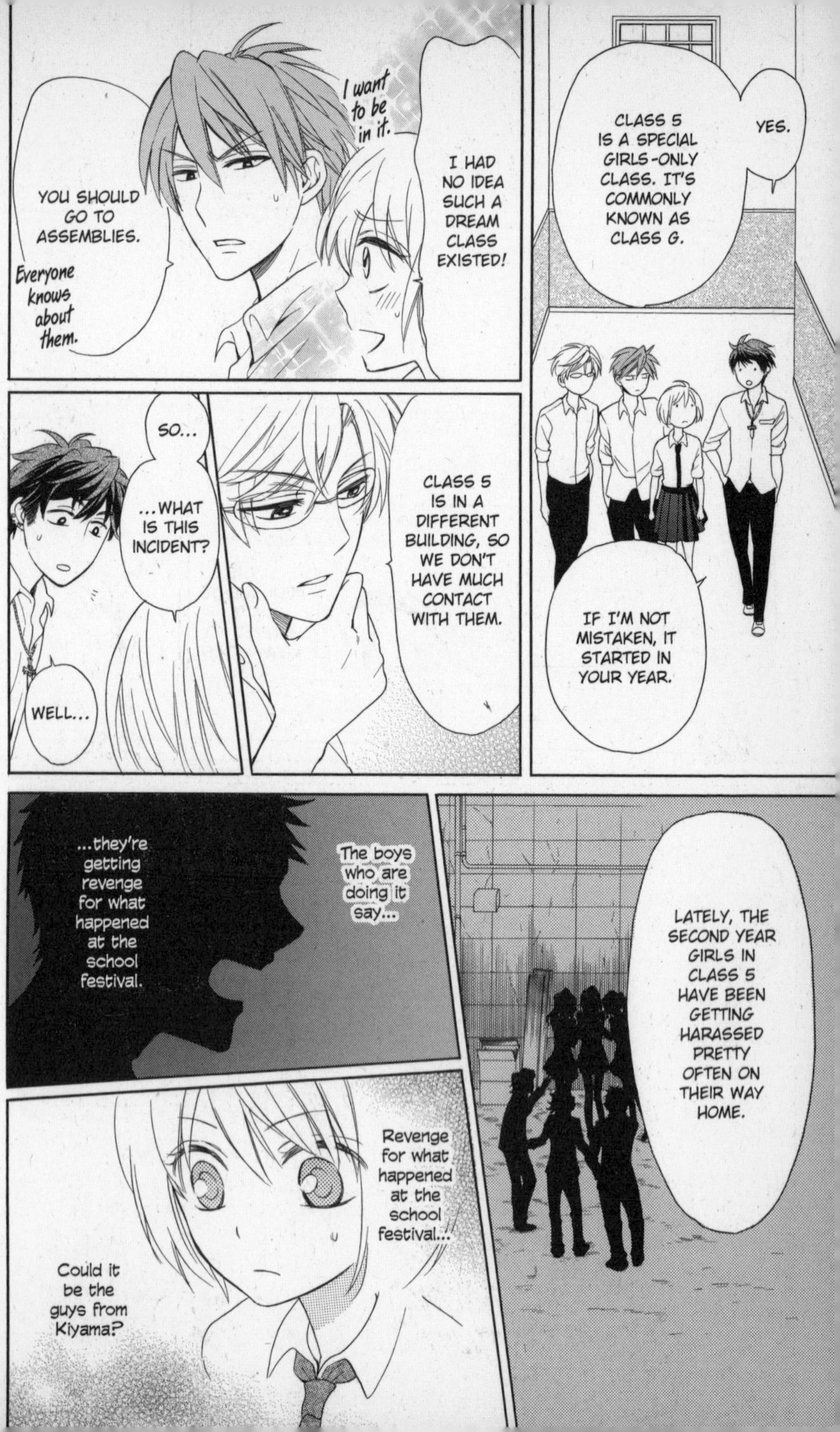
YES.
CLASS 5 IS A SPECIAL GIRLS-ONLY CLASS. IT'S COMMONLY KNOWN AS CLASS G.
IF I'M NOT MISTAKEN, IT STARTED IN YOUR YEAR.
I HAD NO IDEA SUCH A DREAM CLASS EXISTED!
I want to be in it.
YOU SHOULD GO TO ASSEMBLIES.
Everyone knows about them.
CLASS 5 IS IN A DIFFERENT BUILDING, SO WE DON'T HAVE MUCH CONTACT WITH THEM.
SO...
...WHAT IS THIS INCIDENT?
WELL...
LATELY, THE SECOND YEAR GIRLS IN CLASS 5 HAVE BEEN GETTING HARASSED PRETTY OFTEN ON THEIR WAY HOME.
The boys who are doing it say...
...they're getting revenge for what happened at the school festival.
Revenge for what happened at the school festival...
Could it be the guys from Kiyama?

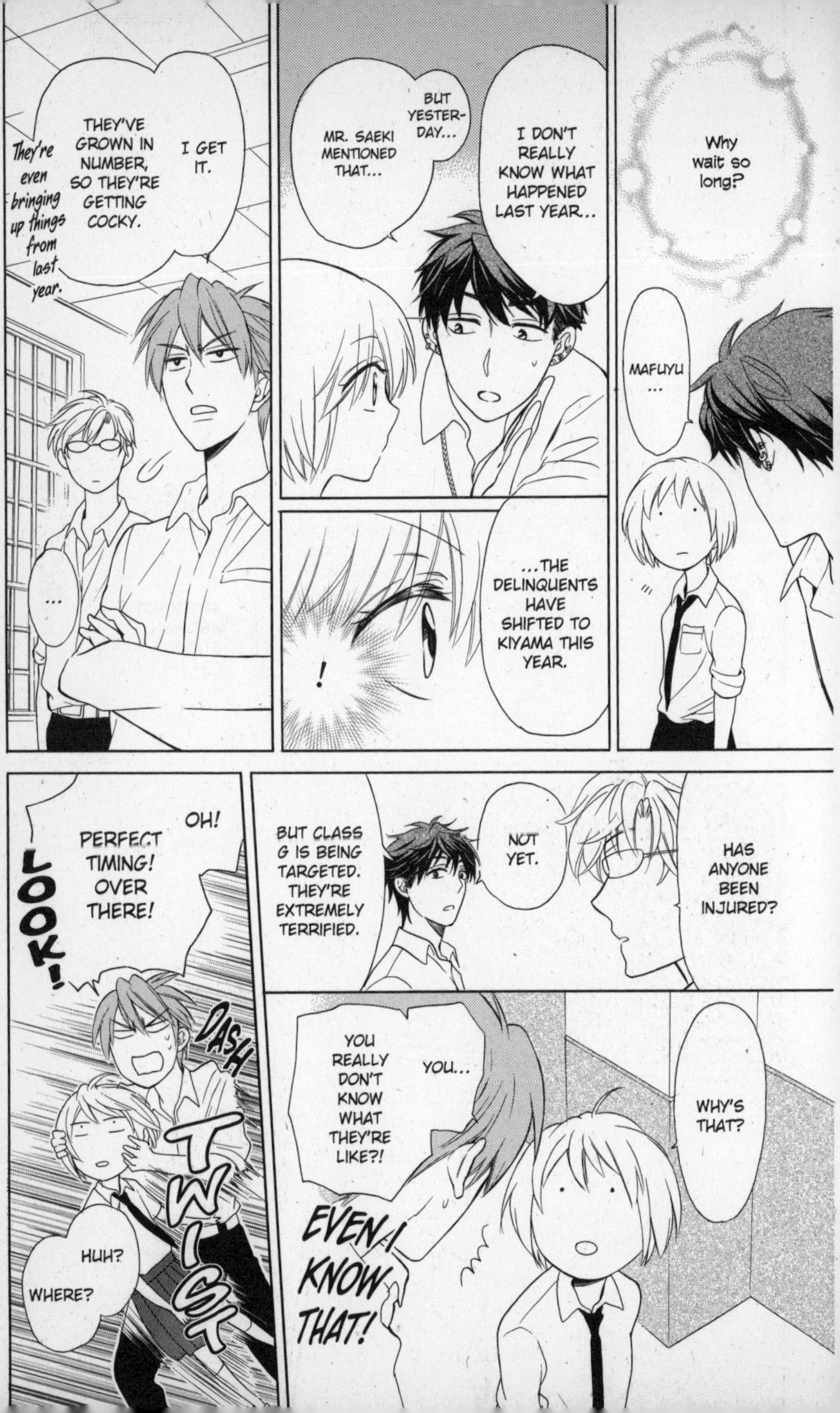
Why wait so long?
MAFUYU...
I DON'T REALLY KNOW WHAT HAPPENED LAST YEAR...
BUT YESTERDAY...
MR. SAEKI MENTIONED THAT...
...THE DELINQUENTS HAVE SHIFTED TO KIYAMA THIS YEAR.
!
I GET IT.
THEY'VE GROWN IN NUMBER, SO THEY'RE GETTING COCKY.
They're even bringing up things from last year.
...
HAS ANYONE BEEN INJURED?
NOT YET.
BUT CLASS G IS BEING TARGETED. THEY'RE EXTREMELY TERRIFIED.
WHY'S THAT?
YOU...
YOU REALLY DON'T KNOW WHAT THEY'RE LIKE?!
EVEN I KNOW THAT!
OH!
PERFECT TIMING! OVER THERE!
LOOK!
DASH
TWIST
HUH?
WHERE?

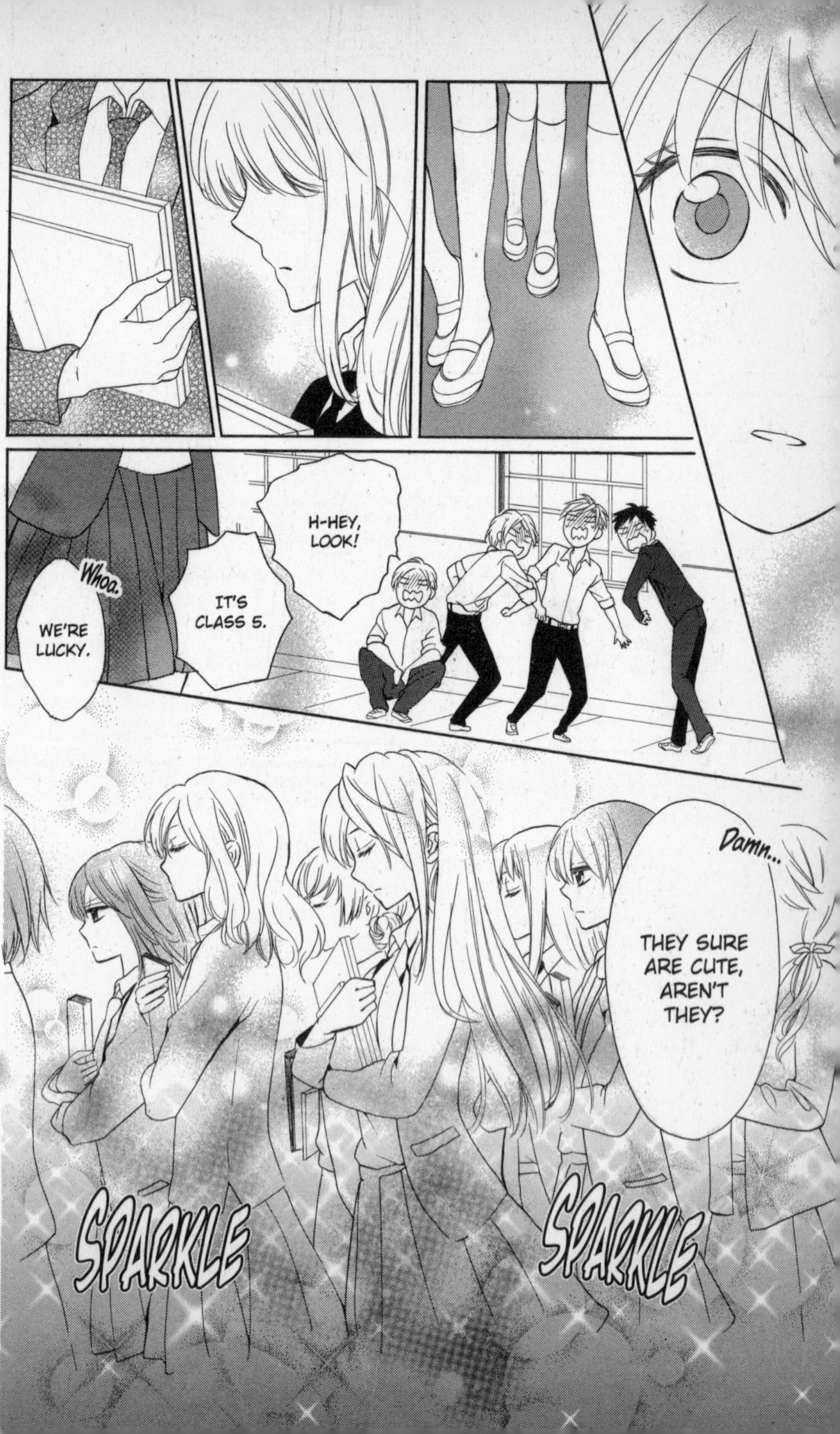
H-HEY, LOOK!
IT'S CLASS 5.
Whoa.
WE'RE LUCKY.
Damn...
THEY SURE ARE CUTE, AREN'T THEY?
SPARKLE
SPARKLE

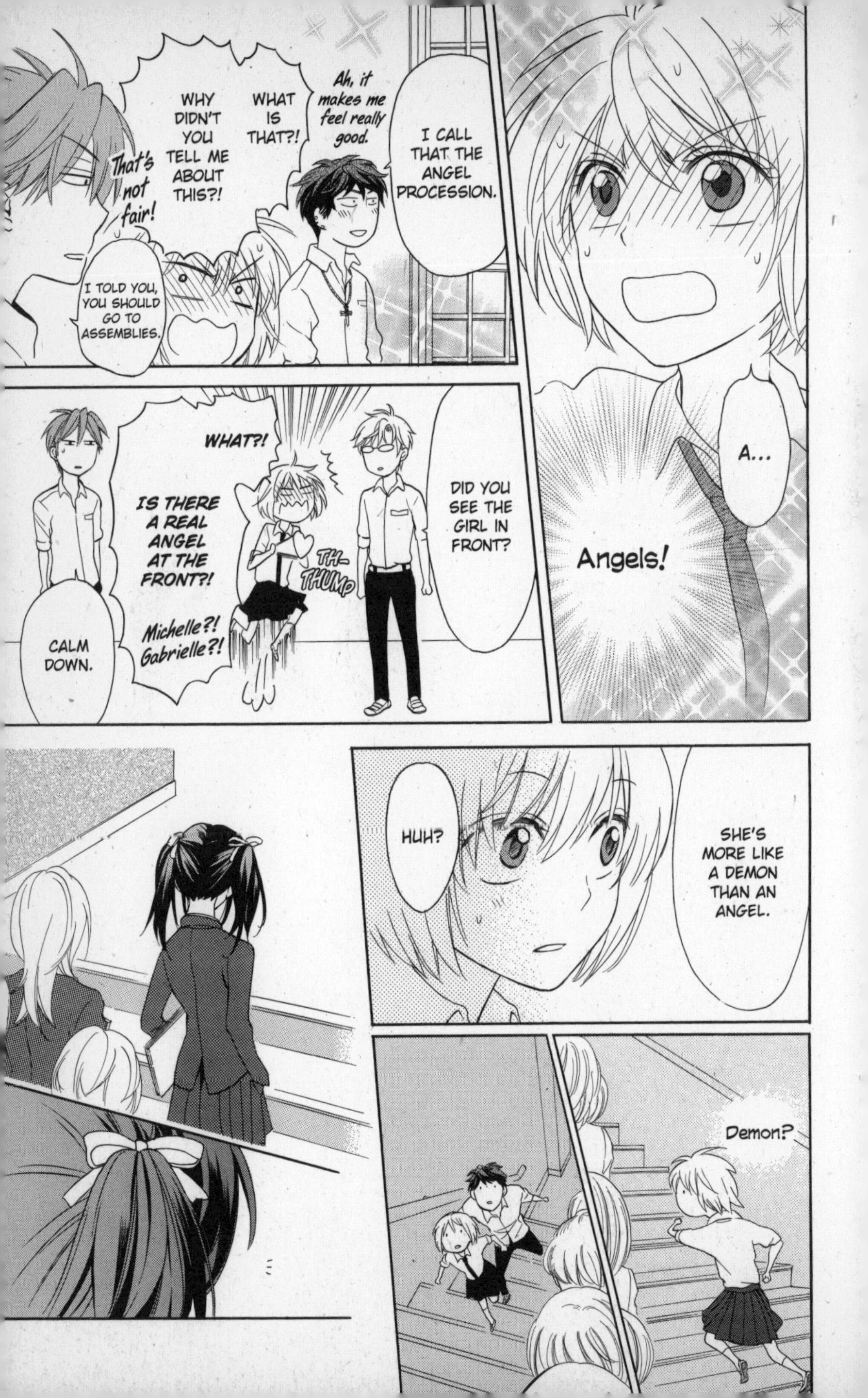
A...
Angels!
I CALL THAT THE ANGEL PROCESSION.
Ah, it makes me feel really good.
WHAT IS THAT?!
WHY DIDN'T YOU TELL ME ABOUT THIS?!
That's not fair!
I TOLD YOU, YOU SHOULD GO TO ASSEMBLIES.
DID YOU SEE THE GIRL IN FRONT?
WHAT?!
IS THERE A REAL ANGEL AT THE FRONT?!
TH-THUMP
Michelle?! Gabrielle?!
CALM DOWN.
SHE'S MORE LIKE A DEMON THAN AN ANGEL.
HUH?
Demon?

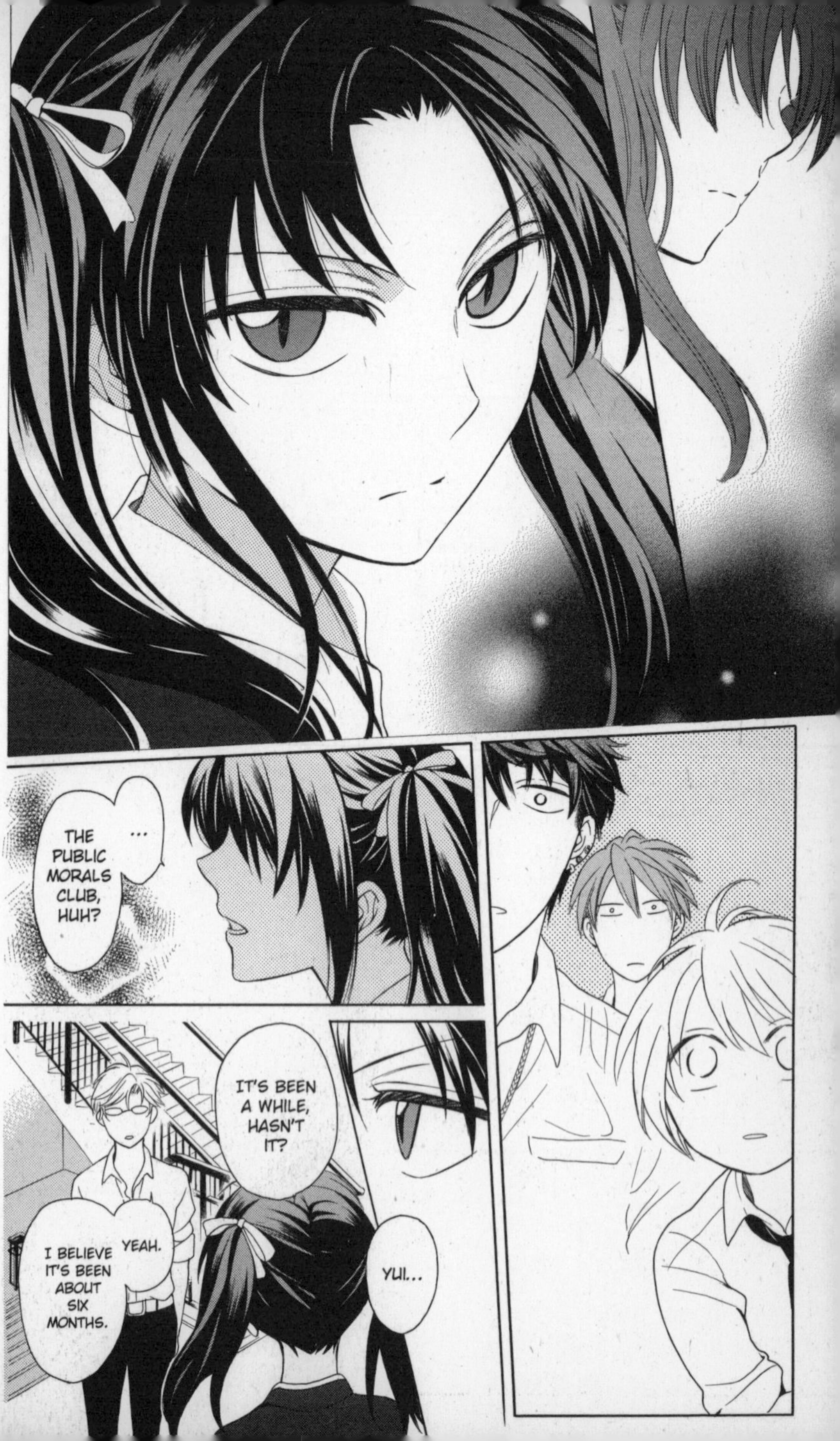
...
THE PUBLIC MORALS CLUB, HUH?
IT'S BEEN A WHILE, HASN'T IT?
YUI...
YEAH.
I BELIEVE IT'S BEEN ABOUT SIX MONTHS.

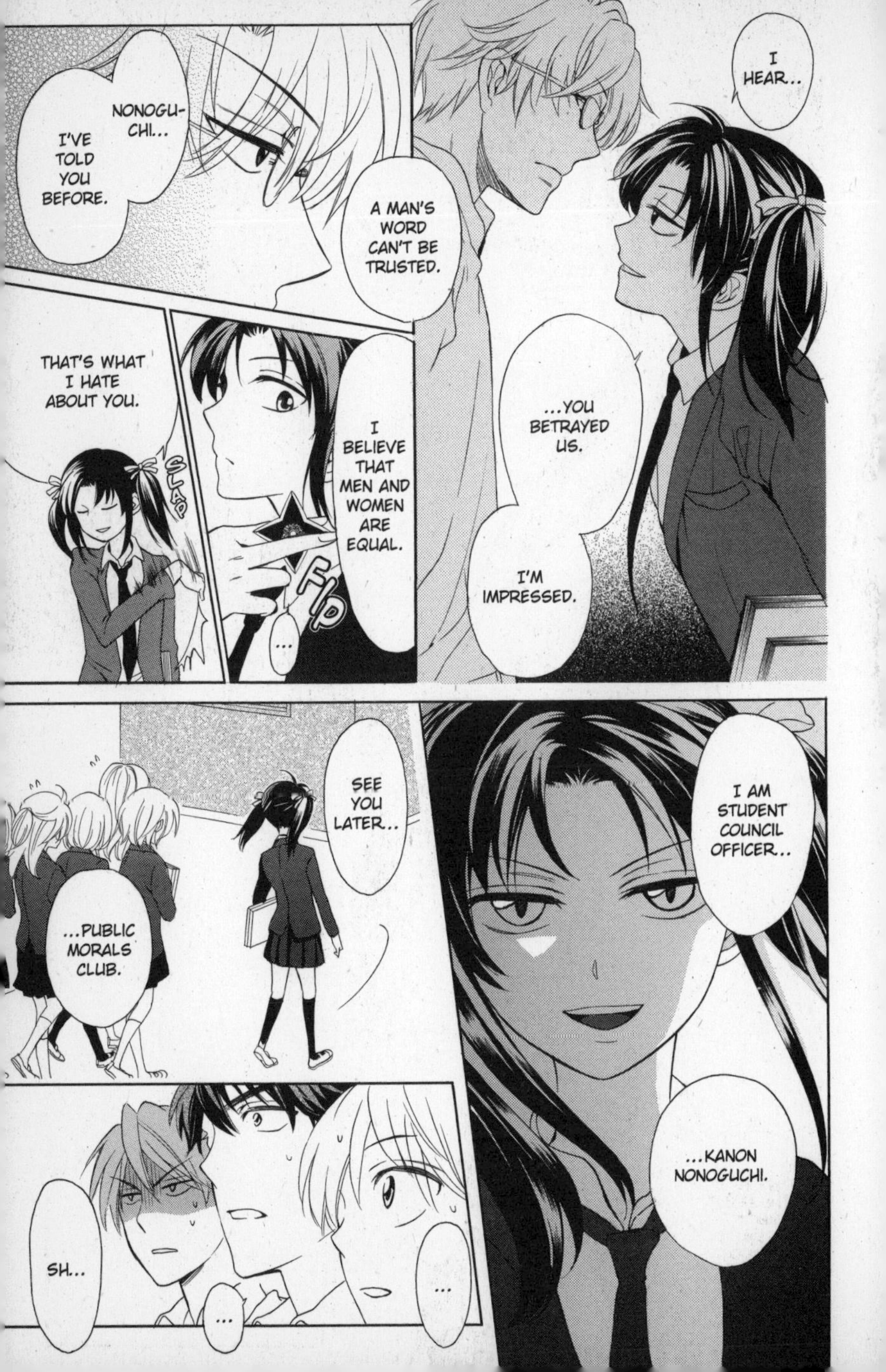
I HEAR...
...YOU BETRAYED US.
I'M IMPRESSED.
NONOGU-CHI...
I'VE TOLD YOU BEFORE.
A MAN'S WORD CAN'T BE TRUSTED.
I BELIEVE THAT MEN AND WOMEN ARE EQUAL.
FLIP
...
SLAP
THAT'S WHAT I HATE ABOUT YOU.
I AM STUDENT COUNCIL OFFICER...
...KANON NONOGUCHI.
SEE YOU LATER...
...PUBLIC MORALS CLUB.
...
...
SH...

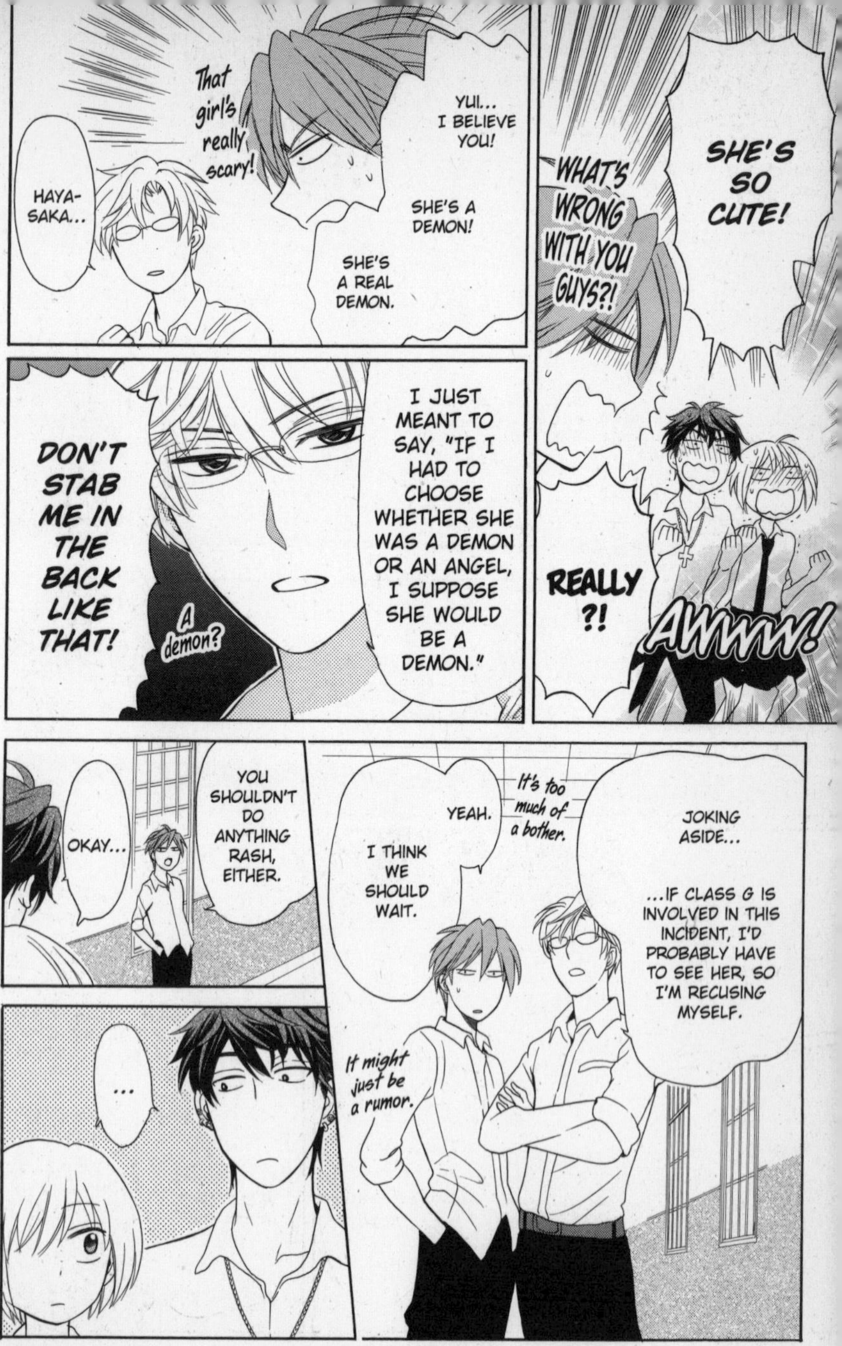
SHE'S SO CUTE!
WHAT'S WRONG WITH YOU GUYS?!
REALLY?!
AWWW!
YUI... I BELIEVE YOU!
That girl's really scary!
SHE'S A DEMON!
SHE'S A REAL DEMON.
HAYA-SAKA...
I JUST MEANT TO SAY, "IF I HAD TO CHOOSE WHETHER SHE WAS A DEMON OR AN ANGEL, I SUPPOSE SHE WOULD BE A DEMON."
A demon?
DON'T STAB ME IN THE BACK LIKE THAT!
JOKING ASIDE...
...IF CLASS G IS INVOLVED IN THIS INCIDENT, I'D PROBABLY HAVE TO SEE HER, SO I'M RECUSING MYSELF.
It's too much of a bother.
YEAH.
I THINK WE SHOULD WAIT.
It might just be a rumor.
YOU SHOULDN'T DO ANYTHING RASH, EITHER.
OKAY...
...

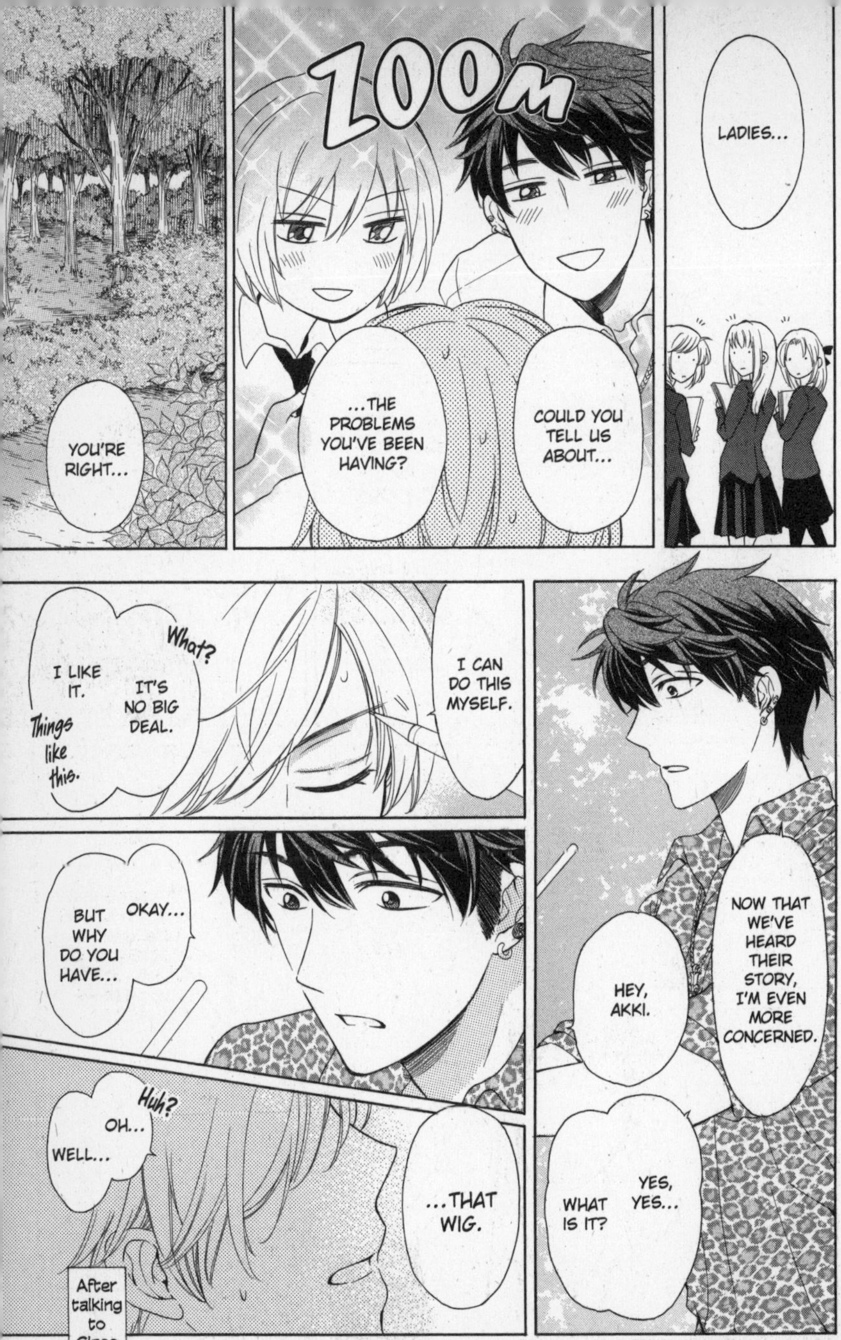
LADIES...
ZOOM
COULD YOU TELL US ABOUT...
...THE PROBLEMS YOU'VE BEEN HAVING?
YOU'RE RIGHT...
NOW THAT WE'VE HEARD THEIR STORY, I'M EVEN MORE CONCERNED.
HEY, AKKI.
YES, YES...
WHAT IS IT?
I CAN DO THIS MYSELF.
What?
IT'S NO BIG DEAL.
I LIKE IT.
Things like this.
OKAY...
BUT WHY DO YOU HAVE...
...THAT WIG.
Huh?
OH...
WELL...
After talking to Class G...

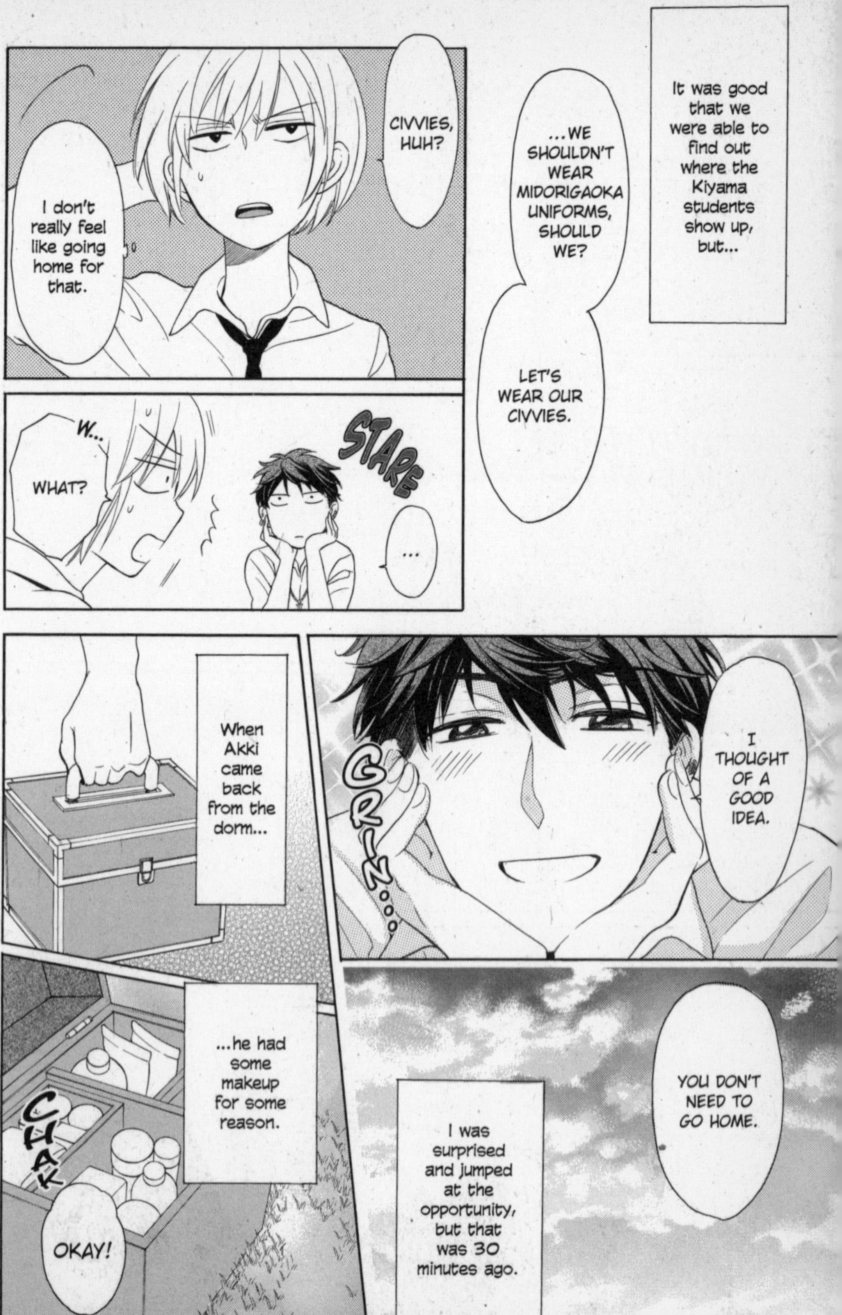
It was good that we were able to find out where the Kiyama students show up, but...
...WE SHOULDN'T WEAR MIDORIGAOKA UNIFORMS, SHOULD WE?
LET'S WEAR OUR CIVVIES.
CIVVIES, HUH?
I don't really feel like going home for that.
STARE
...
W... WHAT?
I THOUGHT OF A GOOD IDEA.
GRIN...
When Akki came back from the dorm...
YOU DON'T NEED TO GO HOME.
I was surprised and jumped at the opportunity, but that was 30 minutes ago.
...he had some makeup for some reason.
CHAK
OKAY!

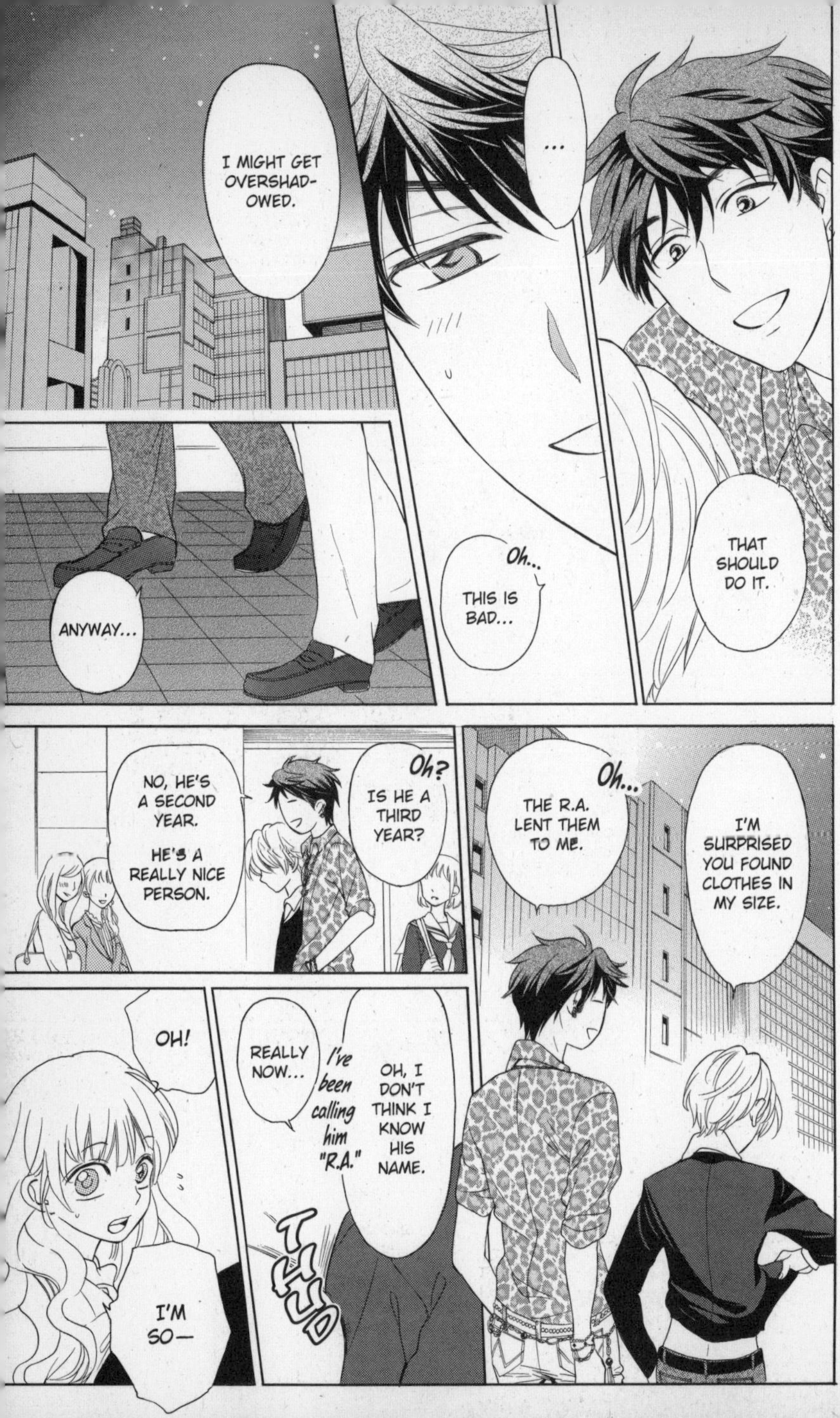
THAT SHOULD DO IT.
...
Oh... THIS IS BAD...
I MIGHT GET OVERSHADOWED.
ANYWAY...
I'M SURPRISED YOU FOUND CLOTHES IN MY SIZE.
Oh... THE R.A. LENT THEM TO ME.
Oh? IS HE A THIRD YEAR?
NO, HE'S A SECOND YEAR.
HE'S A REALLY NICE PERSON.
OH, I DON'T THINK I KNOW HIS NAME.
I've been calling him "R.A."
REALLY NOW...
THUD
OH!
I'M SO—

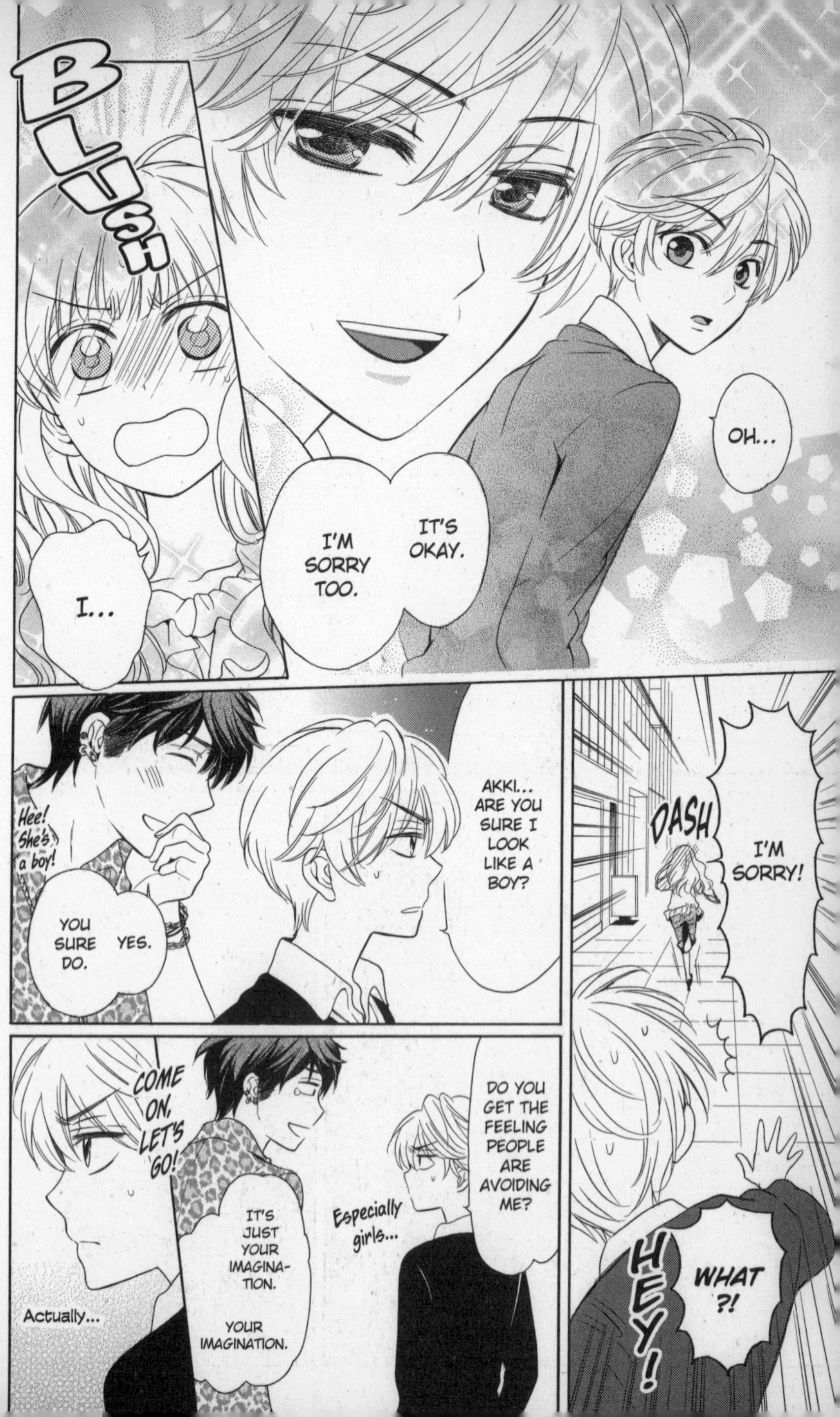
OH...
IT'S OKAY.
I'M SORRY TOO.
BLUSH
I...
I'M SORRY!
DASH
HEY!
WHAT?!
AKKI... ARE YOU SURE I LOOK LIKE A BOY?
Hee! She's a boy!
YES.
YOU SURE DO.
DO YOU GET THE FEELING PEOPLE ARE AVOIDING ME?
Especially girls...
COME ON, LET'S GO!
IT'S JUST YOUR IMAGINATION.
YOUR IMAGINATION.
Actually...

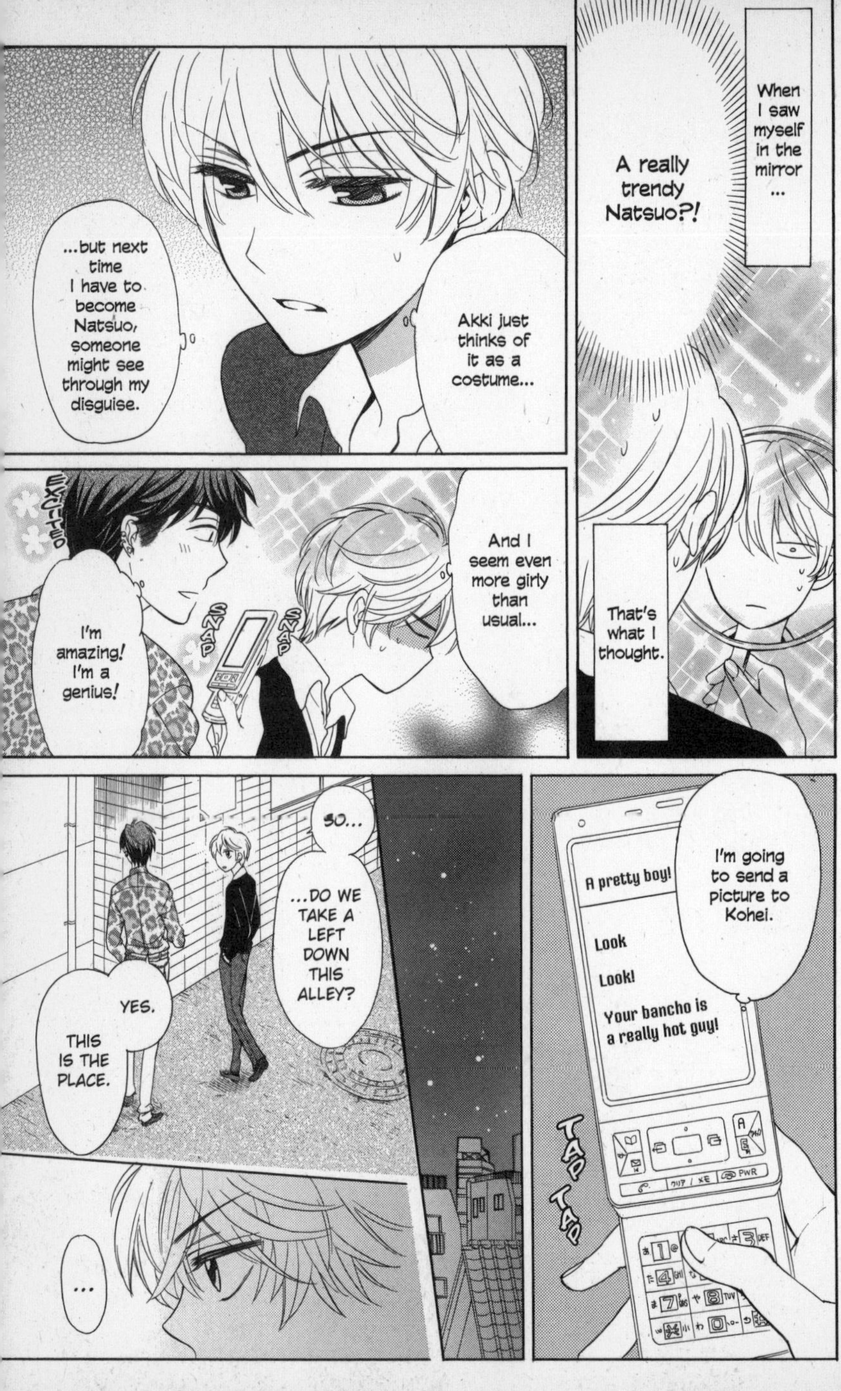
When I saw myself in the mirror ...
A really trendy Natsuo?!
That's what I thought.
Akki just thinks of it as a costume...
...but next time I have to become Natsuo, someone might see through my disguise.
And I seem even more girly than usual...
SNAP
SNAP
EXCITED
I'm amazing! I'm a genius!
I'm going to send a picture to Kohei.
A pretty boy!
Look
Look!
Your bancho is a really hot guy!
TAP TAP
SO...
...DO WE TAKE A LEFT DOWN THIS ALLEY?
YES.
THIS IS THE PLACE.
...

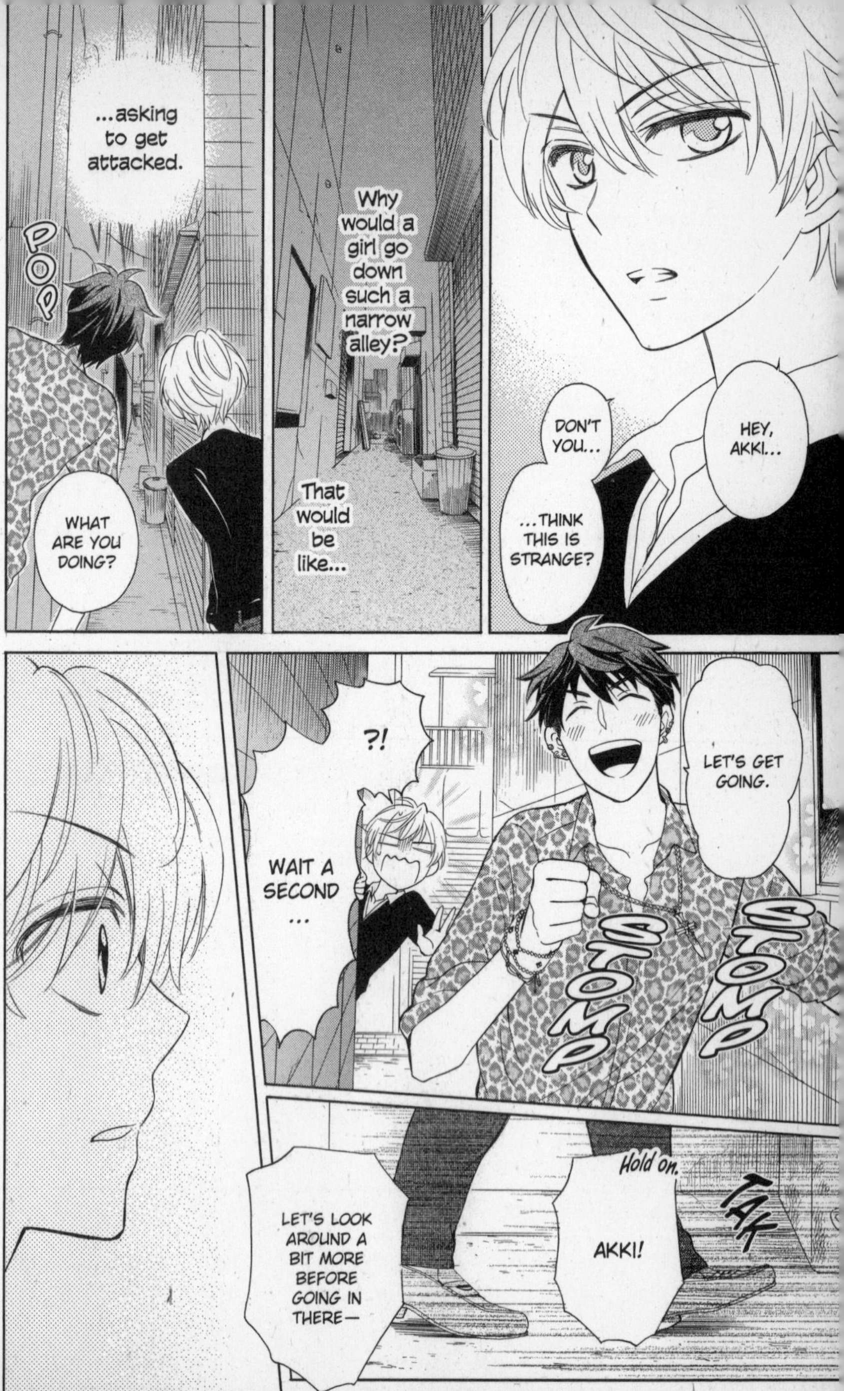
HEY, AKKI...
DON'T YOU...
...THINK THIS IS STRANGE?
Why would a girl go down such a narrow alley?
That would be like...
...asking to get attacked.
POP
WHAT ARE YOU DOING?
LET'S GET GOING.
STOMP STOMP
?!
WAIT A SECOND ...
Hold on.
TAK
AKKI!
LET'S LOOK AROUND A BIT MORE BEFORE GOING IN THERE—

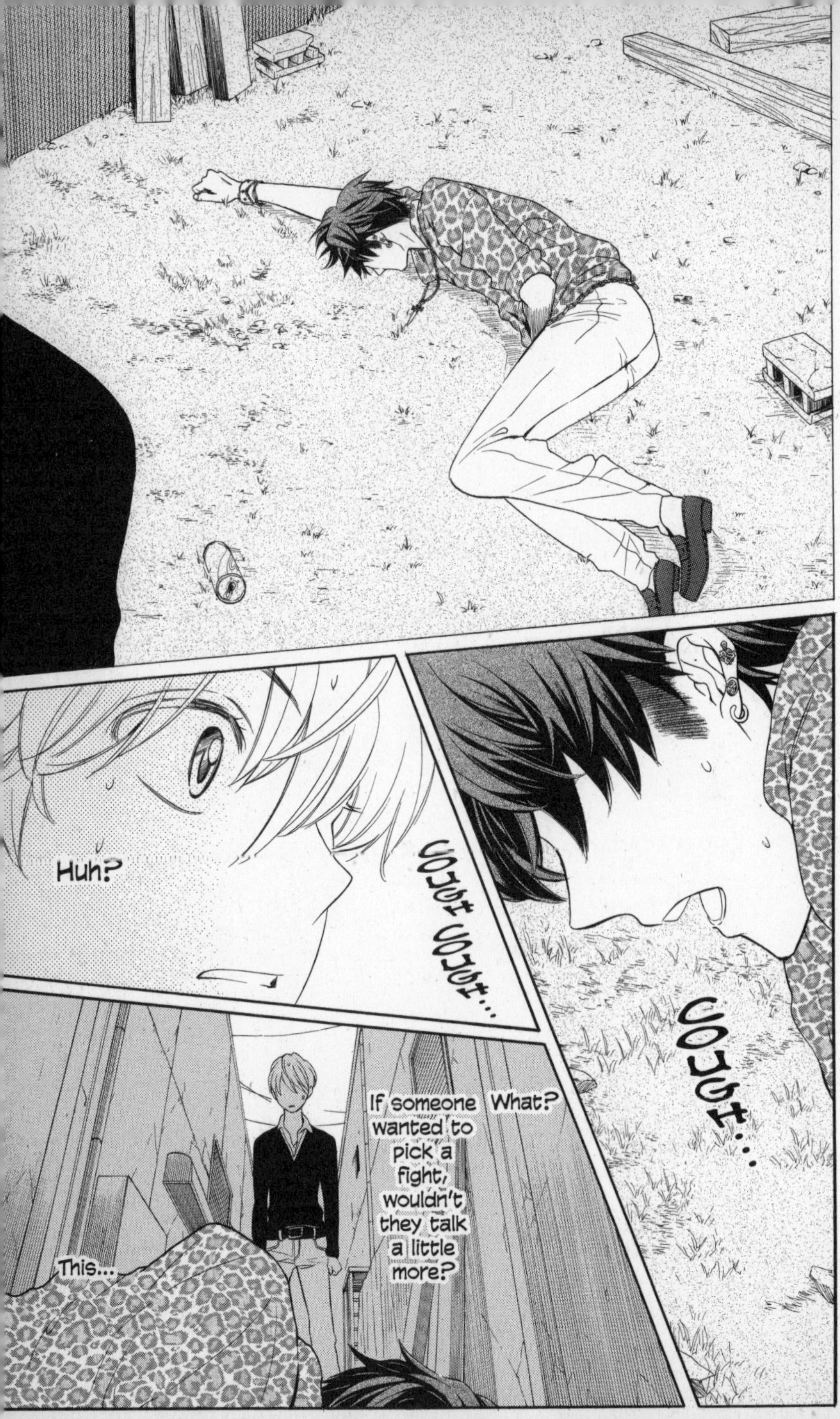
COUGH...
COUGH COUGH...
Huh?
What?
If someone wanted to pick a fight, wouldn't they talk a little more?
This...

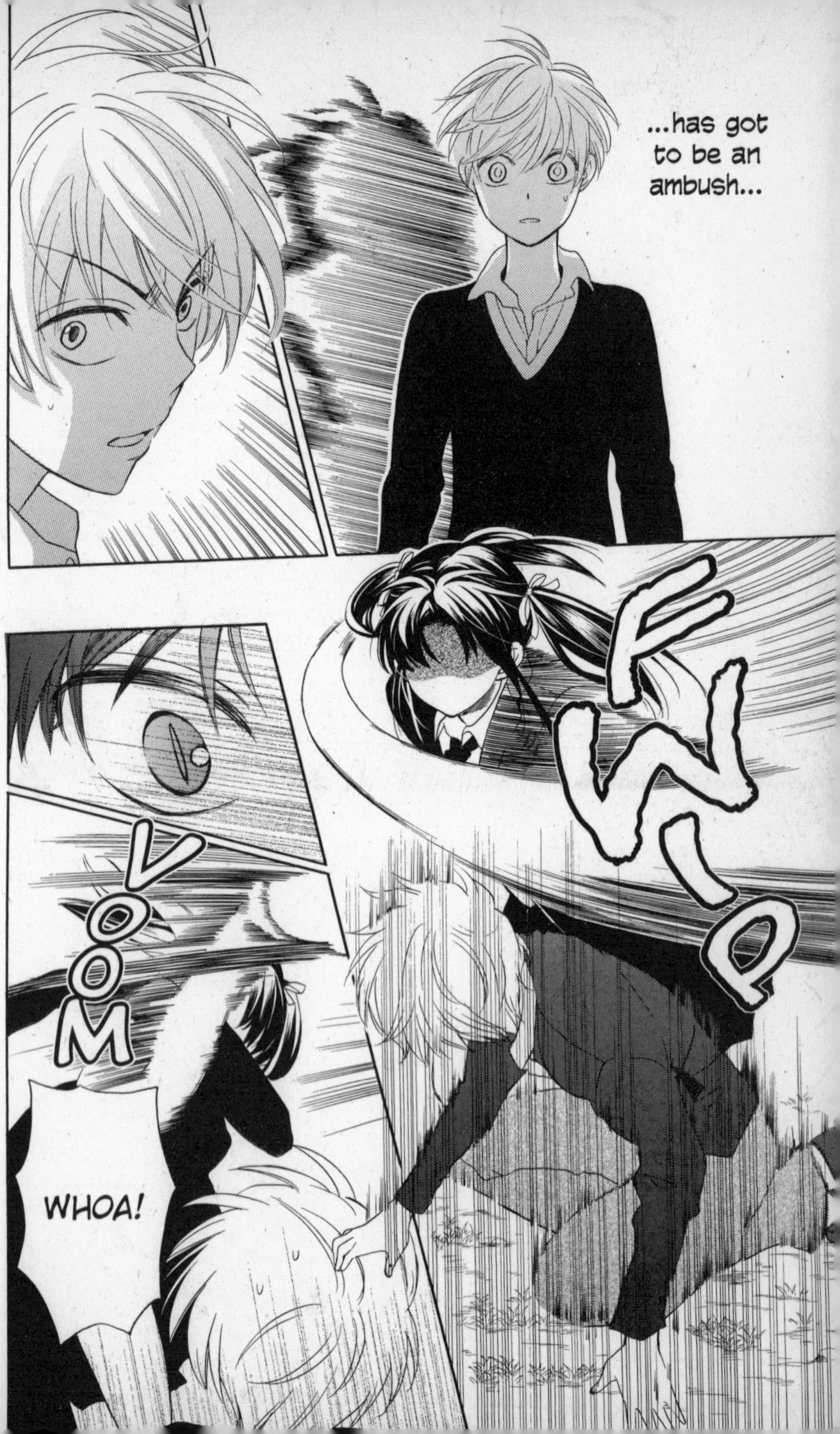
...has got to be an ambush...
FWIP
VOOM
WHOA!

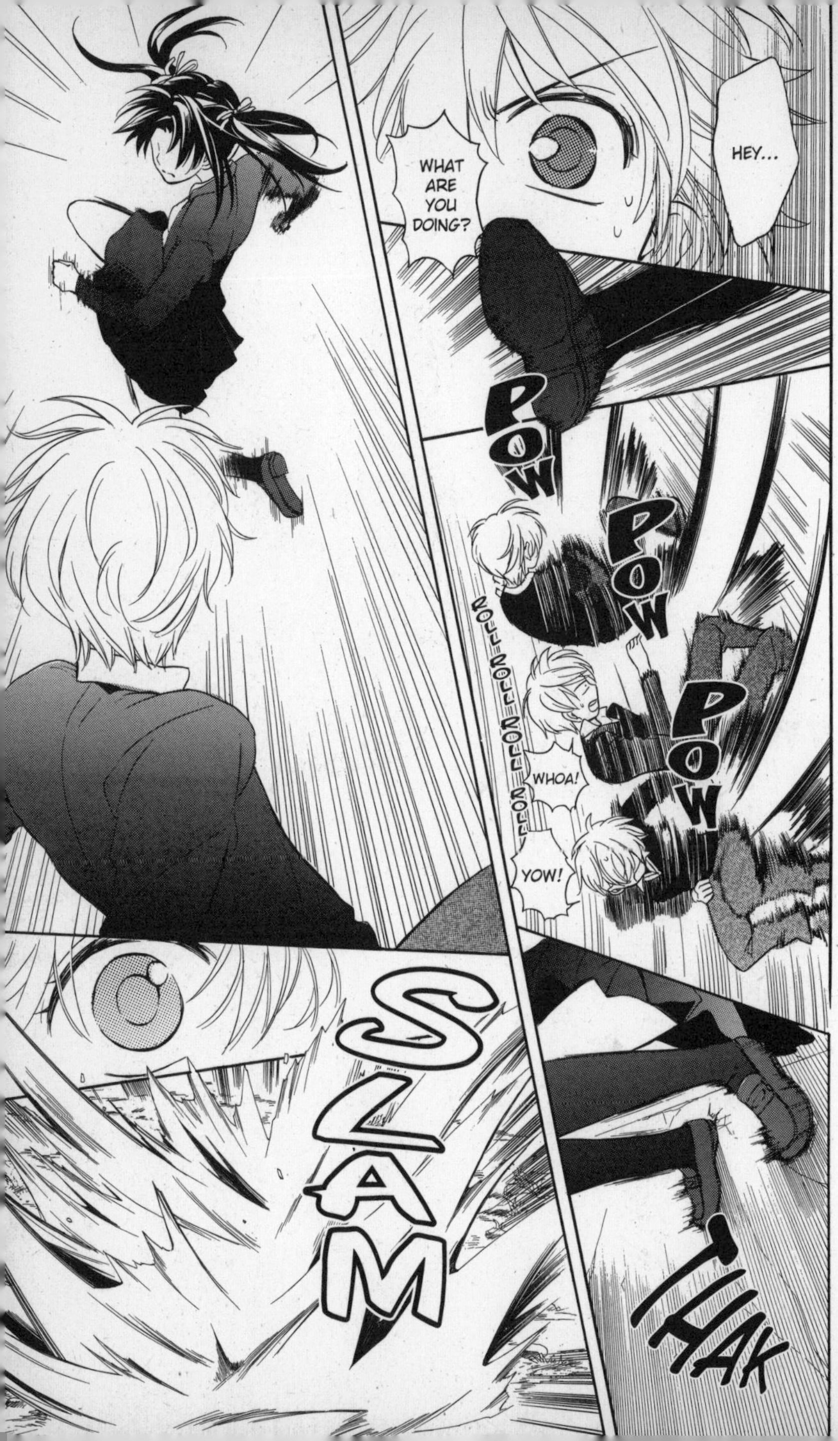
HEY...
WHAT ARE YOU DOING?
POW
POW
POW
ROLL ROLL ROLL ROLL
WHOA!
YOW!
THAK
SLAM

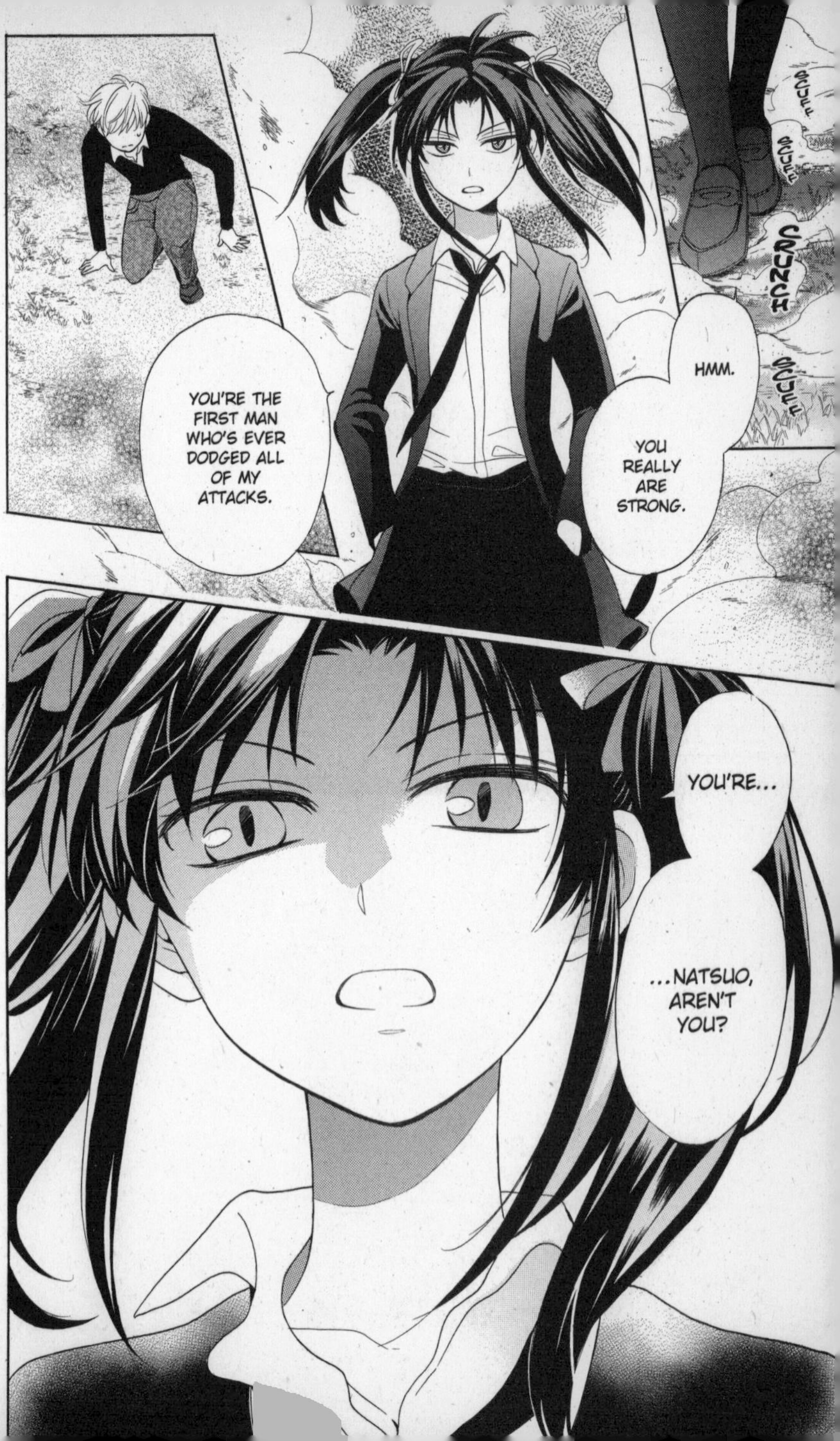
SCUFF
SCUFF
CRUNCH
SCUFF
HMM.
YOU REALLY ARE STRONG.
YOU'RE THE FIRST MAN WHO'S EVER DODGED ALL OF MY ATTACKS.
YOU'RE...
...NATSUO, AREN'T YOU?

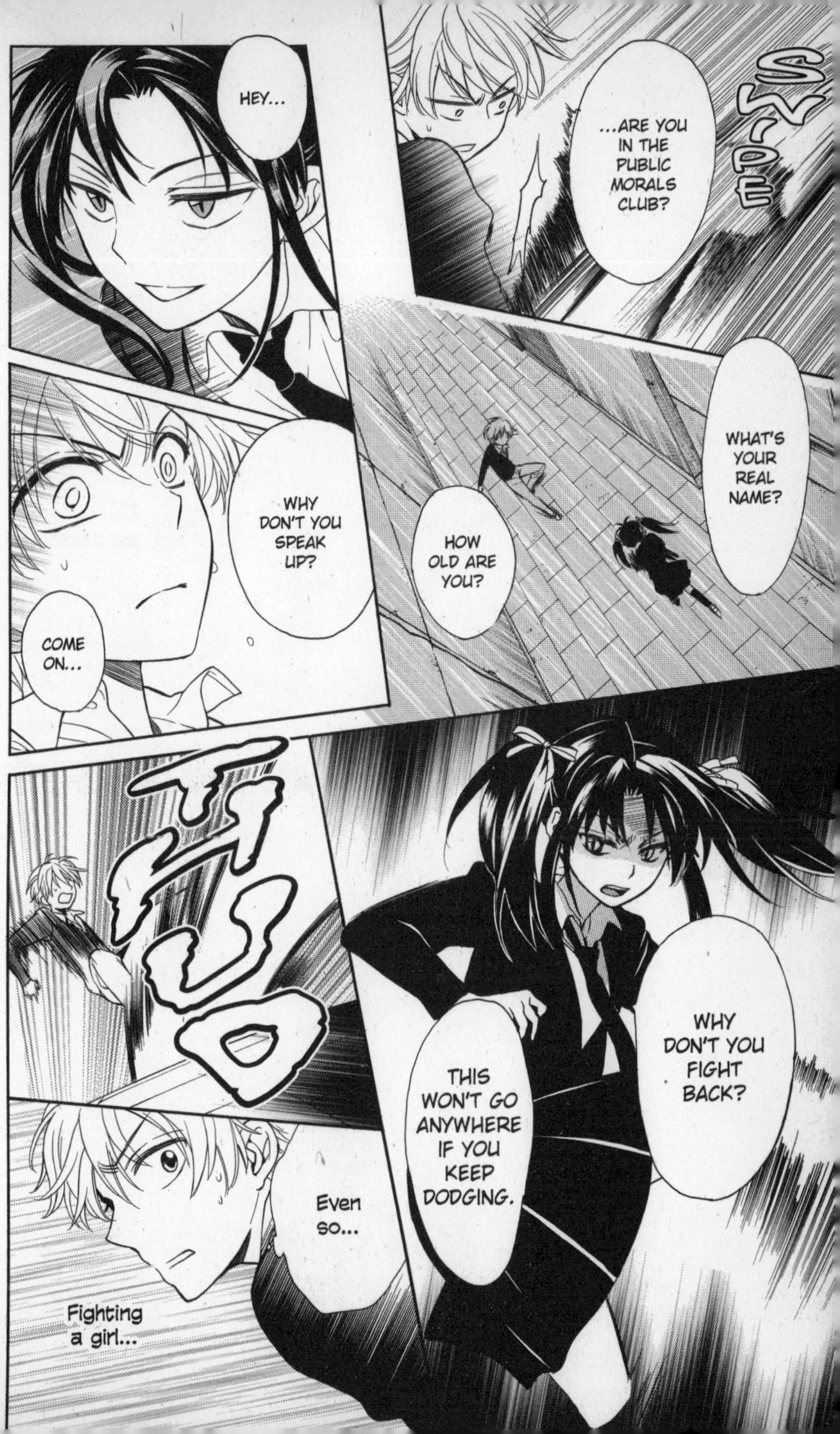
SWIPE
...ARE YOU IN THE PUBLIC MORALS CLUB?
HEY...
WHAT'S YOUR REAL NAME?
HOW OLD ARE YOU?
WHY DON'T YOU SPEAK UP?
COME ON...
WHY DON'T YOU FIGHT BACK?
THIS WON'T GO ANYWHERE IF YOU KEEP DODGING.
Even so...
Fighting a girl...

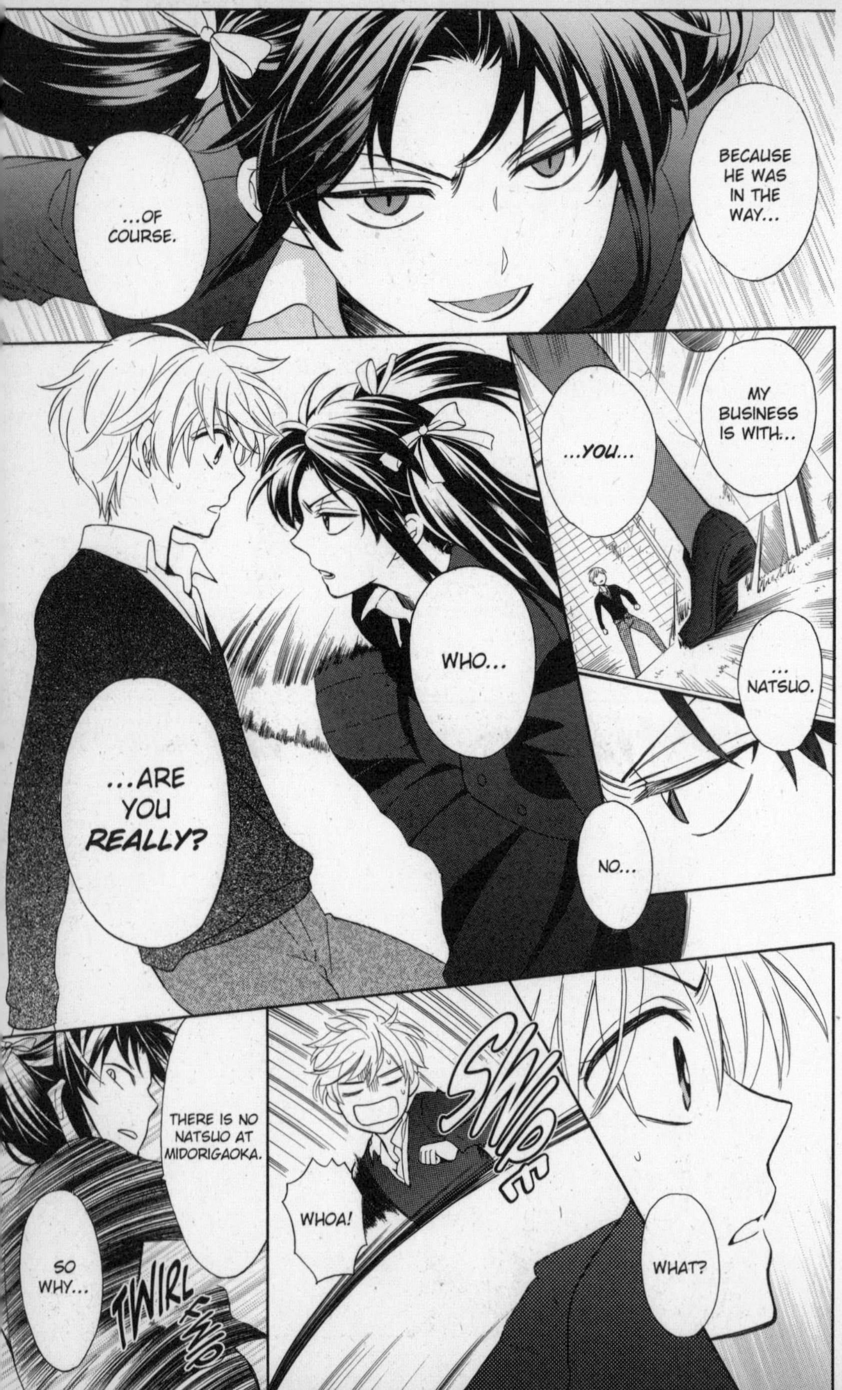
BECAUSE HE WAS IN THE WAY...
...OF COURSE.
MY BUSINESS IS WITH...
...YOU...
...NATSUO.
NO...
WHO...
...ARE YOU REALLY?
WHAT?
SWIPE
WHOA!
THERE IS NO NATSUO AT MIDORIGAOKA.
SO WHY...
TWIRL
FWIP

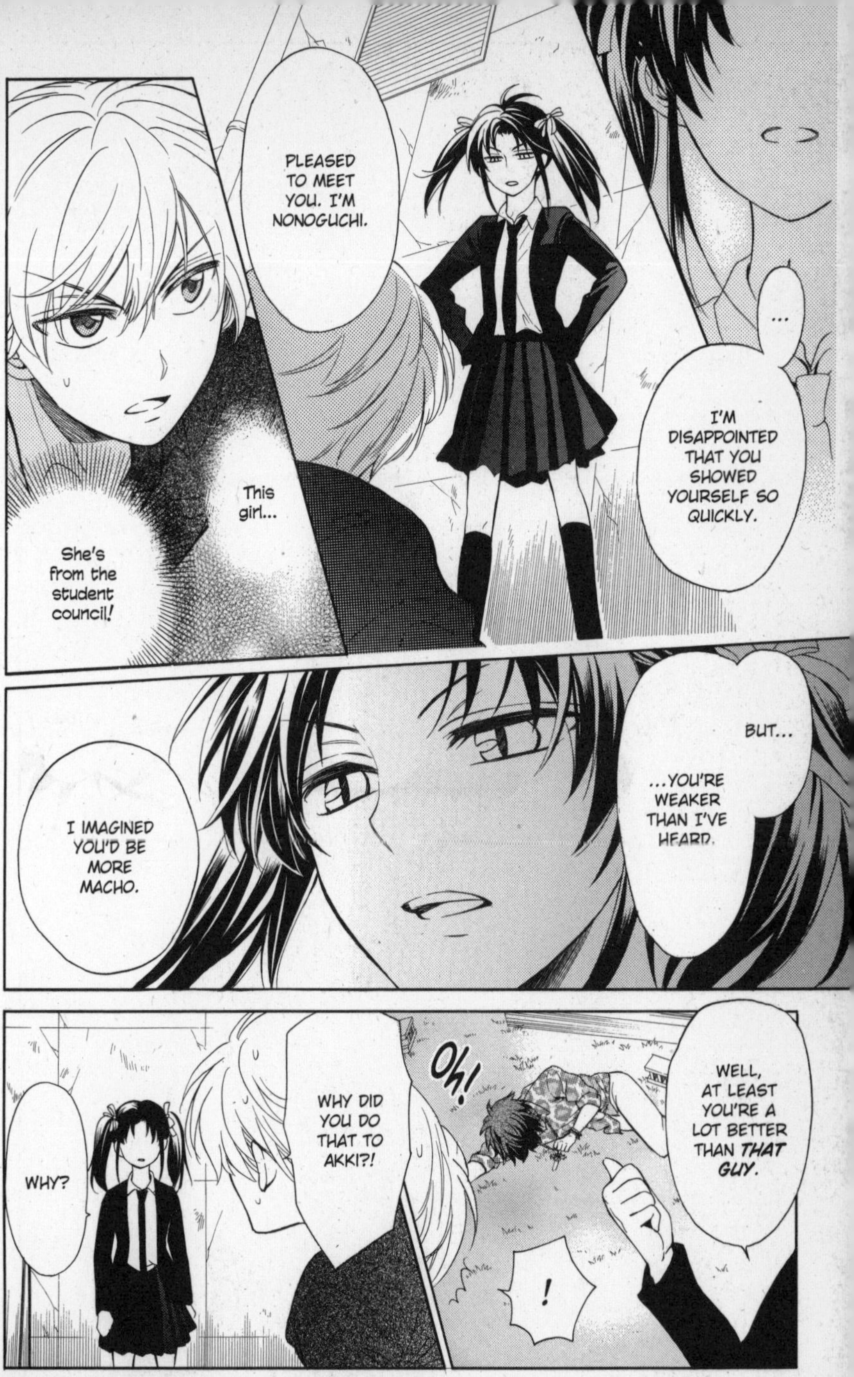
...
I'M DISAPPOINTED THAT YOU SHOWED YOURSELF SO QUICKLY.
PLEASED TO MEET YOU. I'M NONOGUCHI.
This girl...
She's from the student council!
BUT...
...YOU'RE WEAKER THAN I'VE HEARD.
I IMAGINED YOU'D BE MORE MACHO.
WELL, AT LEAST YOU'RE A LOT BETTER THAN THAT GUY.
!
OH!
WHY DID YOU DO THAT TO AKKI?!
WHY?

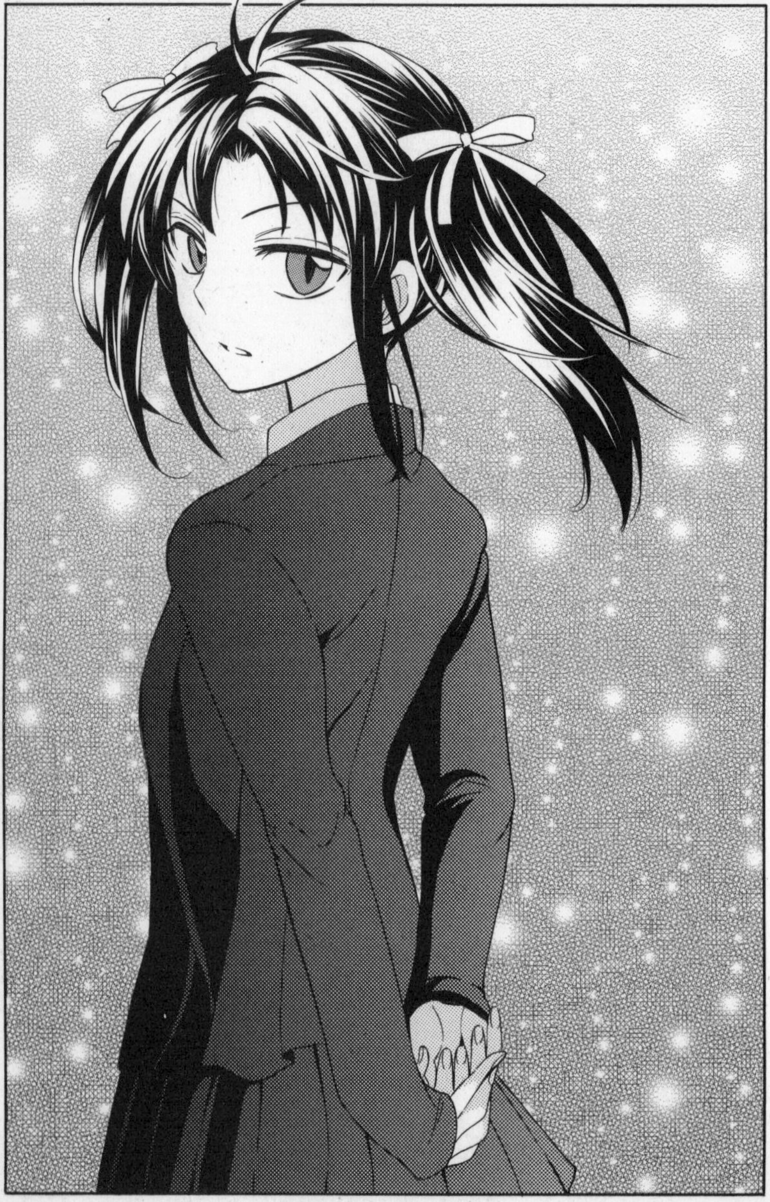

Chapter 71

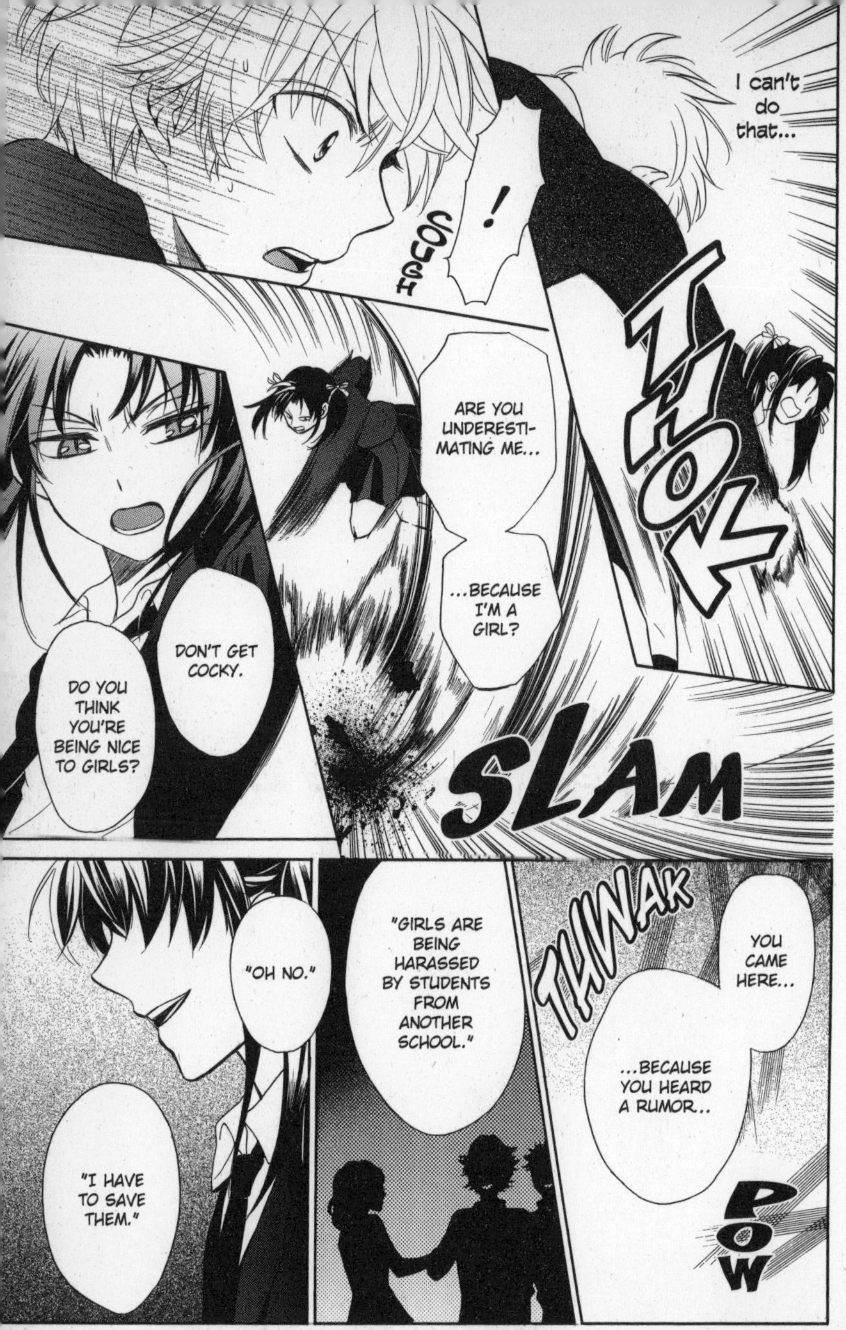
I can't do that...
!
COUGH
THOK
ARE YOU UNDERESTI-MATING ME...
...BECAUSE I'M A GIRL?
SLAM
DON'T GET COCKY.
DO YOU THINK YOU'RE BEING NICE TO GIRLS?
THWAK
YOU CAME HERE...
...BECAUSE YOU HEARD A RUMOR..
POW
"GIRLS ARE BEING HARASSED BY STUDENTS FROM ANOTHER SCHOOL."
"OH NO."
"I HAVE TO SAVE THEM."

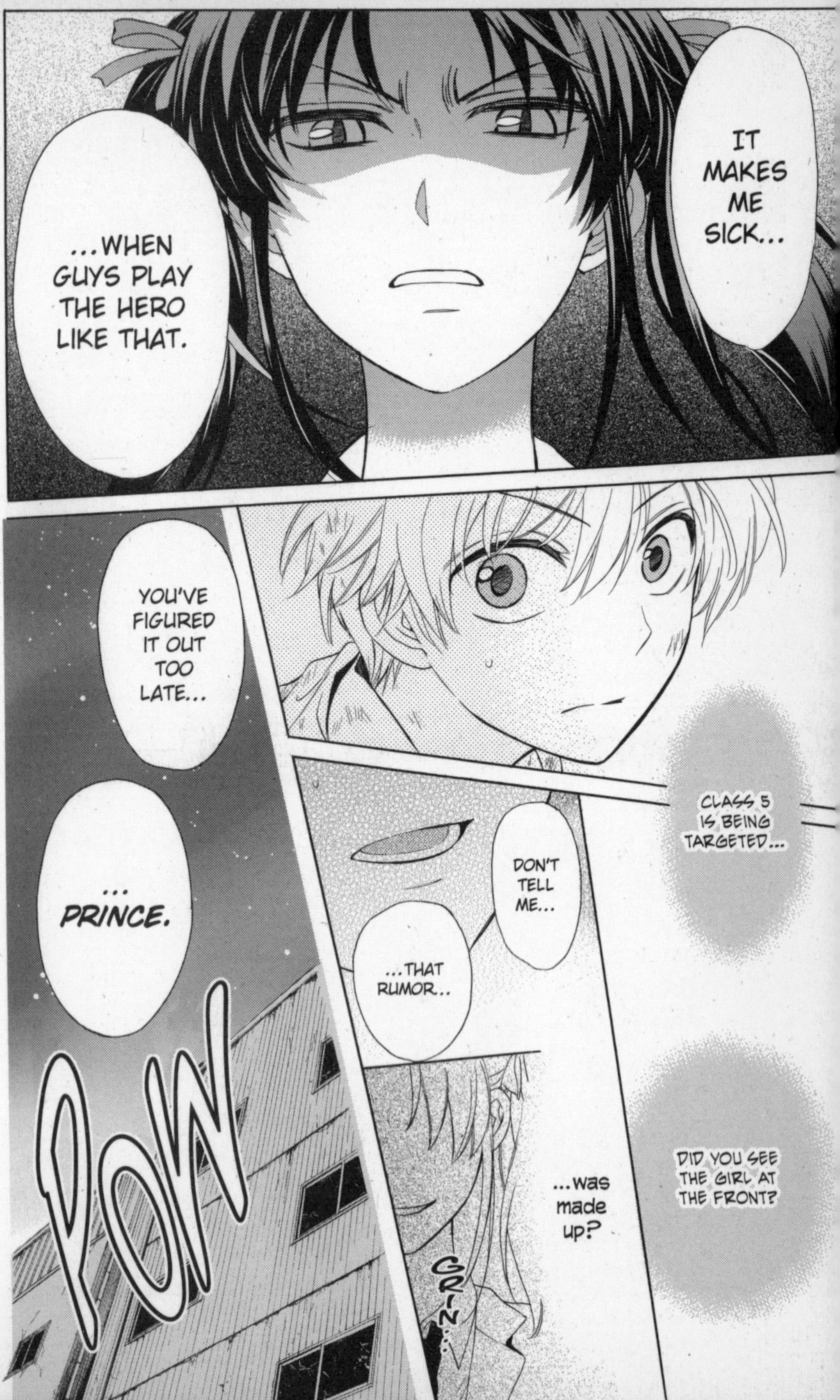
IT MAKES ME SICK...
...WHEN GUYS PLAY THE HERO LIKE THAT.
CLASS 5 IS BEING TARGETED...
DON'T TELL ME...
...THAT RUMOR...
DID YOU SEE THE GIRL AT THE FRONT?
...was made up?
GRIN...
YOU'VE FIGURED IT OUT TOO LATE...
... PRINCE.
POW

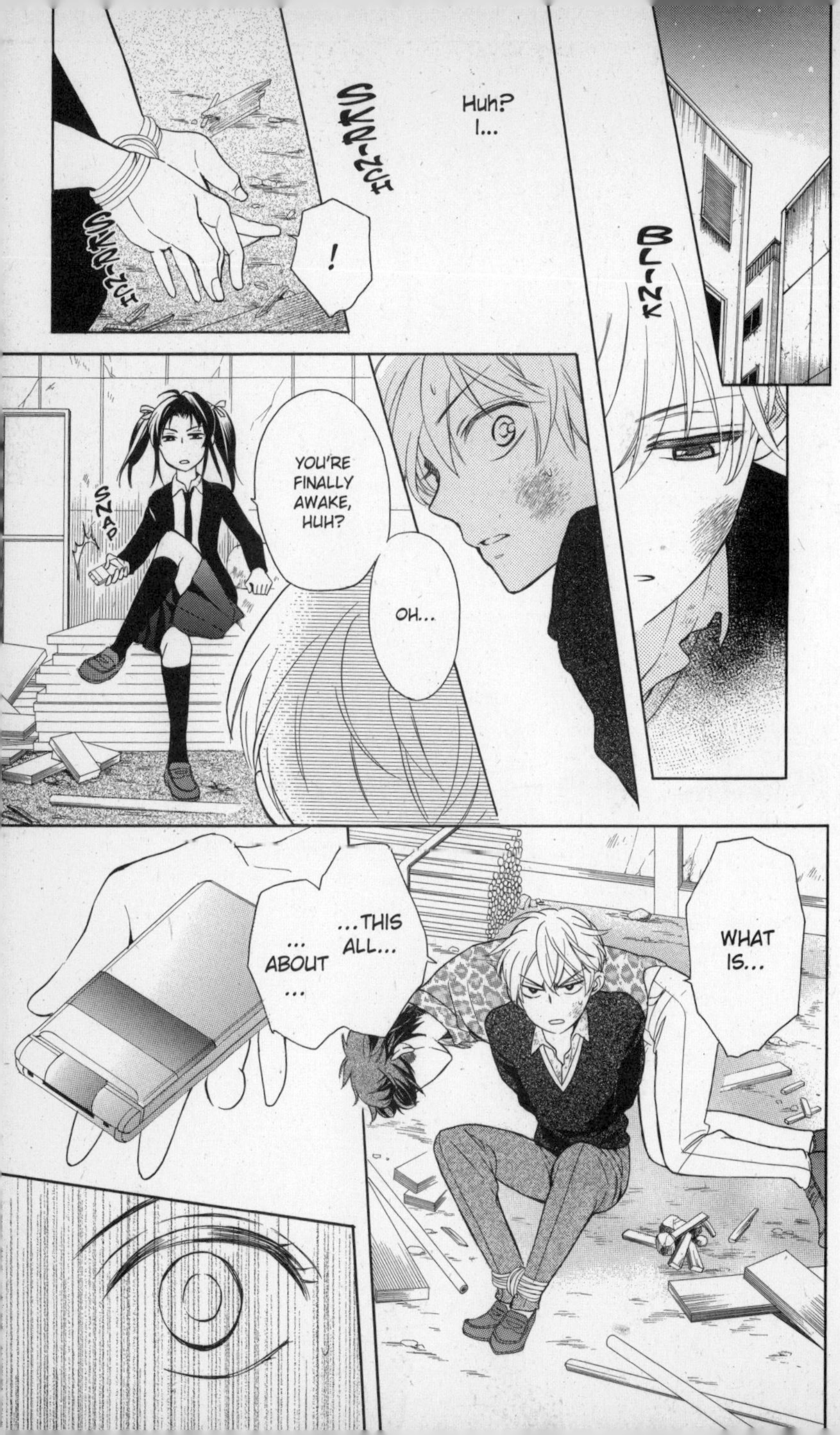

Huh? I...
BLINK
SKRINCH
!
SKRINCH
YOU'RE FINALLY AWAKE, HUH?
SNAP
OH...
WHAT IS...
...THIS ALL...
... ABOUT ...

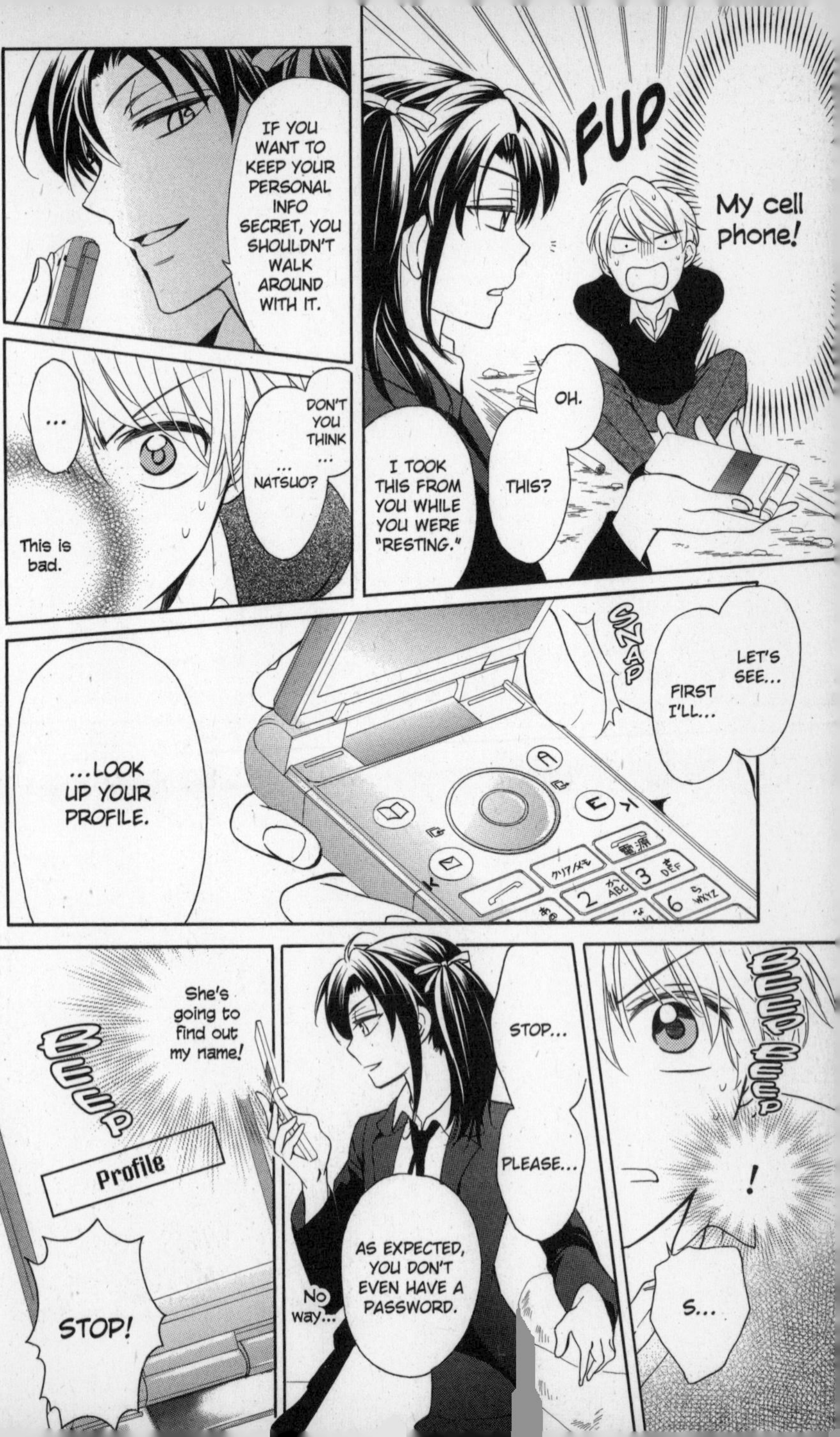
FUP
My cell phone!
OH.
THIS?
I TOOK THIS FROM YOU WHILE YOU WERE "RESTING."
IF YOU WANT TO KEEP YOUR PERSONAL INFO SECRET, YOU SHOULDN'T WALK AROUND WITH IT.
DON'T YOU THINK ... NATSUO?
...
This is bad.
SNAP
LET'S SEE...
FIRST I'LL...
...LOOK UP YOUR PROFILE.
BEEP BEEP
!
S...
STOP...
PLEASE...
AS EXPECTED, YOU DON'T EVEN HAVE A PASSWORD.
No way...
She's going to find out my name!
BEEP
Profile
STOP!

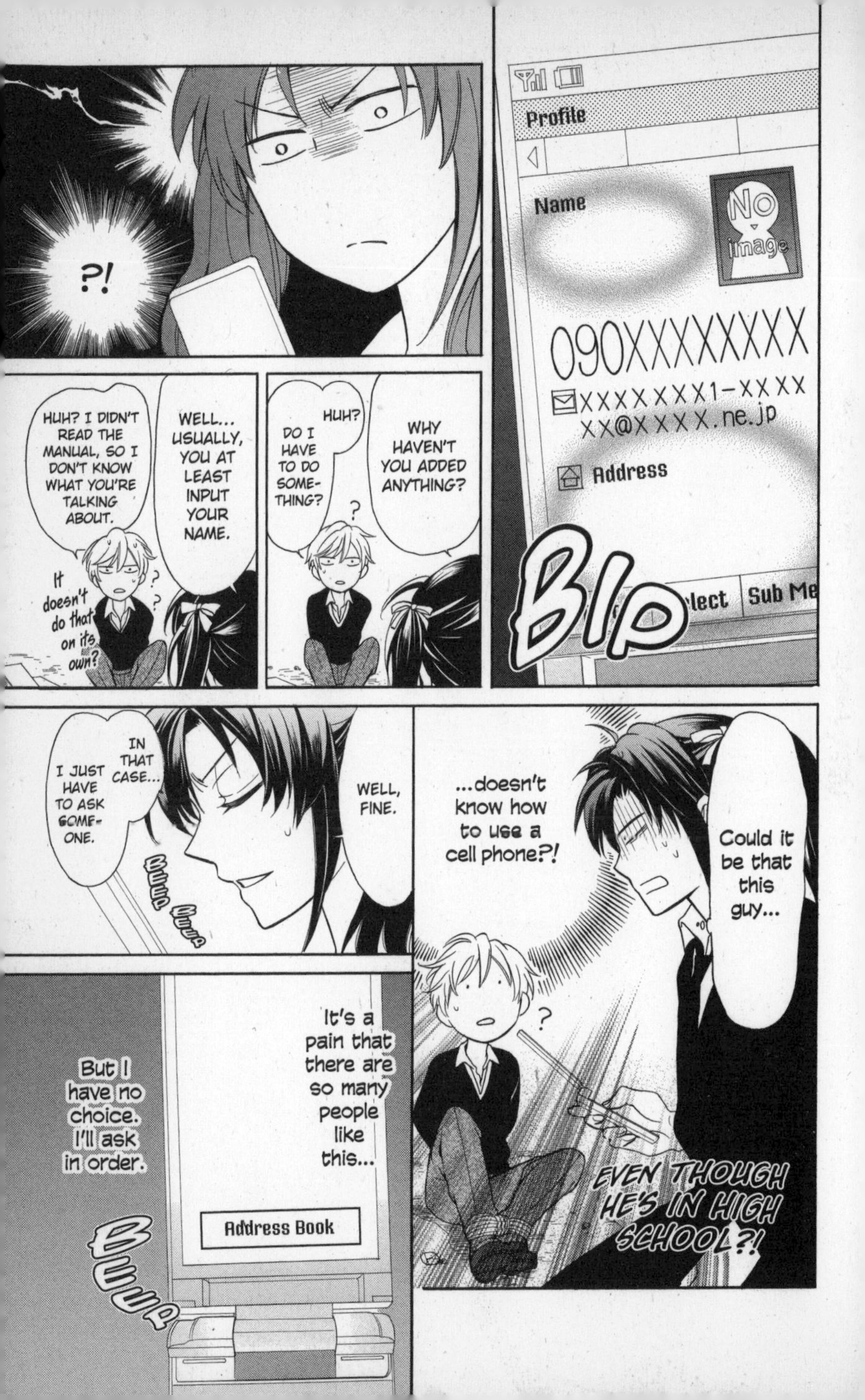

Profile
Name
No image
090XXXXXXXX
XXXXXXX1-XXXX
XX@XXXX.ne.jp
Address
BIP
?!
WHY HAVEN'T YOU ADDED ANYTHING?
HUH? DO I HAVE TO DO SOMETHING?
?
WELL... USUALLY, YOU AT LEAST INPUT YOUR NAME.
HUH? I DIDN'T READ THE MANUAL, SO I DON'T KNOW WHAT YOU'RE TALKING ABOUT.
It doesn't do that on its own?
? ?
Could it be that this guy...
...doesn't know how to use a cell phone?!
?
EVEN THOUGH HE'S IN HIGH SCHOOL?!
WELL, FINE.
IN THAT CASE...
I JUST HAVE TO ASK SOMEONE.
BEEP BEEP
It's a pain that there are so many people like this...
But I have no choice. I'll ask in order.
Address Book
BEEP

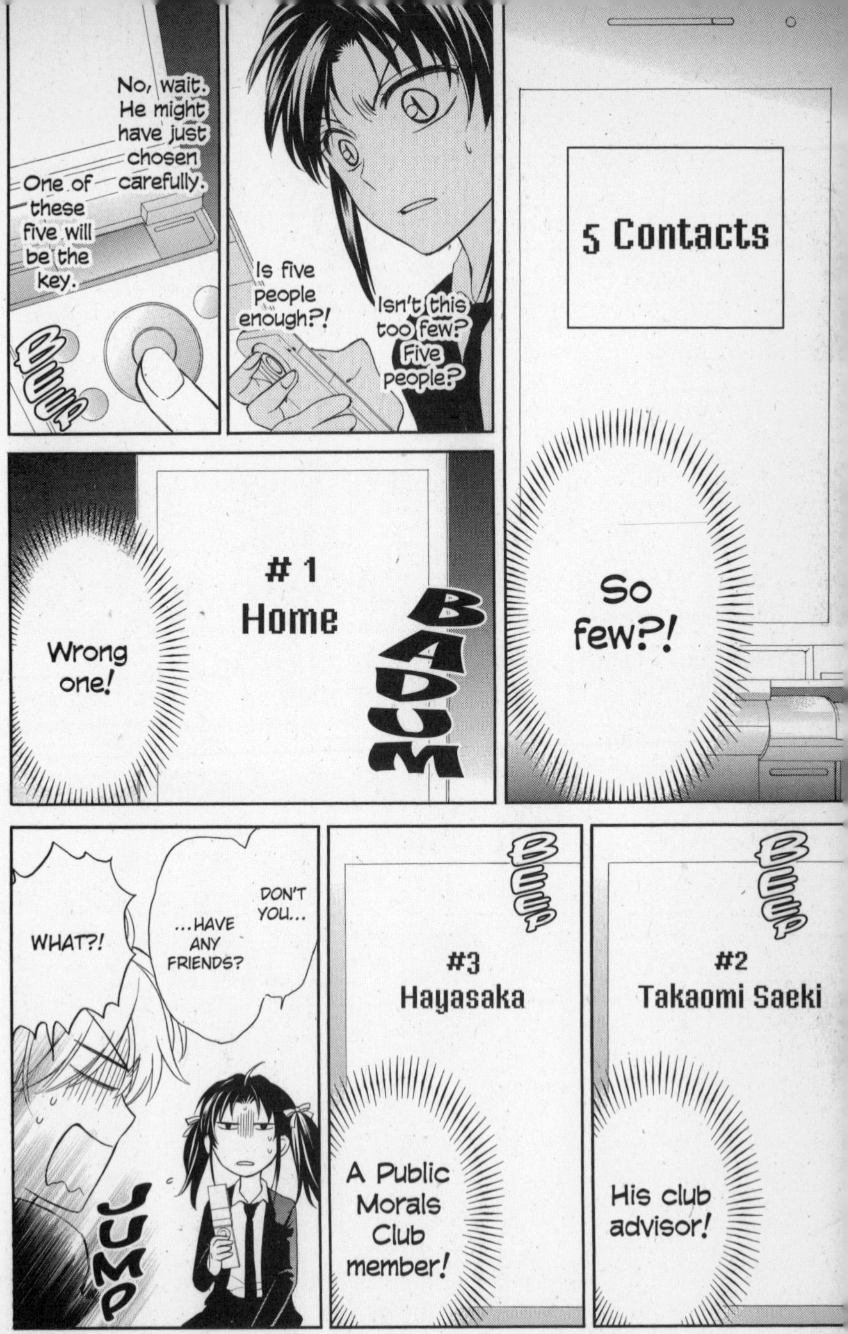
5 Contacts
So few?!
Isn't this too few? Five people?
Is five people enough?!
No, wait. He might have just chosen carefully.
One of these five will be the key.
BEEP
#1 Home
BADUM
Wrong one!
BEEP
#2 Takaomi Saeki
His club advisor!
BEEP
#3 Hayasaka
A Public Morals Club member!
DON'T YOU...
...HAVE ANY FRIENDS?
WHAT?!
JUMP

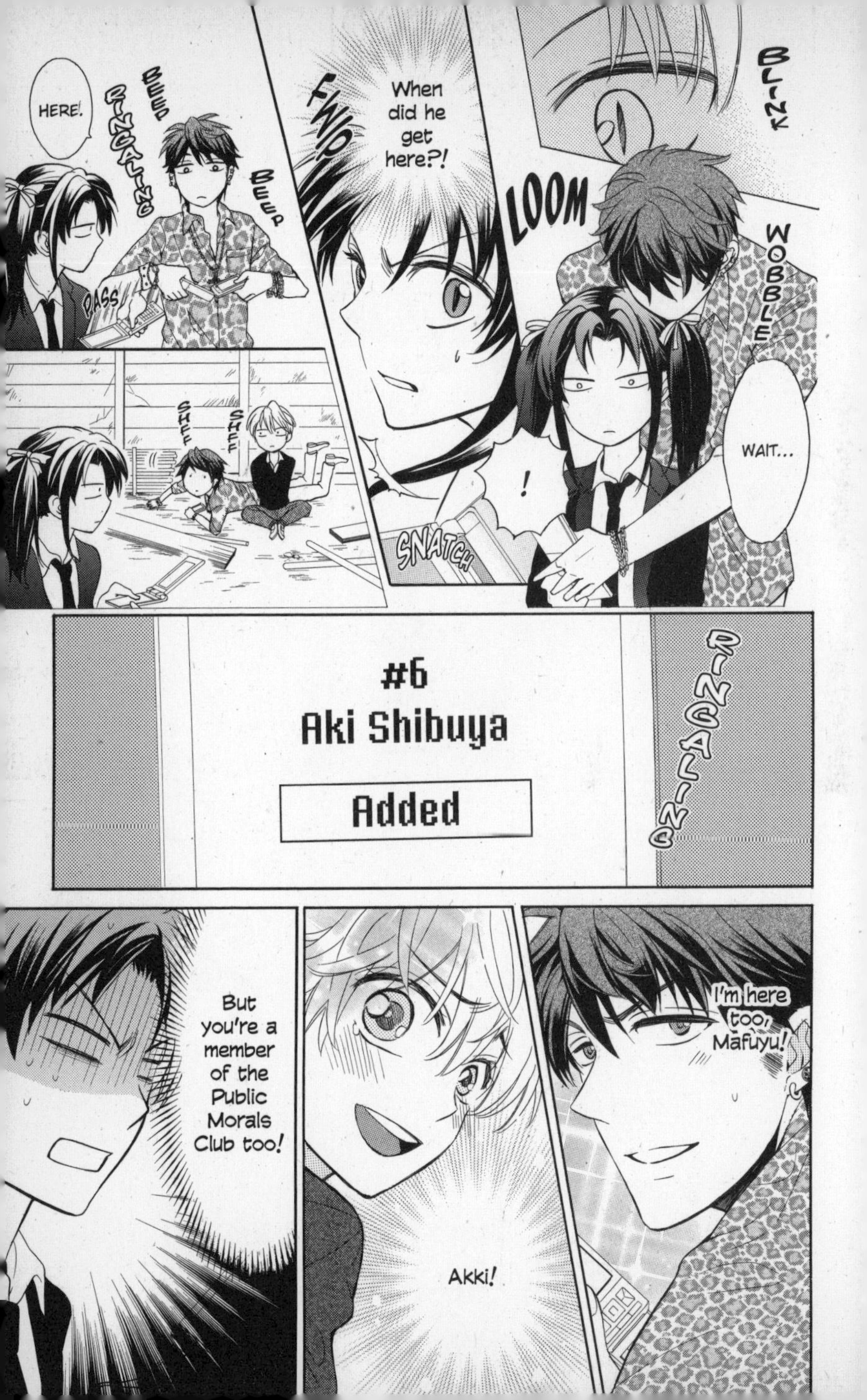
BLINK
LOOM
WOBBLE
WAIT...
FWIP
When did he get here?!
!
SNATCH
HERE!
BEEP
RINGALING
BEEP
PASS
SHEFF
SHEFF
RINGALING
#6
Aki Shibuya
Added
I'm here too, Mafuyu!
Akki!
But you're a member of the Public Morals Club too!

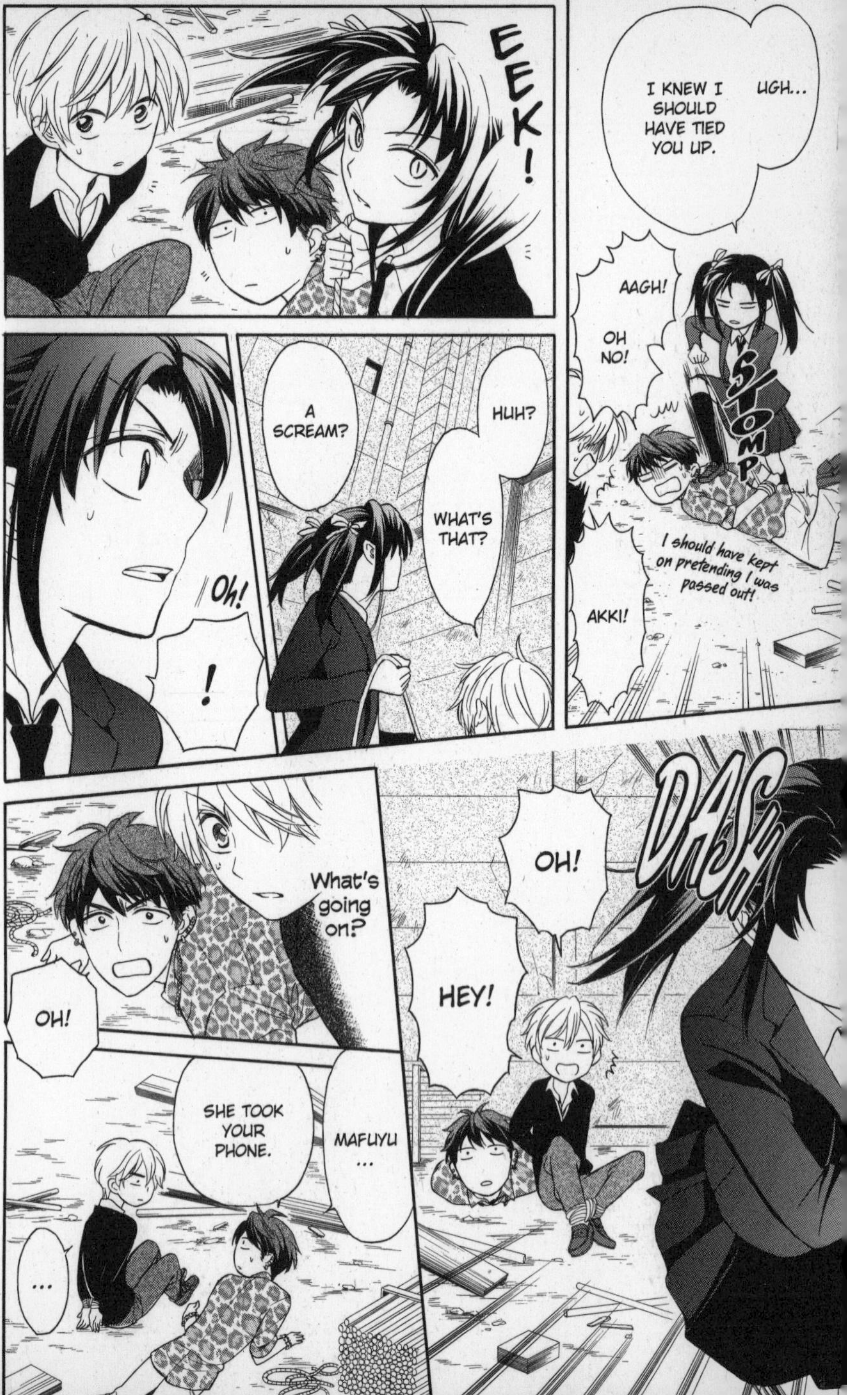
UGH...
I KNEW I SHOULD HAVE TIED YOU UP.
AAGH!
OH NO!
STOMP
I should have kept on pretending I was passed out!
AKKI!
EEK!
HUH?
A SCREAM?
WHAT'S THAT?
Oh!
!
DASH
OH!
HEY!
What's going on?
OH!
MAFUYU ...
SHE TOOK YOUR PHONE.
...

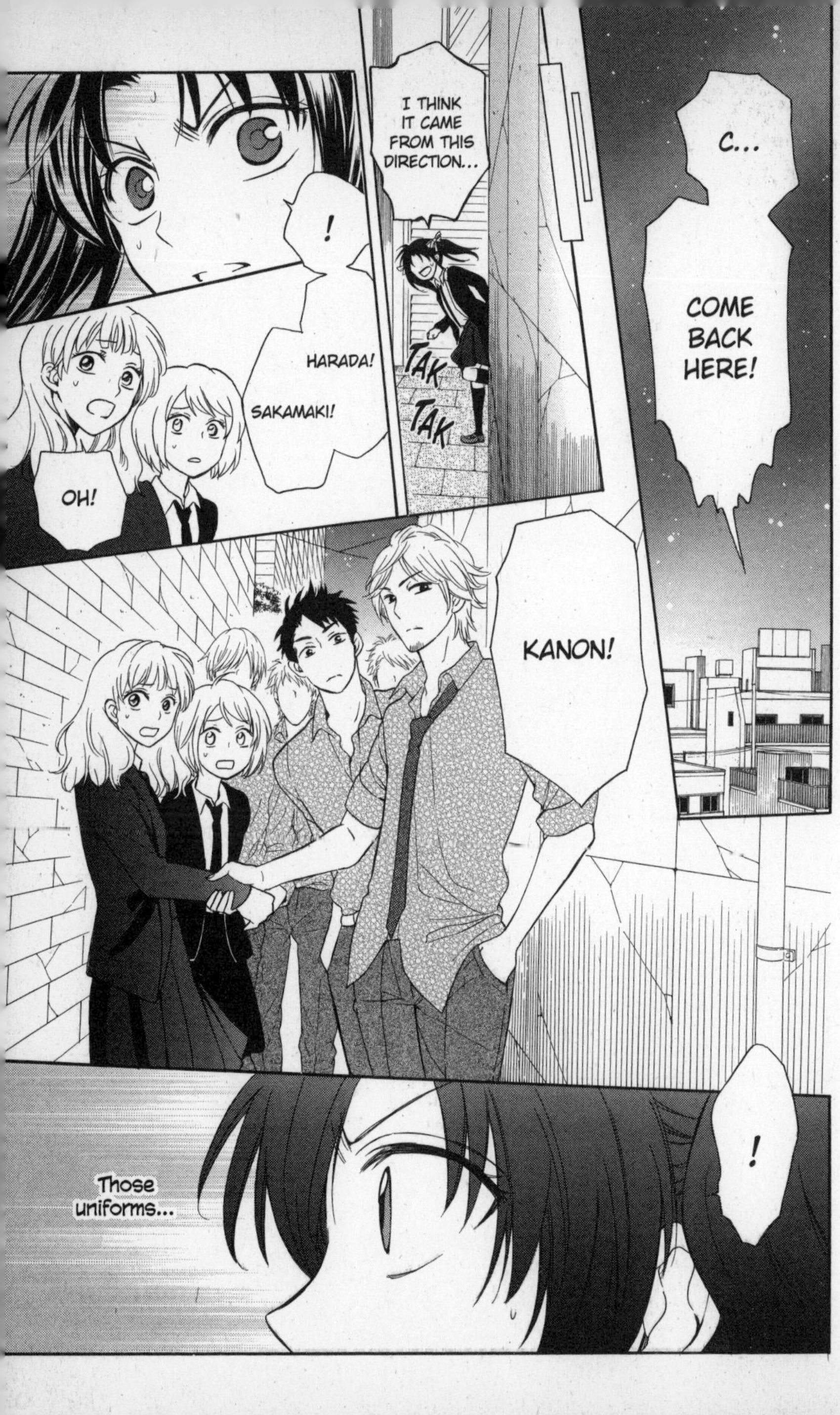
C...
COME BACK HERE!
I THINK IT CAME FROM THIS DIRECTION...
TAK TAK
!
HARADA!
SAKAMAKI!
OH!
KANON!
!
Those uniforms...

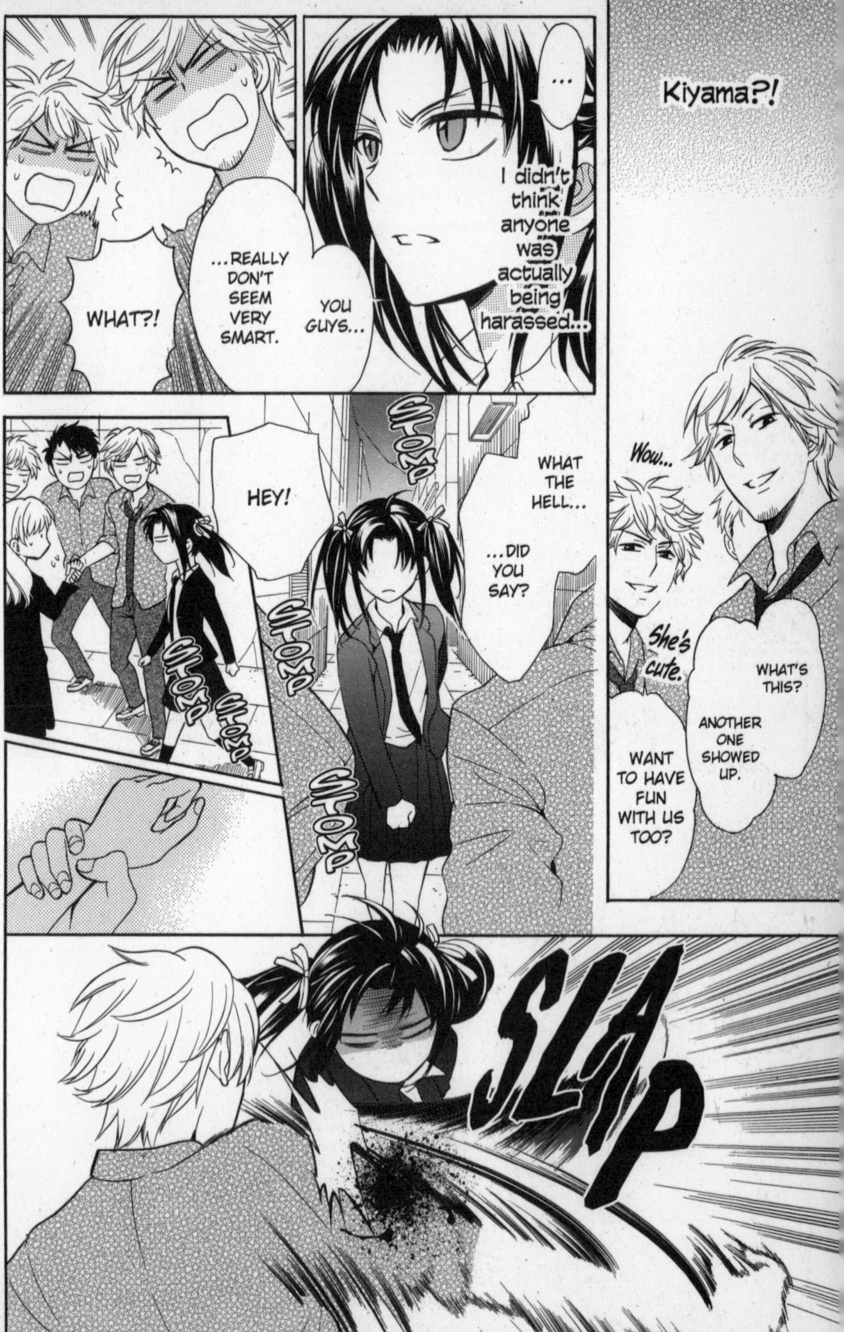
Kiyama?!
Wow...
She's cute.
WHAT'S THIS?
ANOTHER ONE SHOWED UP.
WANT TO HAVE FUN WITH US TOO?
...
I didn't think anyone was actually being harassed...
YOU GUYS...
...REALLY DON'T SEEM VERY SMART.
WHAT?!
WHAT THE HELL...
...DID YOU SAY?
STOMP
STOMP
STOMP
HEY!
STOMP
STOMP
STOMP
SLAP

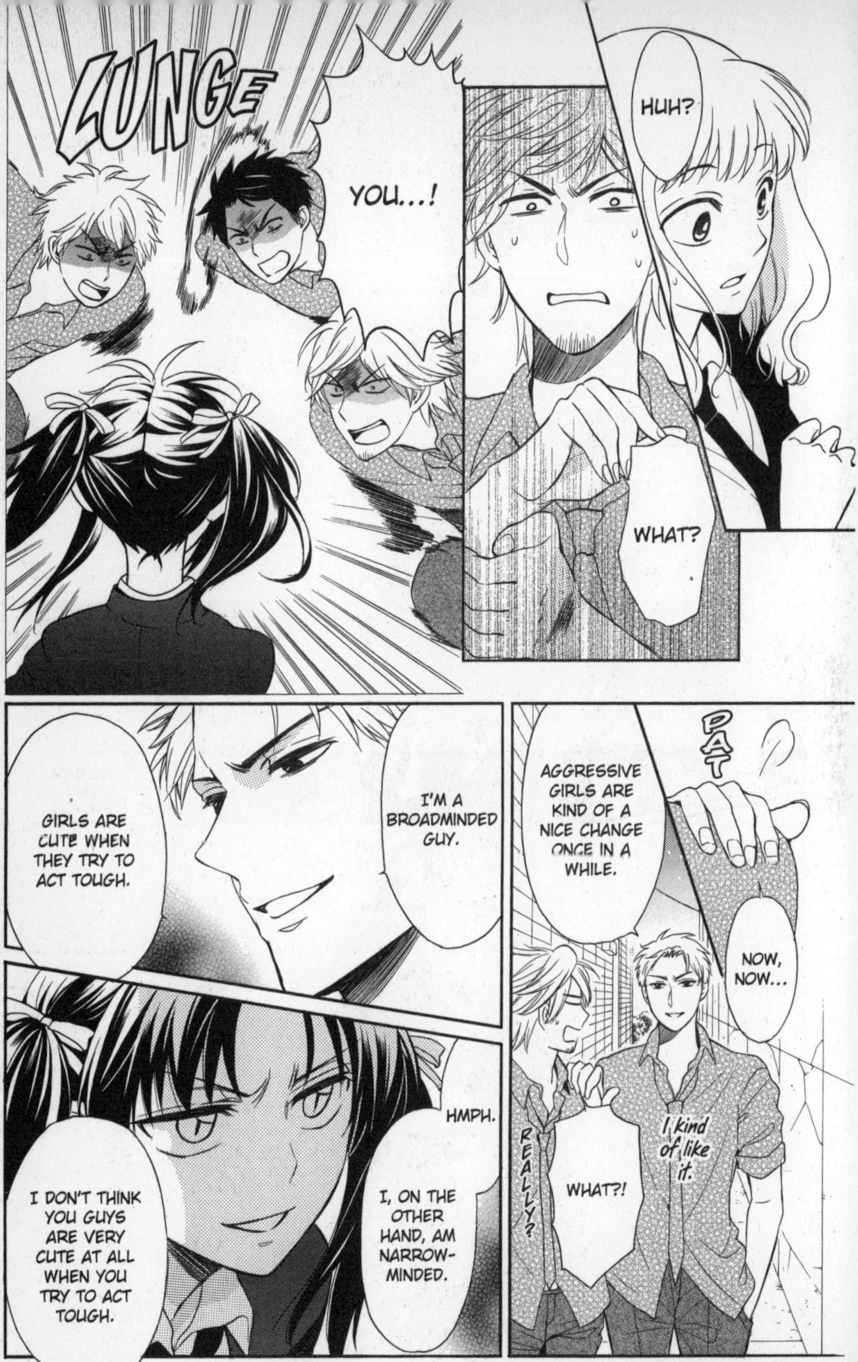
HUH?
WHAT?
LUNGE
YOU...!
PAT
AGGRESSIVE GIRLS ARE KIND OF A NICE CHANGE ONCE IN A WHILE.
NOW, NOW...
I kind of like it.
WHAT?!
REALLY?
I'M A BROADMINDED GUY.
GIRLS ARE CUTE WHEN THEY TRY TO ACT TOUGH.
HMPH.
I, ON THE OTHER HAND, AM NARROW-MINDED.
I DON'T THINK YOU GUYS ARE VERY CUTE AT ALL WHEN YOU TRY TO ACT TOUGH.

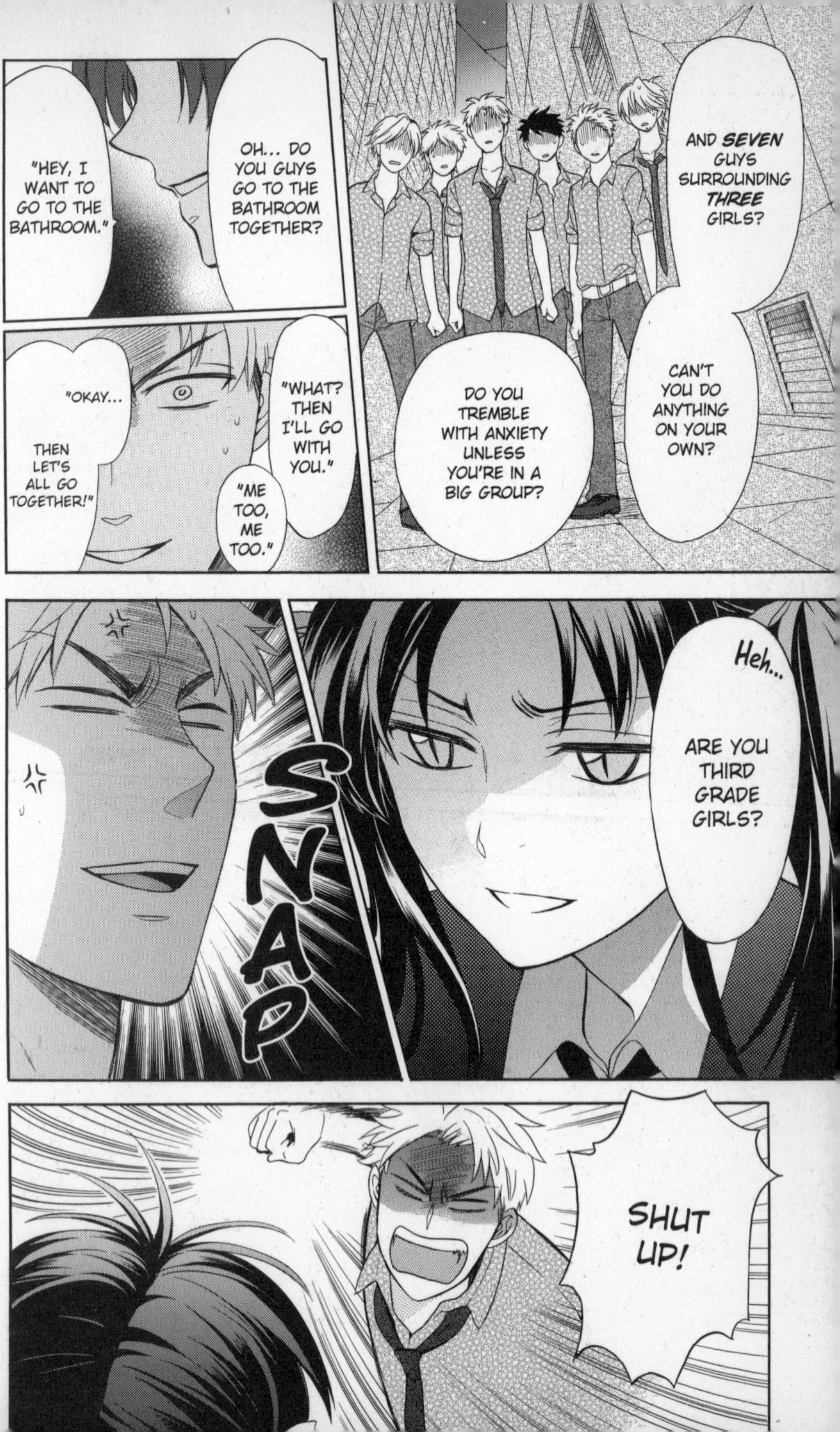

AND SEVEN GUYS SURROUNDING THREE GIRLS?
CAN'T YOU DO ANYTHING ON YOUR OWN?
DO YOU TREMBLE WITH ANXIETY UNLESS YOU'RE IN A BIG GROUP?
OH... DO YOU GUYS GO TO THE BATHROOM TOGETHER?
"HEY, I WANT TO GO TO THE BATHROOM."
"WHAT? THEN I'LL GO WITH YOU."
"ME TOO, ME TOO."
"OKAY... THEN LET'S ALL GO TOGETHER!"
Heh...
ARE YOU THIRD GRADE GIRLS?
SNAP
SHUT UP!

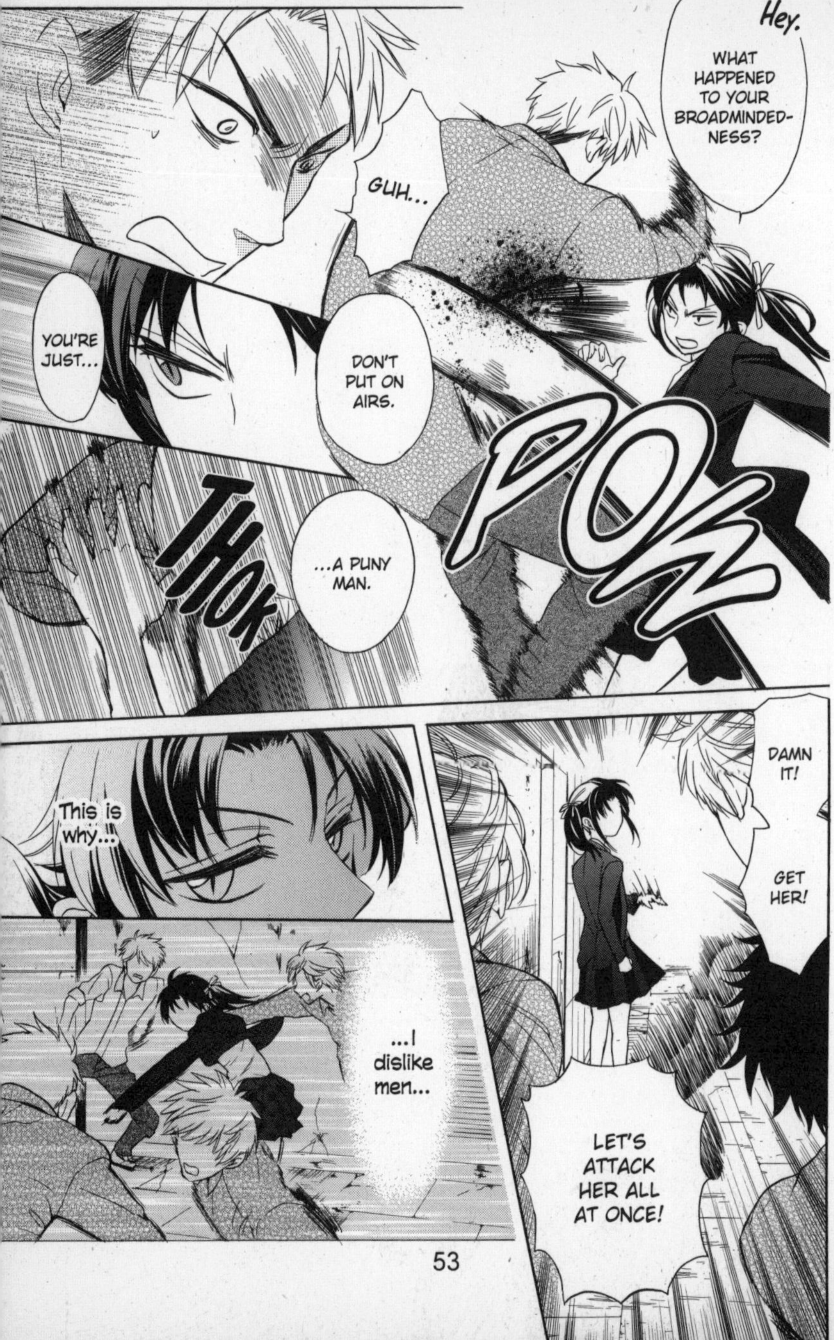
Hey.
WHAT HAPPENED TO YOUR BROADMINDED-NESS?
GUH...
DON'T PUT ON AIRS.
YOU'RE JUST...
POW
THOK
...A PUNY MAN.
DAMN IT!
GET HER!
LET'S ATTACK HER ALL AT ONCE!
This is why...
...I dislike men...

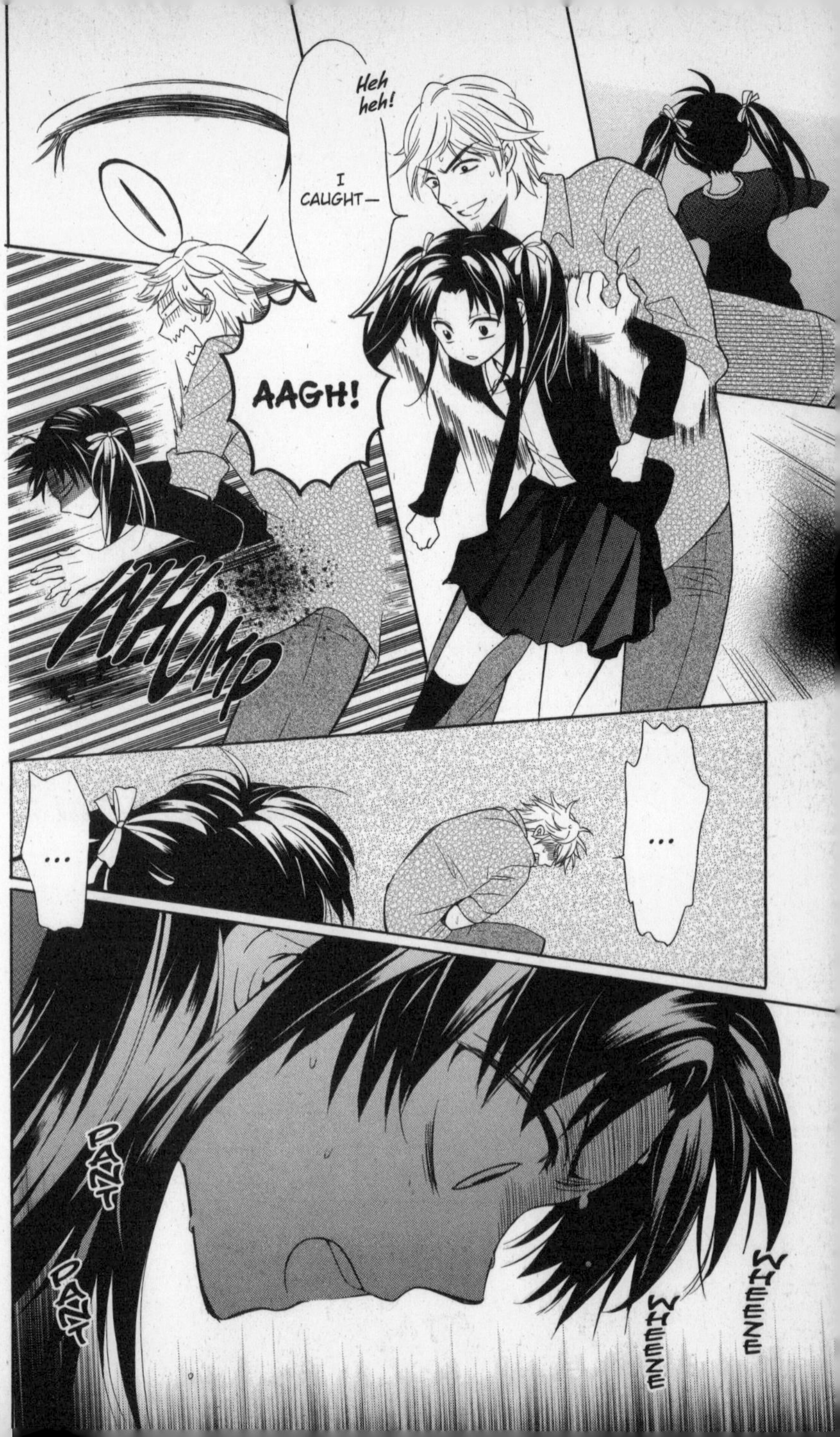
Heh heh!
I CAUGHT—
AAGH!
WHOMP
...
...
WHEEZE
WHEEZE
PANT
PANT

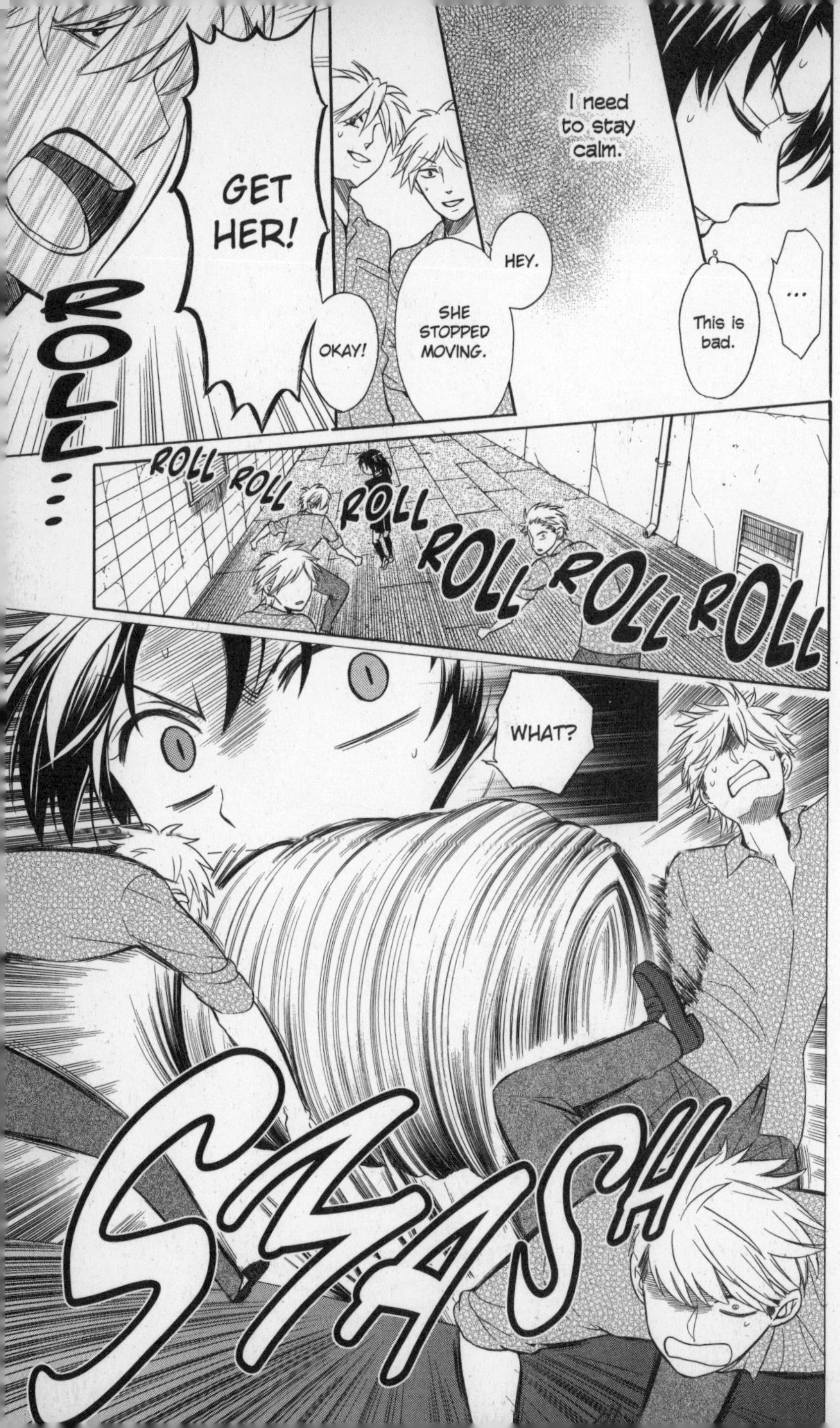
...
This is bad.
I need to stay calm.
HEY.
SHE STOPPED MOVING.
OKAY!
GET HER!
ROLL...
ROLL ROLL ROLL ROLL ROLL ROLL ROLL
WHAT?
SMASH

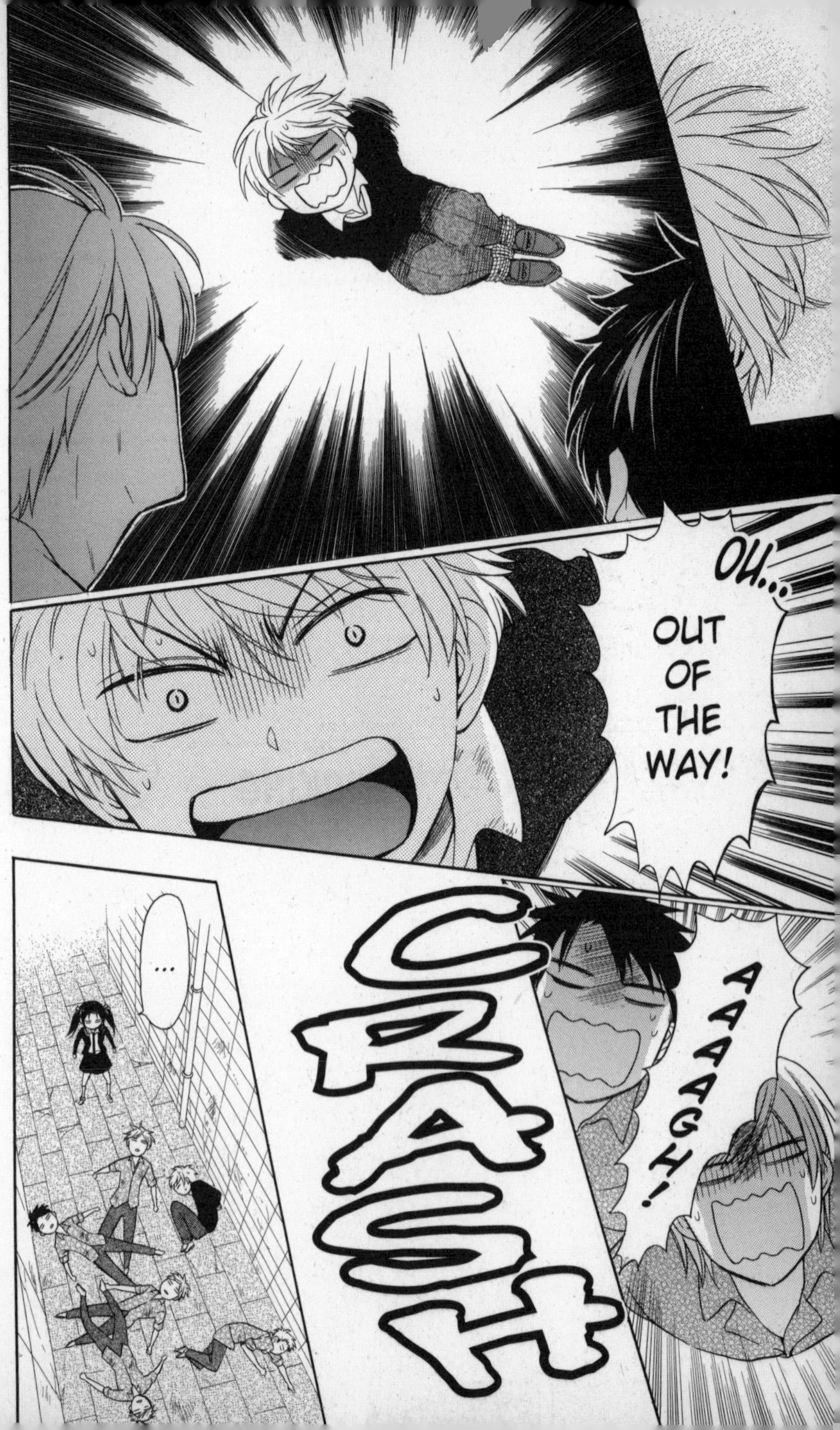
OU...
OUT OF THE WAY!
AAAAAGH!
CRASH
...

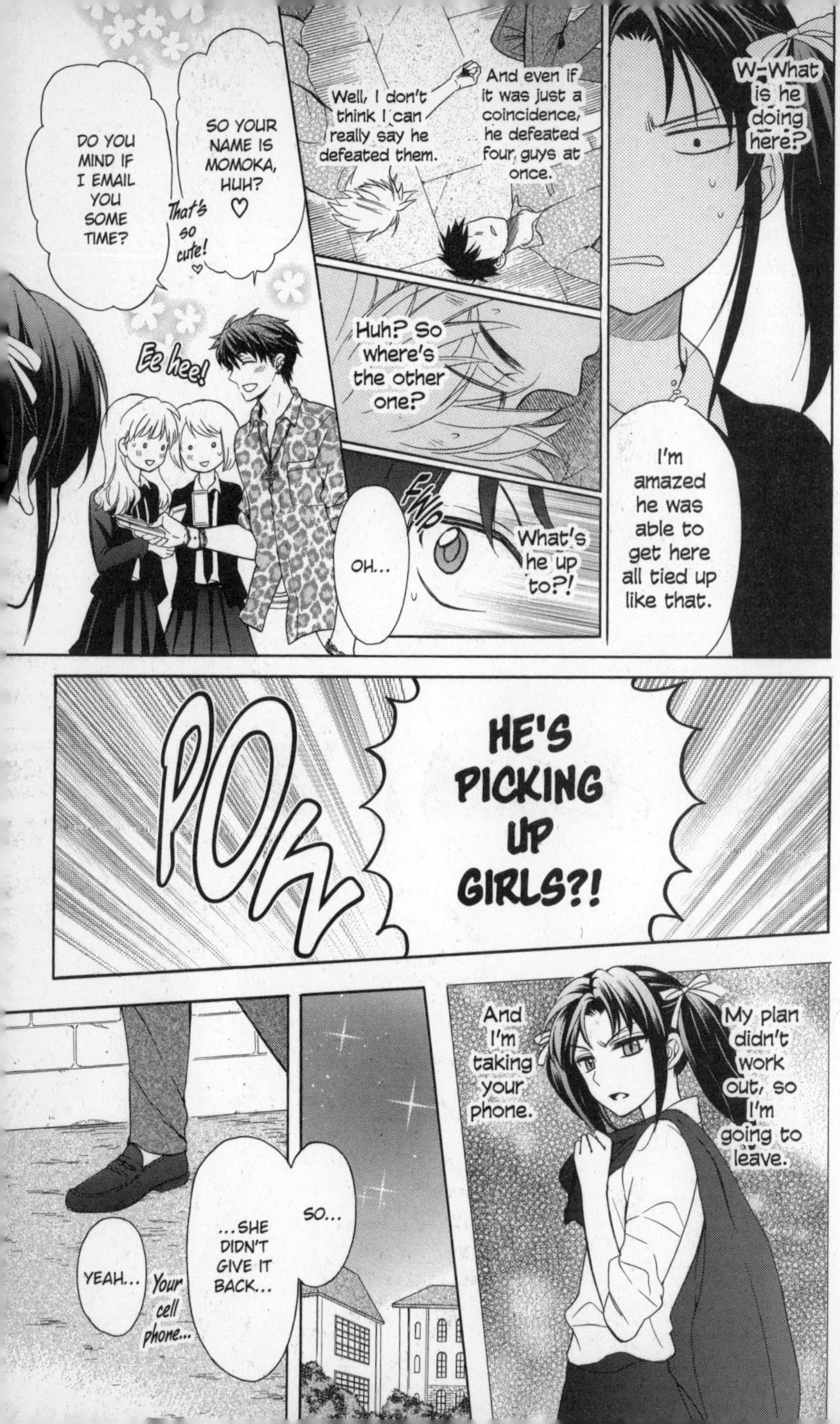
W-What is he doing here?
I'm amazed he was able to get here all tied up like that.
And even if it was just a coincidence, he defeated four guys at once.
Well, I don't think I can really say he defeated them.
Huh? So where's the other one?
What's he up to?!
FWIP
OH...
SO YOUR NAME IS MOMOKA, HUH? ♡
That's so cute! ♡
DO YOU MIND IF I EMAIL YOU SOME TIME?
Ee hee!
HE'S PICKING UP GIRLS?!
POW
My plan didn't work out, so I'm going to leave.
And I'm taking your phone.
SO...
...SHE DIDN'T GIVE IT BACK...
YEAH...
Your cell phone...

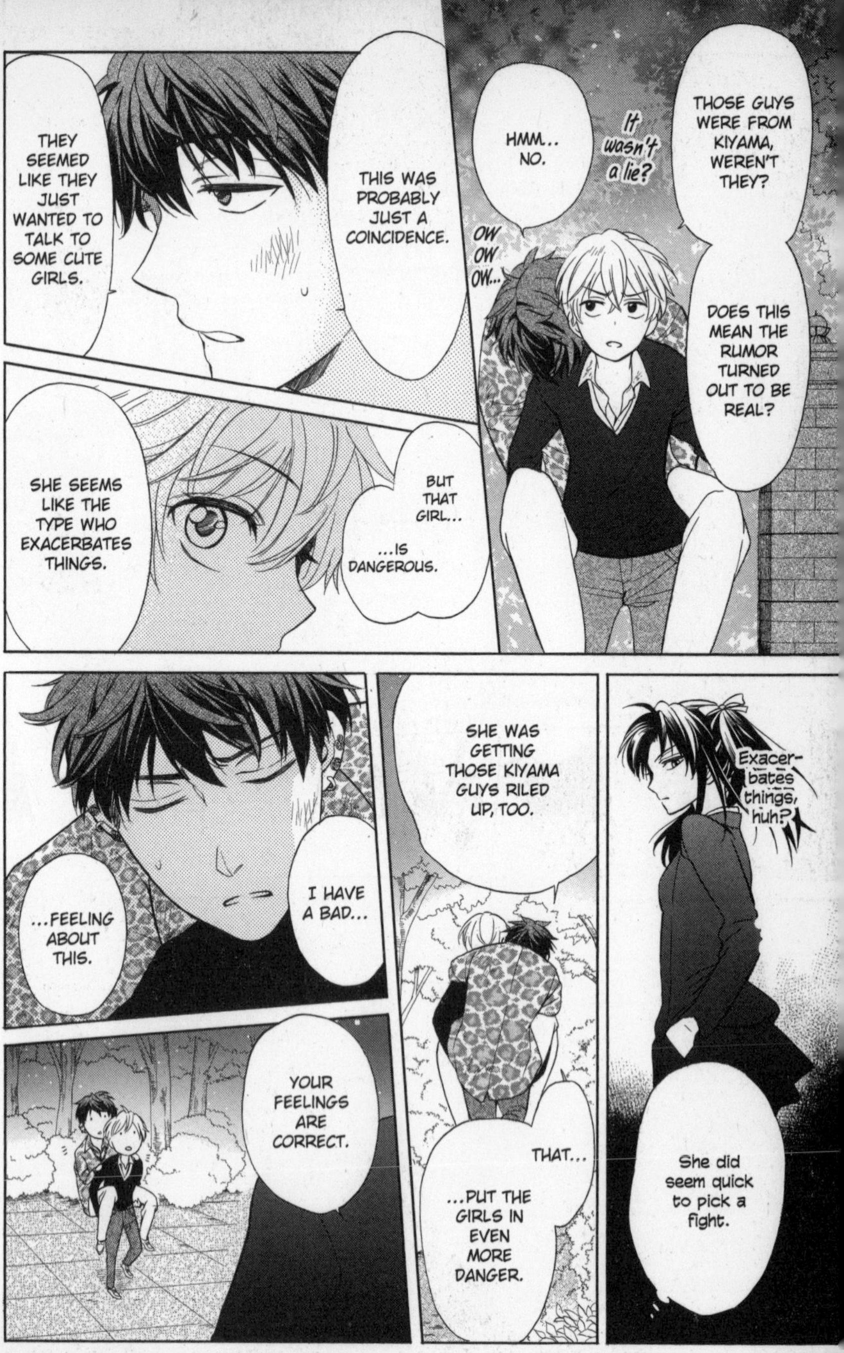
THOSE GUYS WERE FROM KIYAMA, WEREN'T THEY?
DOES THIS MEAN THE RUMOR TURNED OUT TO BE REAL?
It wasn't a lie?
HMM... NO.
OW OW OW...
THIS WAS PROBABLY JUST A COINCIDENCE.
THEY SEEMED LIKE THEY JUST WANTED TO TALK TO SOME CUTE GIRLS.
BUT THAT GIRL...
...IS DANGEROUS.
SHE SEEMS LIKE THE TYPE WHO EXACERBATES THINGS.
Exacer-bates things, huh?
She did seem quick to pick a fight.
SHE WAS GETTING THOSE KIYAMA GUYS RILED UP, TOO.
THAT...
...PUT THE GIRLS IN EVEN MORE DANGER.
I HAVE A BAD...
...FEELING ABOUT THIS.
YOUR FEELINGS ARE CORRECT.

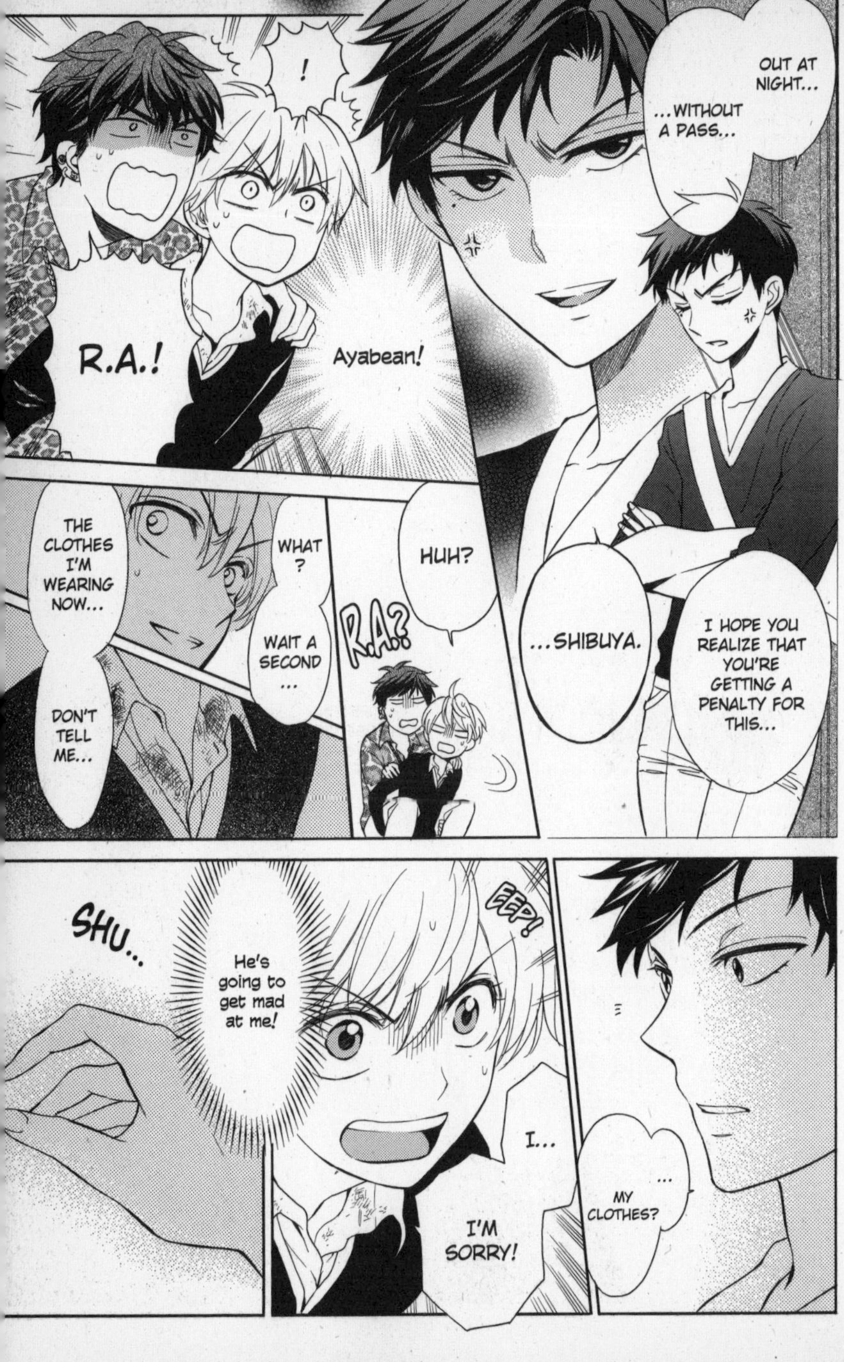
OUT AT NIGHT...
...WITHOUT A PASS...
...SHIBUYA.
I HOPE YOU REALIZE THAT YOU'RE GETTING A PENALTY FOR THIS...
!
R.A.!
Ayabean!
HUH?
R.A.?
WHAT?
WAIT A SECOND...
THE CLOTHES I'M WEARING NOW...
DON'T TELL ME...
...
MY CLOTHES?
EEP!
I...
I'M SORRY!
He's going to get mad at me!
SHU...

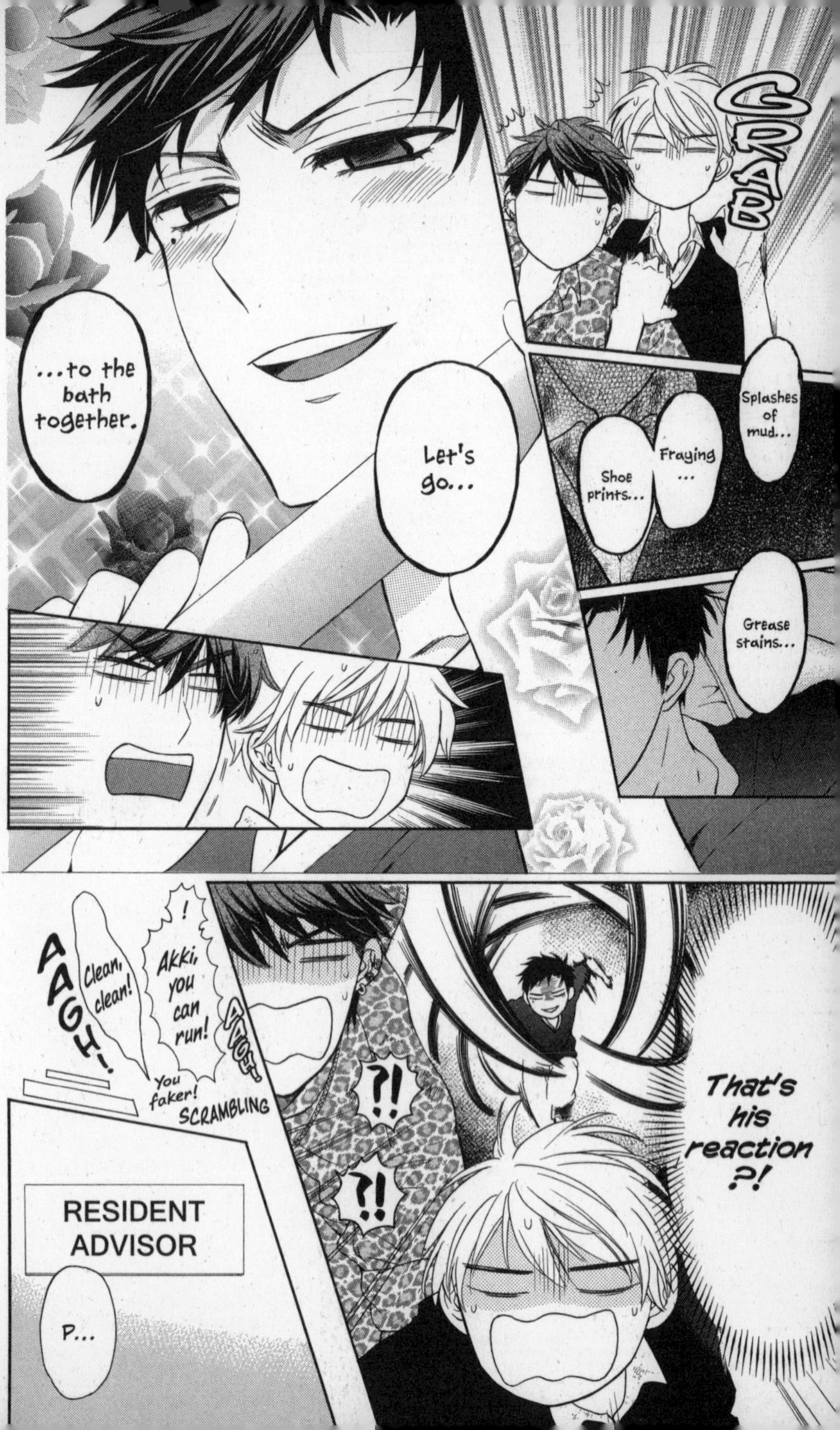
GRAB
Splashes of mud...
Fraying...
Shoe prints...
Grease stains...
Let's go...
...to the bath together.
That's his reaction?!
?!
?!
!
Akki, you can run!
You faker!
SCRAMBLING
Clean, clean!
AAGH!
RESIDENT ADVISOR
P...

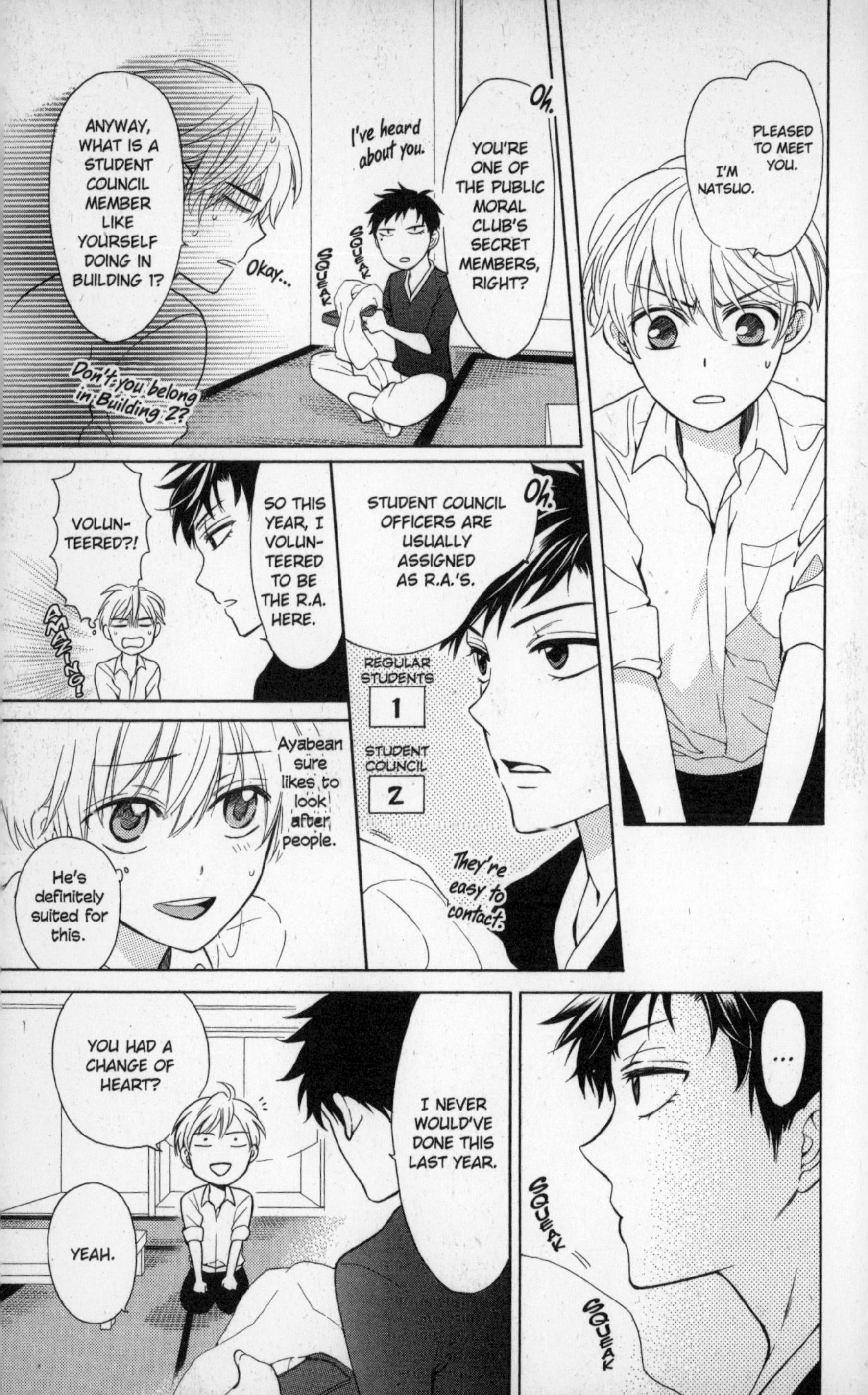
PLEASED TO MEET YOU.
I'M NATSUO.
Oh.
YOU'RE ONE OF THE PUBLIC MORAL CLUB'S SECRET MEMBERS, RIGHT?
I've heard about you.
SQUEAK
ANYWAY, WHAT IS A STUDENT COUNCIL MEMBER LIKE YOURSELF DOING IN BUILDING 1?
Okay...
Don't you belong in Building 2?
Oh.
STUDENT COUNCIL OFFICERS ARE USUALLY ASSIGNED AS R.A.'S.
REGULAR STUDENTS
1
STUDENT COUNCIL
2
They're easy to contact.
SO THIS YEAR, I VOLUNTEERED TO BE THE R.A. HERE.
VOLUN-TEERED?!
Ayabean sure likes to look after people.
He's definitely suited for this.
...
SQUEAK
SQUEAK
I NEVER WOULD'VE DONE THIS LAST YEAR.
YOU HAD A CHANGE OF HEART?
YEAH.

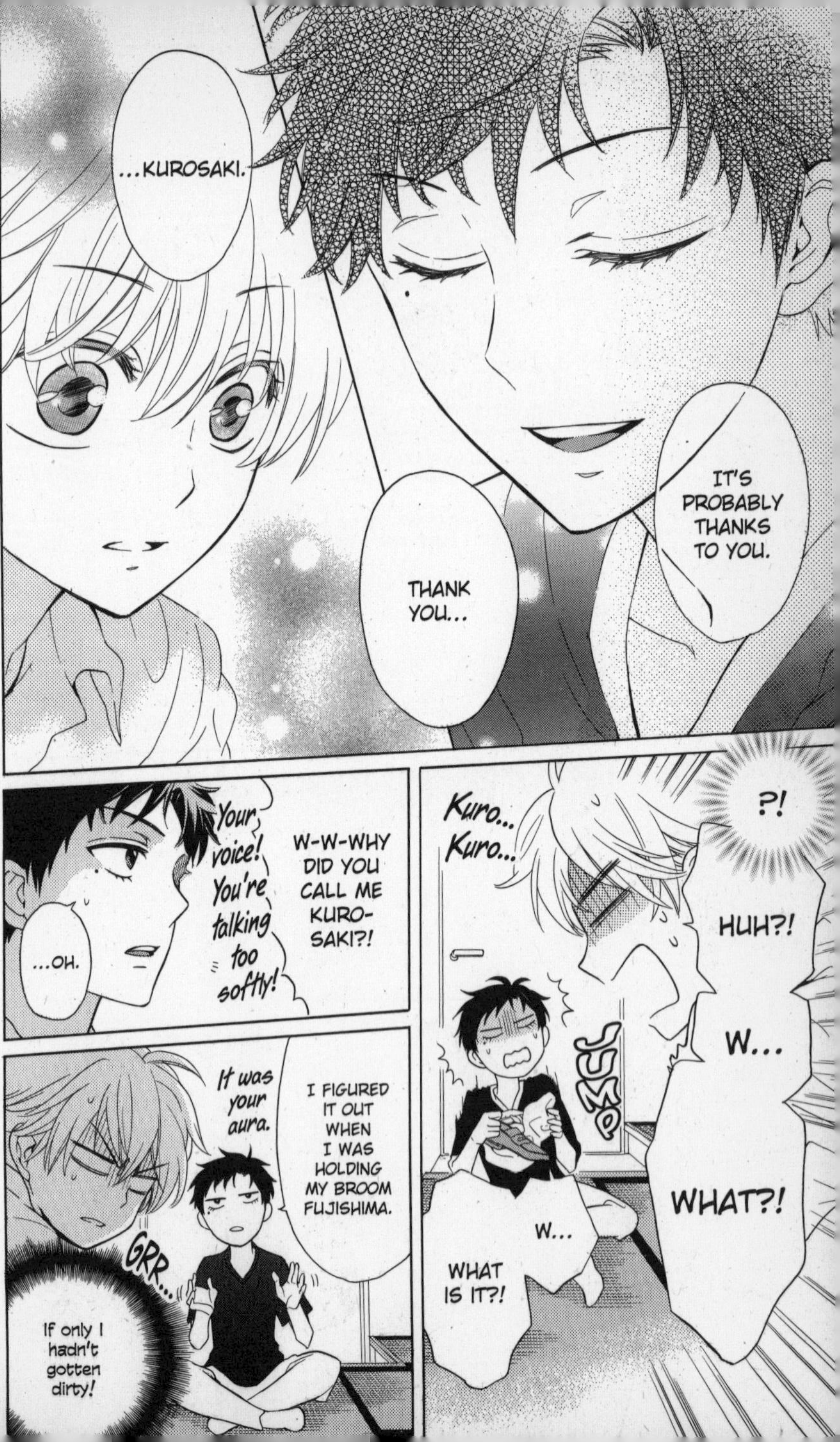
...KUROSAKI.
THANK YOU...
IT'S PROBABLY THANKS TO YOU.
?!
Kuro... Kuro...
HUH?!
W...
WHAT?!
JUMP
W...
WHAT IS IT?!
W-W-WHY DID YOU CALL ME KURO-SAKI?!
Your voice! You're talking too softly!
...OH.
I FIGURED IT OUT WHEN I WAS HOLDING MY BROOM FUJISHIMA.
It was your aura.
GRR...
If only I hadn't gotten dirty!

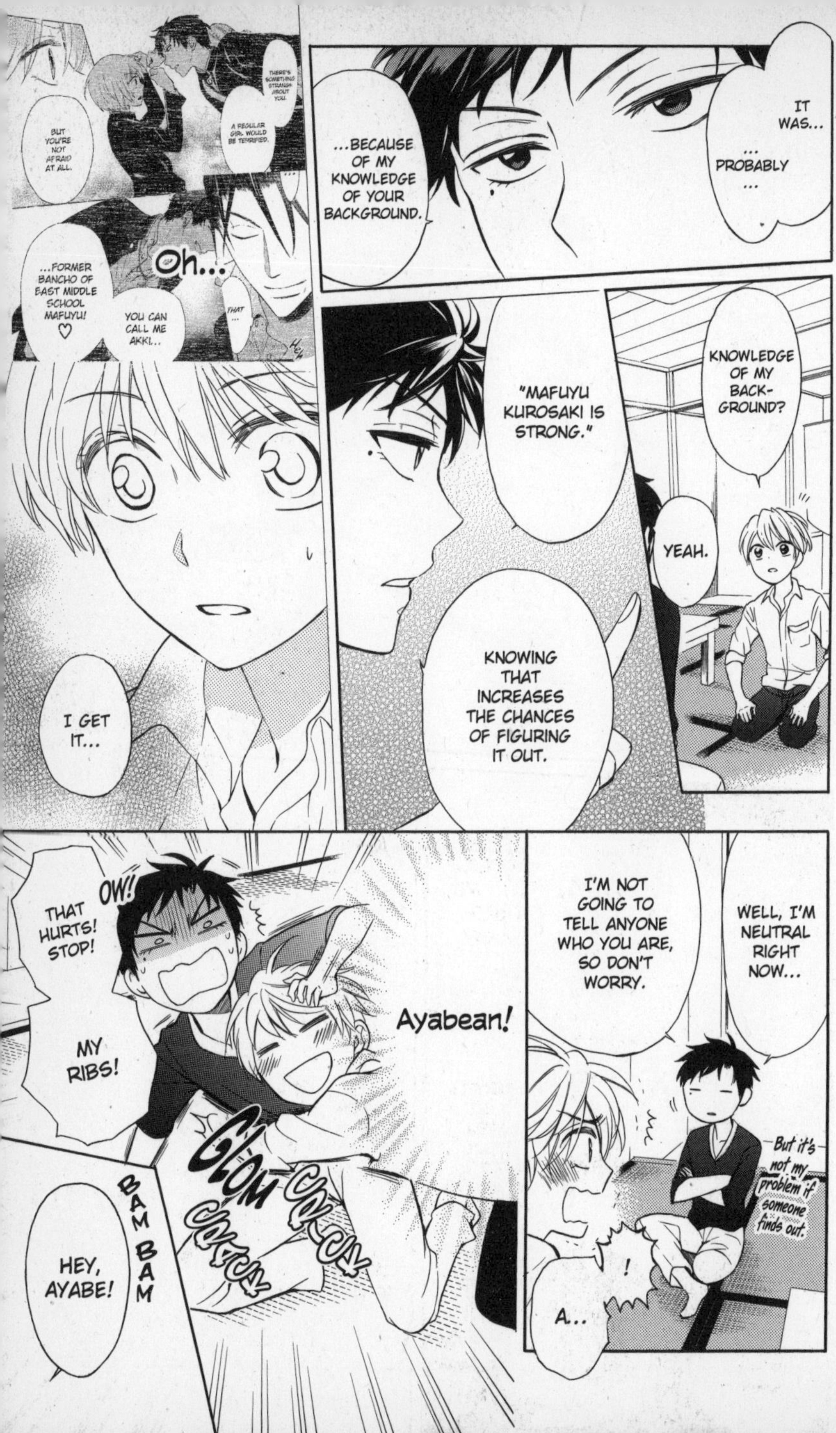
IT WAS... ...PROBABLY...
...BECAUSE OF MY KNOWLEDGE OF YOUR BACKGROUND.
THERE'S SOMETHING STRANGE ABOUT YOU.
A REGULAR GIRL WOULD BE TERRIFIED.
BUT YOU'RE NOT AFRAID AT ALL.
...
THAT...
Oh...
...FORMER BANCHO OF EAST MIDDLE SCHOOL MAFUYU! ♡
YOU CAN CALL ME AKKI...
KNOWLEDGE OF MY BACK-GROUND?
YEAH.
"MAFUYU KUROSAKI IS STRONG."
KNOWING THAT INCREASES THE CHANCES OF FIGURING IT OUT.
I GET IT...
WELL, I'M NEUTRAL RIGHT NOW...
I'M NOT GOING TO TELL ANYONE WHO YOU ARE, SO DON'T WORRY.
But it's not my problem if someone finds out.
!
A...
Ayabean!
OW!
THAT HURTS! STOP!
MY RIBS!
GLOM
CLICK-CLICK
CLICKCLICK
BAM BAM
HEY, AYABE!

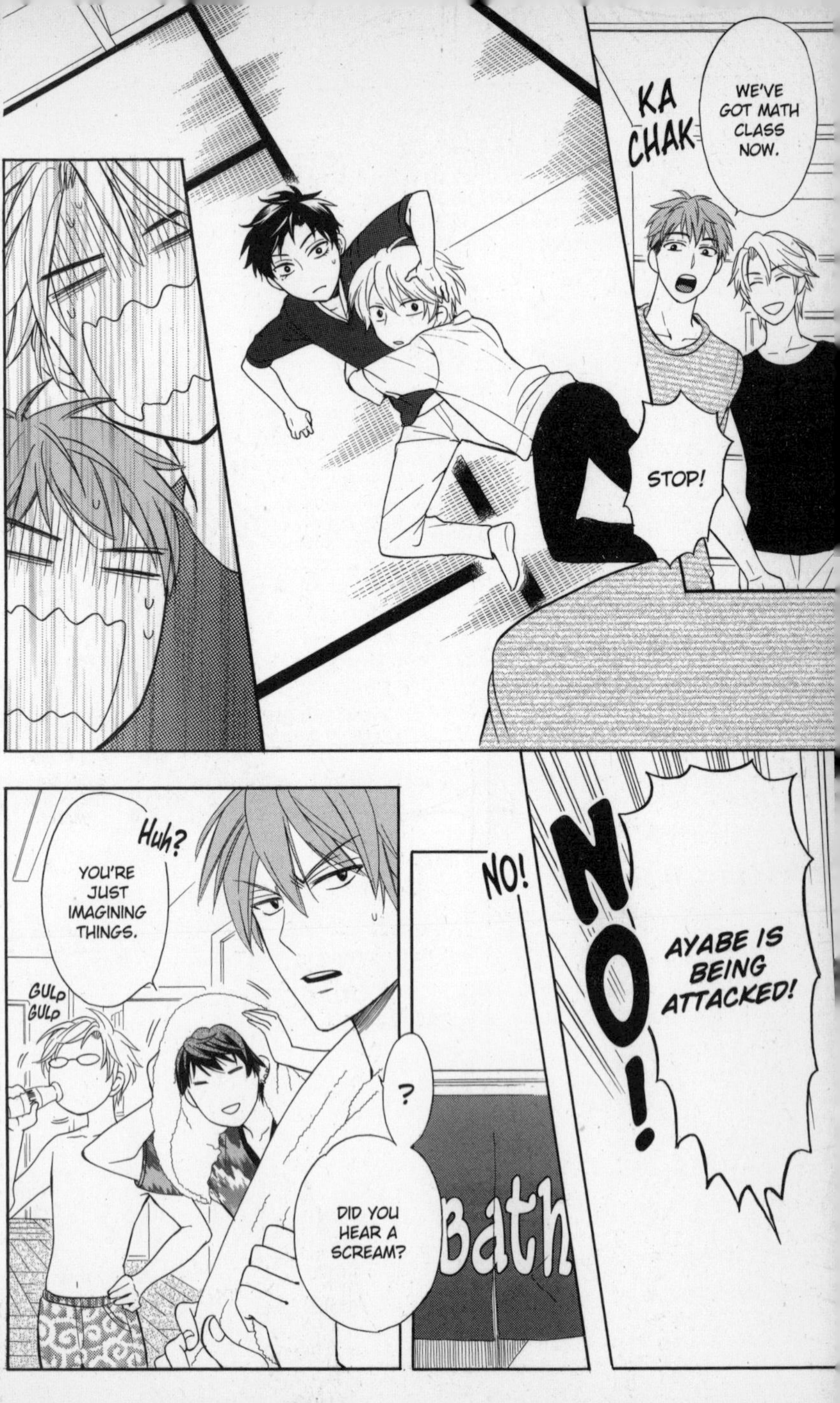
KA CHAK
WE'VE GOT MATH CLASS NOW.
STOP!
NO! NO!
AYABE IS BEING ATTACKED!
DID YOU HEAR A SCREAM?
?
Huh?
YOU'RE JUST IMAGINING THINGS.
GULP GULP
Bath

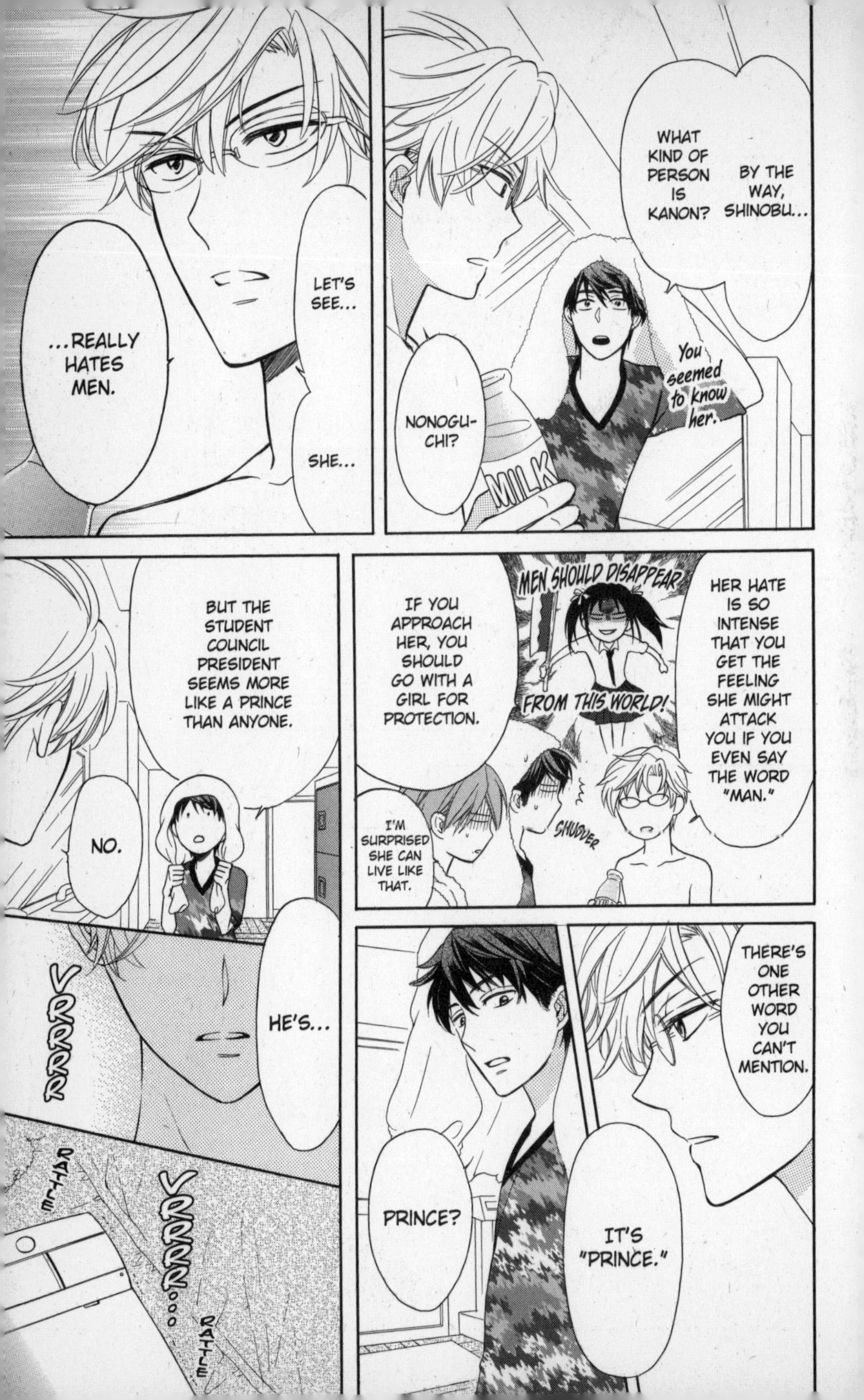
BY THE WAY, SHINOBU...
WHAT KIND OF PERSON IS KANON?
You seemed to know her.
NONOGU-CHI?
LET'S SEE...
SHE...
...REALLY HATES MEN.
HER HATE IS SO INTENSE THAT YOU GET THE FEELING SHE MIGHT ATTACK YOU IF YOU EVEN SAY THE WORD "MAN."
MEN SHOULD DISAPPEAR FROM THIS WORLD!
IF YOU APPROACH HER, YOU SHOULD GO WITH A GIRL FOR PROTECTION.
SHUDDER
I'M SURPRISED SHE CAN LIVE LIKE THAT.
THERE'S ONE OTHER WORD YOU CAN'T MENTION.
IT'S "PRINCE."
PRINCE?
BUT THE STUDENT COUNCIL PRESIDENT SEEMS MORE LIKE A PRINCE THAN ANYONE.
NO.
HE'S...
VRRRR
RATTLE
VRRRR...
RATTLE

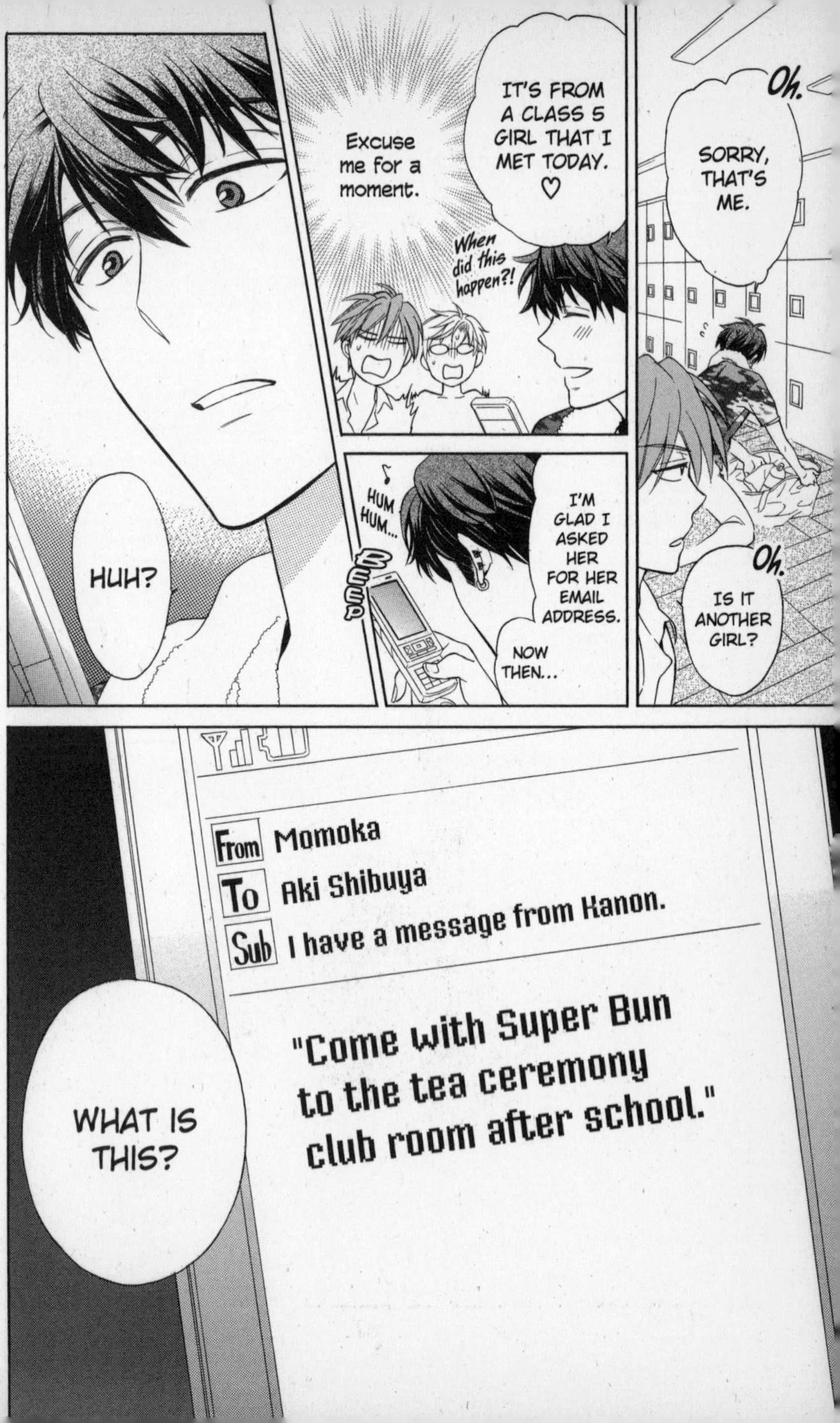
Oh.
SORRY, THAT'S ME.
Oh.
IS IT ANOTHER GIRL?
IT'S FROM A CLASS 5 GIRL THAT I MET TODAY. ♡
Excuse me for a moment.
When did this happen?!
HUM HUM...
I'M GLAD I ASKED HER FOR HER EMAIL ADDRESS.
NOW THEN...
HUH?
From Momoka
To Aki Shibuya
Sub I have a message from Kanon.
"Come with Super Bun to the tea ceremony club room after school."
WHAT IS THIS?

Chapter 72

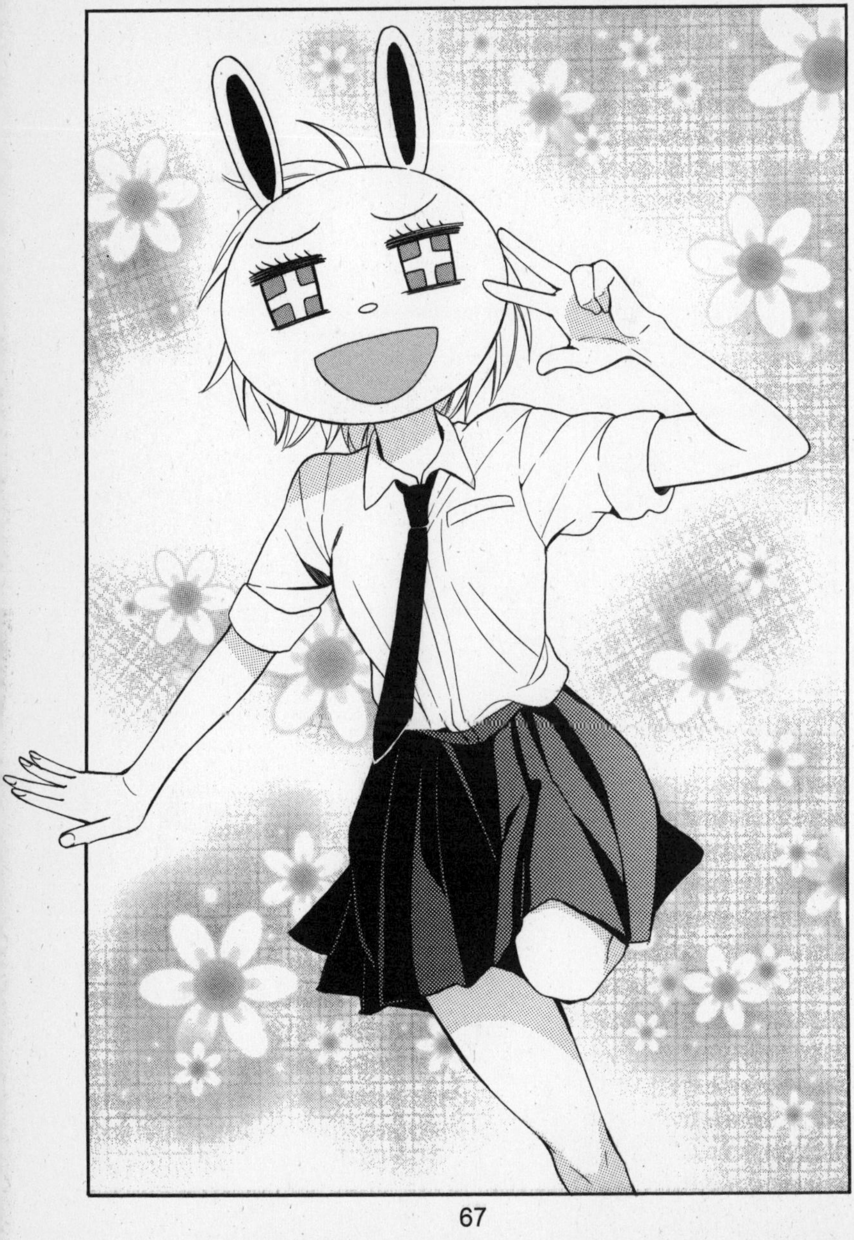

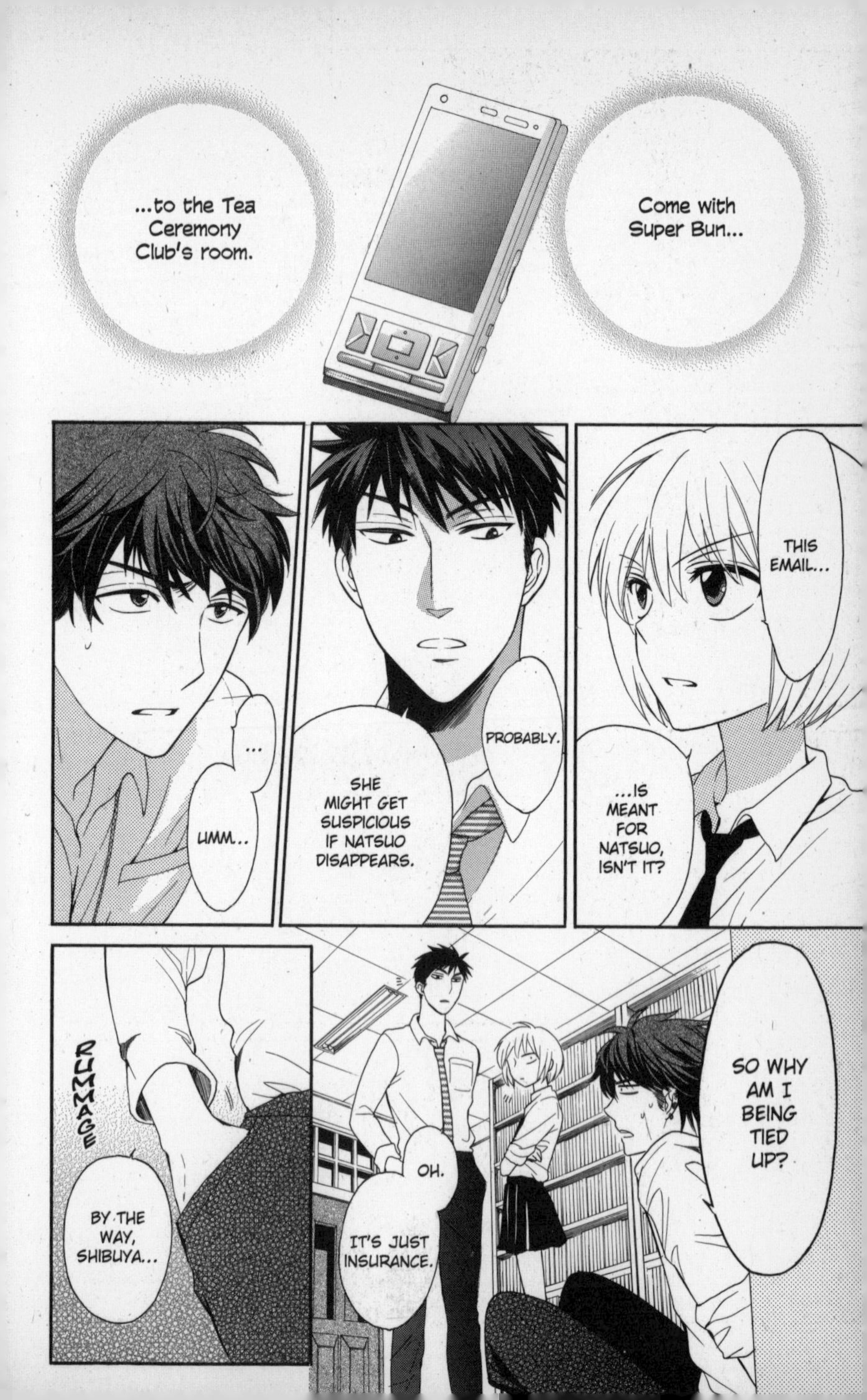
Come with Super Bun...
...to the Tea Ceremony Club's room.
THIS EMAIL...
...IS MEANT FOR NATSUO, ISN'T IT?
PROBABLY.
SHE MIGHT GET SUSPICIOUS IF NATSUO DISAPPEARS.
...
UMM...
SO WHY AM I BEING TIED UP?
OH.
IT'S JUST INSURANCE.
RUMMAGE
BY THE WAY, SHIBUYA...

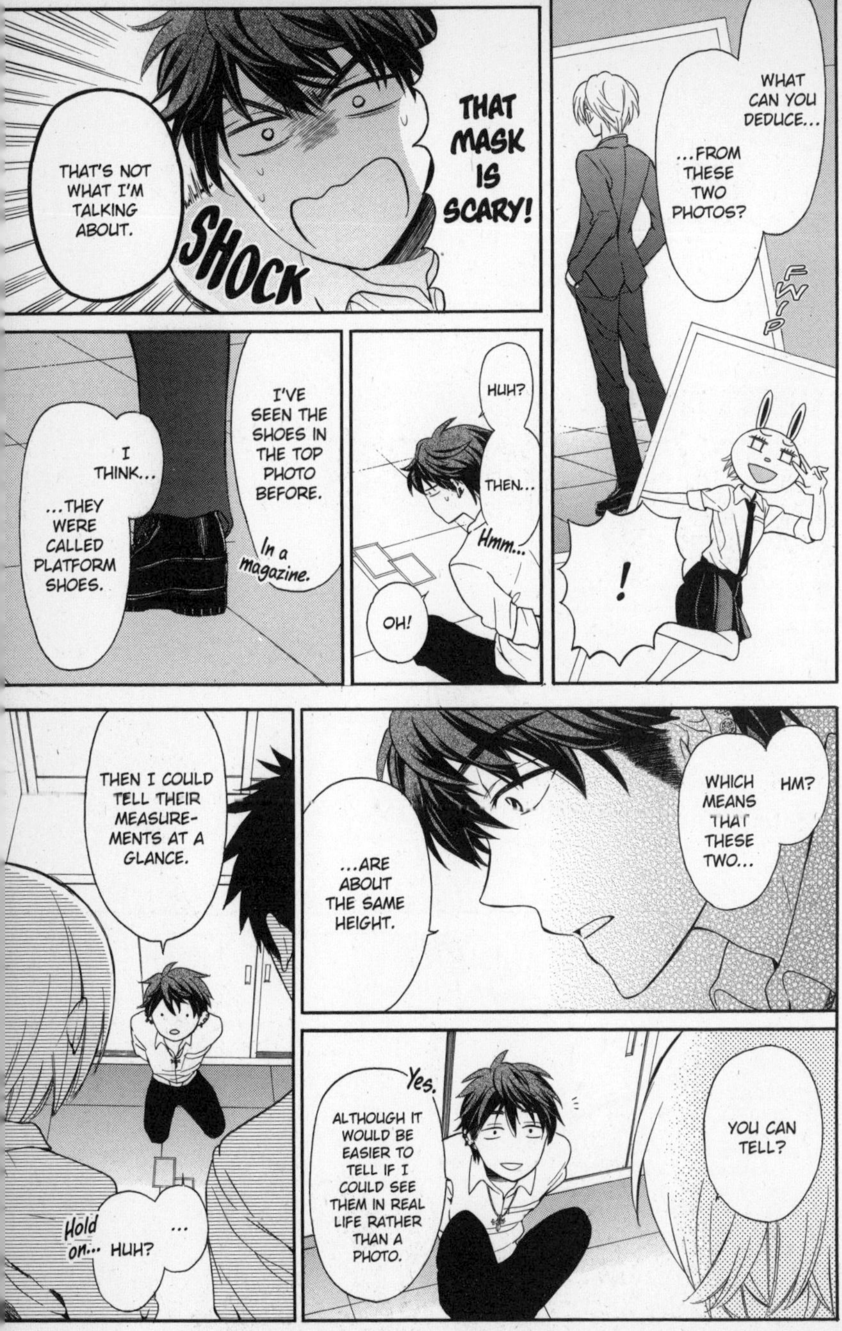
WHAT CAN YOU DEDUCE...
...FROM THESE TWO PHOTOS?
FWIP
!
THAT MASK IS SCARY!
SHOCK
THAT'S NOT WHAT I'M TALKING ABOUT.
HUH?
THEN...
Hmm...
OH!
I'VE SEEN THE SHOES IN THE TOP PHOTO BEFORE.
In a magazine.
I THINK...
...THEY WERE CALLED PLATFORM SHOES.
HM?
WHICH MEANS THAT THESE TWO...
...ARE ABOUT THE SAME HEIGHT.
YOU CAN TELL?
Yes.
ALTHOUGH IT WOULD BE EASIER TO TELL IF I COULD SEE THEM IN REAL LIFE RATHER THAN A PHOTO.
THEN I COULD TELL THEIR MEASUREMENTS AT A GLANCE.
...
Hold on... HUH?

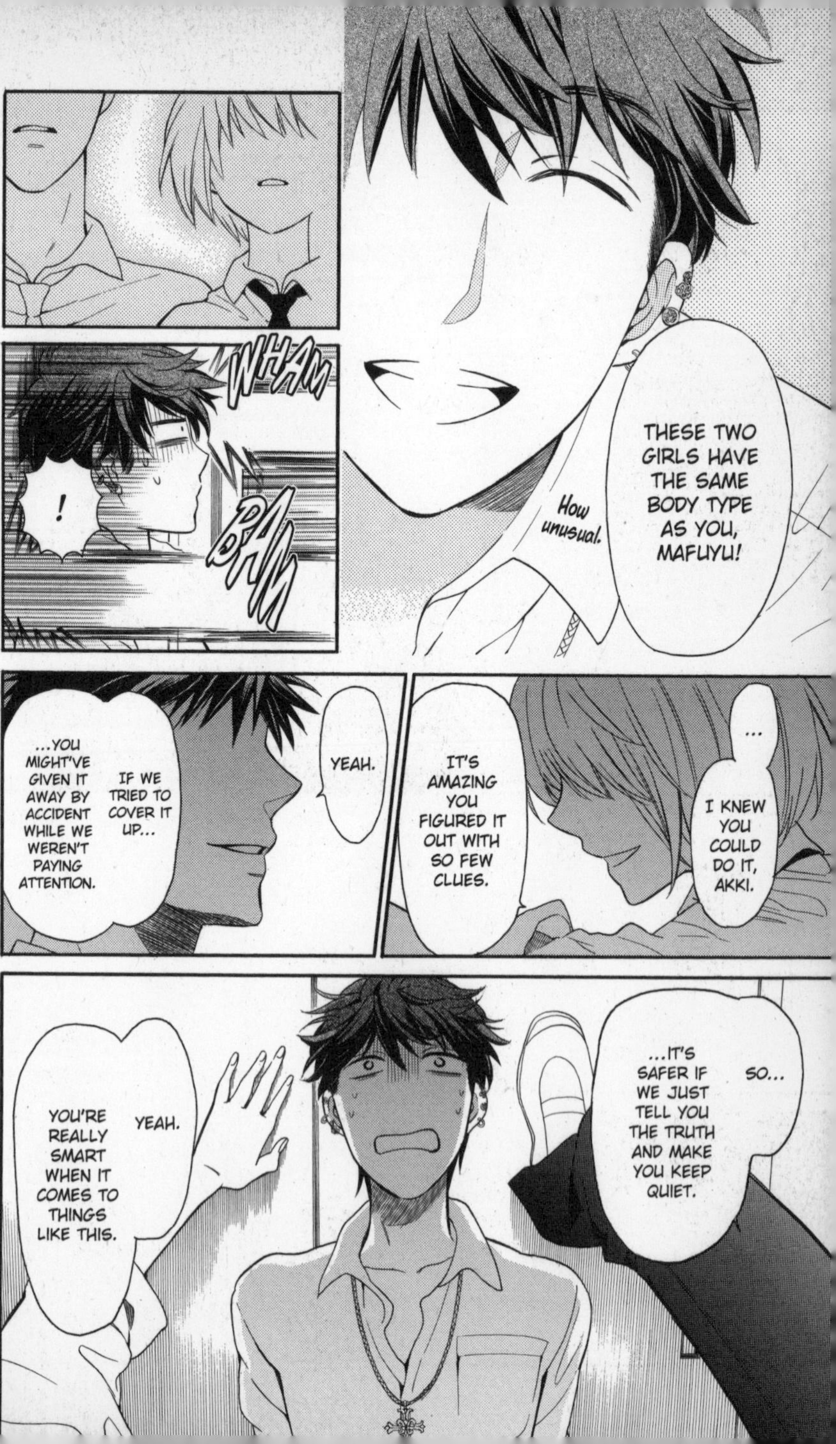
THESE TWO GIRLS HAVE THE SAME BODY TYPE AS YOU, MAFUYU!
How unusual.
WHAM
BAM
!
...
I KNEW YOU COULD DO IT, AKKI.
IT'S AMAZING YOU FIGURED IT OUT WITH SO FEW CLUES.
YEAH.
IF WE TRIED TO COVER IT UP...
...YOU MIGHT'VE GIVEN IT AWAY BY ACCIDENT WHILE WE WEREN'T PAYING ATTENTION.
SO...
...IT'S SAFER IF WE JUST TELL YOU THE TRUTH AND MAKE YOU KEEP QUIET.
YEAH.
YOU'RE REALLY SMART WHEN IT COMES TO THINGS LIKE THIS.

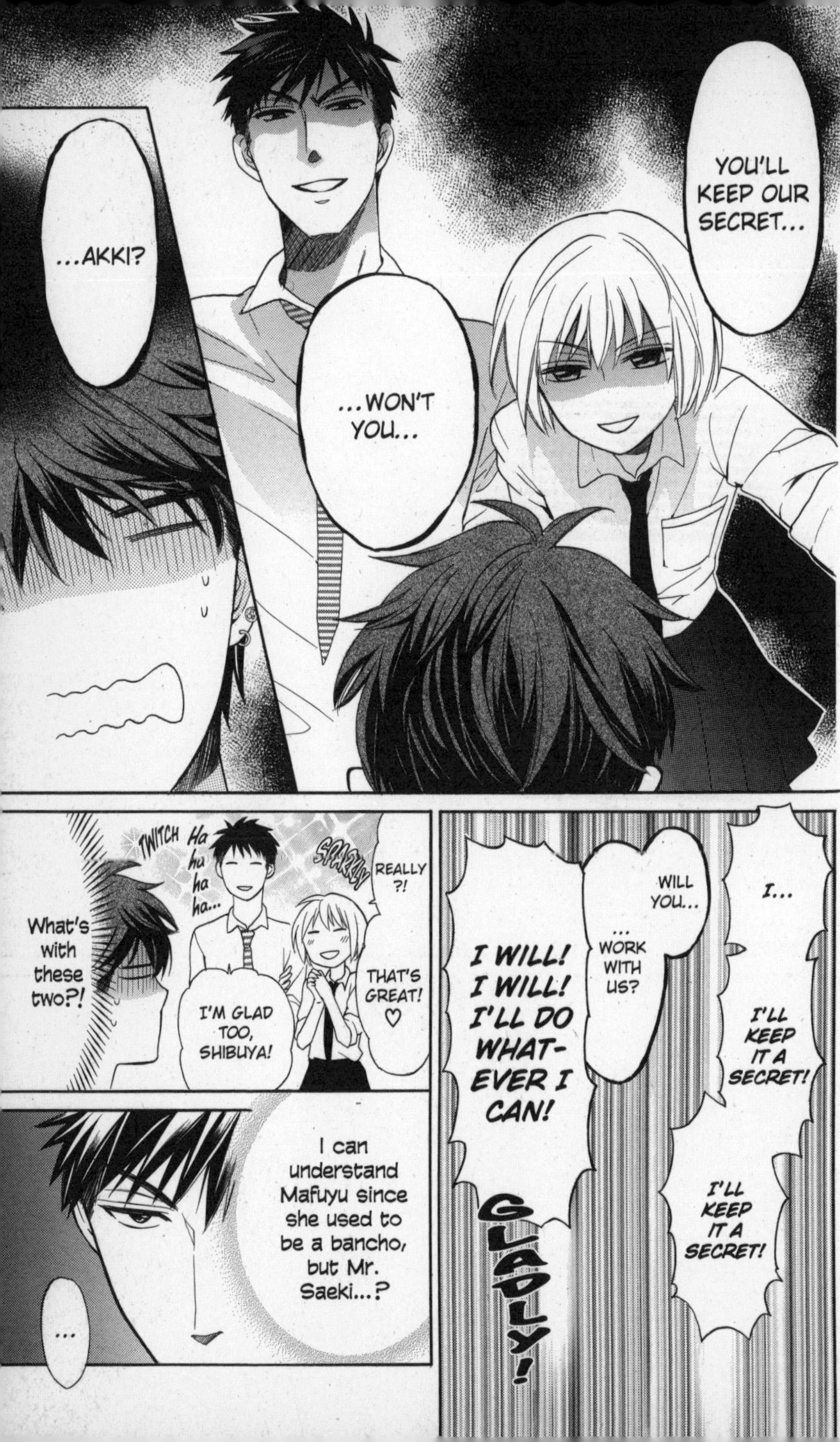
YOU'LL KEEP OUR SECRET...
...WON'T YOU...
...AKKI?
I...
WILL YOU...
...WORK WITH US?
I'LL KEEP IT A SECRET!
I WILL! I WILL! I'LL DO WHATEVER I CAN!
I'LL KEEP IT A SECRET!
GLADLY!
SPARKLY
REALLY?!
THAT'S GREAT! ♡
Ha ha ha ha...
TWITCH
I'M GLAD TOO, SHIBUYA!
What's with these two?!
I can understand Mafuyu since she used to be a bancho, but Mr. Saeki...?
...

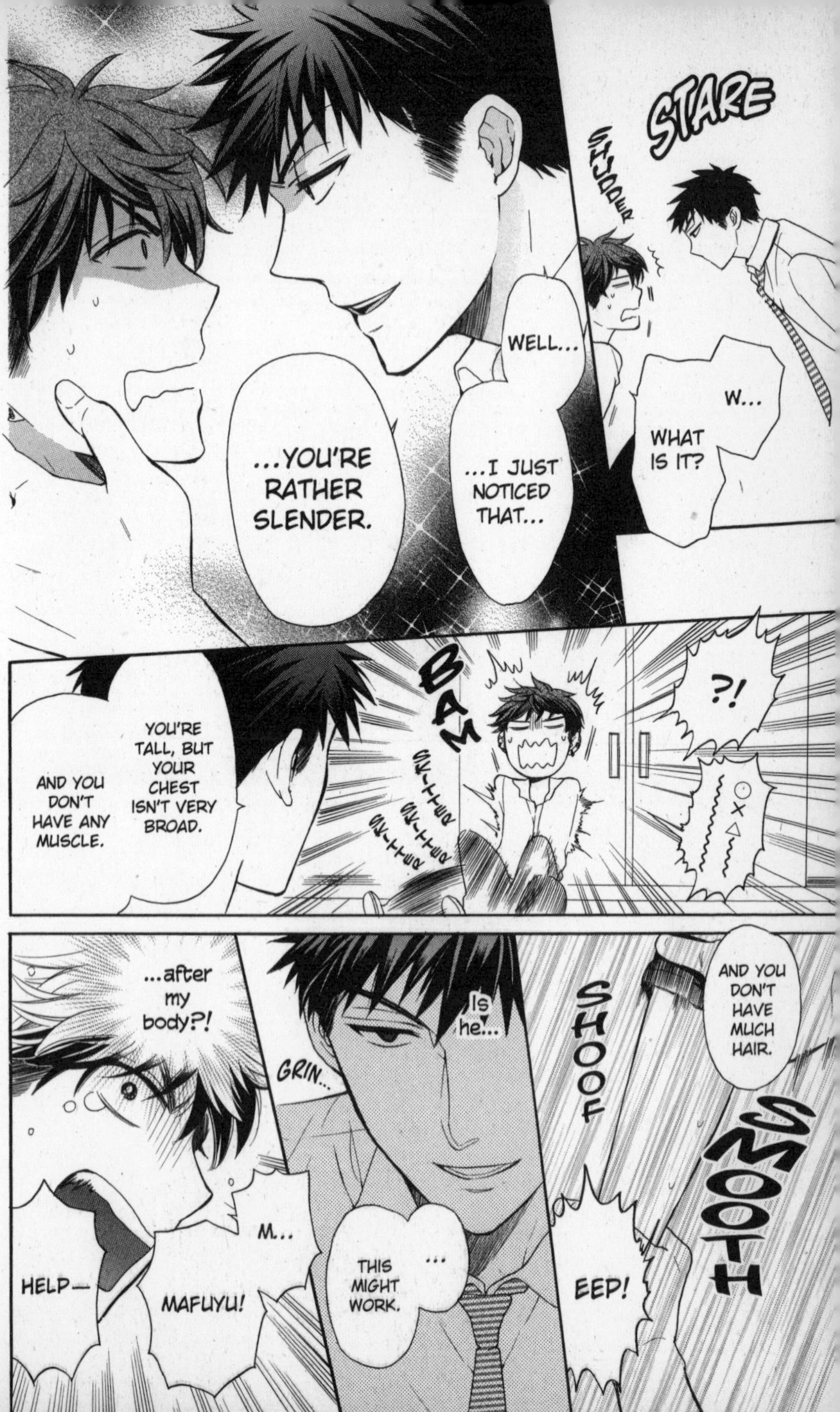
STARE
SHUDDER
W...
WHAT IS IT?
WELL...
...I JUST NOTICED THAT...
...YOU'RE RATHER SLENDER.
?!
BAM
SKITTER SKITTER SKITTER
YOU'RE TALL, BUT YOUR CHEST ISN'T VERY BROAD.
AND YOU DON'T HAVE ANY MUSCLE.
AND YOU DON'T HAVE MUCH HAIR.
SHOOF
SMOOTH
EEP!
GRIN...
...
THIS MIGHT WORK.
Is he...
...after my body?!
M...
MAFUYU!
HELP—

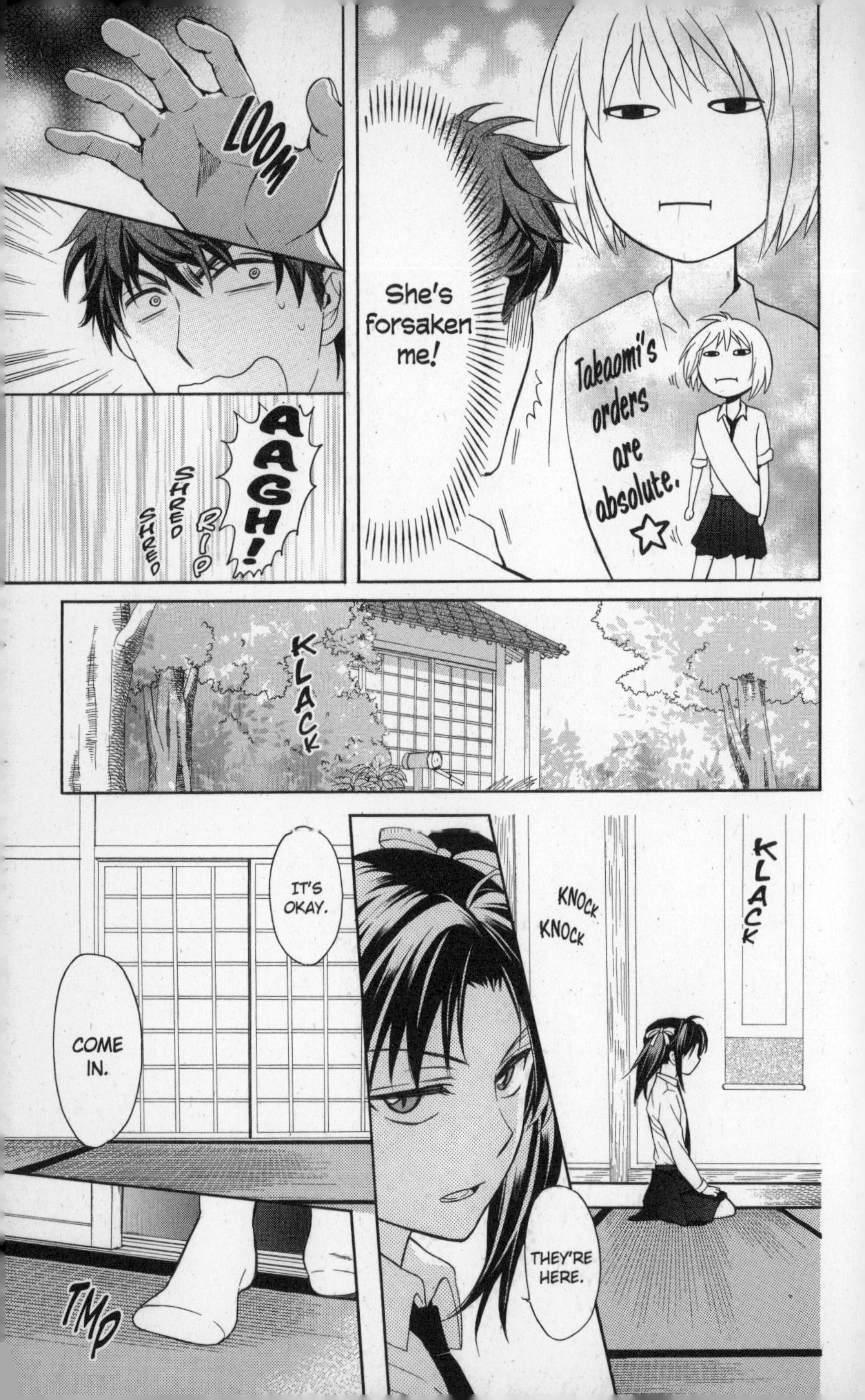

Takaomi's orders are absolute.
She's forsaken me!
LOOM
AAGH!
RIP
SHRED
SHRED
KLACK
KLACK
KNOCK
KNOCK
THEY'RE HERE.
IT'S OKAY.
COME IN.
TMP

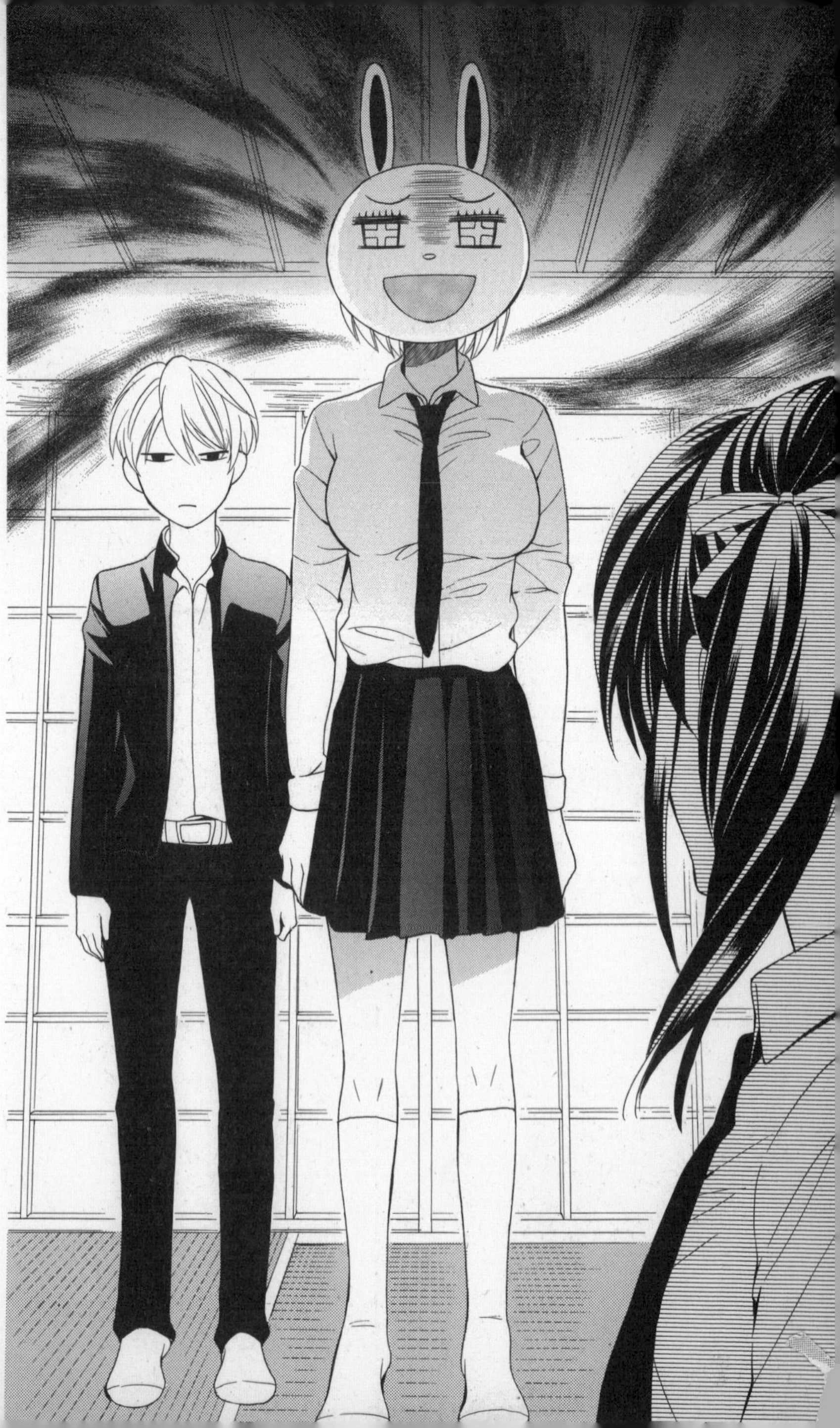

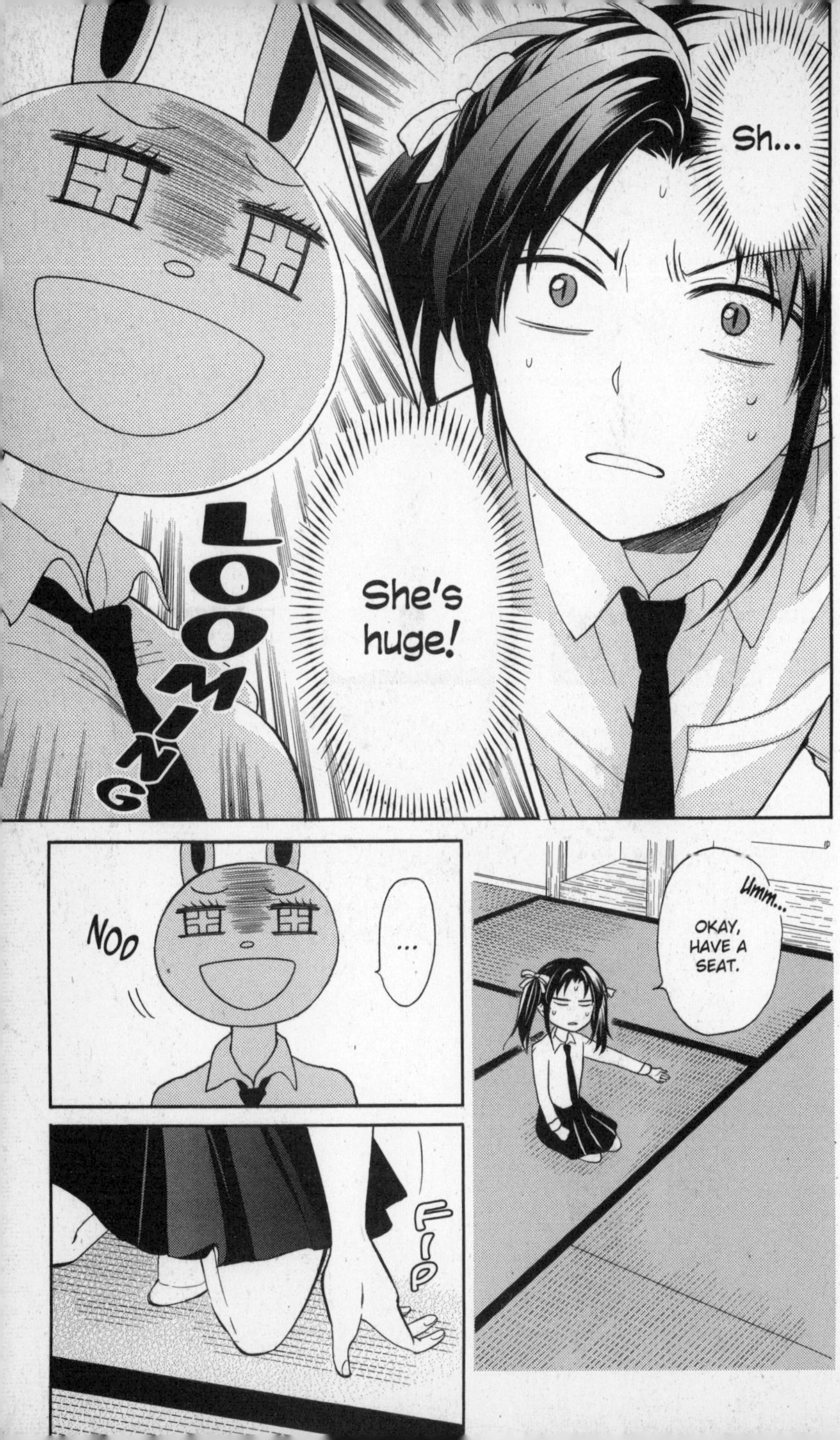
Sh...
She's huge!
LOOMING
Umm...
OKAY, HAVE A SEAT.
...
NOD
FLIP

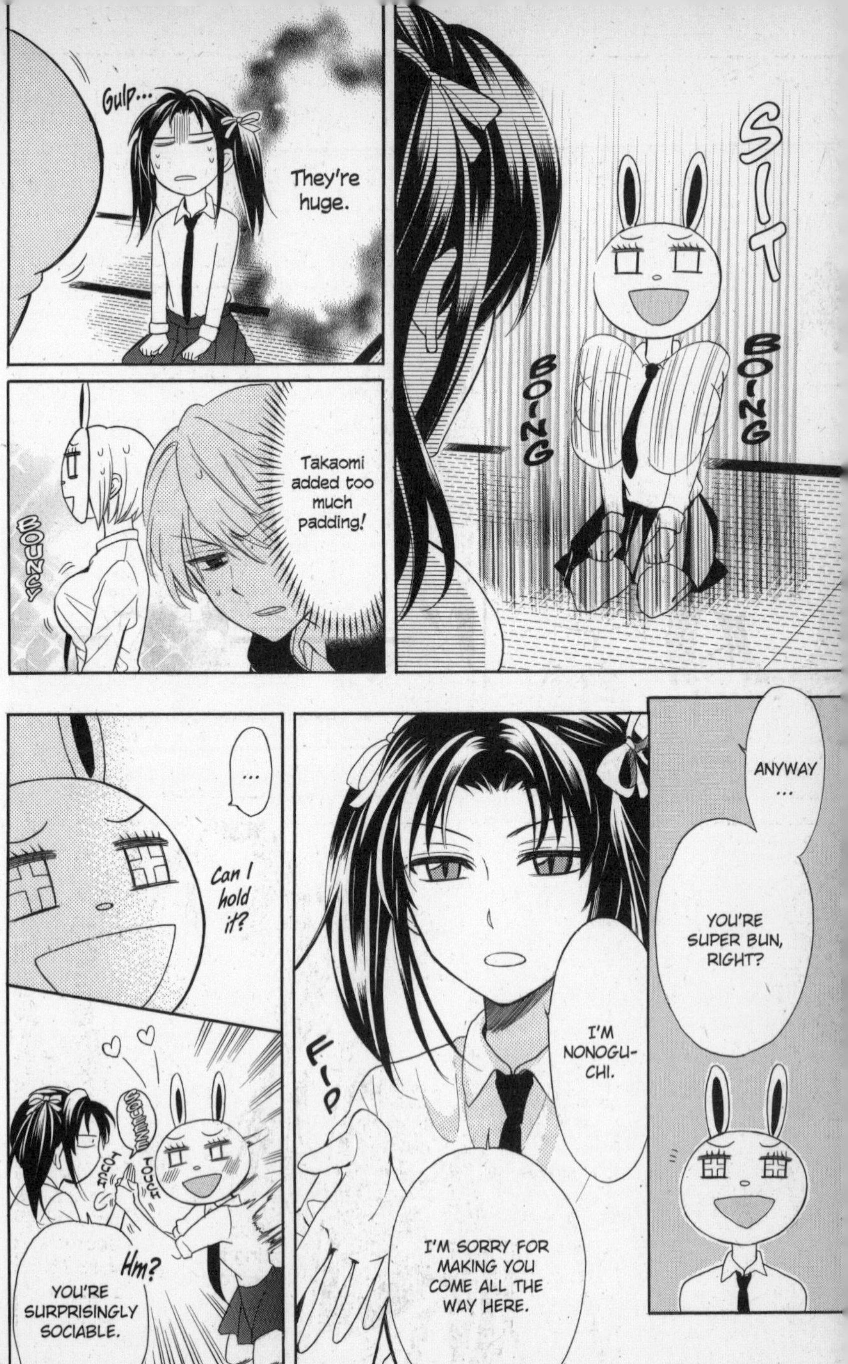
SIT
BOING
BOING
Gulp...
They're huge.
Takaomi added too much padding!
BOUNCY
ANYWAY...
YOU'RE SUPER BUN, RIGHT?
I'M NONOGU-CHI.
FLIP
I'M SORRY FOR MAKING YOU COME ALL THE WAY HERE.
...
Can I hold it?
TOUCH
TOUCH
Hm?
YOU'RE SURPRISINGLY SOCIABLE.

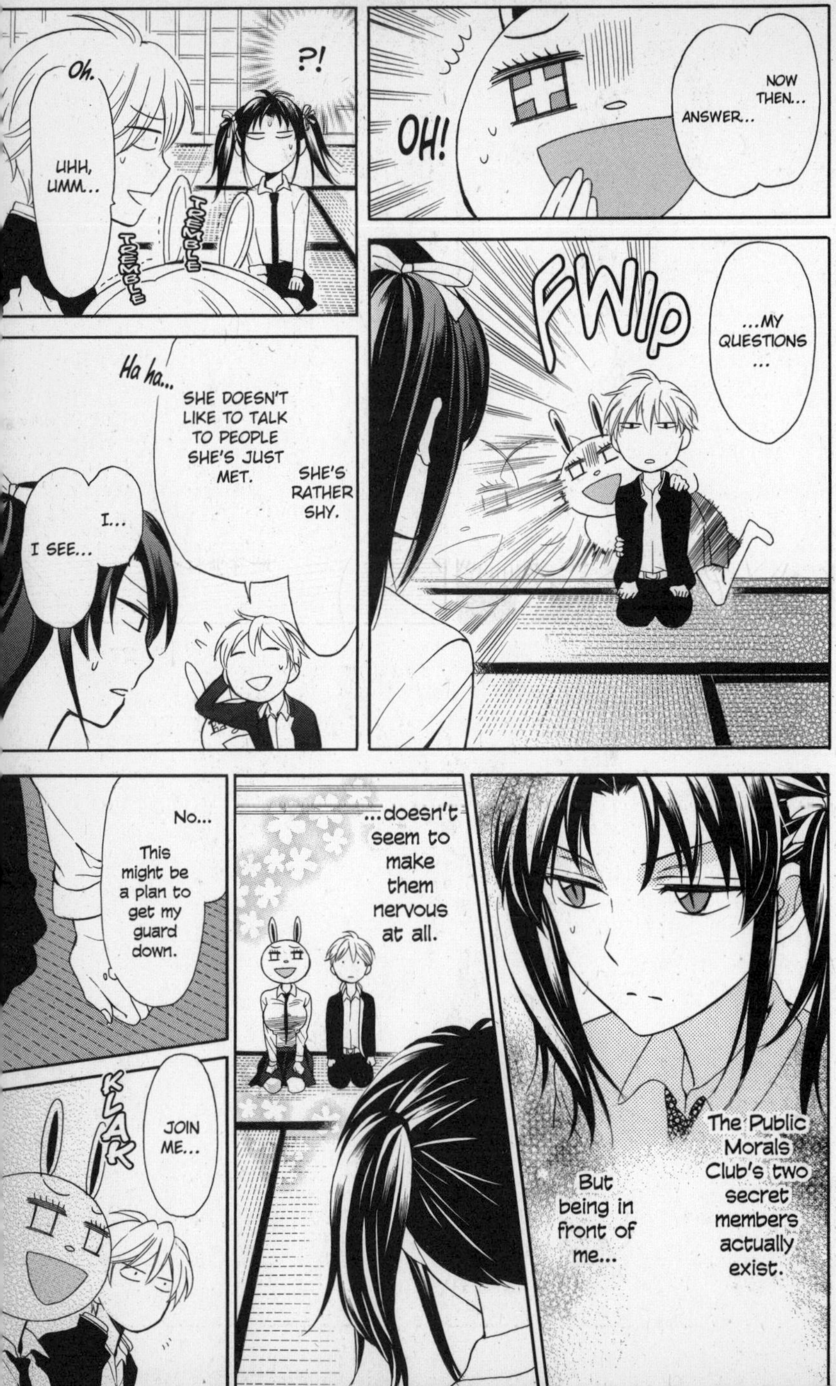
OH!
NOW THEN... ANSWER...
Oh.
?!
UHH, UMM...
TREMBLE
TREMBLE
FWIP
...MY QUESTIONS ...
Ha ha...
SHE DOESN'T LIKE TO TALK TO PEOPLE SHE'S JUST MET.
SHE'S RATHER SHY.
I... I SEE...
The Public Morals Club's two secret members actually exist.
But being in front of me...
...doesn't seem to make them nervous at all.
No...
This might be a plan to get my guard down.
KLAK
JOIN ME...

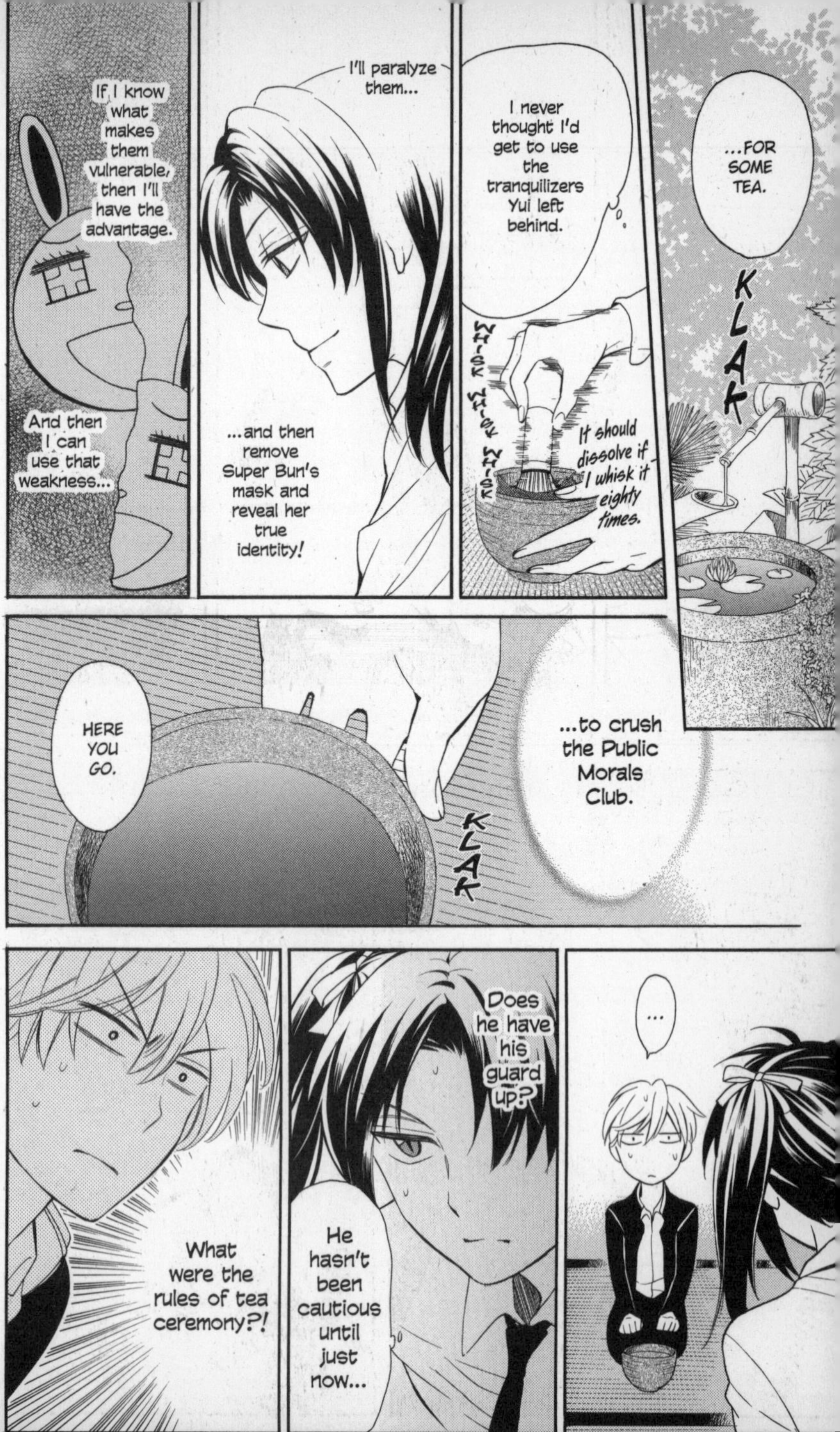
...FOR SOME TEA.
KLAK
I never thought I'd get to use the tranquilizers Yui left behind.
WHISK WHISK WHISK
It should dissolve if I whisk it eighty times.
I'll paralyze them...
...and then remove Super Bun's mask and reveal her true identity!
If I know what makes them vulnerable, then I'll have the advantage.
And then I can use that weakness...
...to crush the Public Morals Club.
KLAK
HERE YOU GO.
...
Does he have his guard up?
He hasn't been cautious until just now...
What were the rules of tea ceremony?!

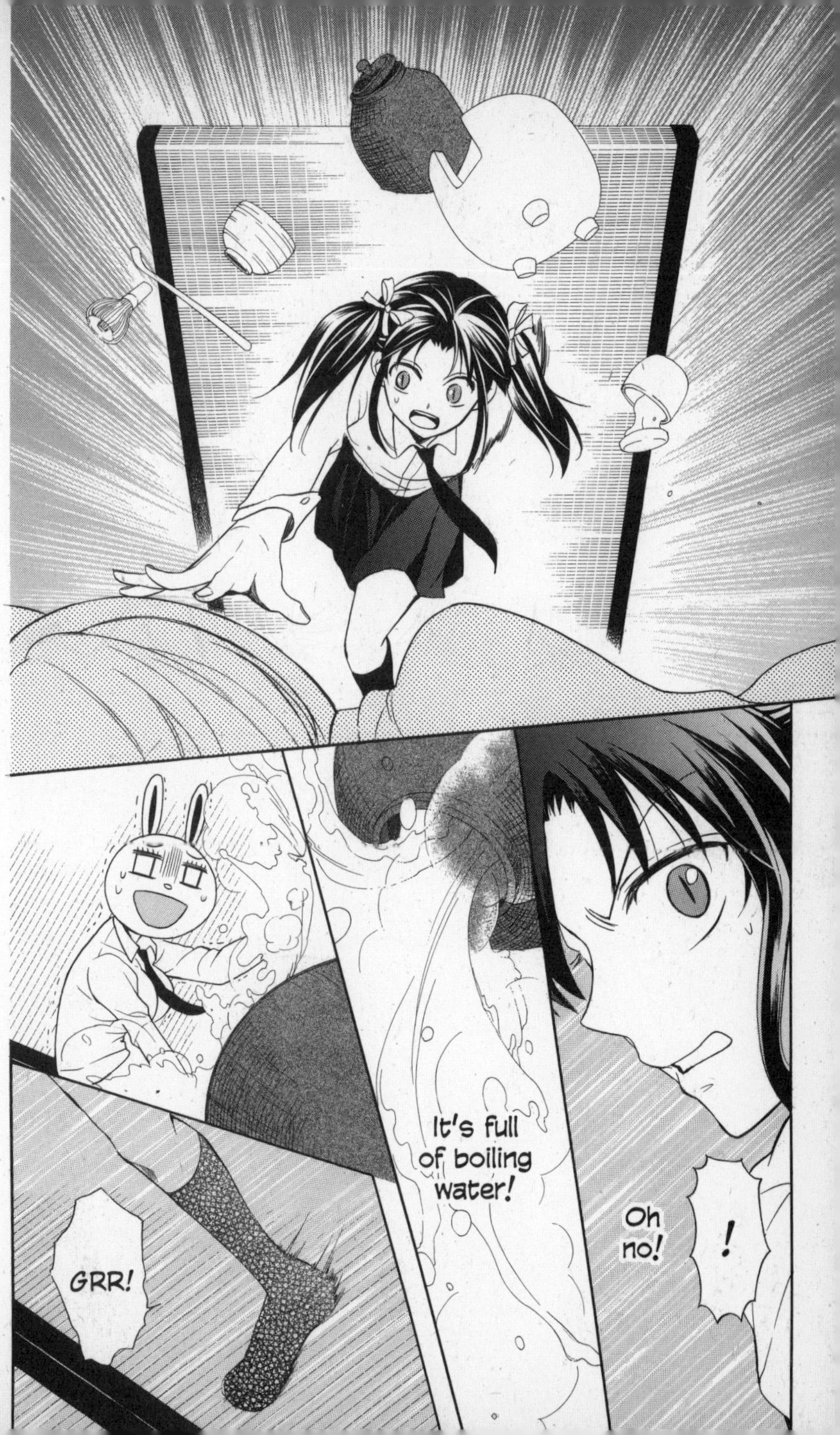
!
Oh no!
It's full of boiling water!
GRR!

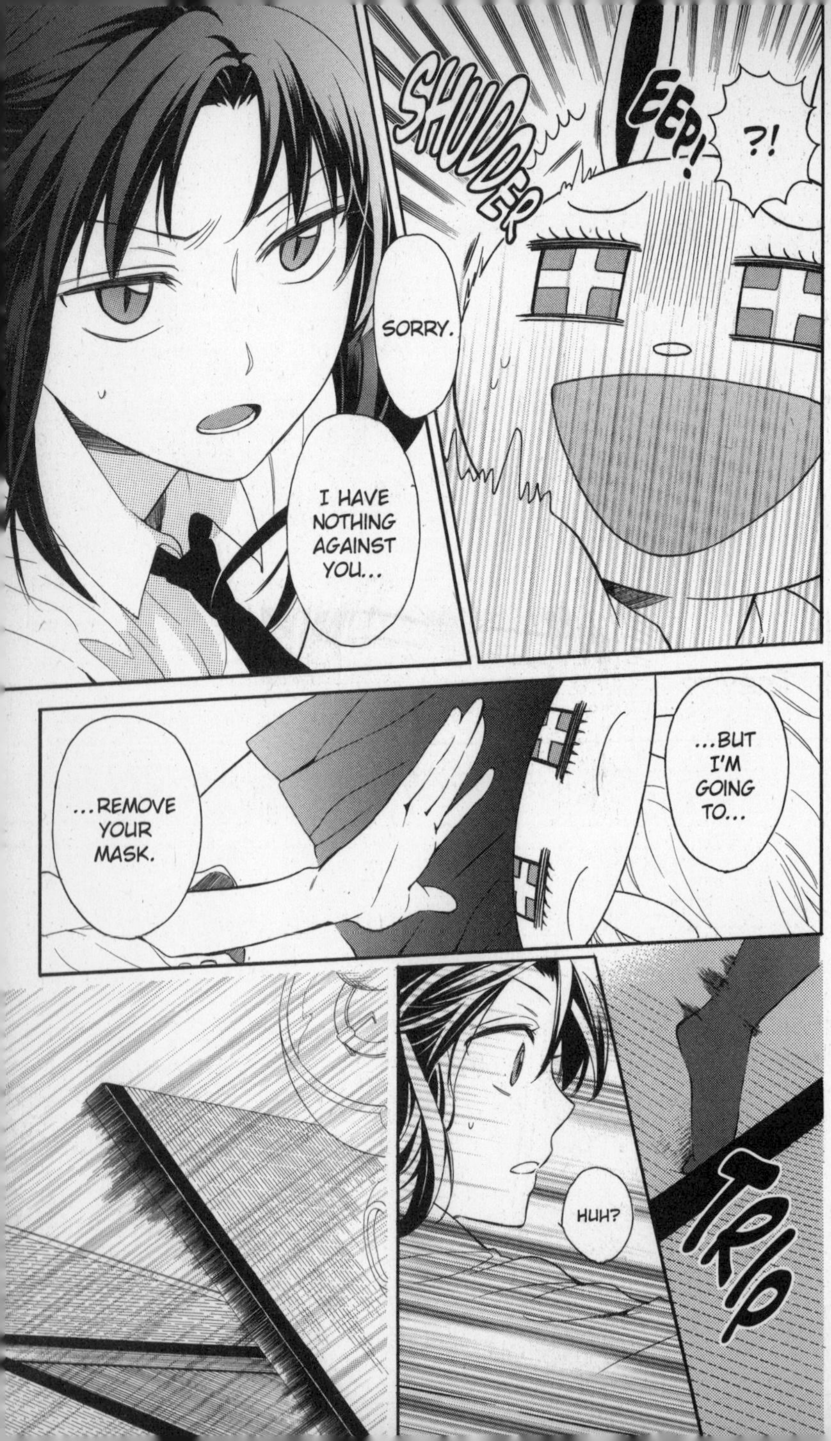

?!
EEP!
SHUDDER
SORRY.
I HAVE NOTHING AGAINST YOU...
...BUT I'M GOING TO...
...REMOVE YOUR MASK.
TRIP
HUH?

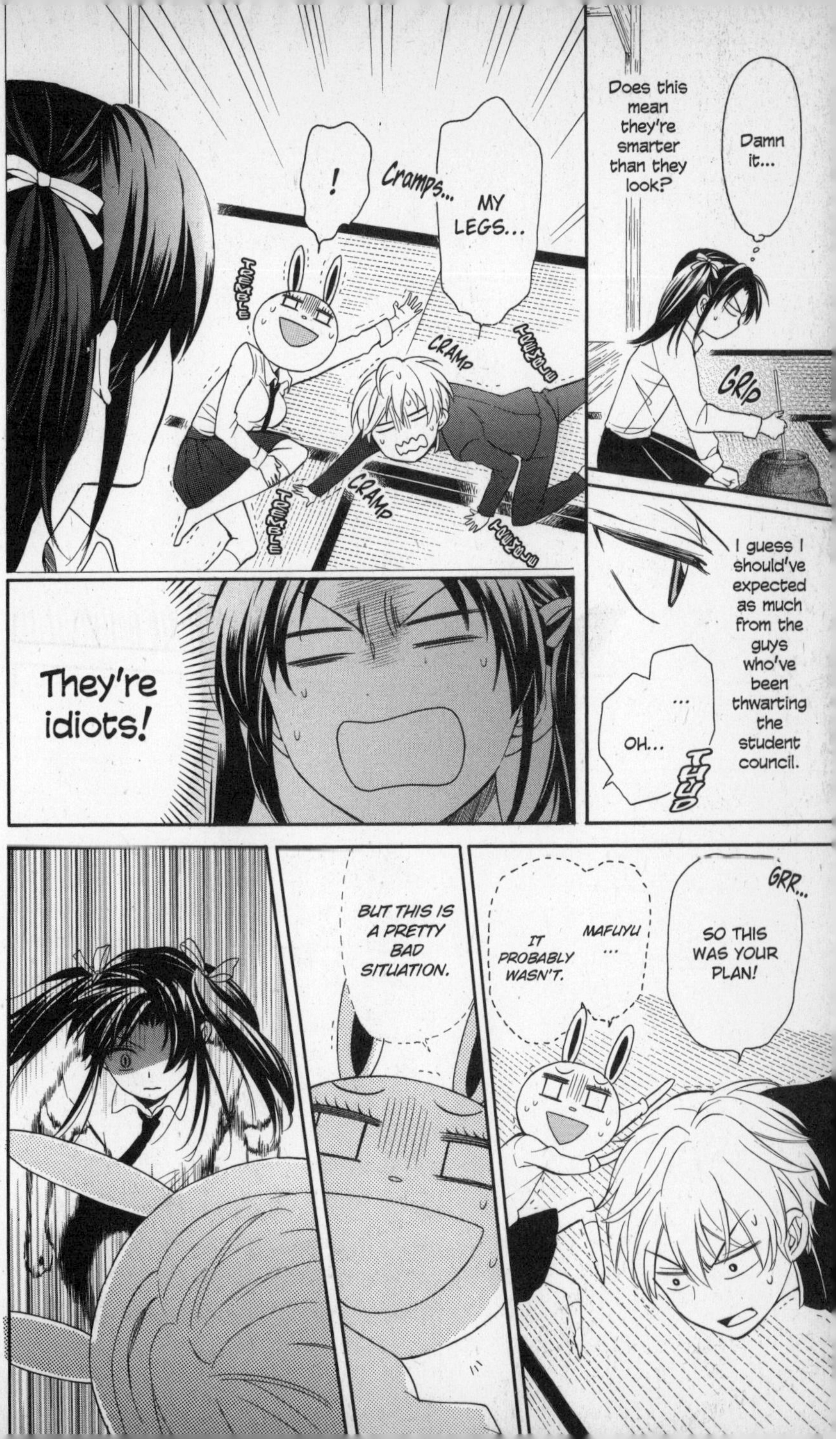

Damn it...
Does this mean they're smarter than they look?
GRIP
I guess I should've expected as much from the guys who've been thwarting the student council.
...
OH...
THUD
MY LEGS...
Cramps...
!
TREMBLE
CRAMP
CRAMP
TREMBLE
They're idiots!
GRR...
SO THIS WAS YOUR PLAN!
MAFUYU...
IT PROBABLY WASN'T.
BUT THIS IS A PRETTY BAD SITUATION.

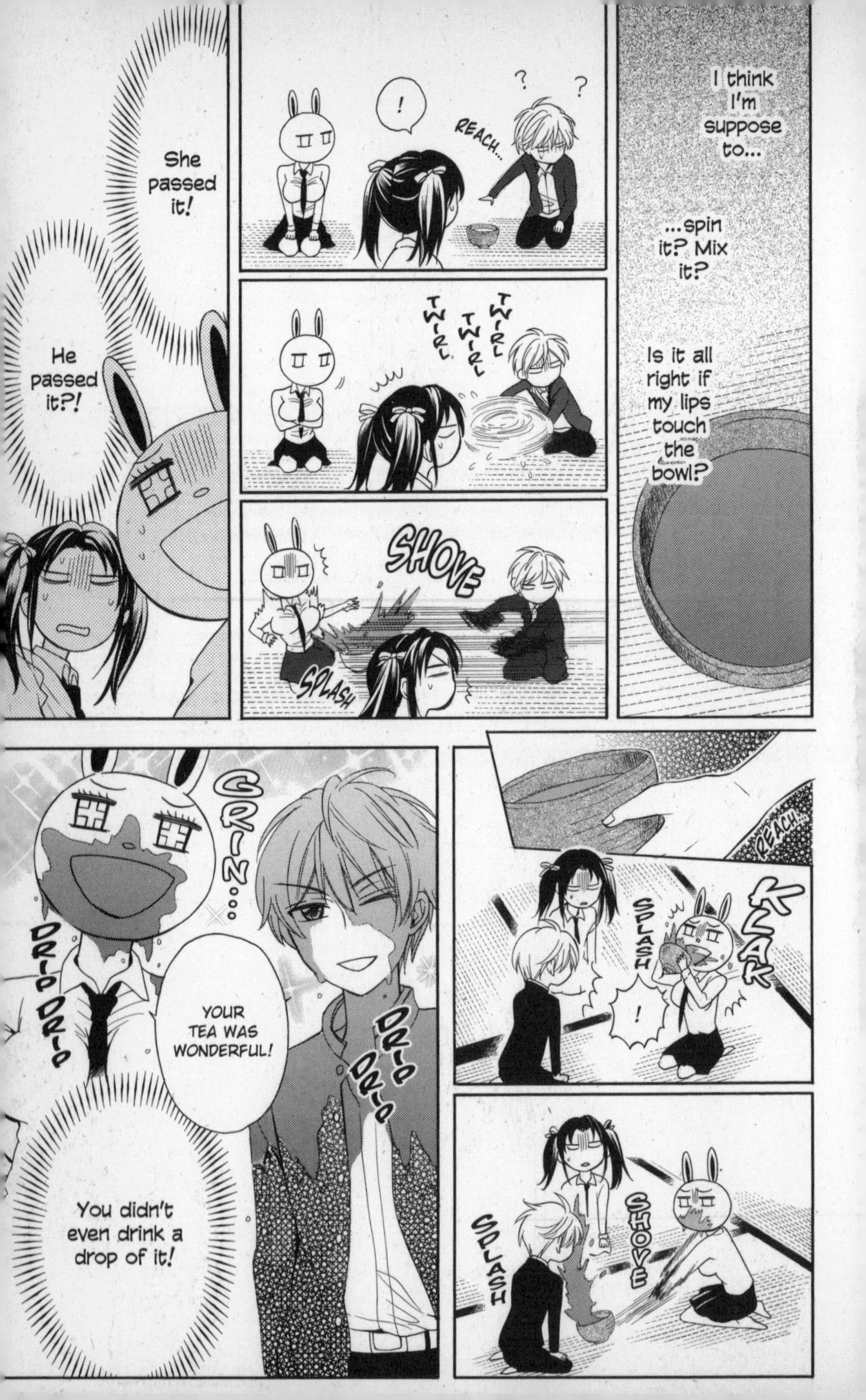

I think I'm suppose to...
...spin it? Mix it?
Is it all right if my lips touch the bowl?
?
?
!
REACH...
TWIRL
TWIRL
TWIRL
SHOVE
SPLASH
She passed it!
He passed it?!
REACH...
KLAK
SPLASH
!
SHOVE
SPLASH
GRIN...
DRIP DRIP
YOUR TEA WAS WONDERFUL!
DRIP DRIP
You didn't even drink a drop of it!

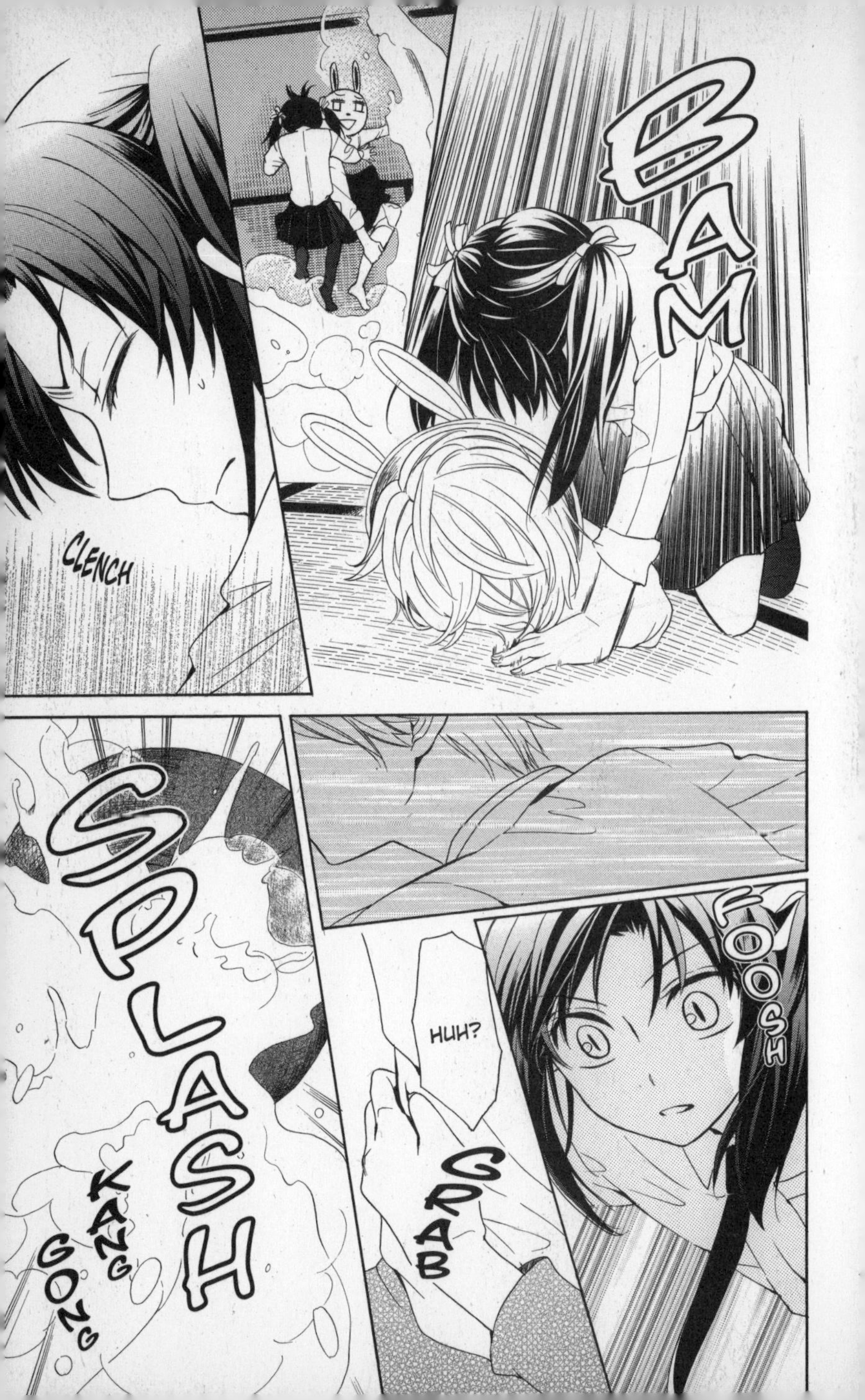
BAM
CLENCH
FOOSH
HUH?
GRAB
SPLASH
KANG
GONG

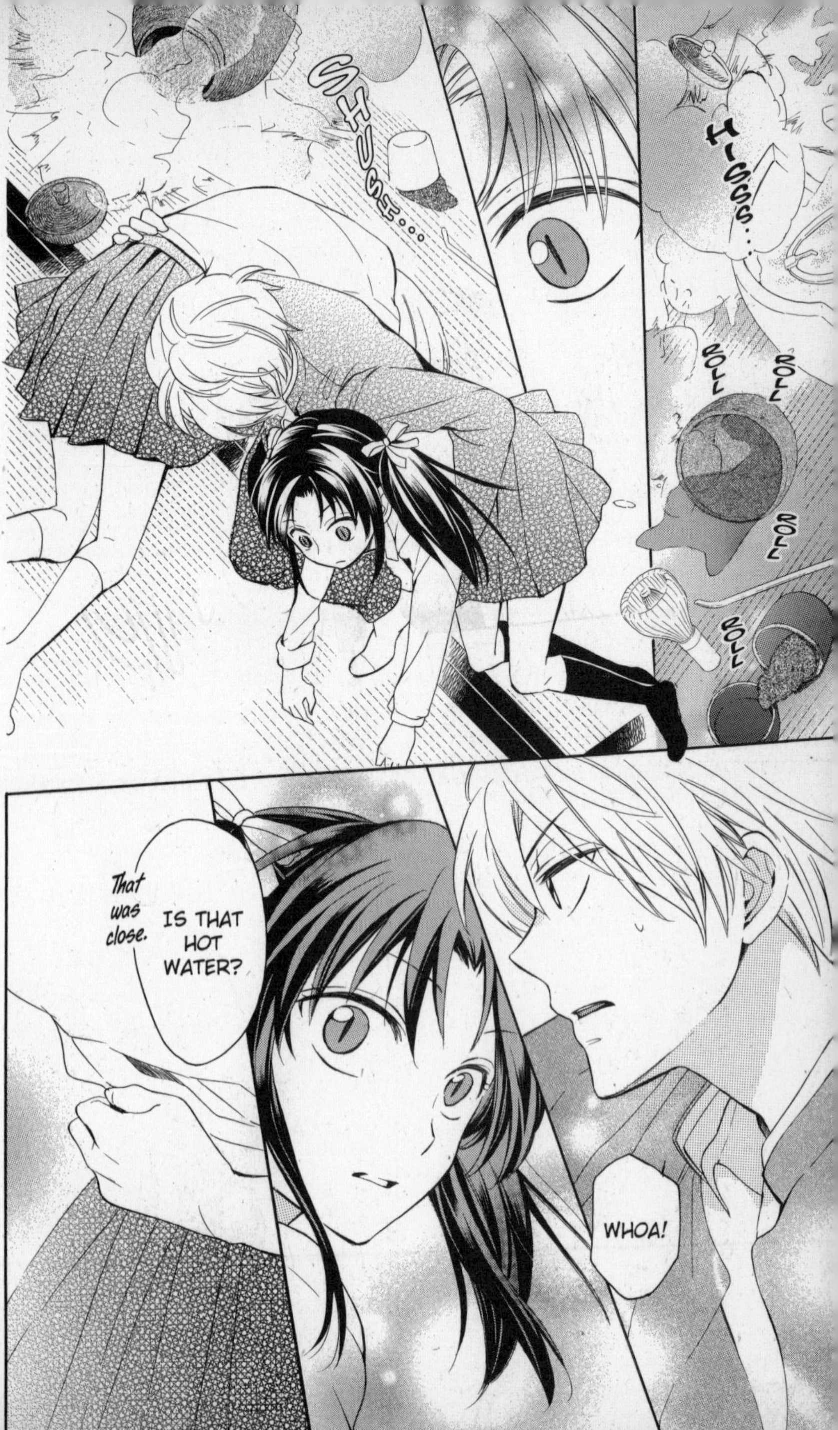
HISSS...
ROLL
ROLL
ROLL
ROLL
SHUSH...
WHOA!
IS THAT HOT WATER?
That was close.

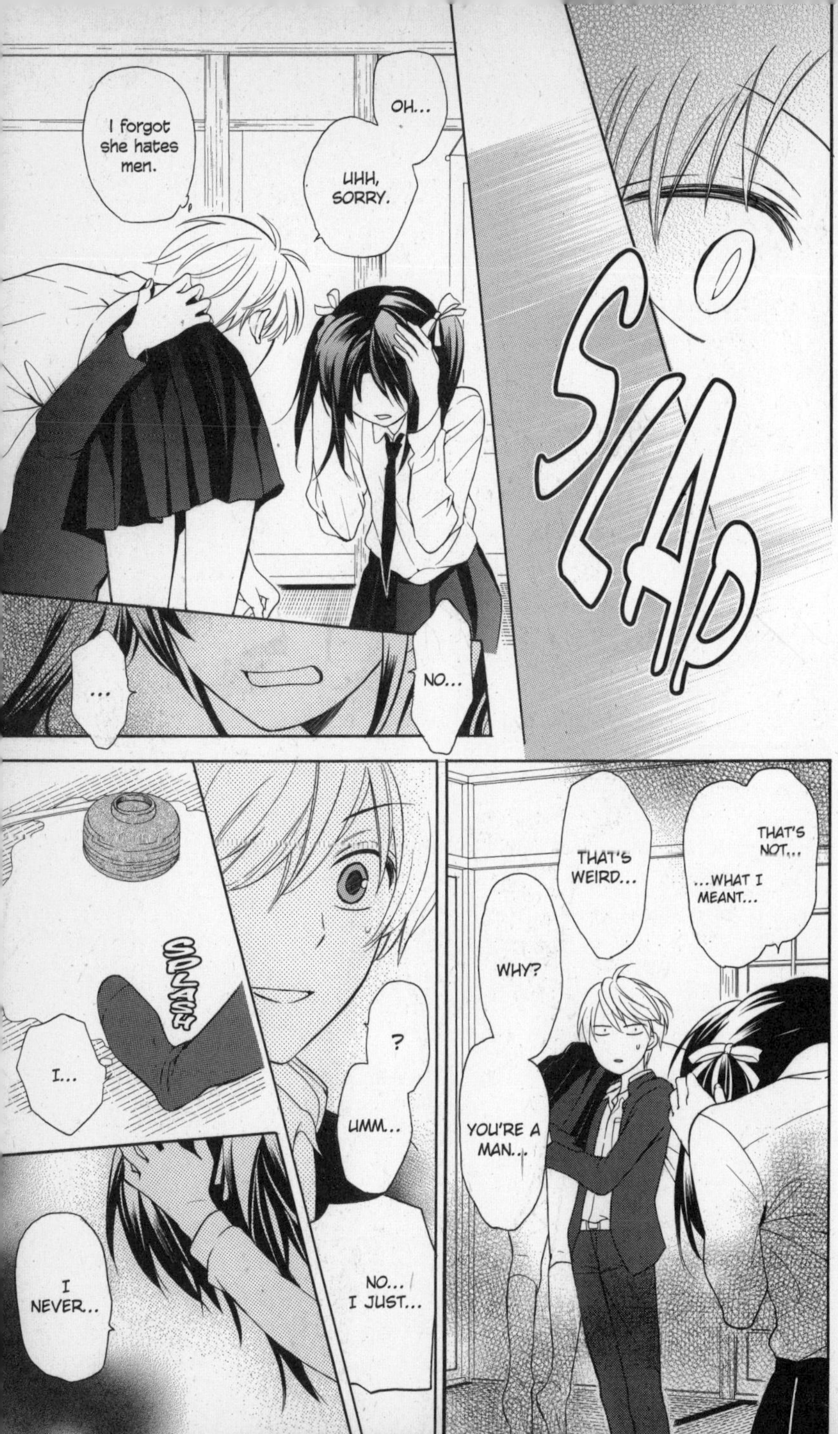
SLAP
OH...
UHH, SORRY.
I forgot she hates men.
NO...
...
THAT'S NOT...
...WHAT I MEANT...
THAT'S WEIRD...
WHY?
YOU'RE A MAN...
?
UMM...
SPLASH
I...
NO... I JUST...
I NEVER...

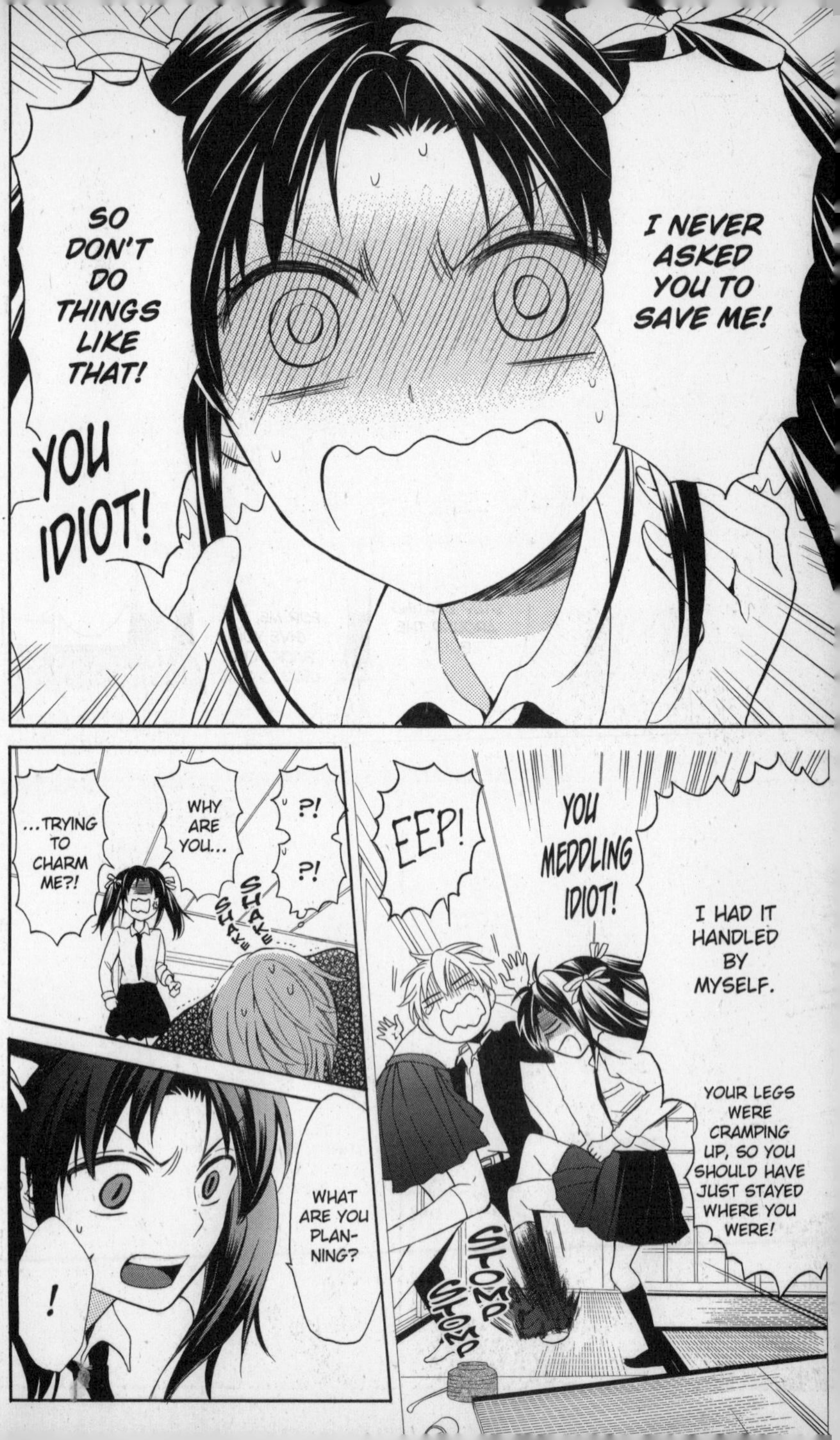
I NEVER ASKED YOU TO SAVE ME!
SO DON'T DO THINGS LIKE THAT!
YOU IDIOT!
I HAD IT HANDLED BY MYSELF.
YOUR LEGS WERE CRAMPING UP, SO YOU SHOULD HAVE JUST STAYED WHERE YOU WERE!
YOU MEDDLING IDIOT!
EEP!
STOMP STOMP
?! ?!
SHAKE SHAKE
WHY ARE YOU...
...TRYING TO CHARM ME?!
WHAT ARE YOU PLAN-NING?
!

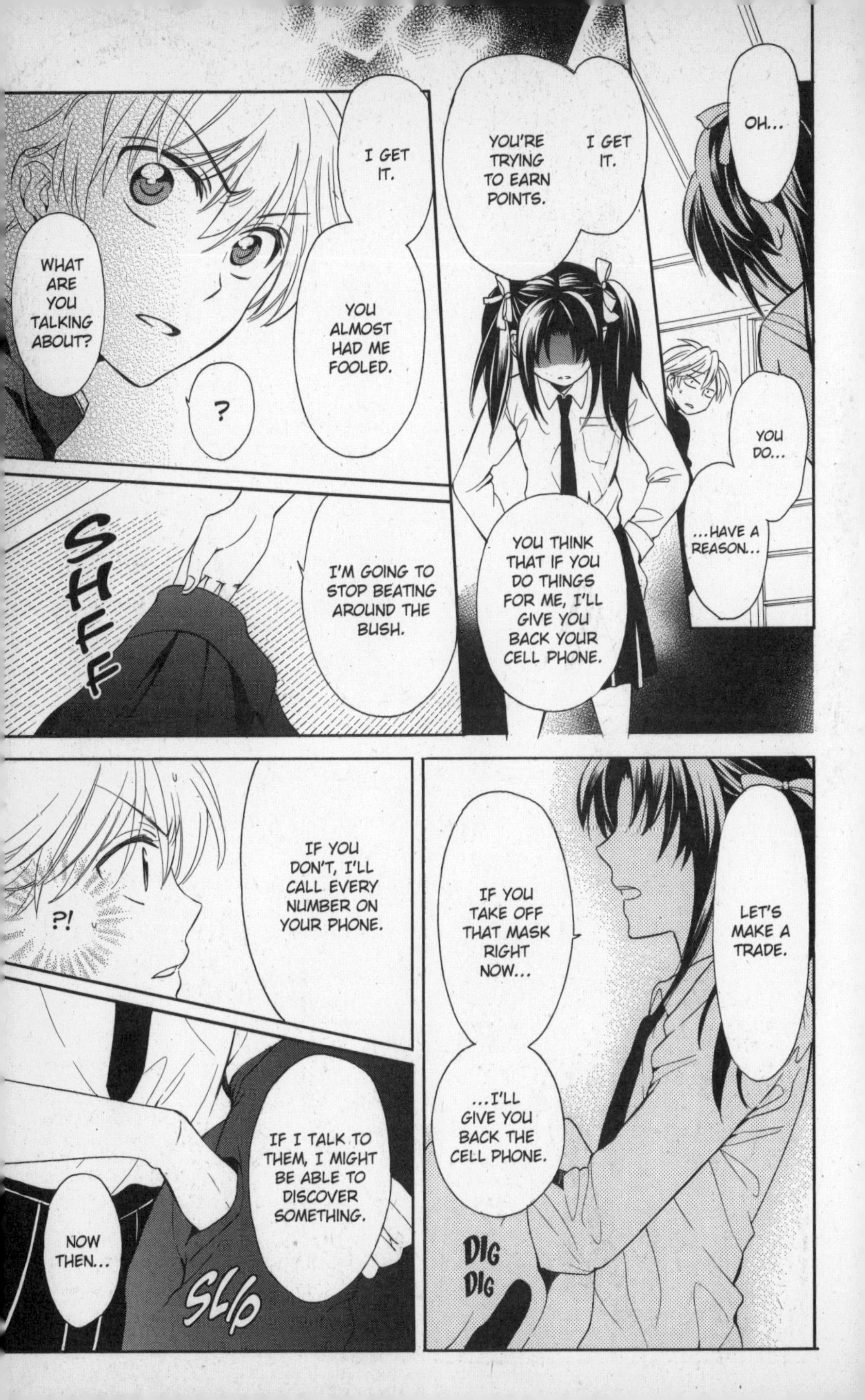
OH...
YOU DO...
...HAVE A REASON...
I GET IT.
YOU'RE TRYING TO EARN POINTS.
YOU THINK THAT IF YOU DO THINGS FOR ME, I'LL GIVE YOU BACK YOUR CELL PHONE.
I GET IT.
YOU ALMOST HAD ME FOOLED.
?
WHAT ARE YOU TALKING ABOUT?
I'M GOING TO STOP BEATING AROUND THE BUSH.
SHFFF
LET'S MAKE A TRADE.
IF YOU TAKE OFF THAT MASK RIGHT NOW...
...I'LL GIVE YOU BACK THE CELL PHONE.
DIG DIG
IF YOU DON'T, I'LL CALL EVERY NUMBER ON YOUR PHONE.
?!
IF I TALK TO THEM, I MIGHT BE ABLE TO DISCOVER SOMETHING.
NOW THEN...
SLIP

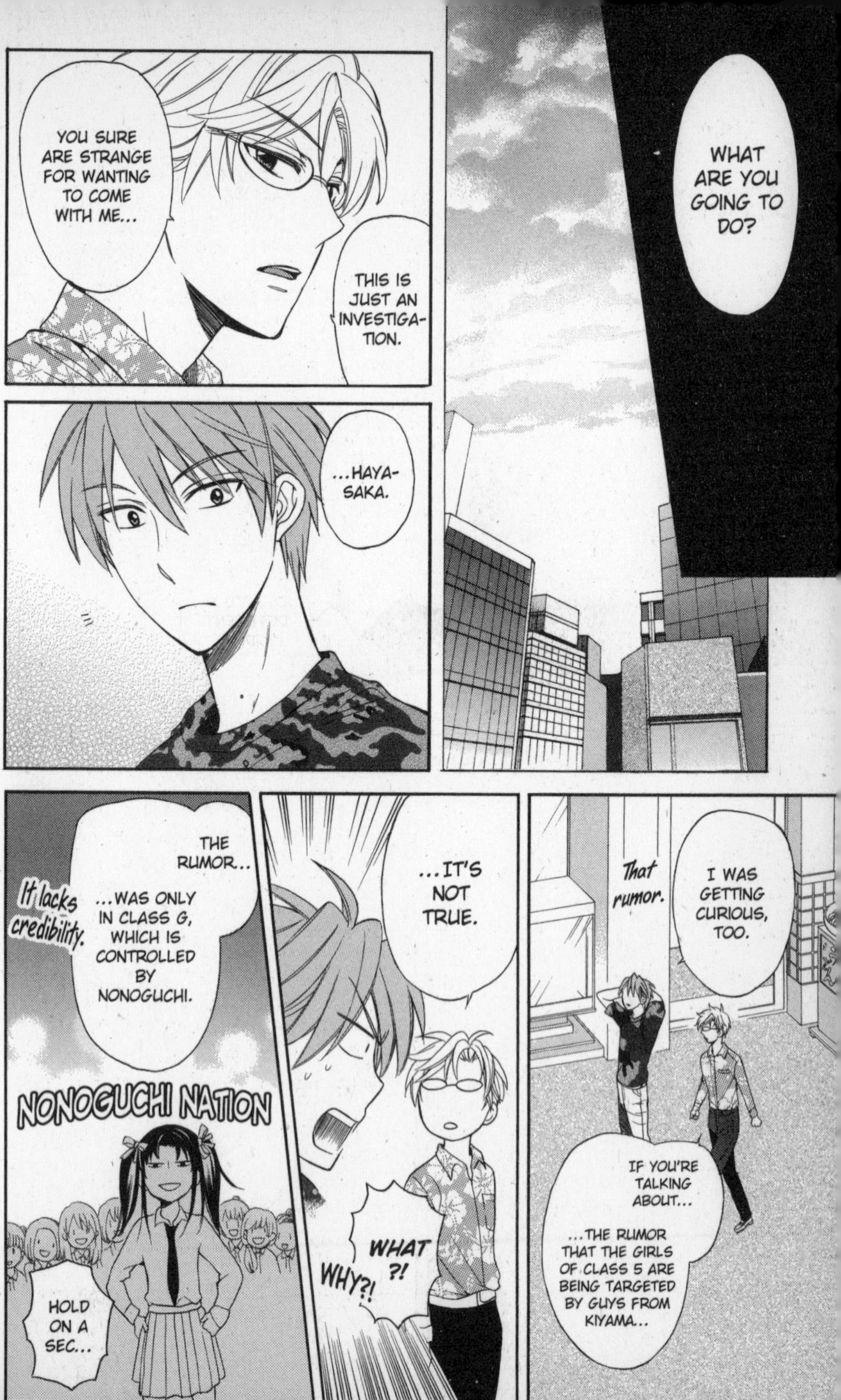
WHAT ARE YOU GOING TO DO?
YOU SURE ARE STRANGE FOR WANTING TO COME WITH ME...
THIS IS JUST AN INVESTIGATION.
...HAYASAKA.
I WAS GETTING CURIOUS, TOO.
That rumor.
IF YOU'RE TALKING ABOUT...
...THE RUMOR THAT THE GIRLS OF CLASS 5 ARE BEING TARGETED BY GUYS FROM KIYAMA...
...IT'S NOT TRUE.
WHAT?!
WHY?!
THE RUMOR...
...WAS ONLY IN CLASS G, WHICH IS CONTROLLED BY NONOGUCHI.
It lacks credibility.
NONOGUCHI NATION
HOLD ON A SEC...

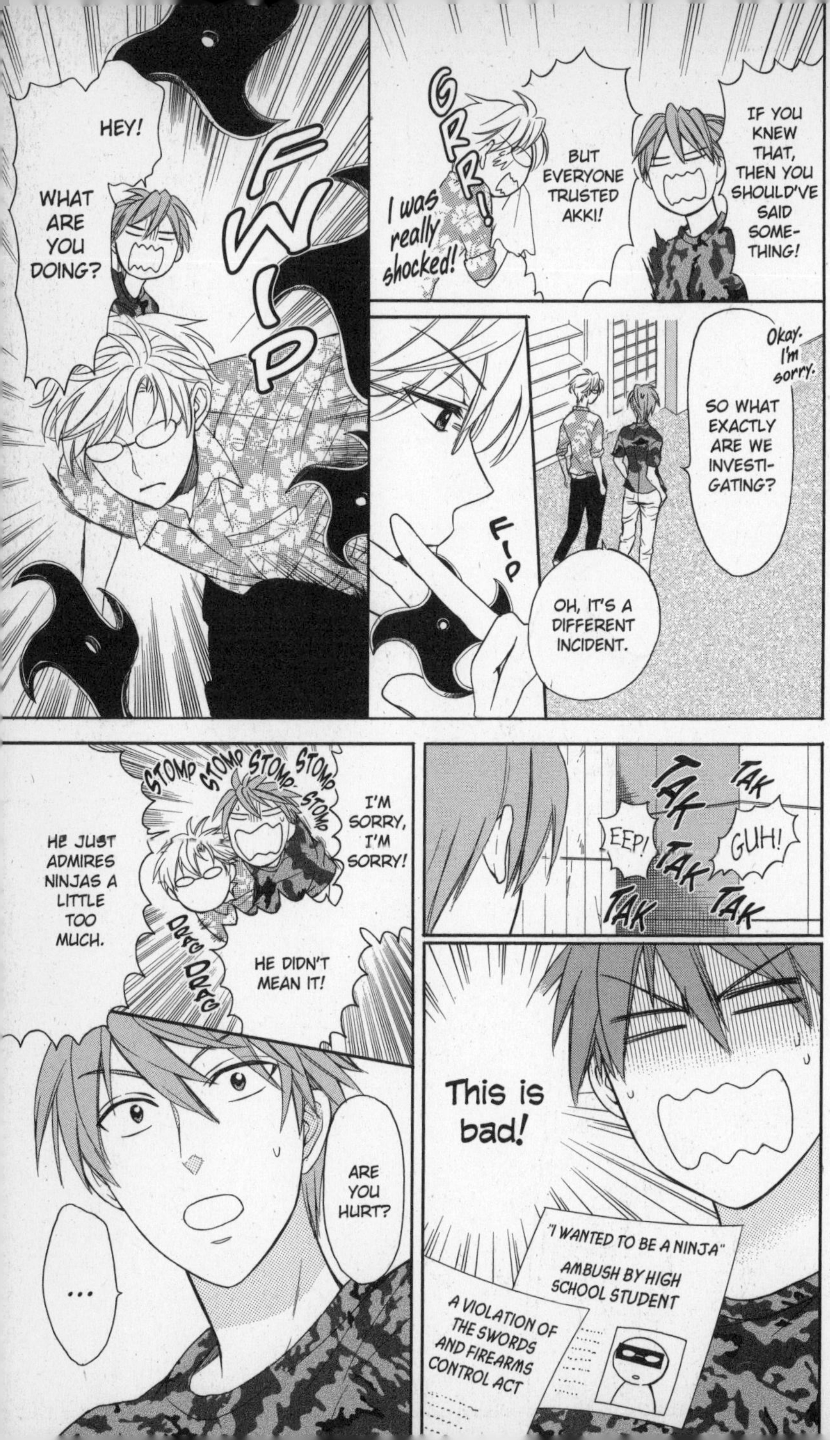
IF YOU KNEW THAT, THEN YOU SHOULD'VE SAID SOMETHING!
BUT EVERYONE TRUSTED AKKI!
GRR!
I was really shocked!
Okay. I'm sorry.
SO WHAT EXACTLY ARE WE INVESTIGATING?
FLIP
OH, IT'S A DIFFERENT INCIDENT.
FWIP
HEY!
WHAT ARE YOU DOING?
TAK TAK TAK TAK TAK TAK
GUH!
EEP!
This is bad!
"I WANTED TO BE A NINJA"
AMBUSH BY HIGH SCHOOL STUDENT
A VIOLATION OF THE SWORDS AND FIREARMS CONTROL ACT
STOMP STOMP STOMP STOMP STOMP
I'M SORRY, I'M SORRY!
HE JUST ADMIRES NINJAS A LITTLE TOO MUCH.
DRAG DRAG
HE DIDN'T MEAN IT!
ARE YOU HURT?
...

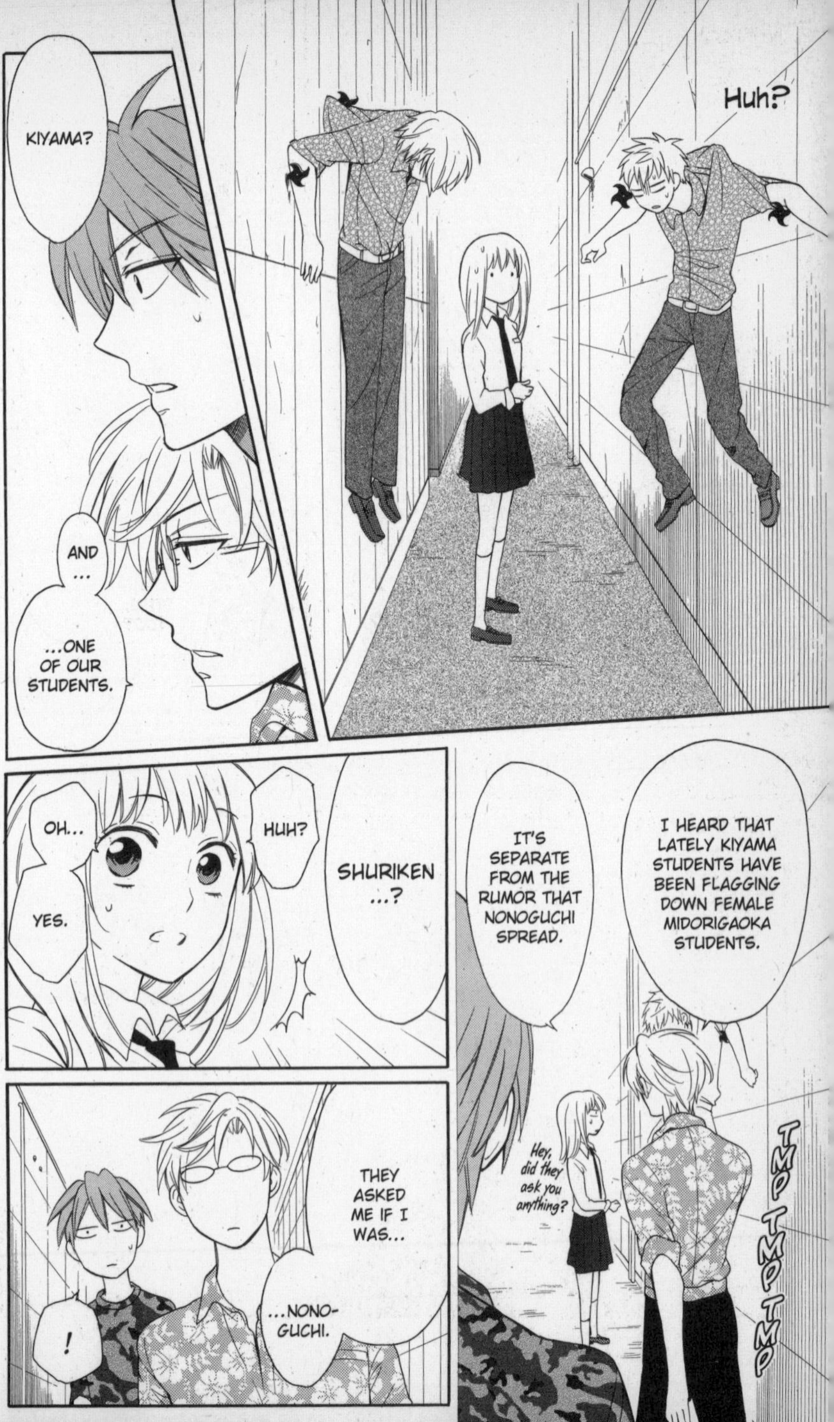
Huh?
KIYAMA?
AND...
...ONE OF OUR STUDENTS.
I HEARD THAT LATELY KIYAMA STUDENTS HAVE BEEN FLAGGING DOWN FEMALE MIDORIGAOKA STUDENTS.
IT'S SEPARATE FROM THE RUMOR THAT NONOGUCHI SPREAD.
Hey, did they ask you anything?
TMP TMP TMP TMP
SHURIKEN ...?
HUH?
OH...
YES.
THEY ASKED ME IF I WAS...
...NONO-GUCHI.
!

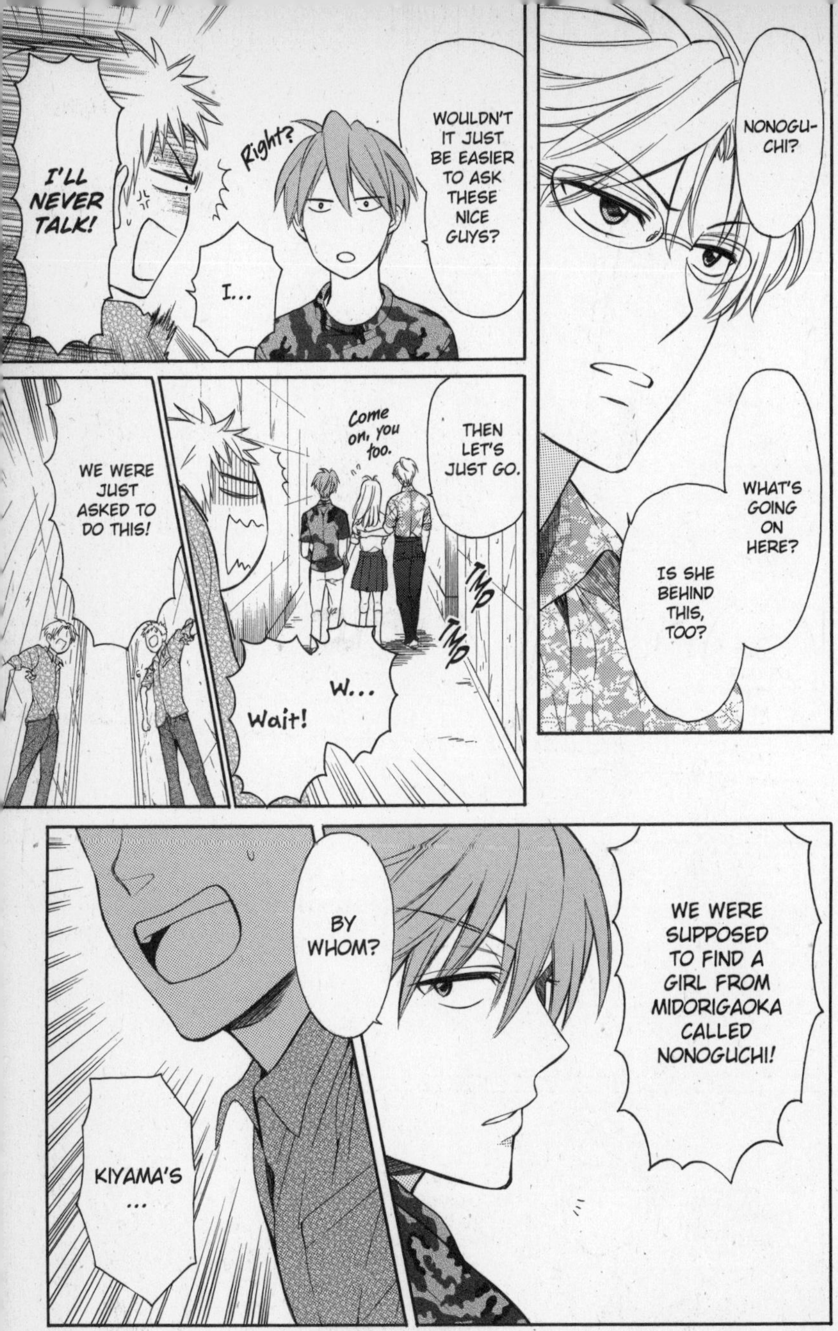
NONOGU-CHI?
WHAT'S GOING ON HERE?
IS SHE BEHIND THIS, TOO?
WOULDN'T IT JUST BE EASIER TO ASK THESE NICE GUYS?
Right?
I...
I'LL NEVER TALK!
THEN LET'S JUST GO.
Come on, you too.
TMP TMP
W...
Wait!
WE WERE JUST ASKED TO DO THIS!
WE WERE SUPPOSED TO FIND A GIRL FROM MIDORIGAOKA CALLED NONOGUCHI!
BY WHOM?
KIYAMA'S ...

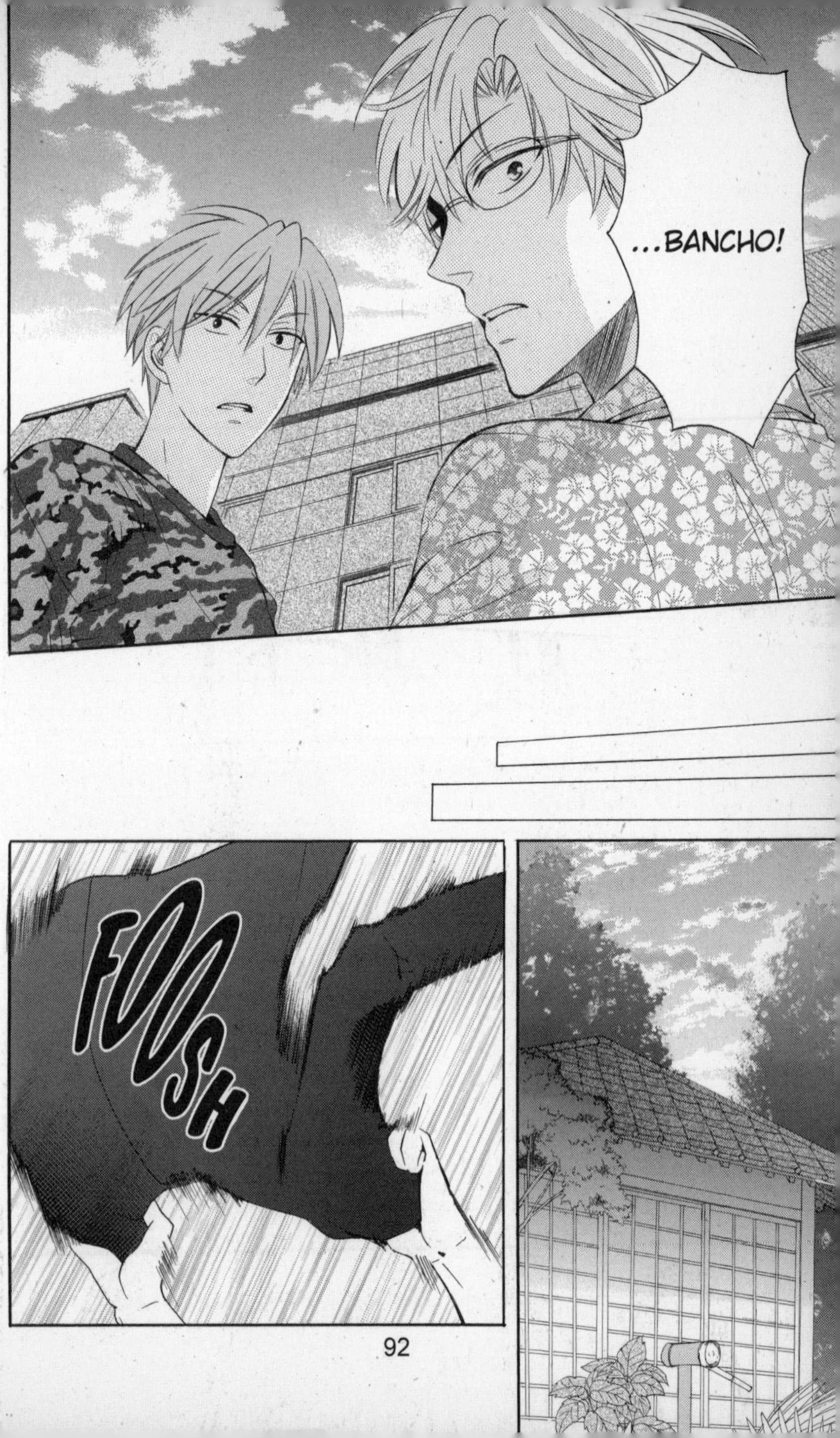
...BANCHO!
FOOSH

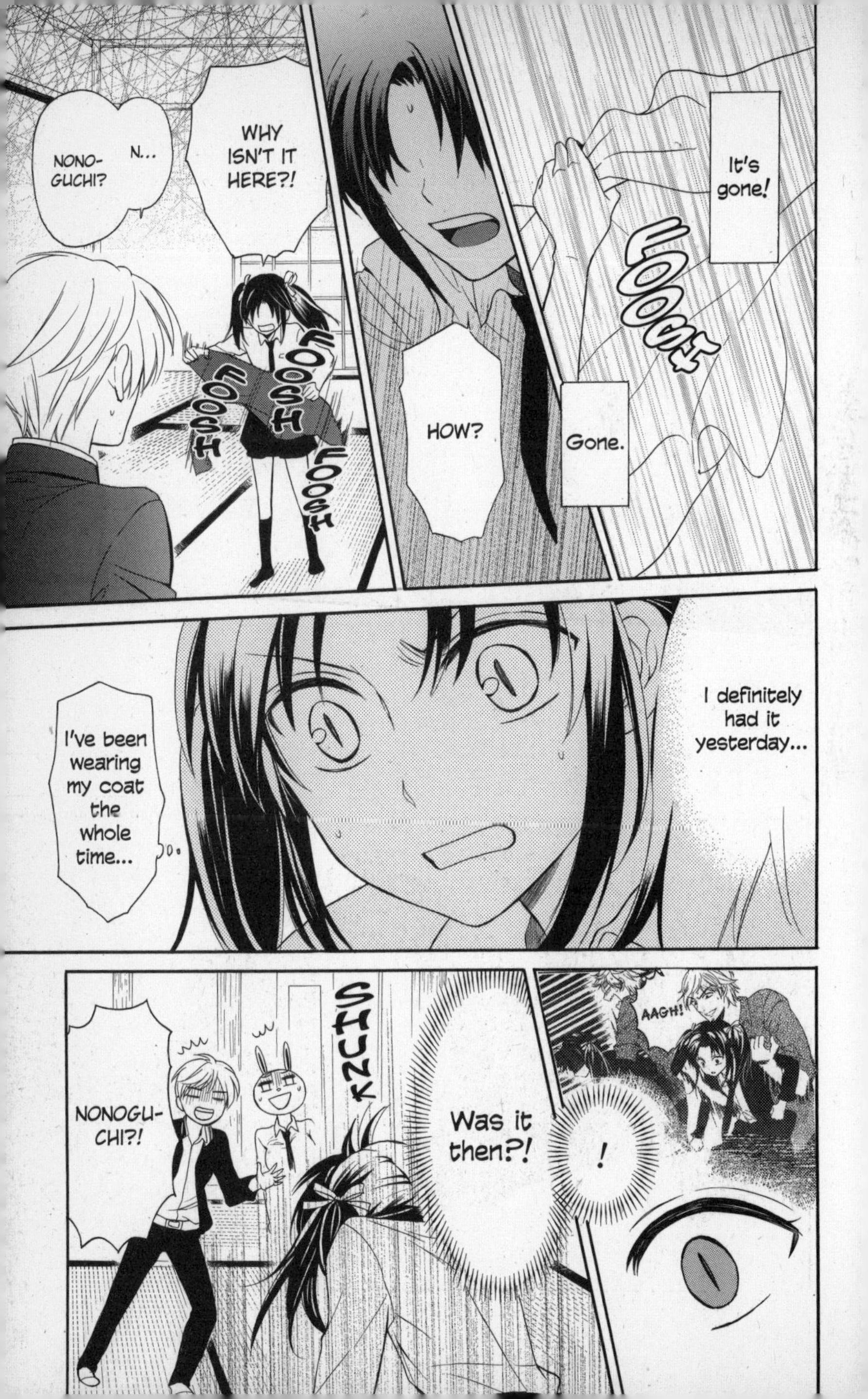
It's gone!
FOOSH
Gone.
HOW?
WHY ISN'T IT HERE?!
N... NONO-GUCHI?
FOOSH
FOOSH
FOOSH
I definitely had it yesterday...
I've been wearing my coat the whole time...
AAGH!
!
Was it then?!
SHUNK
NONOGU-CHI?!

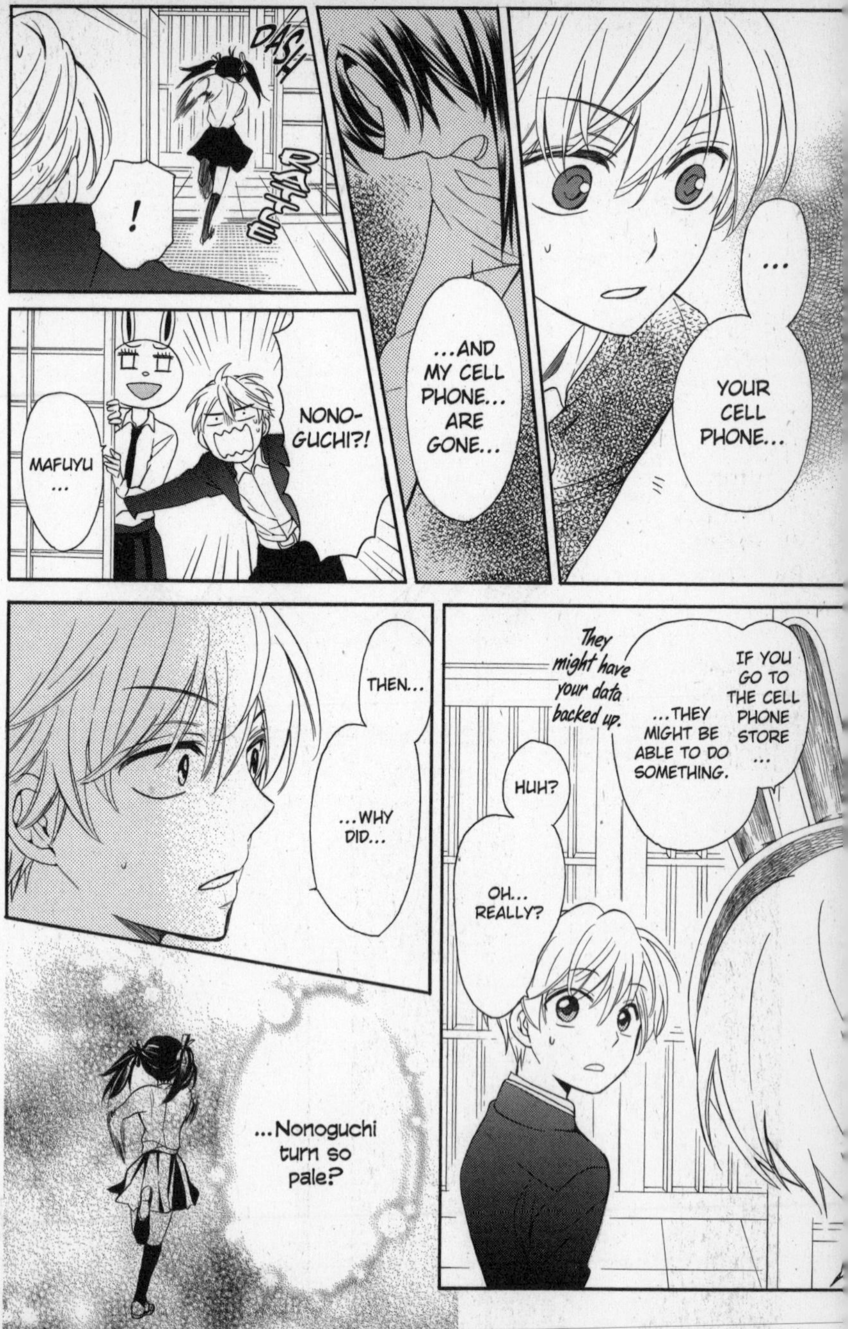
...
YOUR CELL PHONE...
...AND MY CELL PHONE... ARE GONE...
DASH
DASH
!
NONO-GUCHI?!
MAFUYU ...
IF YOU GO TO THE CELL PHONE STORE ...
...THEY MIGHT BE ABLE TO DO SOMETHING.
They might have your data backed up.
HUH?
OH... REALLY?
THEN...
...WHY DID...
...Nonoguchi turn so pale?

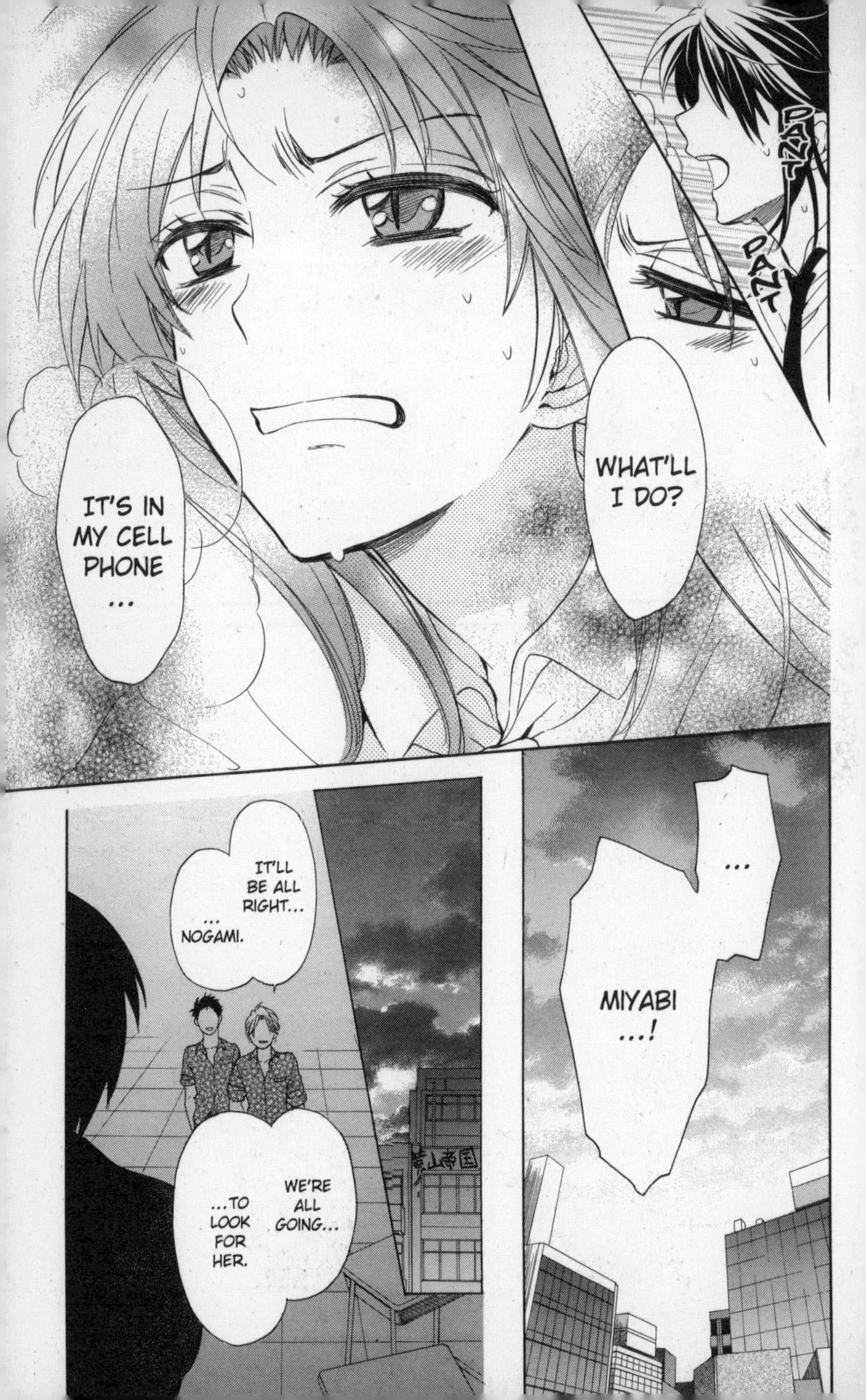
PANT
PANT
PANT
WHAT'LL I DO?
IT'S IN MY CELL PHONE ...
...
MIYABI ...!
IT'LL BE ALL RIGHT... ... NOGAMI.
WE'RE ALL GOING...
...TO LOOK FOR HER.

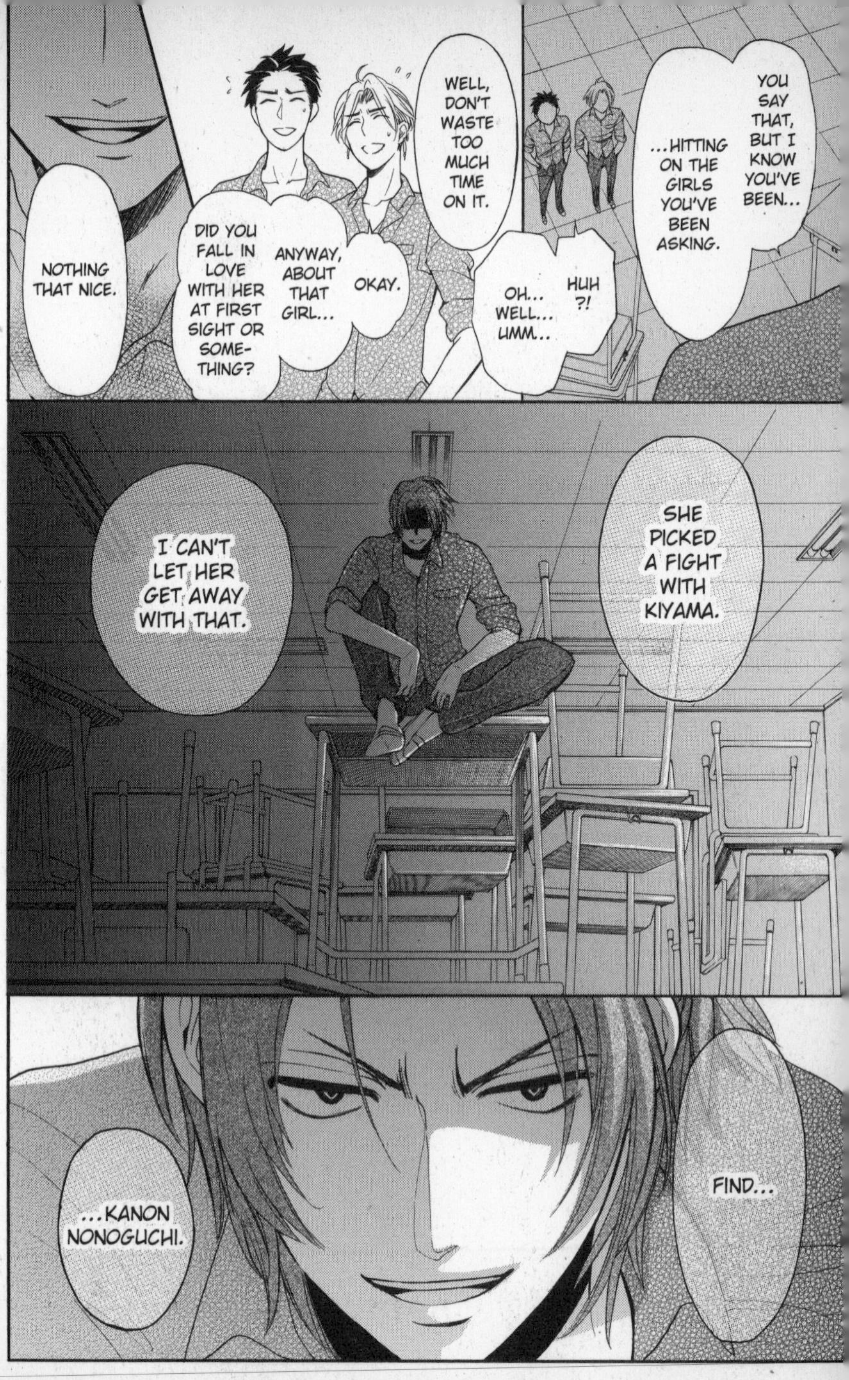
YOU SAY THAT, BUT I KNOW YOU'VE BEEN...
...HITTING ON THE GIRLS YOU'VE BEEN ASKING.
HUH ?!
OH... WELL... UMM...
WELL, DON'T WASTE TOO MUCH TIME ON IT.
OKAY.
ANYWAY, ABOUT THAT GIRL...
DID YOU FALL IN LOVE WITH HER AT FIRST SIGHT OR SOME-THING?
NOTHING THAT NICE.
SHE PICKED A FIGHT WITH KIYAMA.
I CAN'T LET HER GET AWAY WITH THAT.
FIND...
...KANON NONOGUCHI.

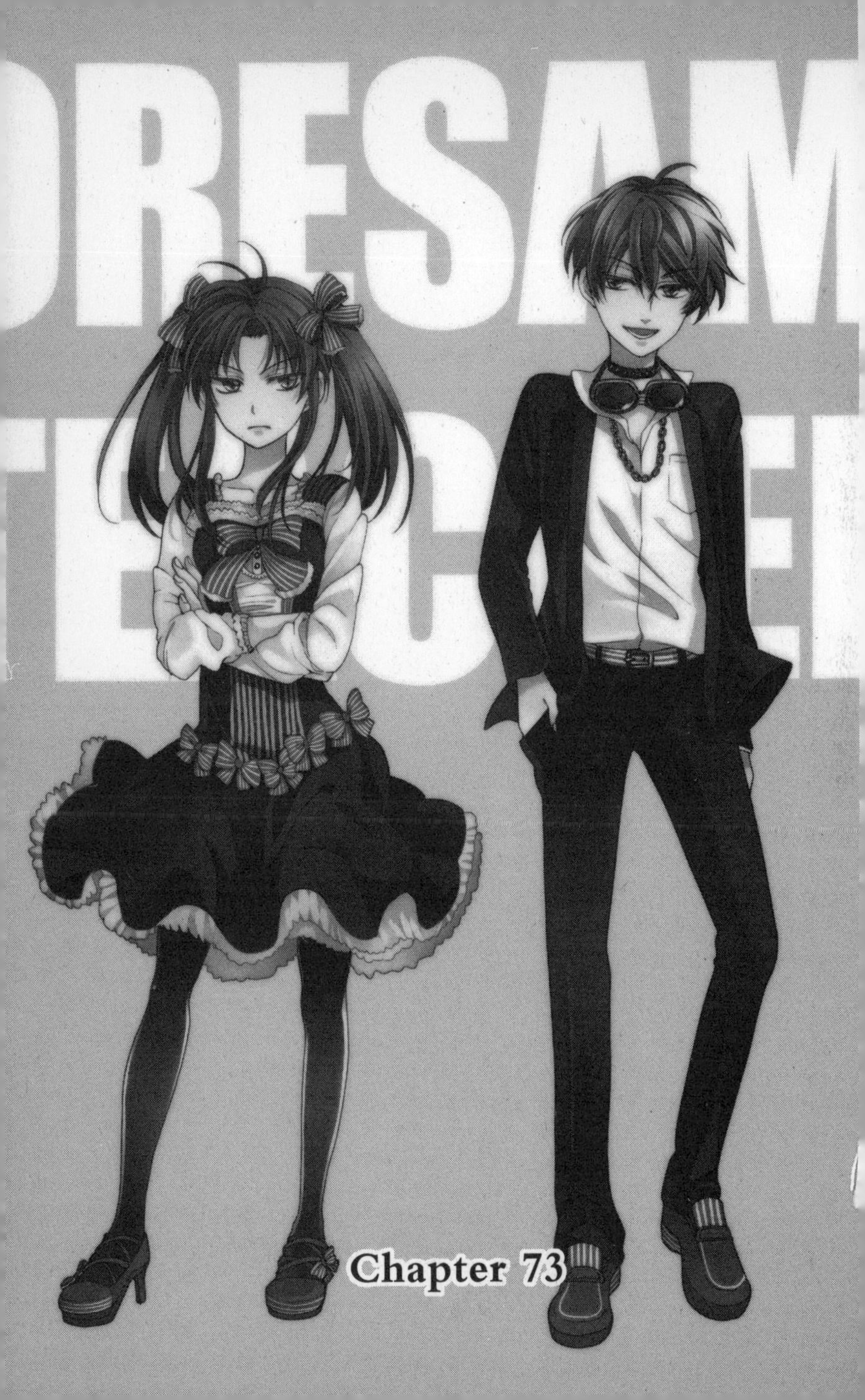

Chapter 73

COME TO DORM 1

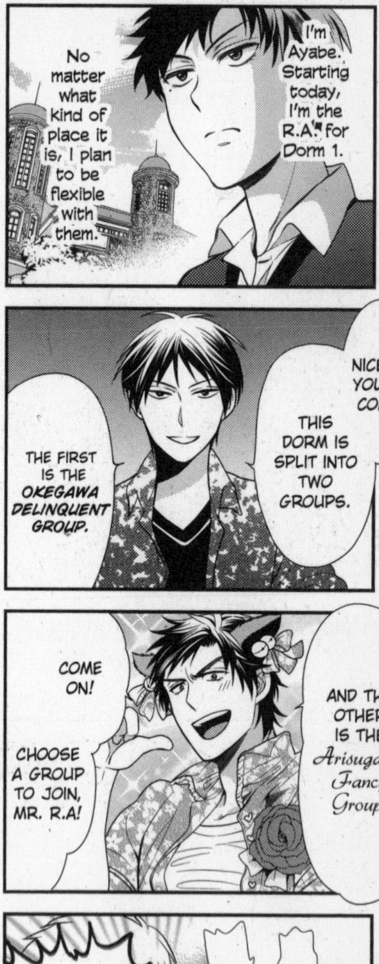
I'm Ayabe. Starting today, I'm the R.A. for Dorm 1.
No matter what kind of place it is, I plan to be flexible with them.
NICE OF YOU TO COME!
THIS DORM IS SPLIT INTO TWO GROUPS.
THE FIRST IS THE *OKEGAWA DELINQUENT GROUP*.
AND THE OTHER IS THE *Arisugawa Fancy Group*!
COME ON!
CHOOSE A GROUP TO JOIN, MR. R.A!
!
!
AYABE!
IT'S A JOKE!
Don't take it seriously!

THE R.A. WAS WATCHING

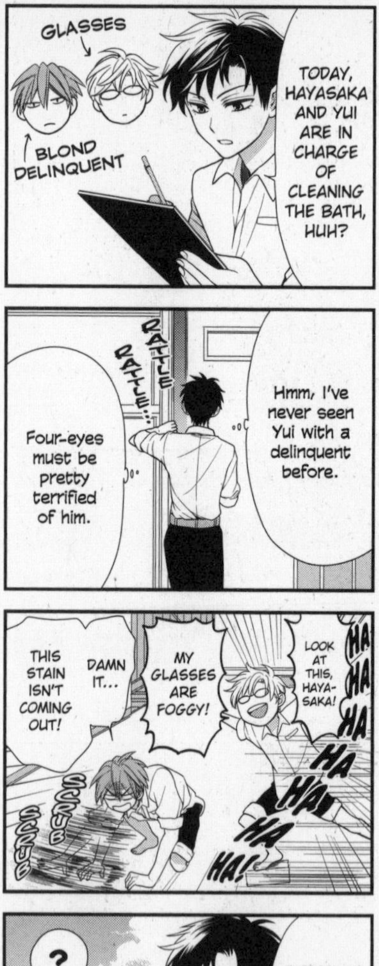
TODAY, HAYASAKA AND YUI ARE IN CHARGE OF CLEANING THE BATH, HUH?
GLASSES
BLOND DELINQUENT
RATTLE
RATTLE...
Hmm, I've never seen Yui with a delinquent before.
Four-eyes must be pretty terrified of him.
HA HA HA HA HA HA HA HA!
LOOK AT THIS, HAYA-SAKA!
MY GLASSES ARE FOGGY!
DAMN IT...
THIS STAIN ISN'T COMING OUT!
SCRUB
SCRUB
I FINALLY REALIZED THAT JUDGING PEOPLE BY HOW THEY LOOK IS SILLY.
?

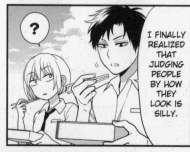

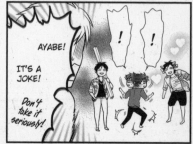

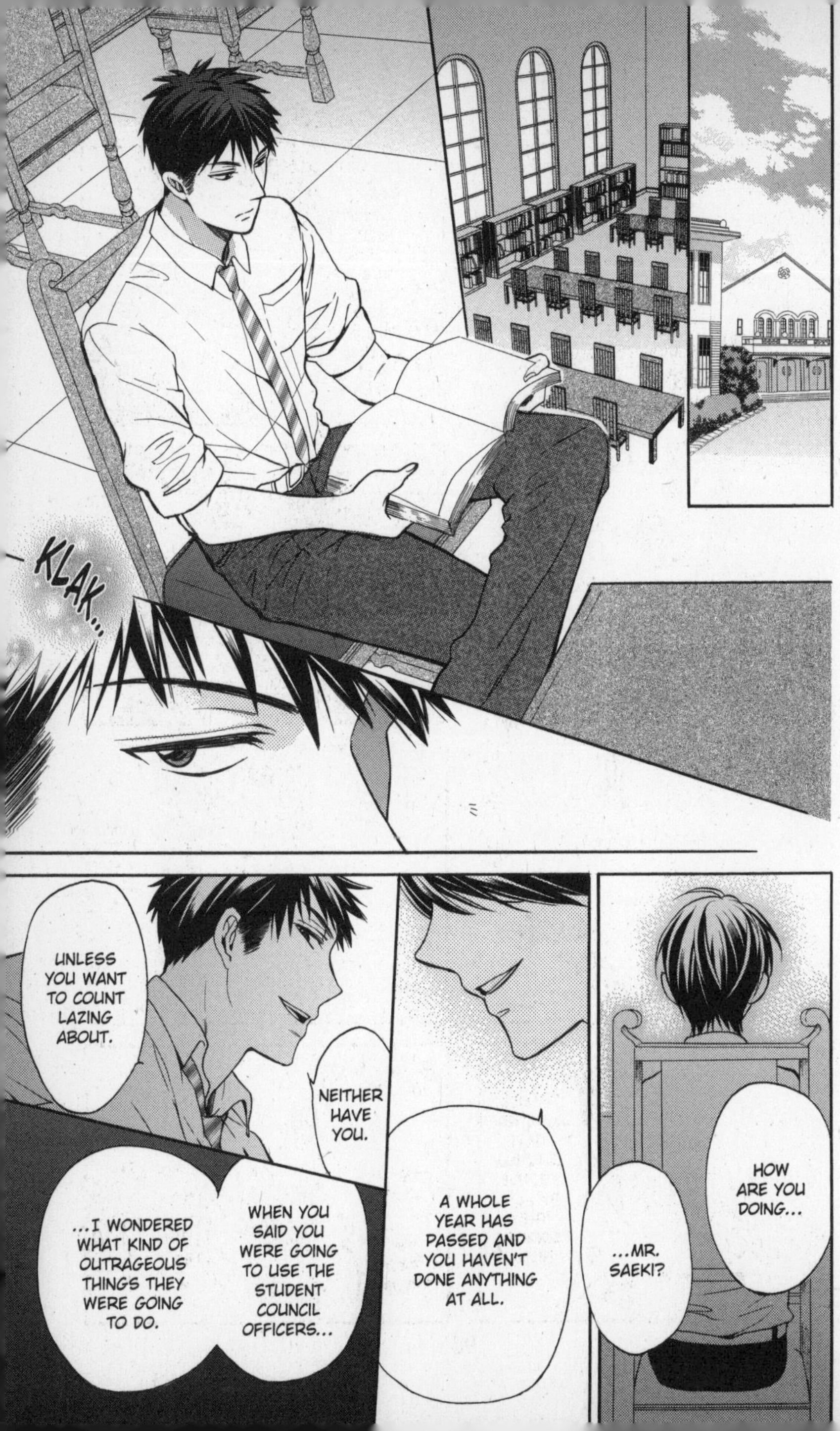
KLAK...
HOW ARE YOU DOING...
...MR. SAEKI?
A WHOLE YEAR HAS PASSED AND YOU HAVEN'T DONE ANYTHING AT ALL.
NEITHER HAVE YOU.
UNLESS YOU WANT TO COUNT LAZING ABOUT.
WHEN YOU SAID YOU WERE GOING TO USE THE STUDENT COUNCIL OFFICERS...
...I WONDERED WHAT KIND OF OUTRAGEOUS THINGS THEY WERE GOING TO DO.

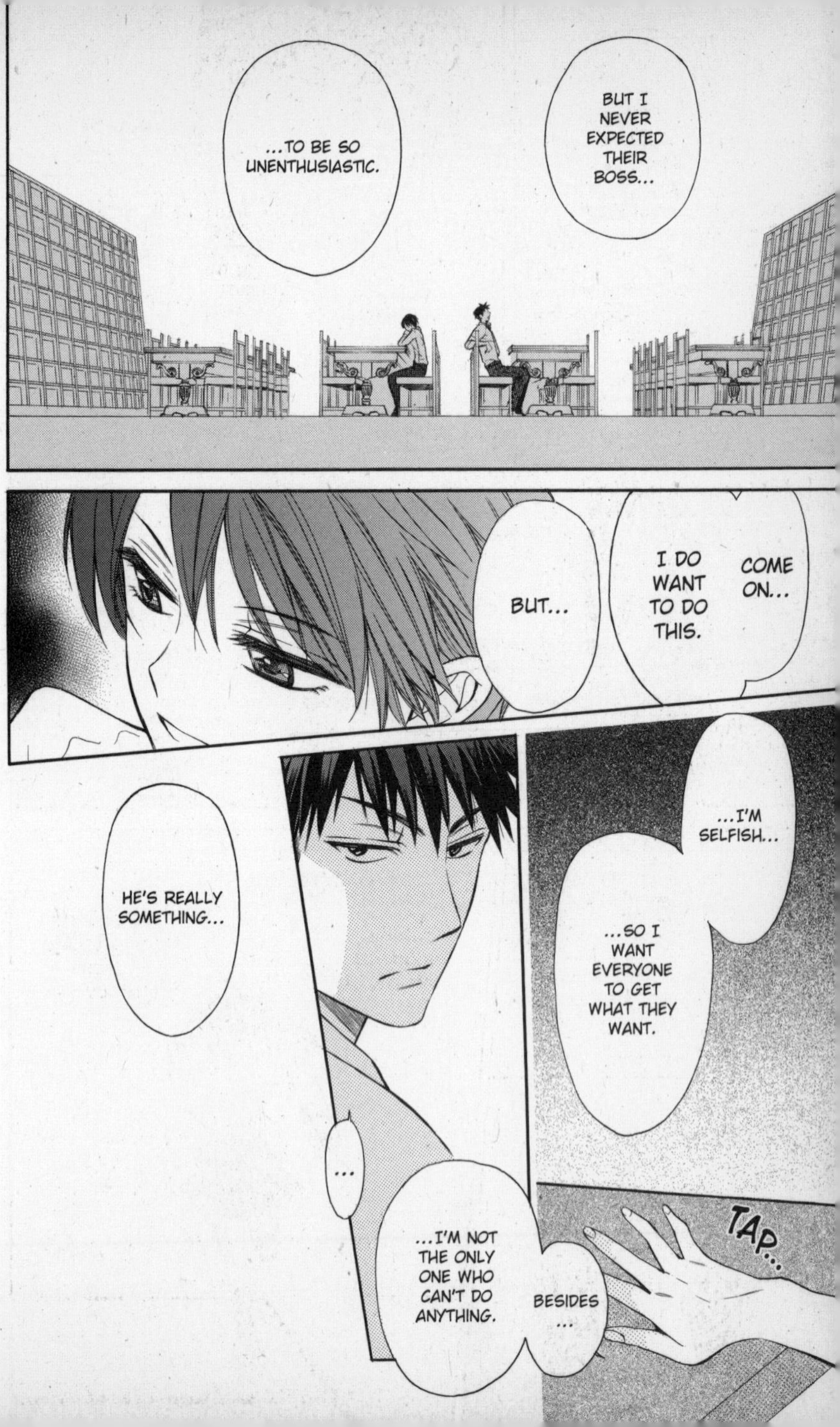
BUT I NEVER EXPECTED THEIR BOSS...
...TO BE SO UNENTHUSIASTIC.
COME ON...
I DO WANT TO DO THIS.
BUT...
...I'M SELFISH...
...SO I WANT EVERYONE TO GET WHAT THEY WANT.
TAP...
BESIDES...
...I'M NOT THE ONLY ONE WHO CAN'T DO ANYTHING.
...
HE'S REALLY SOMETHING...

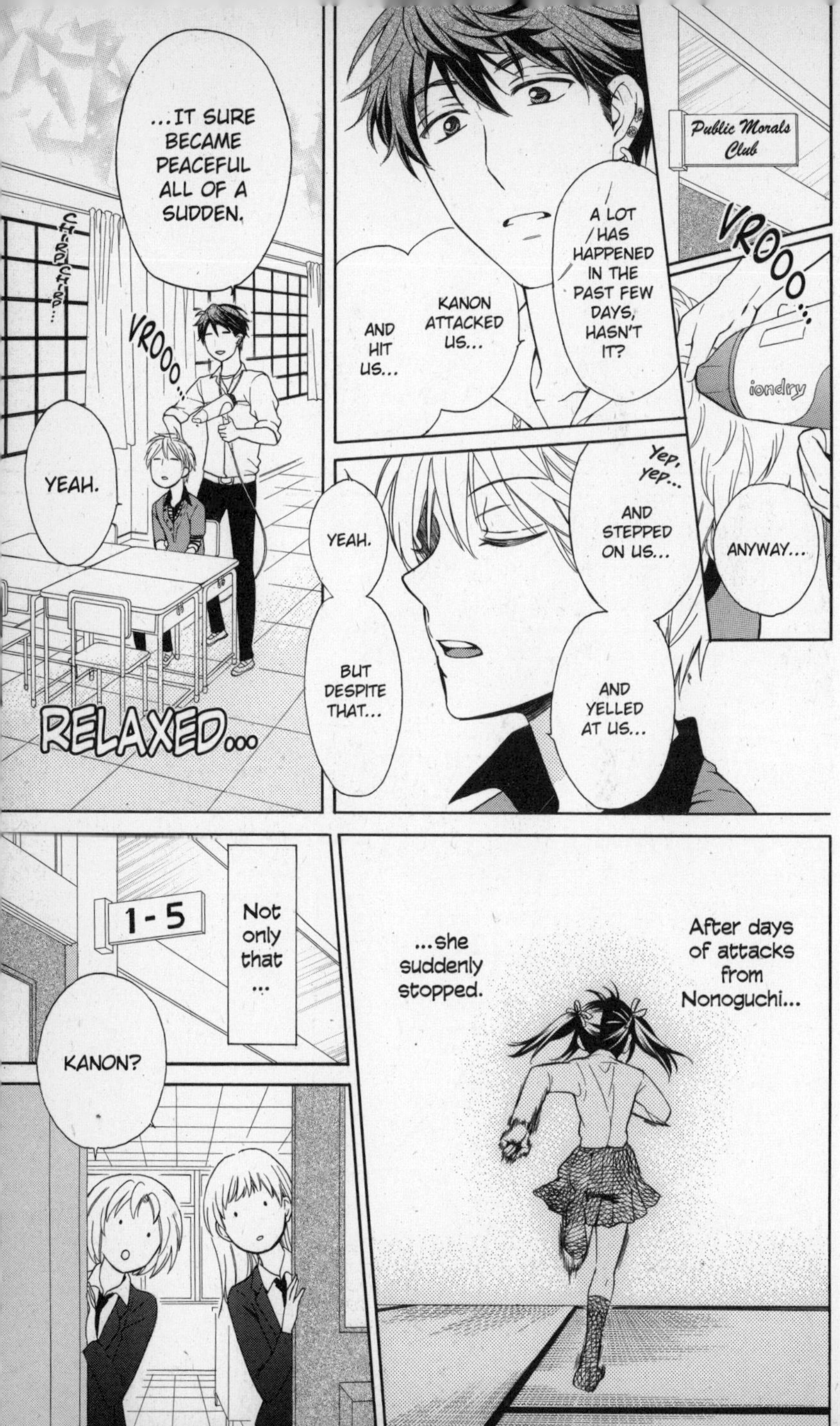
Public Morals Club
VROOO...
iondry
A LOT HAS HAPPENED IN THE PAST FEW DAYS, HASN'T IT?
KANON ATTACKED US...
AND HIT US...
ANYWAY...
Yep, yep...
AND STEPPED ON US...
AND YELLED AT US...
YEAH.
BUT DESPITE THAT...
...IT SURE BECAME PEACEFUL ALL OF A SUDDEN.
CHIRP CHIRP...
VROOO...
YEAH.
RELAXED...
After days of attacks from Nonoguchi...
...she suddenly stopped.
1-5
Not only that...
KANON?

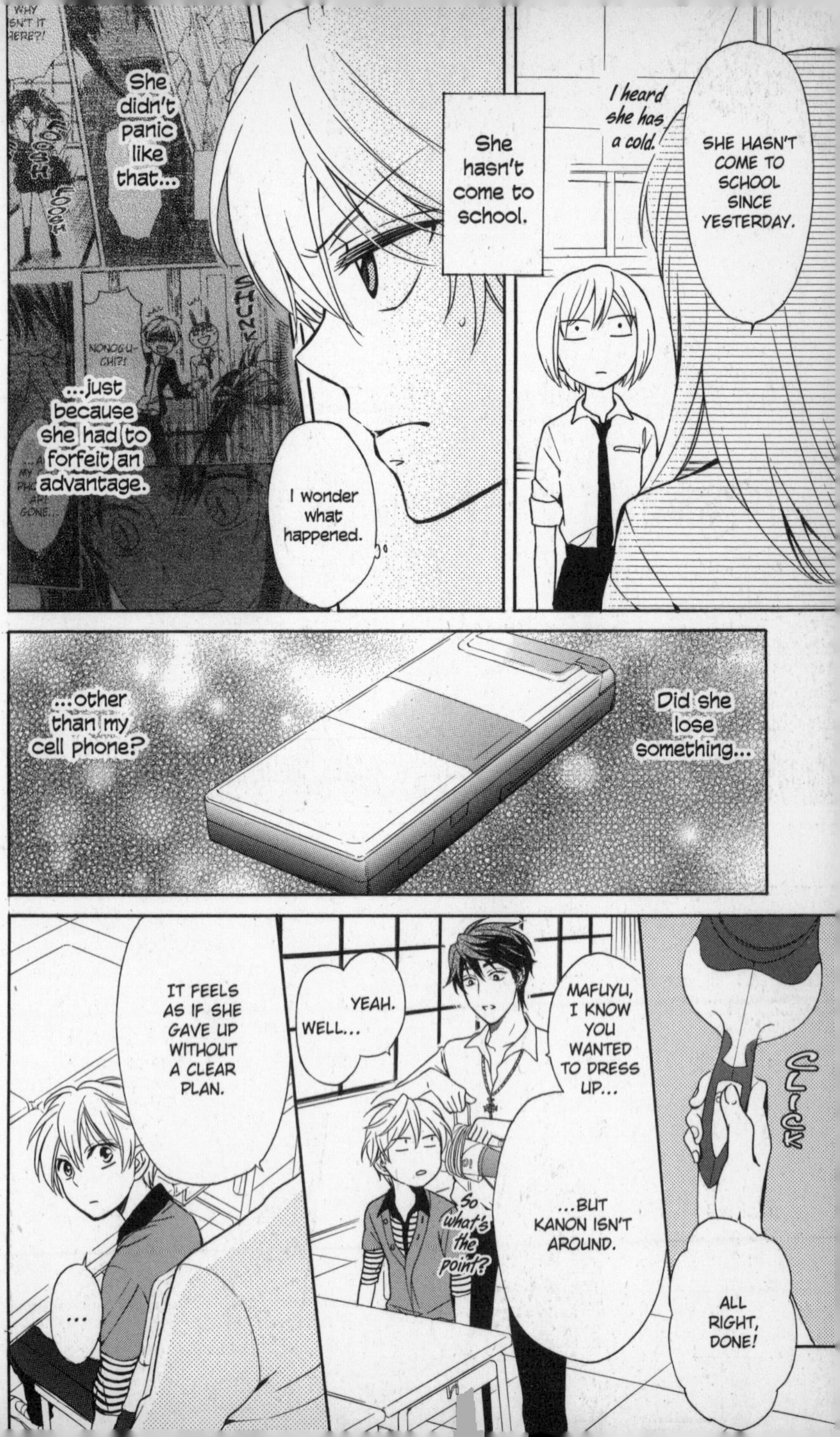

SHE HASN'T COME TO SCHOOL SINCE YESTERDAY.
I heard she has a cold.
She hasn't come to school.
I wonder what happened.
WHY ISN'T IT HERE?!
She didn't panic like that...
WOOSH
WOOSH
NONOGUCHI?!
SHUNK
...just because she had to forfeit an advantage.
Did she lose something...
...other than my cell phone?
CLICK
ALL RIGHT, DONE!
MAFUYU, I KNOW YOU WANTED TO DRESS UP...
...BUT KANON ISN'T AROUND.
So what's the point?
YEAH. WELL...
IT FEELS AS IF SHE GAVE UP WITHOUT A CLEAR PLAN.
...

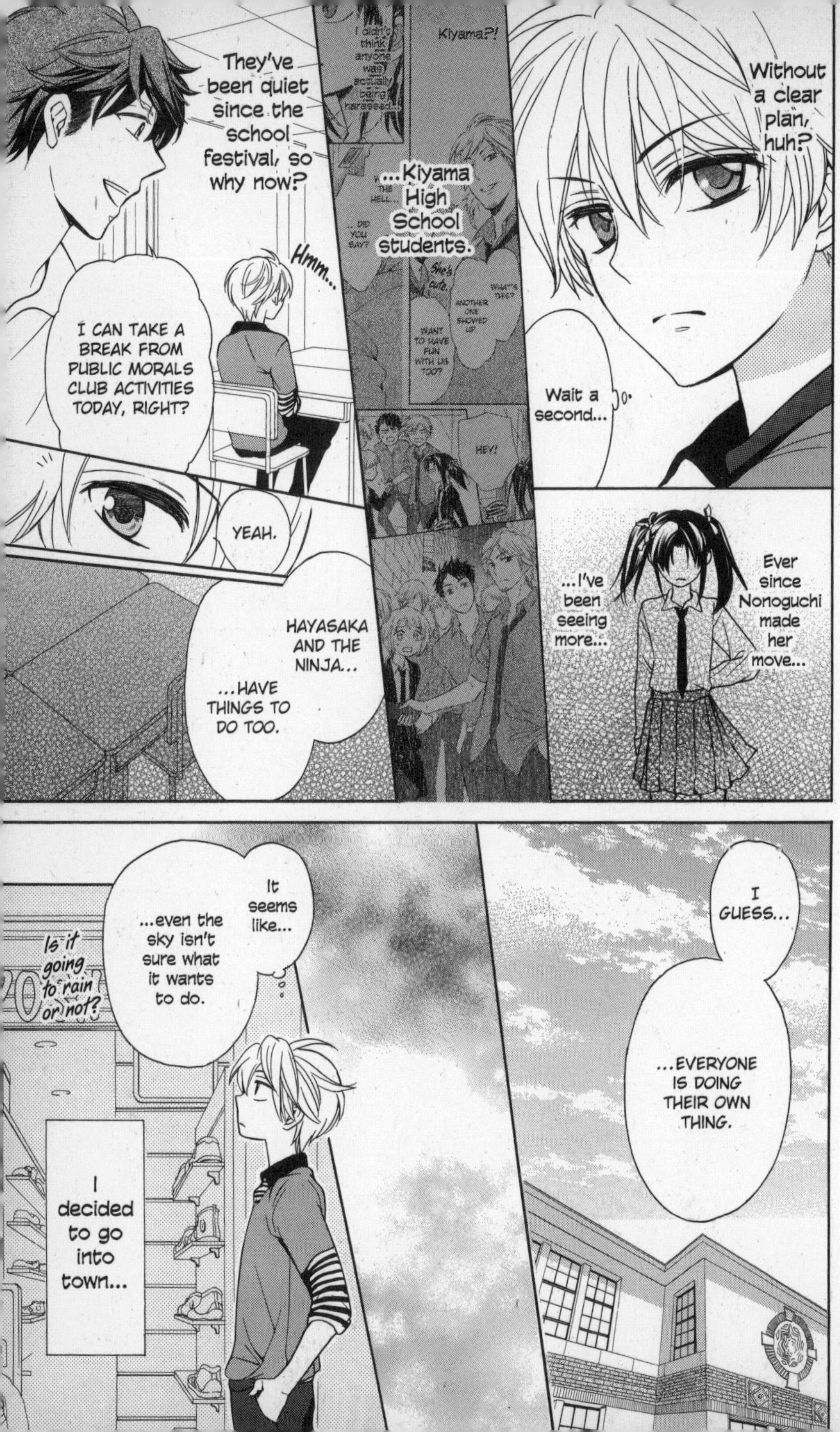
Without a clear plan, huh?
Wait a second...
Kiyama?!
I didn't think anyone was actually being harassed...
...Kiyama High School students.
...DID YOU SAY?
She's cute.
WHAT'S THIS?
ANOTHER ONE SHOWED UP
WANT TO HAVE FUN WITH US TOO?
HEY!
They've been quiet since the school festival, so why now?
Hmm...
I CAN TAKE A BREAK FROM PUBLIC MORALS CLUB ACTIVITIES TODAY, RIGHT?
YEAH.
HAYASAKA AND THE NINJA...
...HAVE THINGS TO DO TOO.
Ever since Nonoguchi made her move...
...I've been seeing more...
I GUESS...
...EVERYONE IS DOING THEIR OWN THING.
It seems like...
...even the sky isn't sure what it wants to do.
Is it going to rain or not?
I decided to go into town...

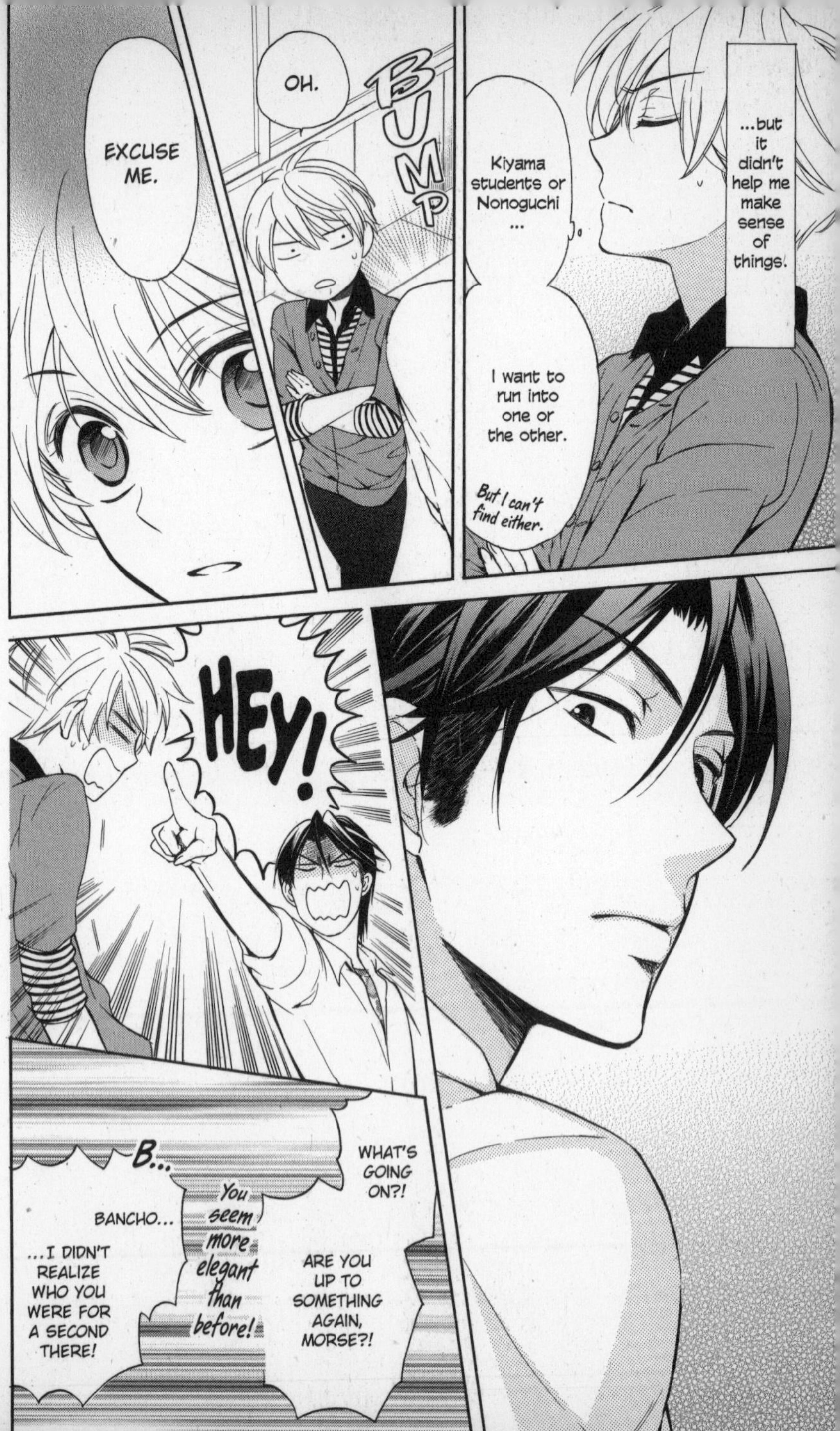
...but it didn't help me make sense of things.
Kiyama students or Nonoguchi ...
I want to run into one or the other.
But I can't find either.
BUMP
OH.
EXCUSE ME.
HEY!
WHAT'S GOING ON?!
ARE YOU UP TO SOMETHING AGAIN, MORSE?!
You seem more elegant than before!
B...
BANCHO...
...I DIDN'T REALIZE WHO YOU WERE FOR A SECOND THERE!

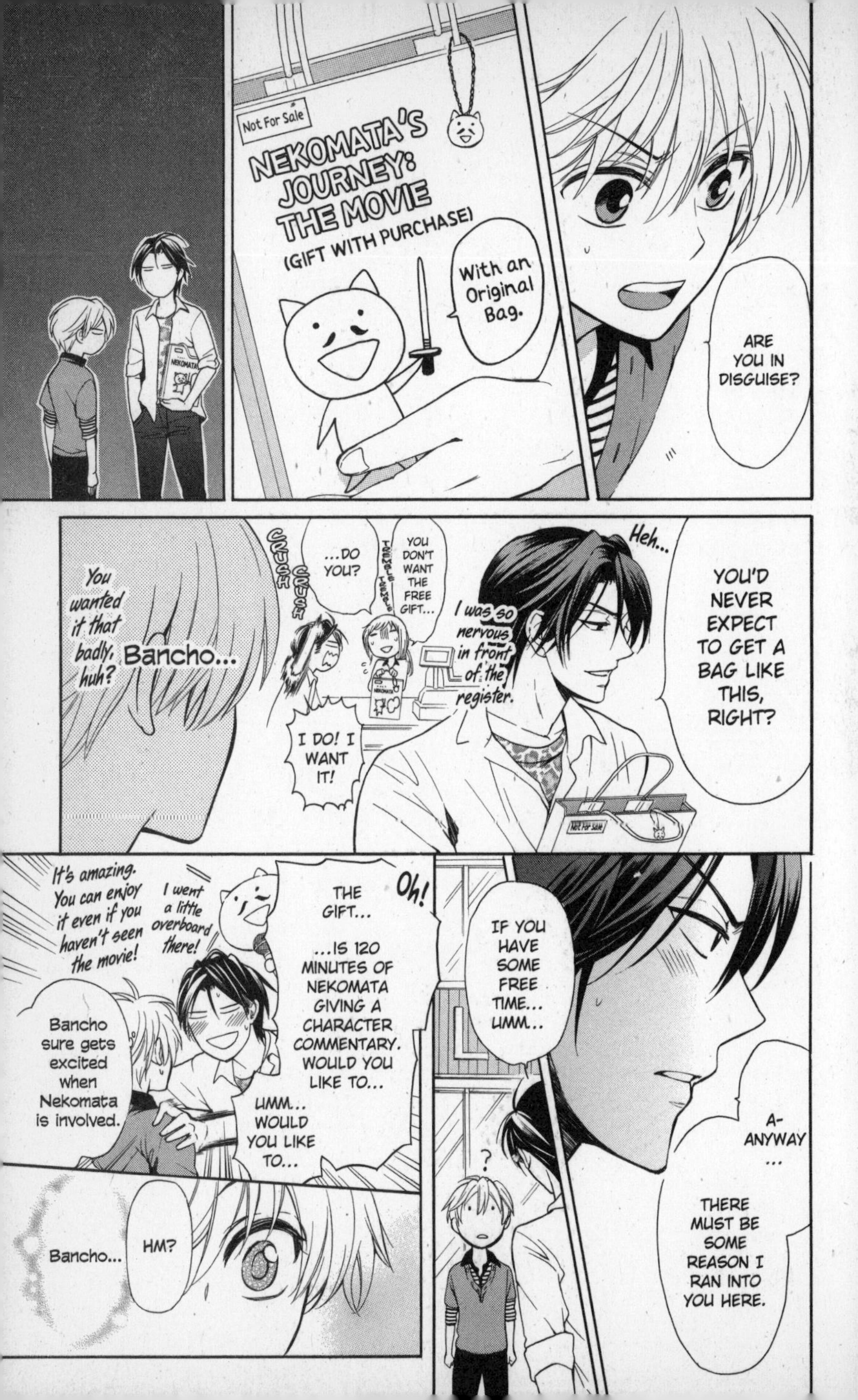
ARE YOU IN DISGUISE?
Not For Sale
NEKOMATA'S JOURNEY: THE MOVIE
(GIFT WITH PURCHASE)
With an Original Bag.
Heh...
YOU'D NEVER EXPECT TO GET A BAG LIKE THIS, RIGHT?
I was so nervous in front of the register.
YOU DON'T WANT THE FREE GIFT...
TREMBLE TREMBLE
...DO YOU?
CRUSH CRUSH
I DO! I WANT IT!
You wanted it that badly, huh?
Bancho...
Not For Sale
IF YOU HAVE SOME FREE TIME... UMM...
A-ANYWAY...
THERE MUST BE SOME REASON I RAN INTO YOU HERE.
?
Oh!
THE GIFT...
...IS 120 MINUTES OF NEKOMATA GIVING A CHARACTER COMMENTARY. WOULD YOU LIKE TO...
UMM... WOULD YOU LIKE TO...
I went a little overboard there!
It's amazing. You can enjoy it even if you haven't seen the movie!
Bancho sure gets excited when Nekomata is involved.
HM?
Bancho...

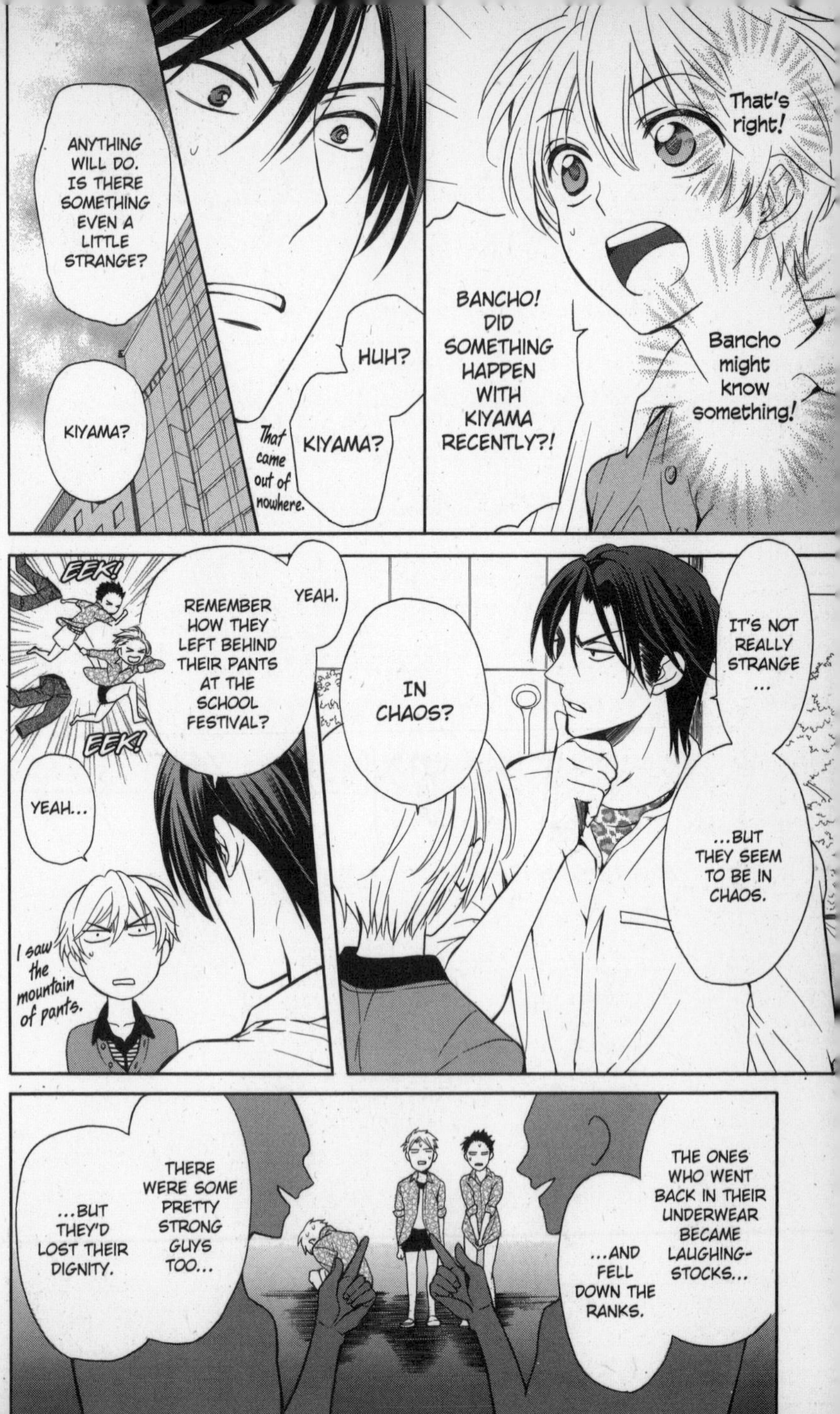
That's right!
Bancho might know something!
BANCHO! DID SOMETHING HAPPEN WITH KIYAMA RECENTLY?!
HUH?
KIYAMA?
That came out of nowhere.
ANYTHING WILL DO. IS THERE SOMETHING EVEN A LITTLE STRANGE?
KIYAMA?
IT'S NOT REALLY STRANGE...
...BUT THEY SEEM TO BE IN CHAOS.
IN CHAOS?
YEAH.
REMEMBER HOW THEY LEFT BEHIND THEIR PANTS AT THE SCHOOL FESTIVAL?
EEK!
EEK!
YEAH...
I saw the mountain of pants.
THE ONES WHO WENT BACK IN THEIR UNDERWEAR BECAME LAUGHING-STOCKS...
...AND FELL DOWN THE RANKS.
THERE WERE SOME PRETTY STRONG GUYS TOO...
...BUT THEY'D LOST THEIR DIGNITY.

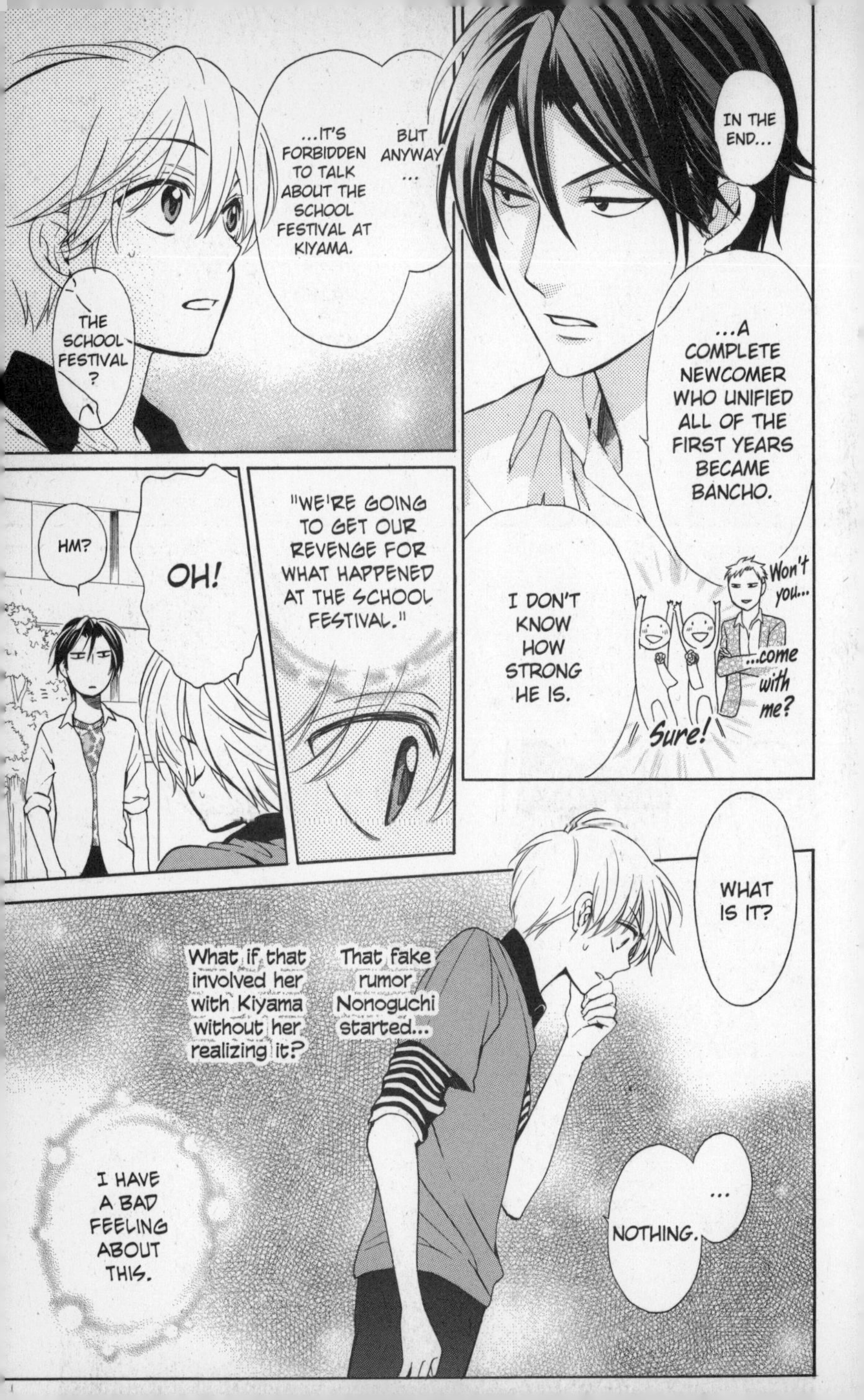
IN THE END...
...A COMPLETE NEWCOMER WHO UNIFIED ALL OF THE FIRST YEARS BECAME BANCHO.
Won't you... ...come with me?
Sure!
I DON'T KNOW HOW STRONG HE IS.
BUT ANYWAY...
...IT'S FORBIDDEN TO TALK ABOUT THE SCHOOL FESTIVAL AT KIYAMA.
THE SCHOOL FESTIVAL?
"WE'RE GOING TO GET OUR REVENGE FOR WHAT HAPPENED AT THE SCHOOL FESTIVAL."
OH!
HM?
WHAT IS IT?
...
NOTHING.
That fake rumor Nonoguchi started...
What if that involved her with Kiyama without her realizing it?
I HAVE A BAD FEELING ABOUT THIS.

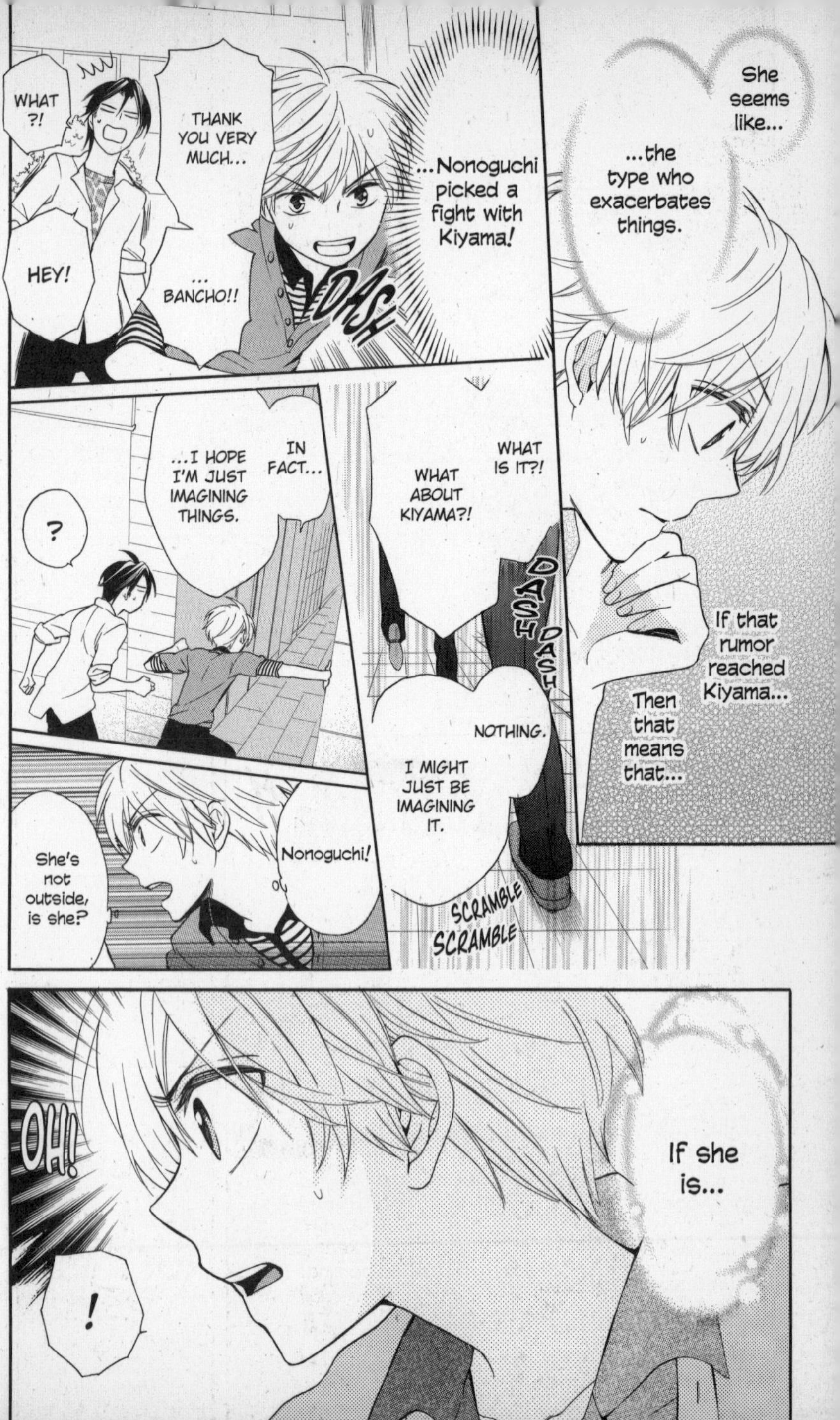
She seems like...
...the type who exacerbates things.
If that rumor reached Kiyama...
Then that means that...
...Nonoguchi picked a fight with Kiyama!
DASH
THANK YOU VERY MUCH...
...BANCHO!!
WHAT?!
HEY!
WHAT IS IT?!
WHAT ABOUT KIYAMA?!
DASH DASH
NOTHING.
I MIGHT JUST BE IMAGINING IT.
SCRAMBLE SCRAMBLE
IN FACT...
...I HOPE I'M JUST IMAGINING THINGS.
?
Nonoguchi!
She's not outside, is she?
If she is...
OH!
!

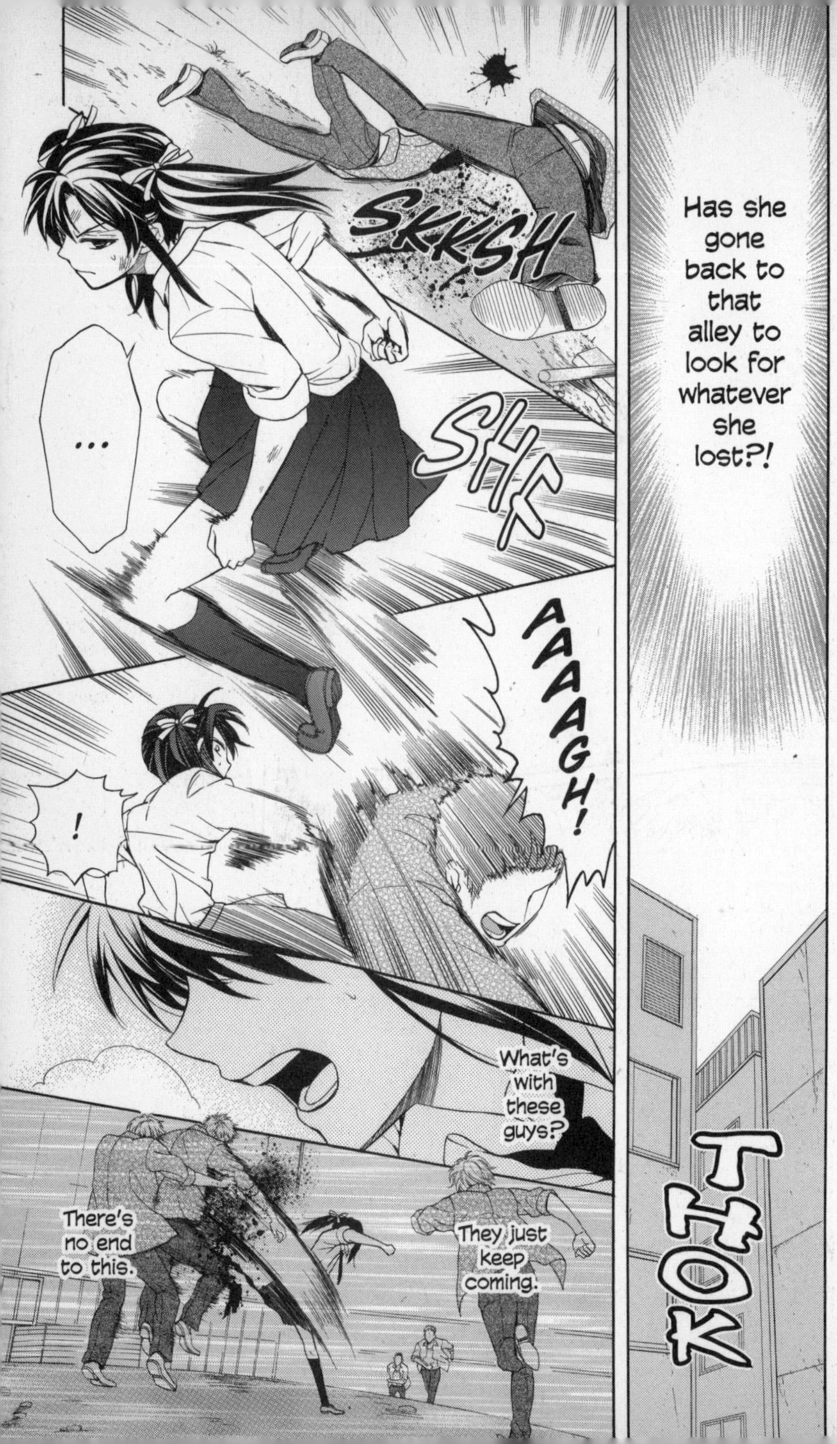
Has she gone back to that alley to look for whatever she lost?!
THOK
SKKSH
SHK
...
AAAAAGH!
!
What's with these guys?
They just keep coming.
There's no end to this.

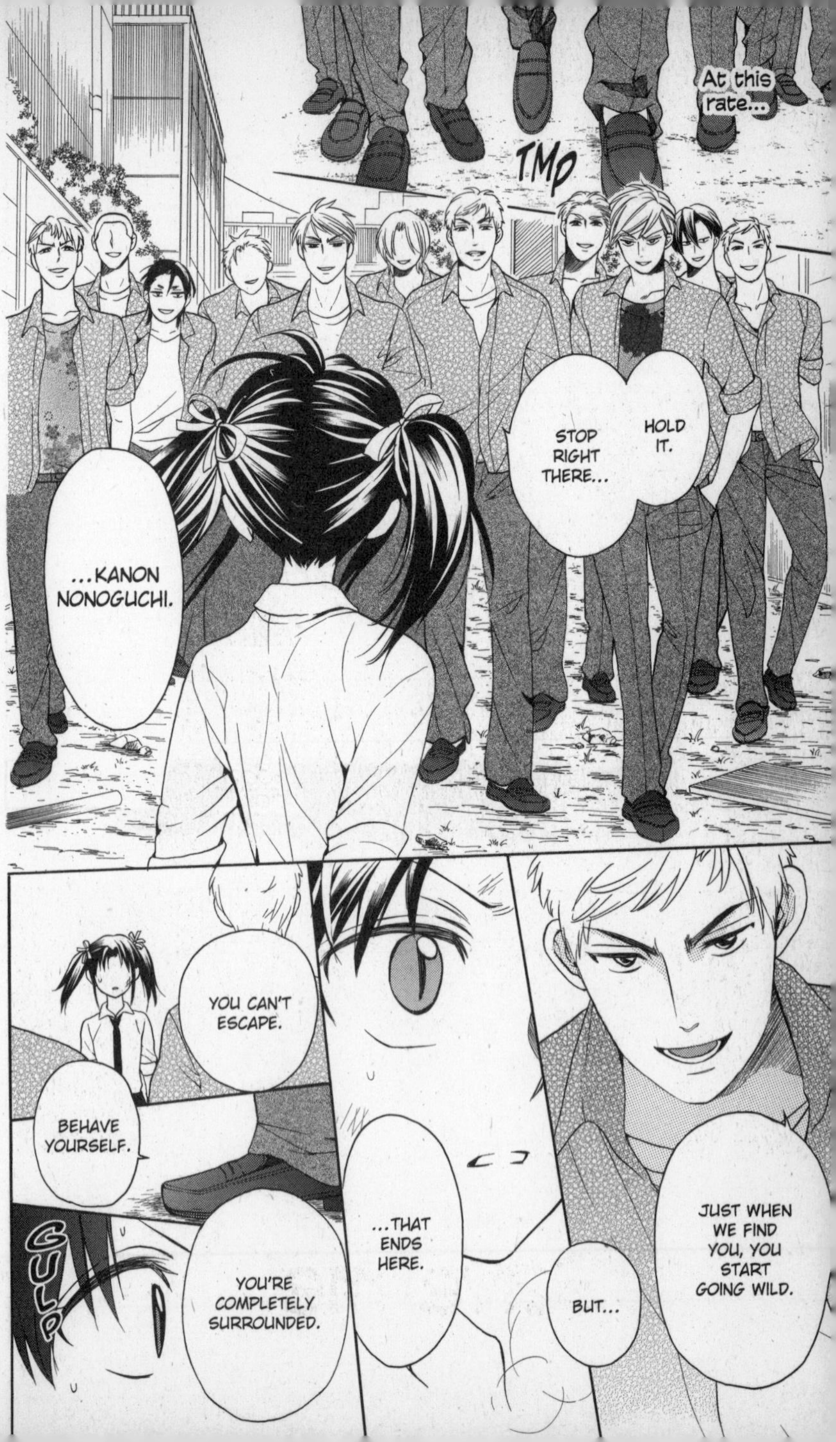
At this rate...
TMP
HOLD IT.
STOP RIGHT THERE...
...KANON NONOGUCHI.
JUST WHEN WE FIND YOU, YOU START GOING WILD.
BUT...
...THAT ENDS HERE.
YOU'RE COMPLETELY SURROUNDED.
YOU CAN'T ESCAPE.
BEHAVE YOURSELF.
GULP

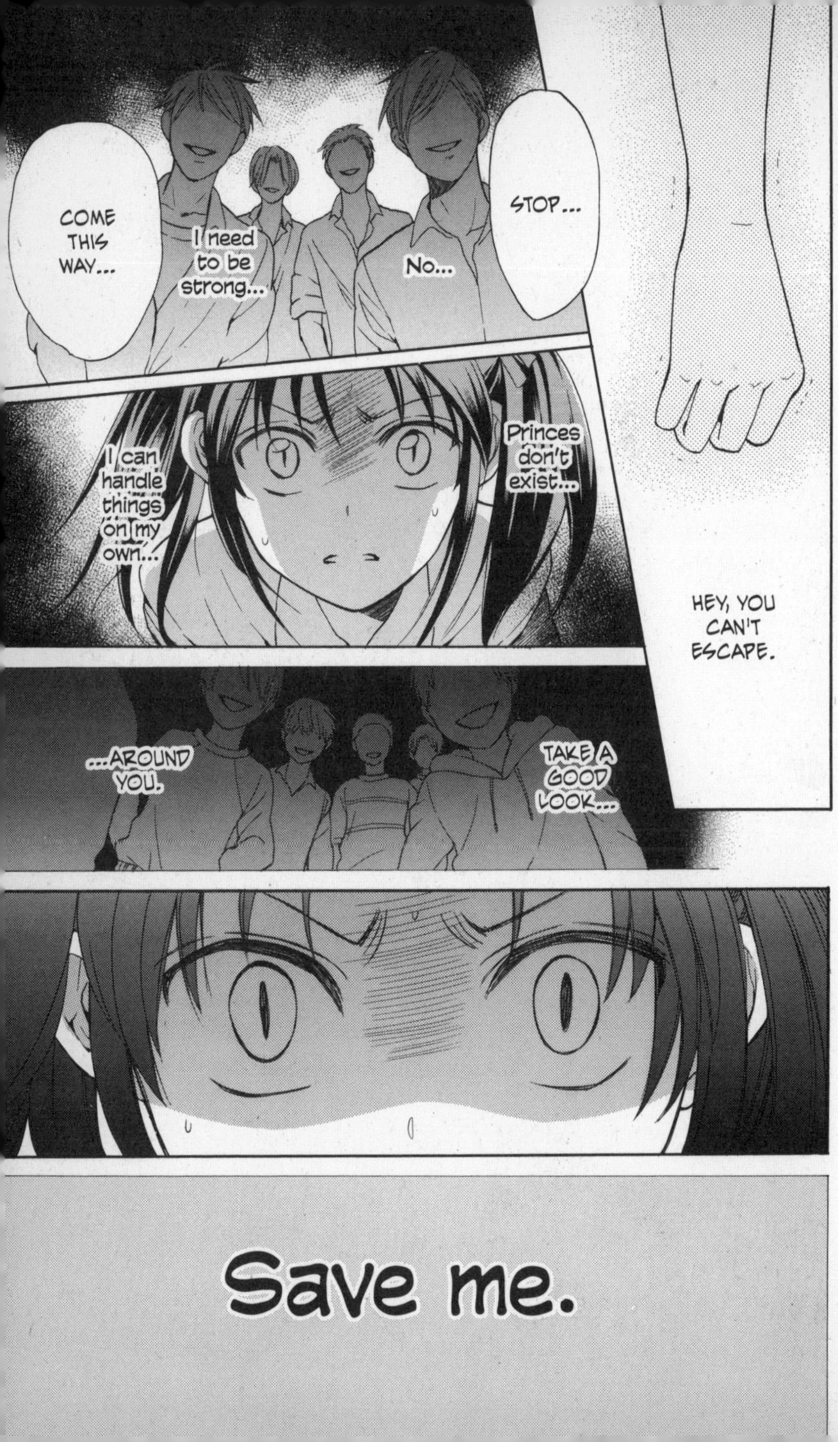
HEY, YOU CAN'T ESCAPE.
STOP...
No...
I need to be strong...
COME THIS WAY...
Princes don't exist...
I can handle things on my own...
TAKE A GOOD LOOK...
...AROUND YOU.
Save me.

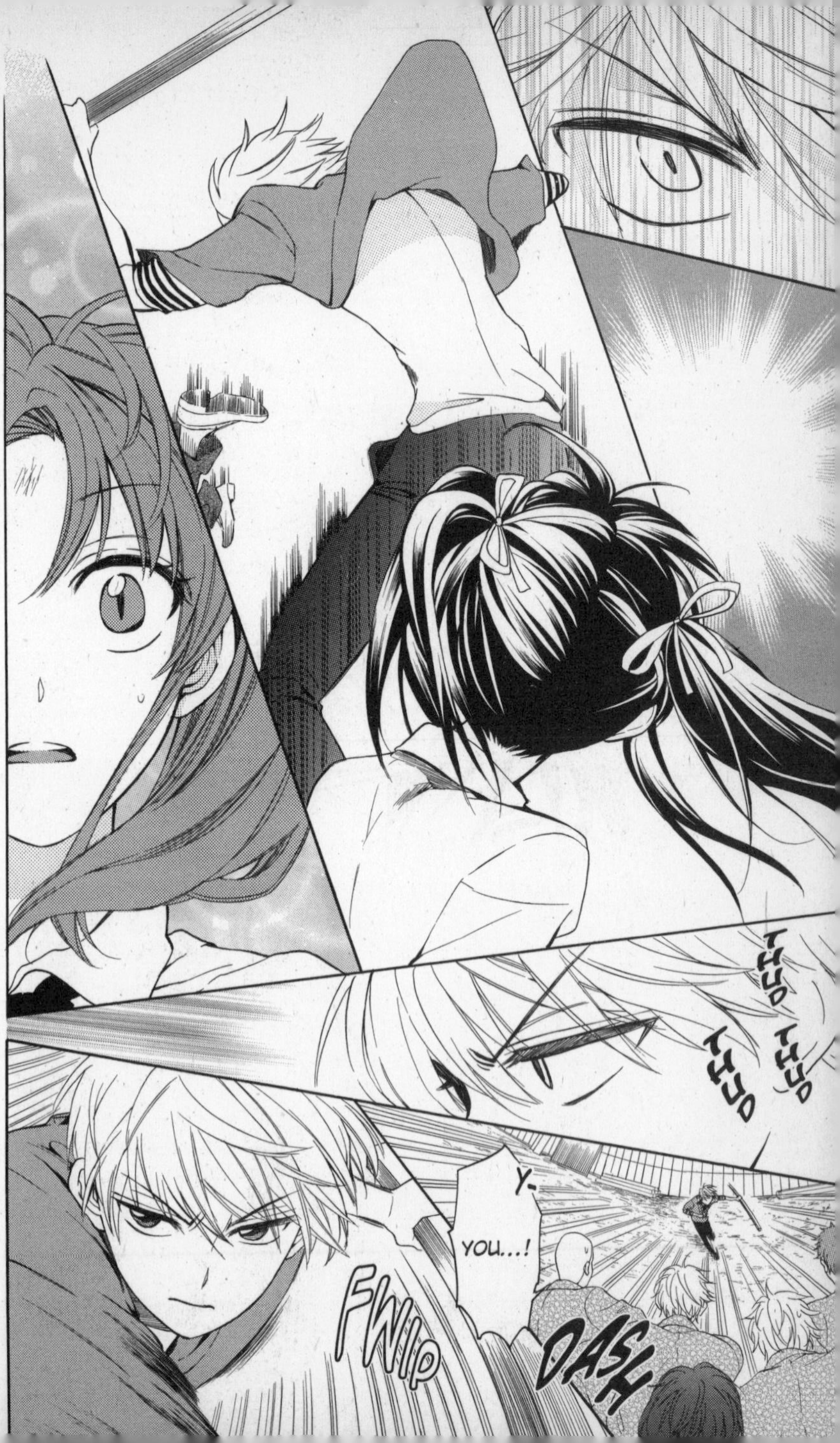
THUD THUD THUD
Y-
YOU...!
FWIP
DASH

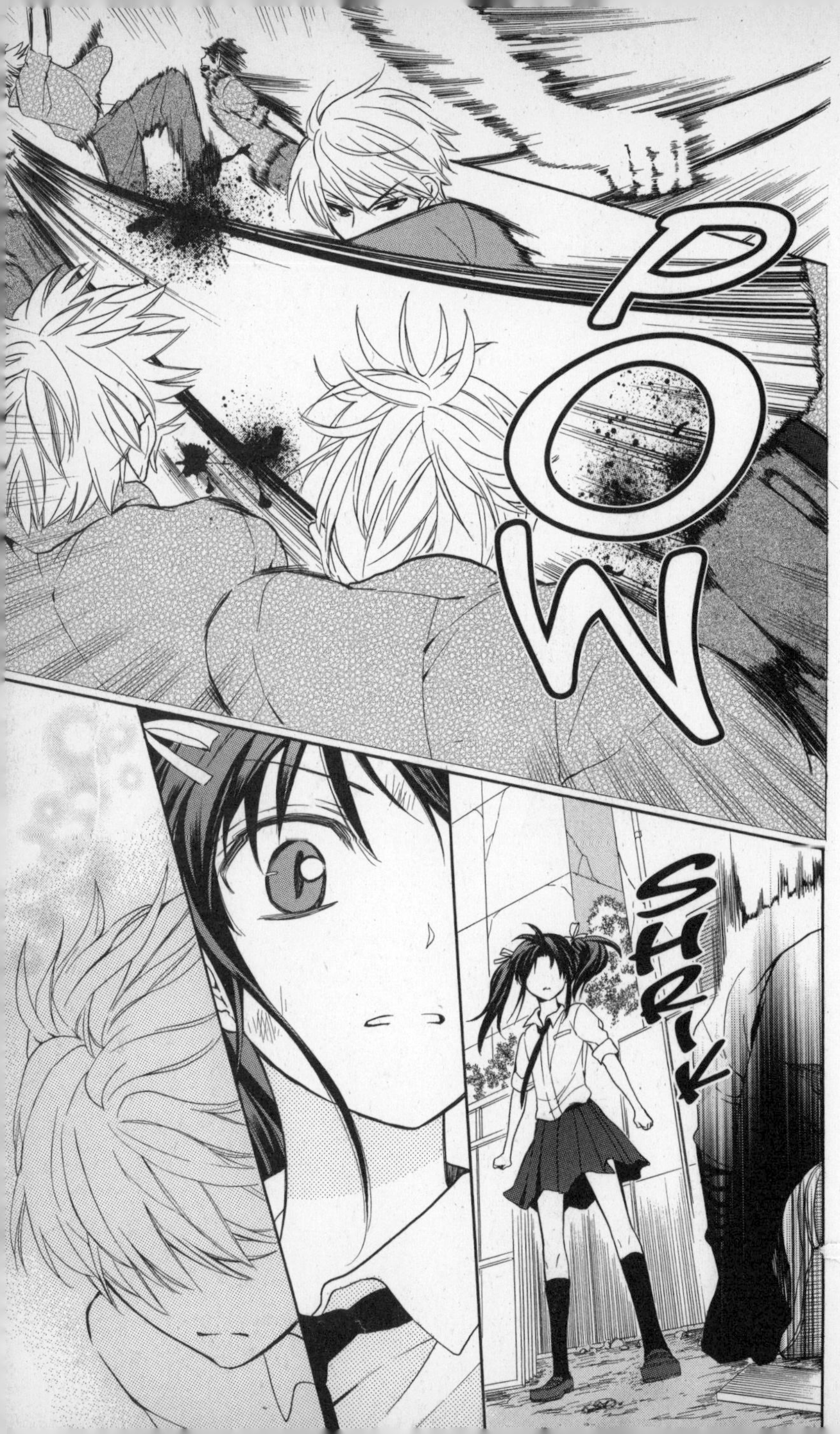
POW
SHRIK

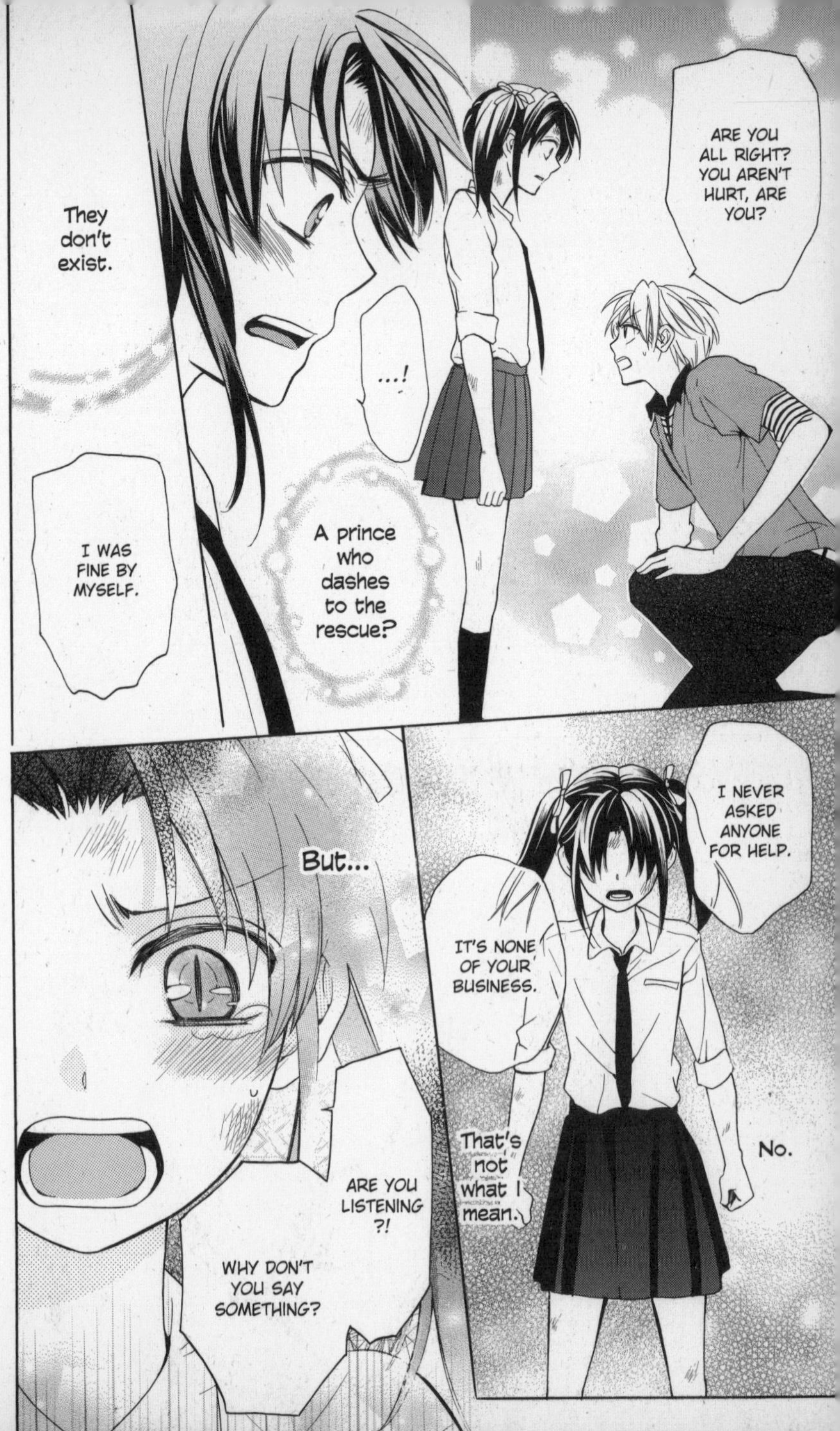
ARE YOU ALL RIGHT? YOU AREN'T HURT, ARE YOU?
...!
A prince who dashes to the rescue?
They don't exist.
I WAS FINE BY MYSELF.
I NEVER ASKED ANYONE FOR HELP.
IT'S NONE OF YOUR BUSINESS.
No.
That's not what I mean.
But...
ARE YOU LISTENING?!
WHY DON'T YOU SAY SOMETHING?

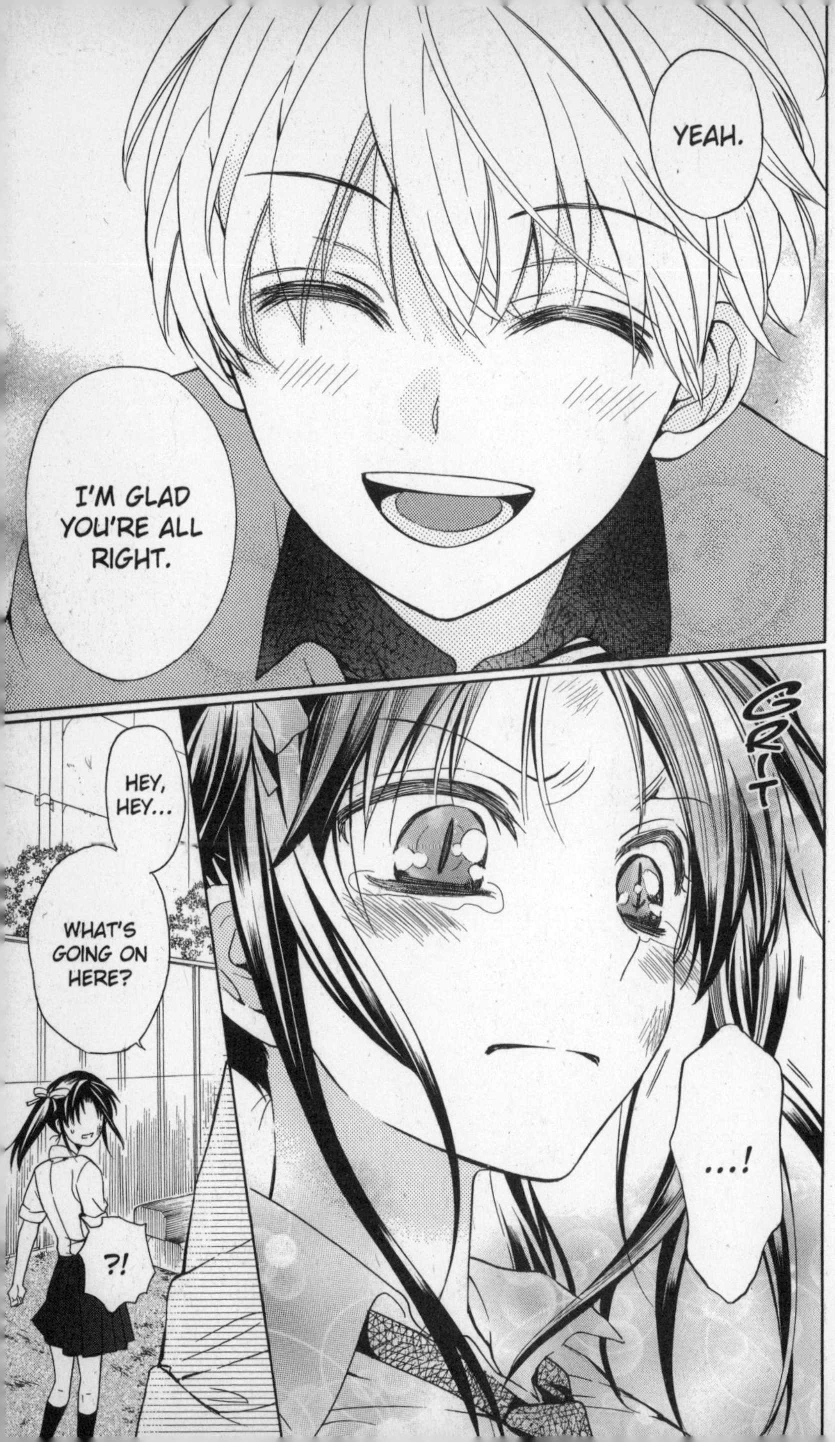
YEAH.
I'M GLAD YOU'RE ALL RIGHT.
GRIT
...!
HEY, HEY...
WHAT'S GOING ON HERE?
?!

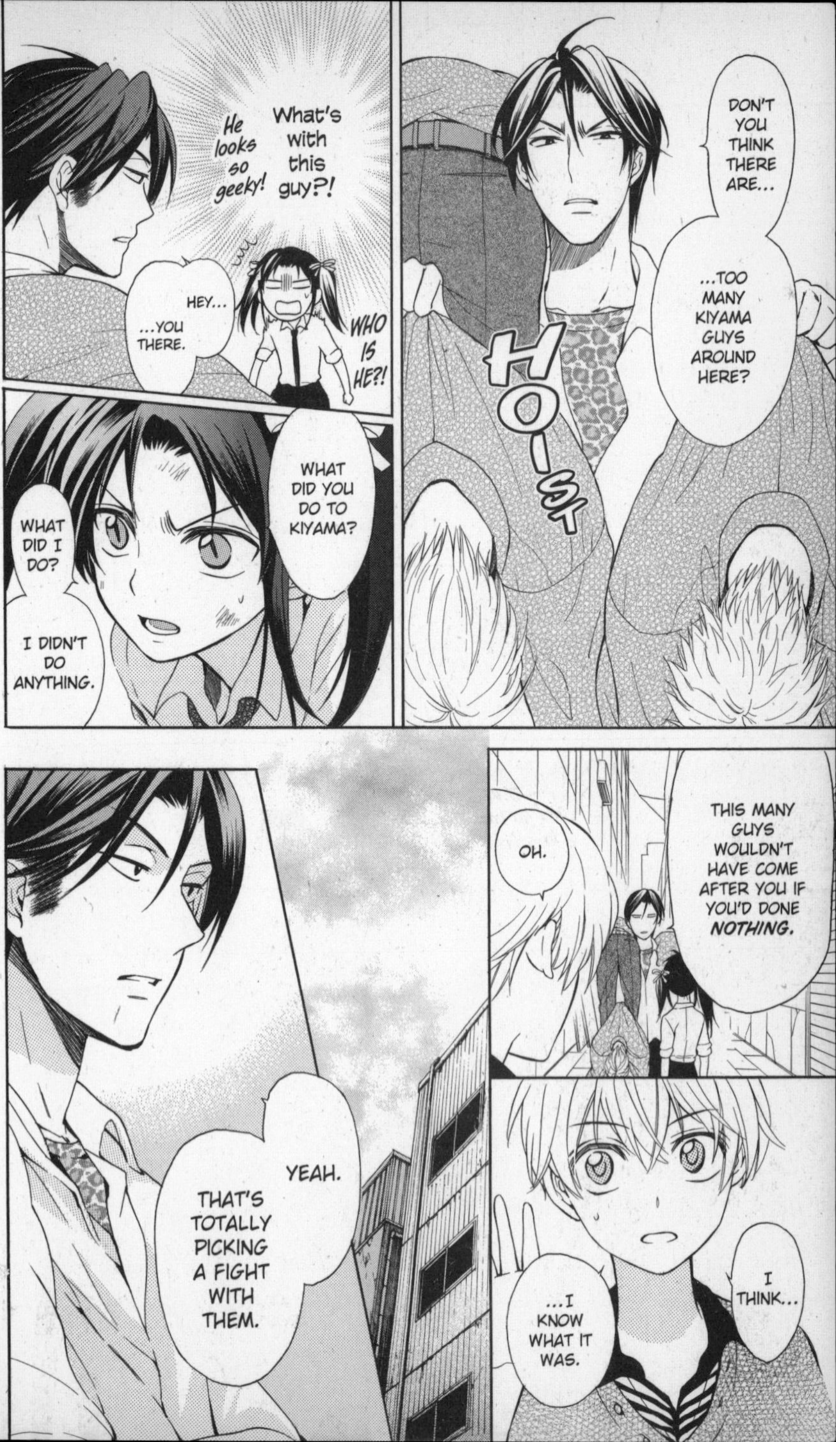
DON'T YOU THINK THERE ARE...
...TOO MANY KIYAMA GUYS AROUND HERE?
HOIST
What's with this guy?!
He looks so geeky!
WHO IS HE?!
HEY...
...YOU THERE.
WHAT DID YOU DO TO KIYAMA?
WHAT DID I DO?
I DIDN'T DO ANYTHING.
THIS MANY GUYS WOULDN'T HAVE COME AFTER YOU IF YOU'D DONE NOTHING.
OH.
I THINK...
...I KNOW WHAT IT WAS.
YEAH.
THAT'S TOTALLY PICKING A FIGHT WITH THEM.

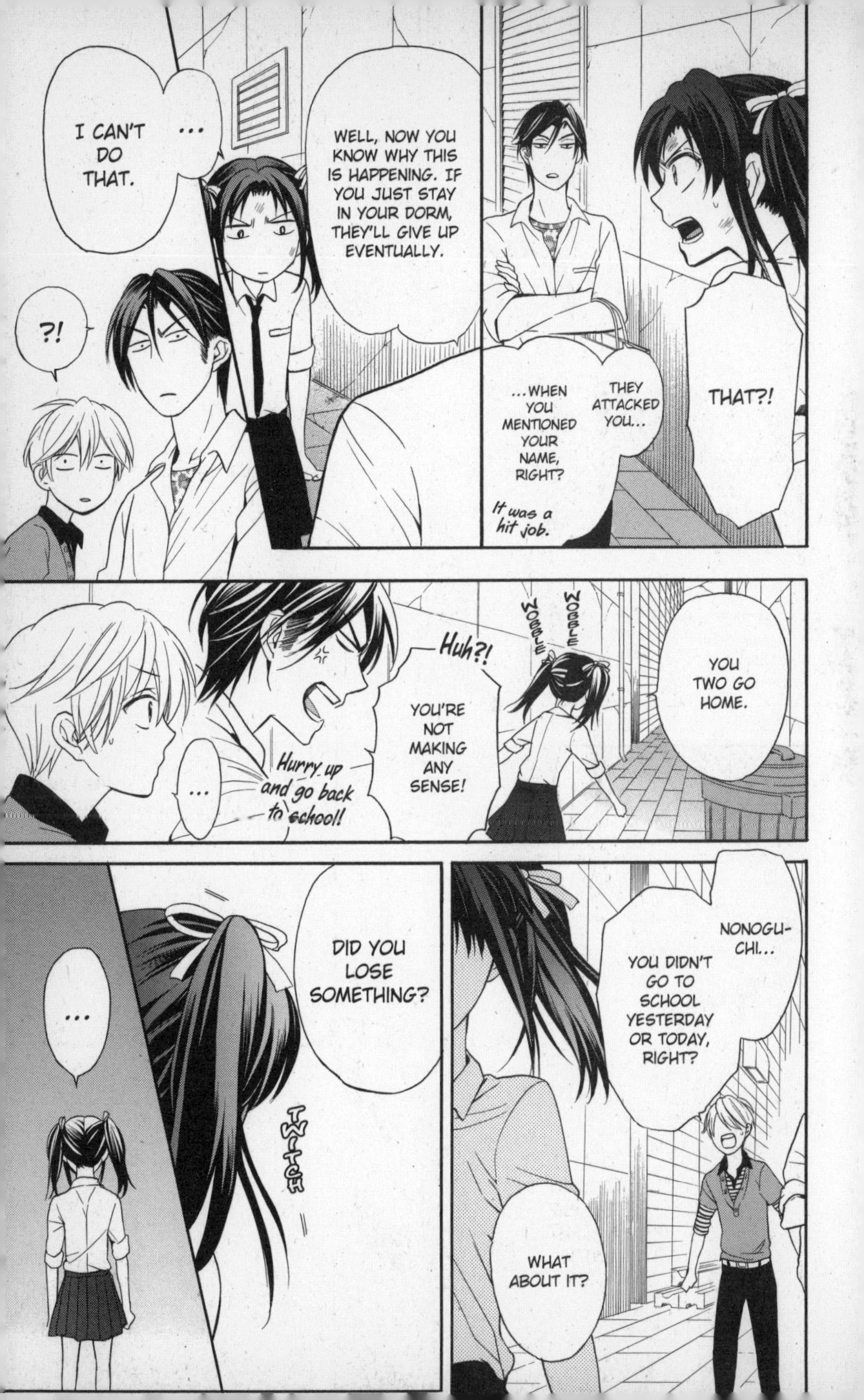
THAT?!
THEY ATTACKED YOU...
...WHEN YOU MENTIONED YOUR NAME, RIGHT?
It was a hit job.
WELL, NOW YOU KNOW WHY THIS IS HAPPENING. IF YOU JUST STAY IN YOUR DORM, THEY'LL GIVE UP EVENTUALLY.
...
I CAN'T DO THAT.
?!
YOU TWO GO HOME.
WOBBLE WOBBLE
Huh?!
YOU'RE NOT MAKING ANY SENSE!
Hurry up and go back to school!
...
NONOGU-CHI...
YOU DIDN'T GO TO SCHOOL YESTERDAY OR TODAY, RIGHT?
WHAT ABOUT IT?
DID YOU LOSE SOMETHING?
TWITCH
...

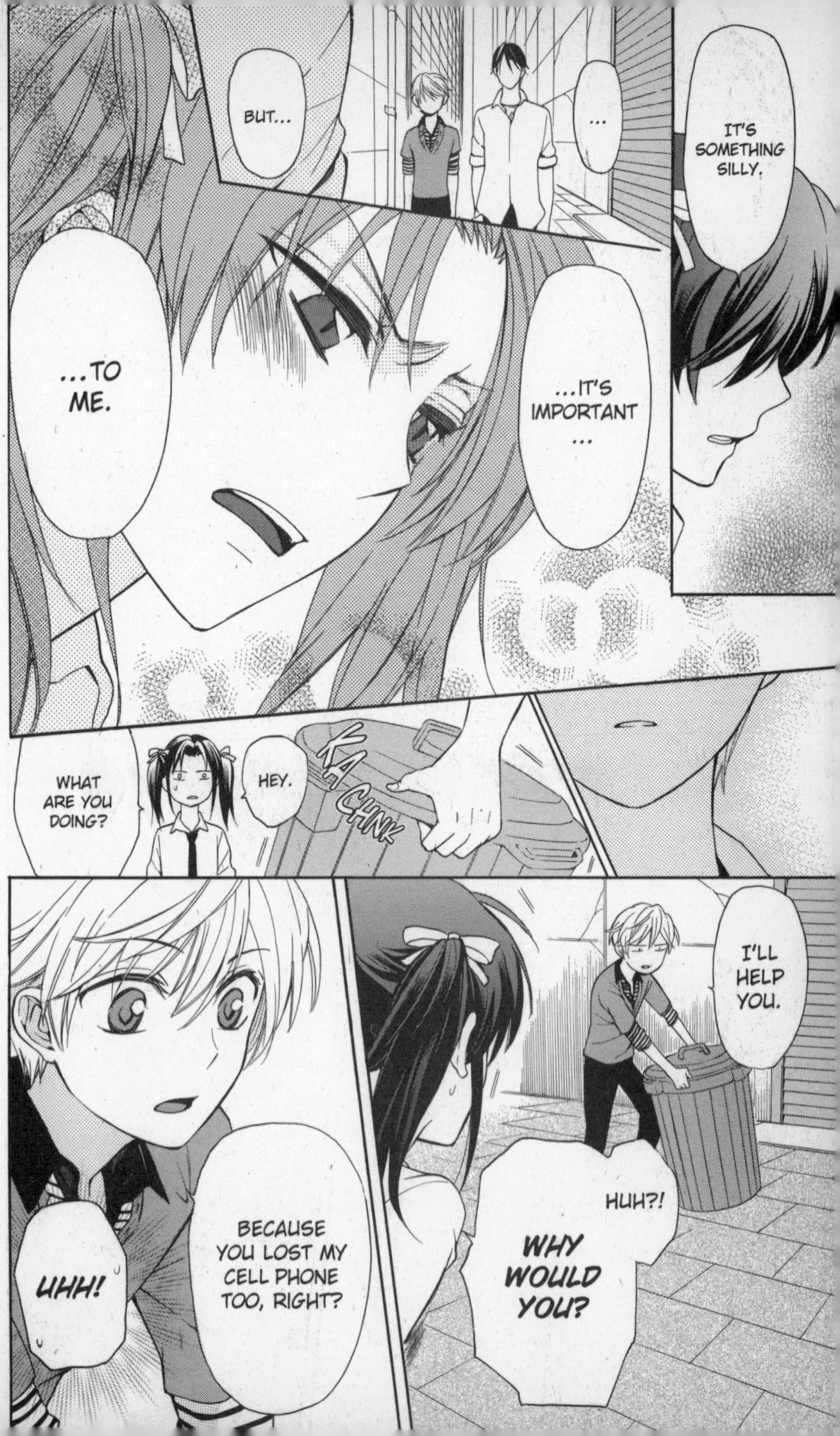
IT'S SOMETHING SILLY.
...
BUT...
...IT'S IMPORTANT ...
...TO ME.
KA CHNK
HEY.
WHAT ARE YOU DOING?
I'LL HELP YOU.
HUH?!
WHY WOULD YOU?
BECAUSE YOU LOST MY CELL PHONE TOO, RIGHT?
UHH!

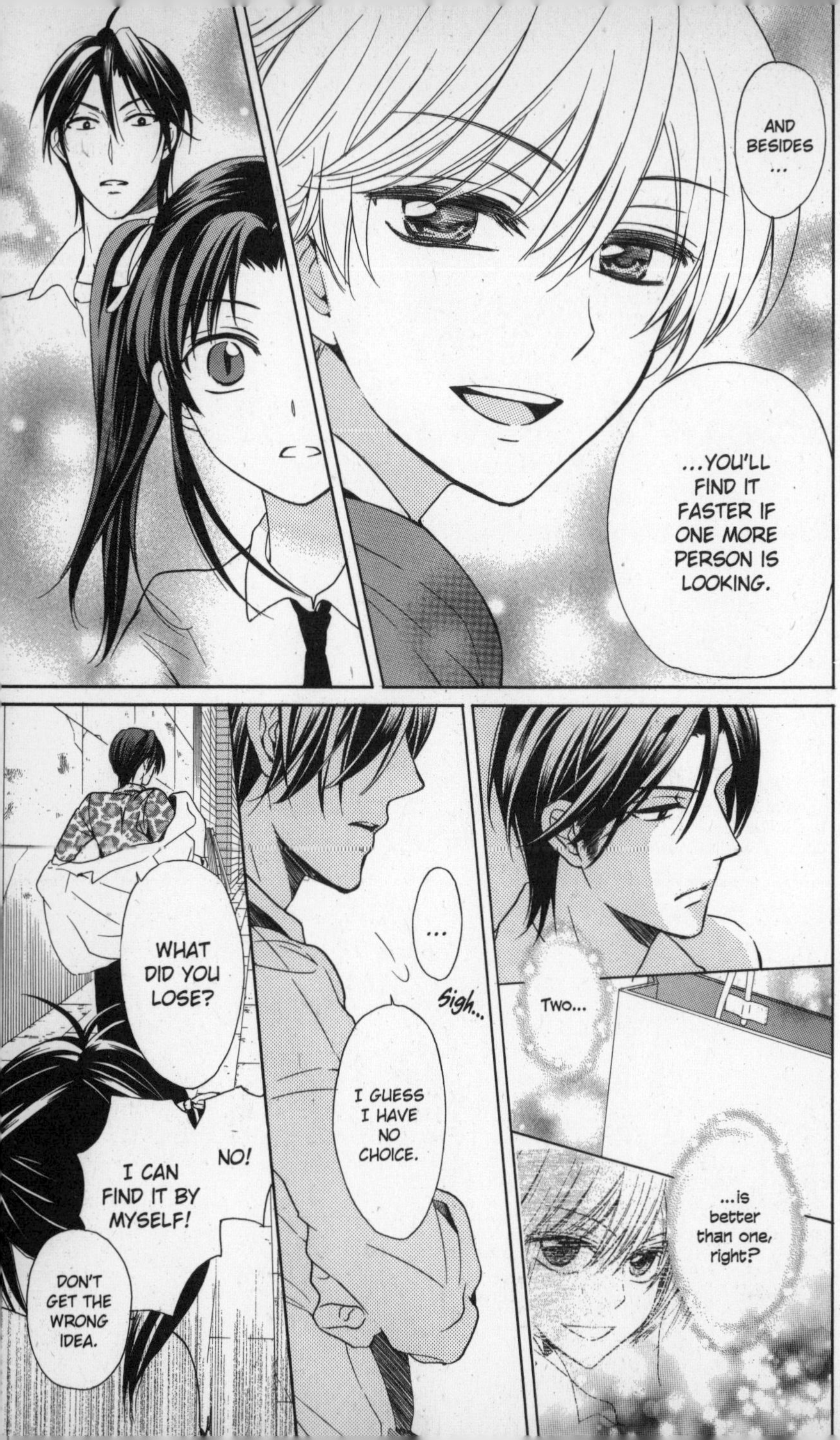
AND BESIDES ...
...YOU'LL FIND IT FASTER IF ONE MORE PERSON IS LOOKING.
Two...
...is better than one, right?
...
Sigh...
I GUESS I HAVE NO CHOICE.
WHAT DID YOU LOSE?
NO!
I CAN FIND IT BY MYSELF!
DON'T GET THE WRONG IDEA.

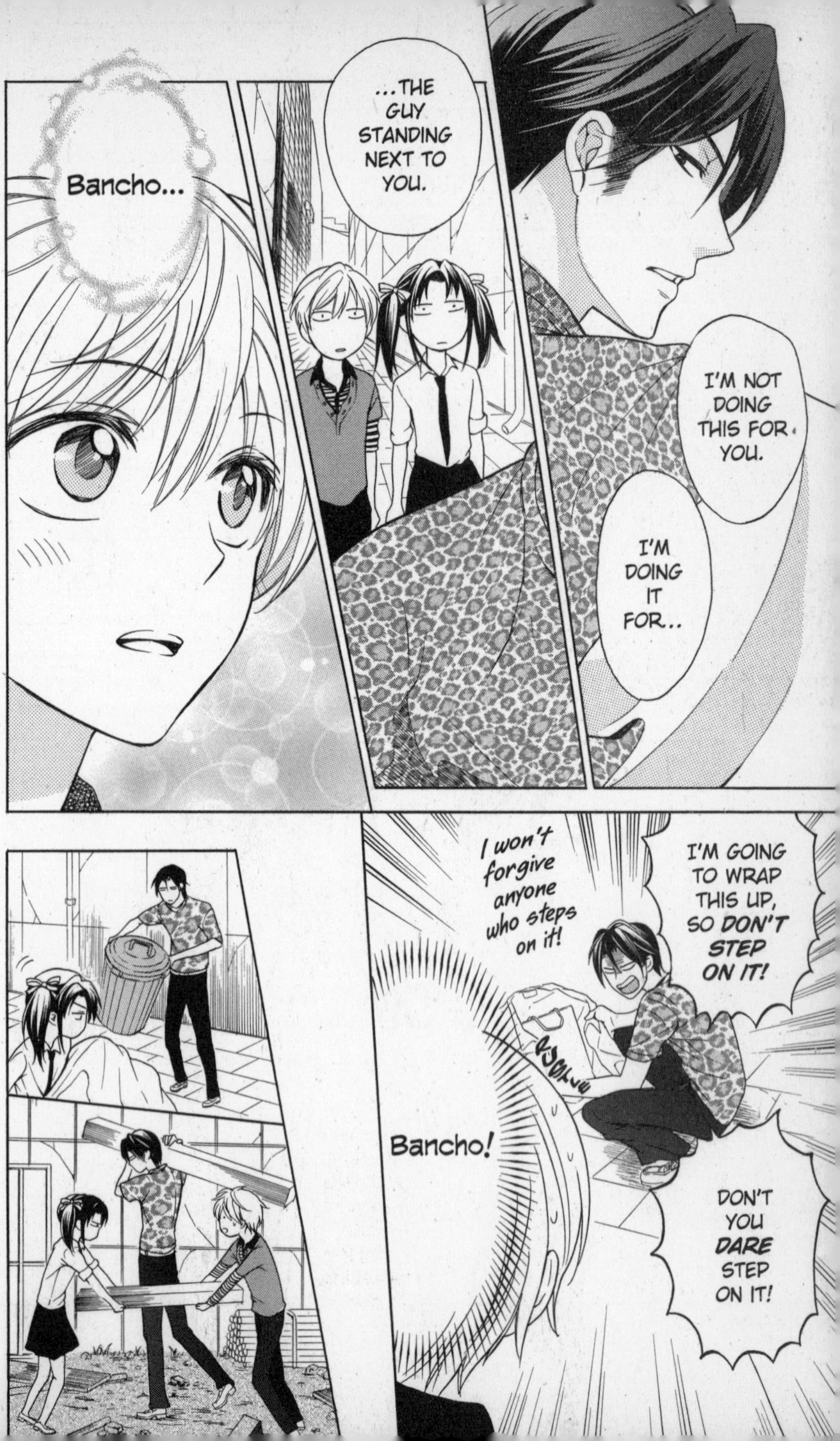
I'M NOT DOING THIS FOR YOU.
I'M DOING IT FOR...
...THE GUY STANDING NEXT TO YOU.
Bancho...
I'M GOING TO WRAP THIS UP, SO **DON'T STEP ON IT!**
I won't forgive anyone who steps on it!
Bancho!
DON'T YOU **DARE** STEP ON IT!

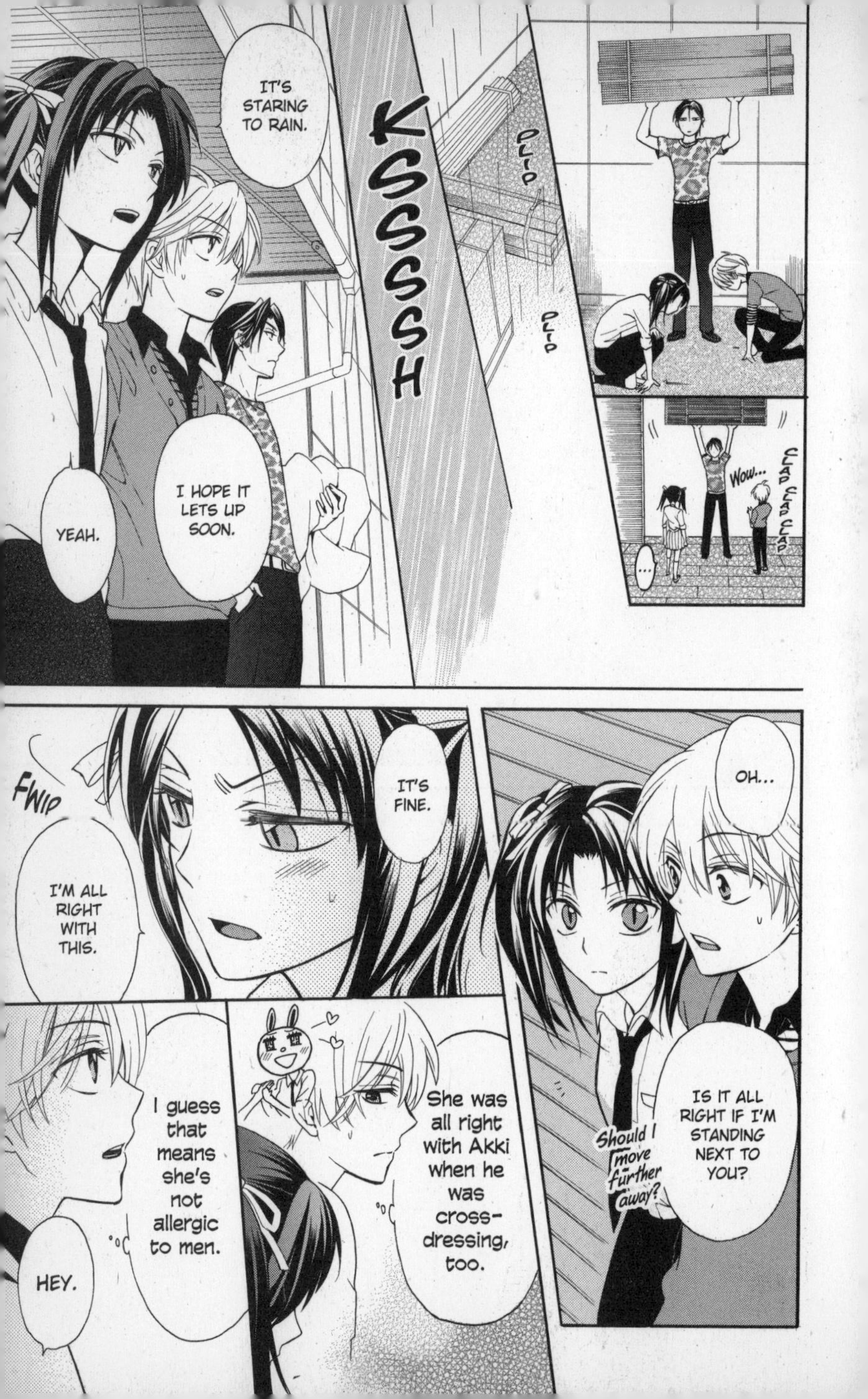

Wow...
CLAP CLAP CLAP
...
KSSSSH
PLIP
PLIP
IT'S STARING TO RAIN.
I HOPE IT LETS UP SOON.
YEAH.
OH...
IS IT ALL RIGHT IF I'M STANDING NEXT TO YOU?
Should I move further away?
IT'S FINE.
FWIP
I'M ALL RIGHT WITH THIS.
She was all right with Akki when he was cross-dressing, too.
I guess that means she's not allergic to men.
HEY.

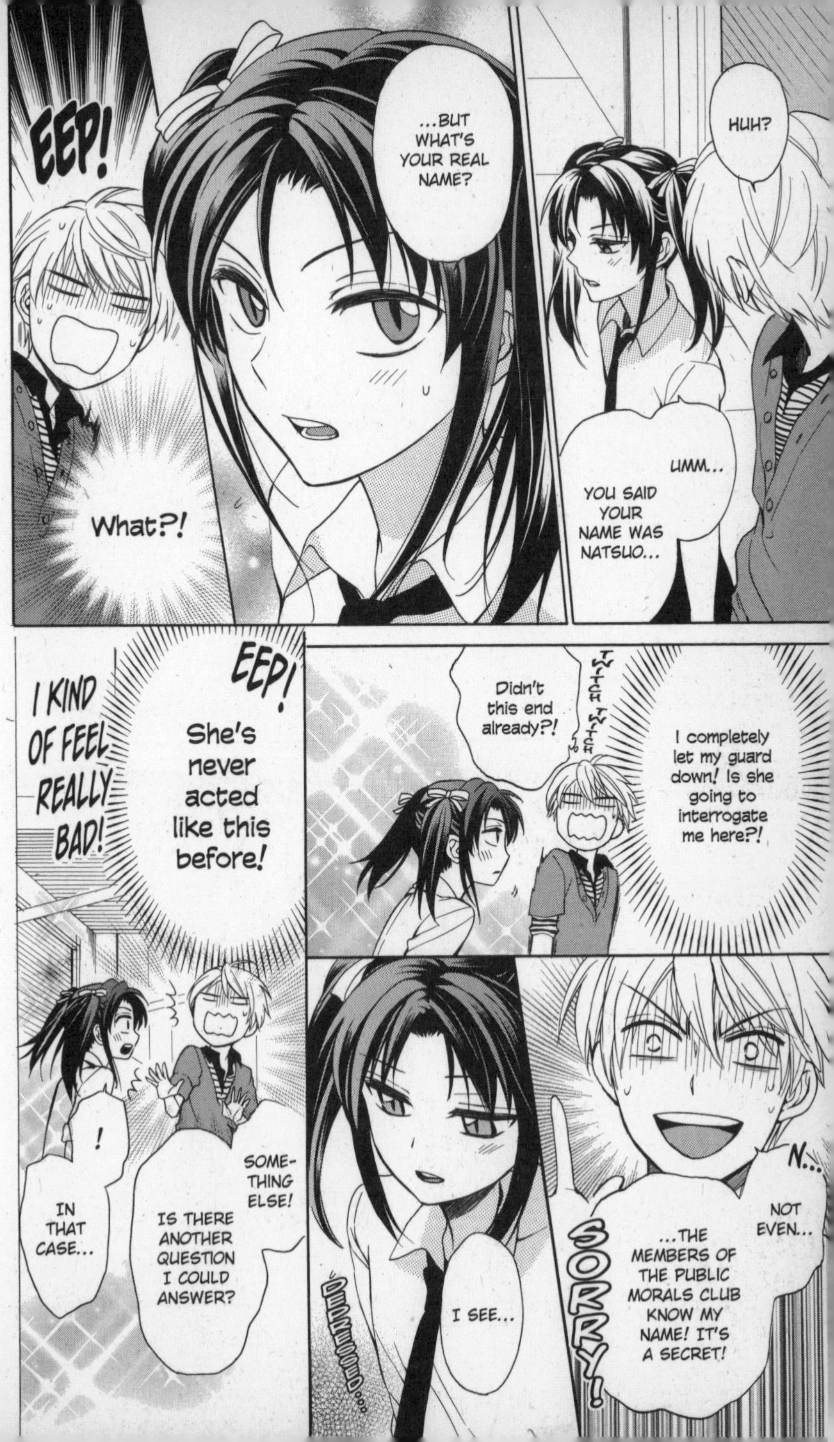
HUH?
UMM...
YOU SAID YOUR NAME WAS NATSUO...
...BUT WHAT'S YOUR REAL NAME?
EEP!
What?!
TWITCH TWITCH
Didn't this end already?!
I completely let my guard down! Is she going to interrogate me here?!
N...
NOT EVEN...
...THE MEMBERS OF THE PUBLIC MORALS CLUB KNOW MY NAME! IT'S A SECRET!
SORRY!
I SEE...
EEP!
She's never acted like this before!
I KIND OF FEEL REALLY BAD!
SOMETHING ELSE!
IS THERE ANOTHER QUESTION I COULD ANSWER?
!
IN THAT CASE...

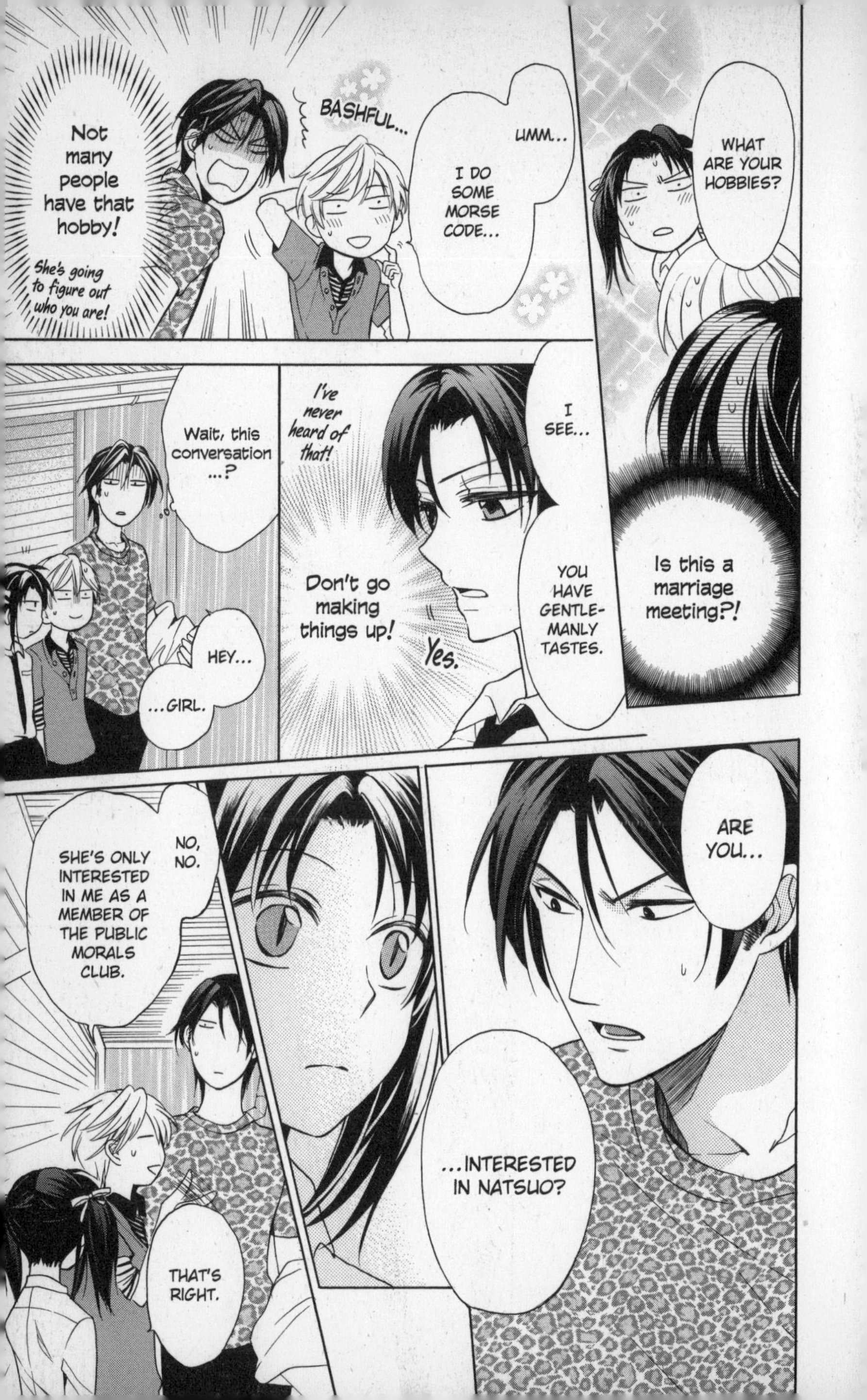
WHAT ARE YOUR HOBBIES?
Is this a marriage meeting?!
UMM...
I DO SOME MORSE CODE...
BASHFUL...
Not many people have that hobby!
She's going to figure out who you are!
I SEE...
YOU HAVE GENTLEMANLY TASTES.
I've never heard of that!
Don't go making things up!
Yes.
Wait, this conversation ...?
HEY...
...GIRL.
ARE YOU...
...INTERESTED IN NATSUO?
NO, NO.
SHE'S ONLY INTERESTED IN ME AS A MEMBER OF THE PUBLIC MORALS CLUB.
THAT'S RIGHT.

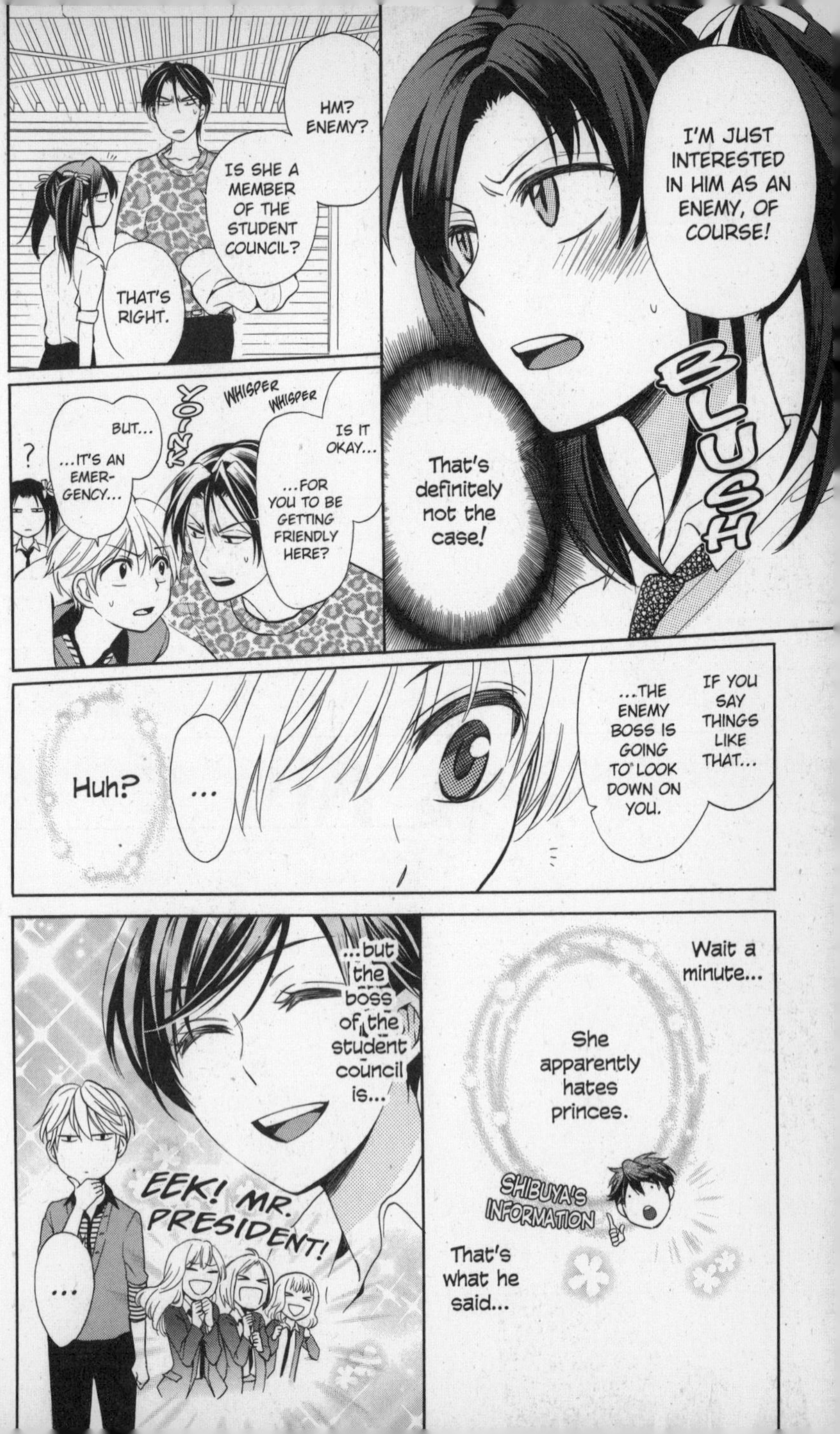
I'M JUST INTERESTED IN HIM AS AN ENEMY, OF COURSE!
BLUSH
That's definitely not the case!
HM? ENEMY?
IS SHE A MEMBER OF THE STUDENT COUNCIL?
THAT'S RIGHT.
WHISPER WHISPER
IS IT OKAY...
...FOR YOU TO BE GETTING FRIENDLY HERE?
YOINK
BUT...
...IT'S AN EMERGENCY...
?
IF YOU SAY THINGS LIKE THAT...
...THE ENEMY BOSS IS GOING TO LOOK DOWN ON YOU.
...
Huh?
Wait a minute...
She apparently hates princes.
SHIBUYA'S INFORMATION
That's what he said...
...but the boss of the student council is...
EEK! MR. PRESIDENT!
...

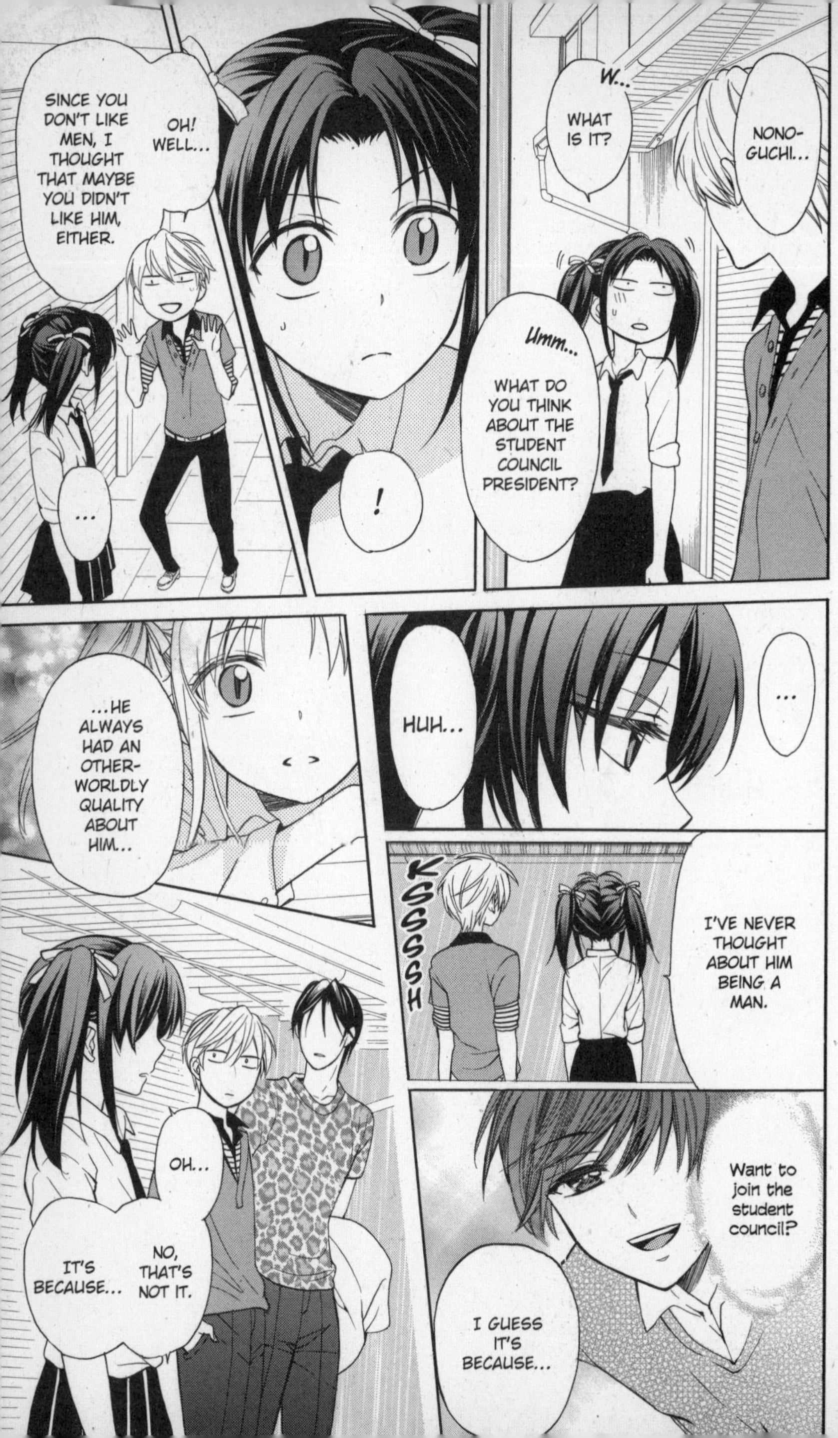
NONO-GUCHI...
W... WHAT IS IT?
Umm...
WHAT DO YOU THINK ABOUT THE STUDENT COUNCIL PRESIDENT?
!
OH! WELL...
SINCE YOU DON'T LIKE MEN, I THOUGHT THAT MAYBE YOU DIDN'T LIKE HIM, EITHER.
...
...
HUH...
...HE ALWAYS HAD AN OTHER-WORLDLY QUALITY ABOUT HIM...
KSSSSH
I'VE NEVER THOUGHT ABOUT HIM BEING A MAN.
Want to join the student council?
I GUESS IT'S BECAUSE...
OH...
NO, THAT'S NOT IT.
IT'S BECAUSE...

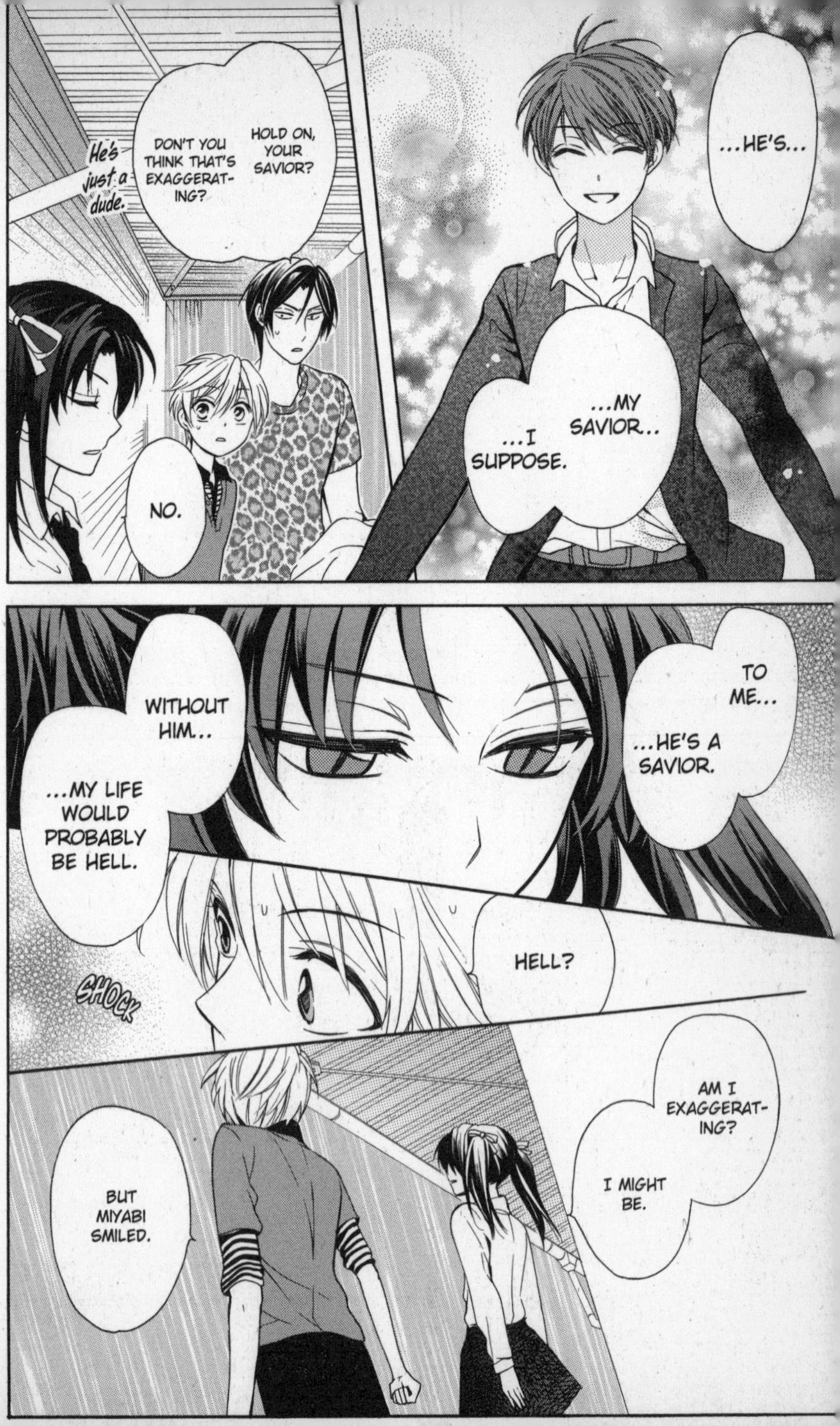
...HE'S...
...MY SAVIOR...
...I SUPPOSE.
HOLD ON, YOUR SAVIOR?
DON'T YOU THINK THAT'S EXAGGERAT-ING?
He's just a dude.
NO.
TO ME...
...HE'S A SAVIOR.
WITHOUT HIM...
...MY LIFE WOULD PROBABLY BE HELL.
HELL?
SHOCK
AM I EXAGGERAT-ING?
I MIGHT BE.
BUT MIYABI SMILED.

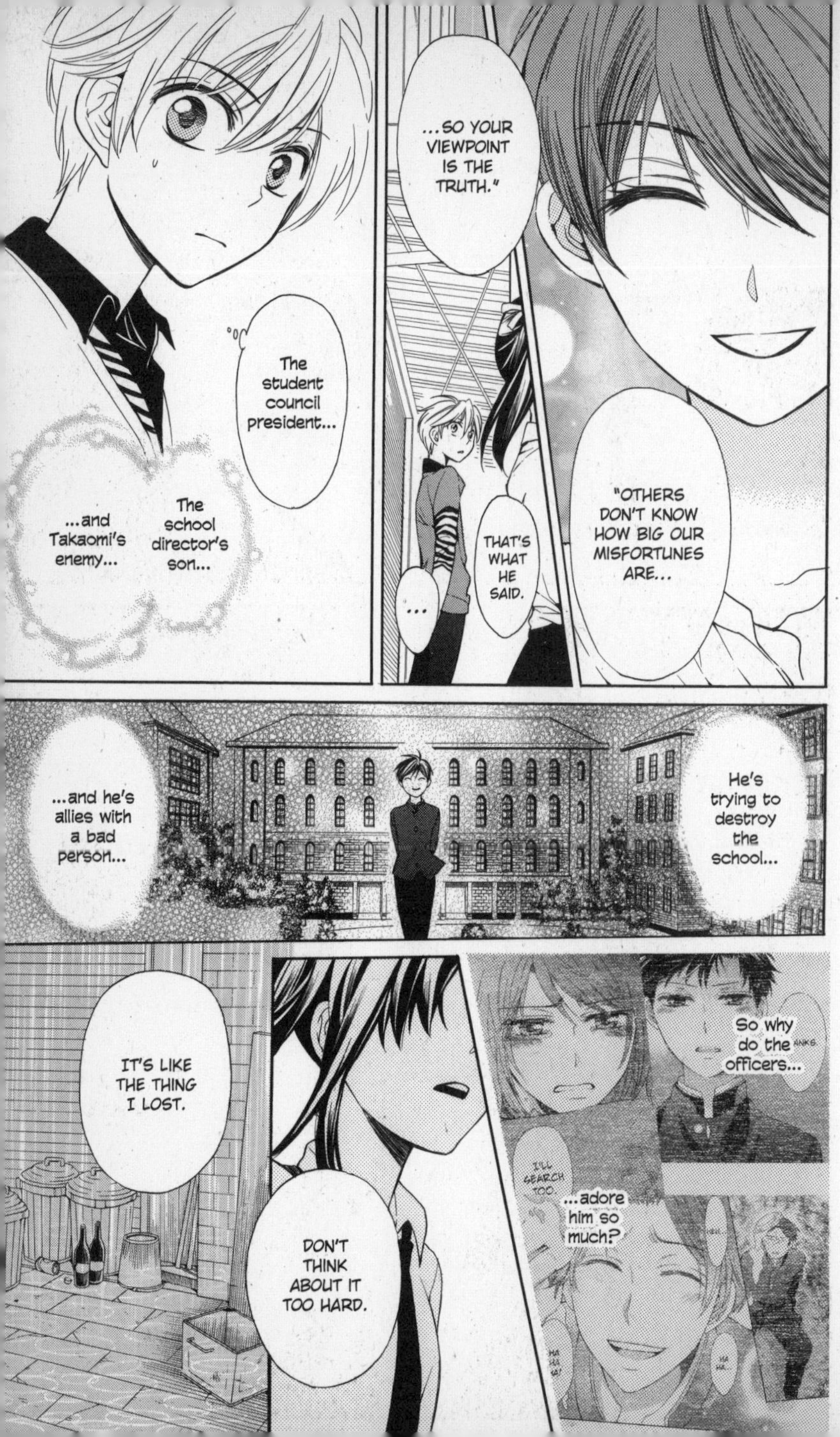
"OTHERS DON'T KNOW HOW BIG OUR MISFORTUNES ARE...
...SO YOUR VIEWPOINT IS THE TRUTH."
THAT'S WHAT HE SAID.
...
The student council president...
The school director's son...
...and Takaomi's enemy...
He's trying to destroy the school...
...and he's allies with a bad person...
So why do the officers...
I'LL SEARCH TOO
...adore him so much?
DON'T THINK ABOUT IT TOO HARD.
IT'S LIKE THE THING I LOST.

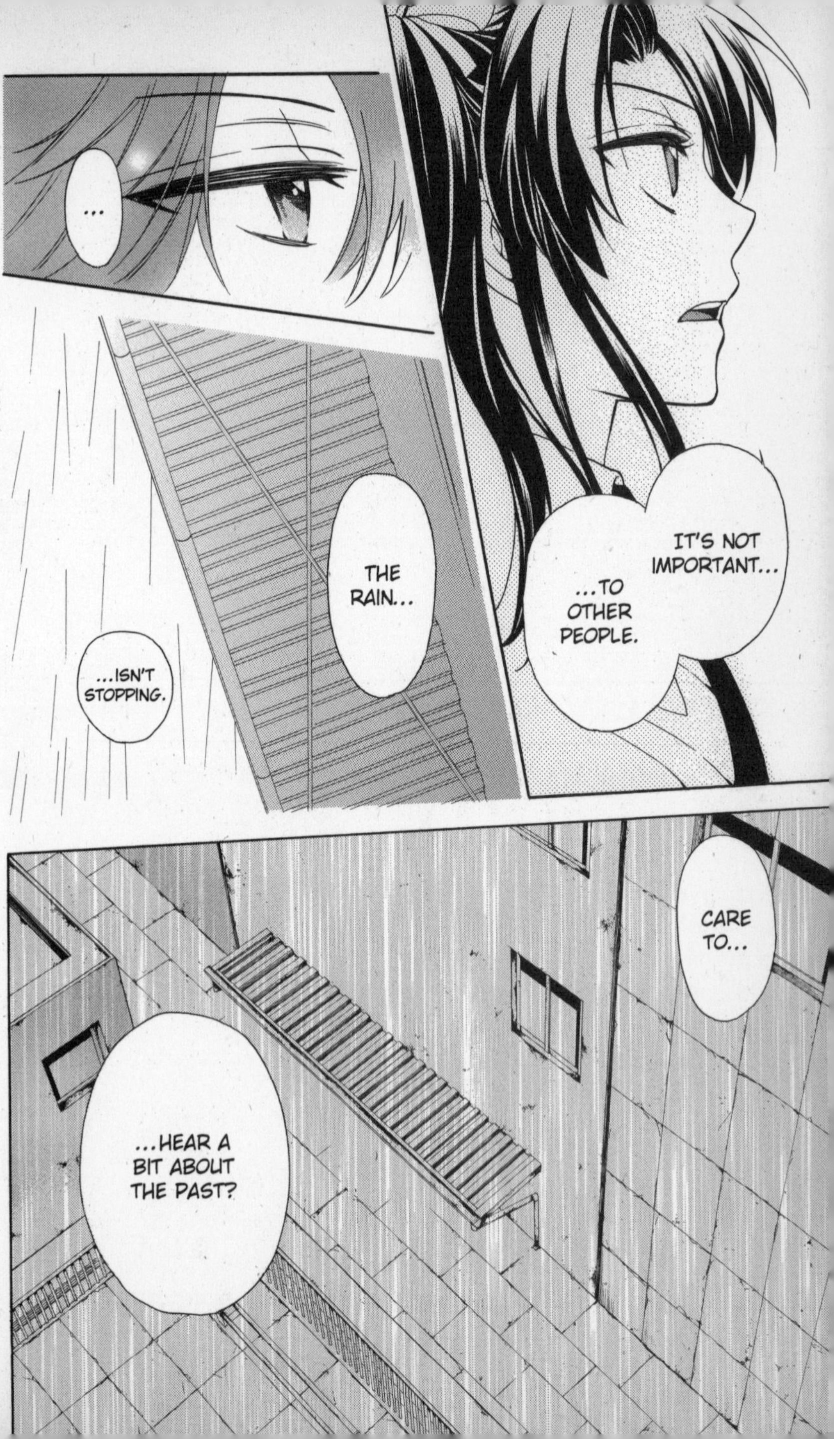
IT'S NOT IMPORTANT...
...TO OTHER PEOPLE.
...
THE RAIN...
...ISN'T STOPPING.
CARE TO...
...HEAR A BIT ABOUT THE PAST?

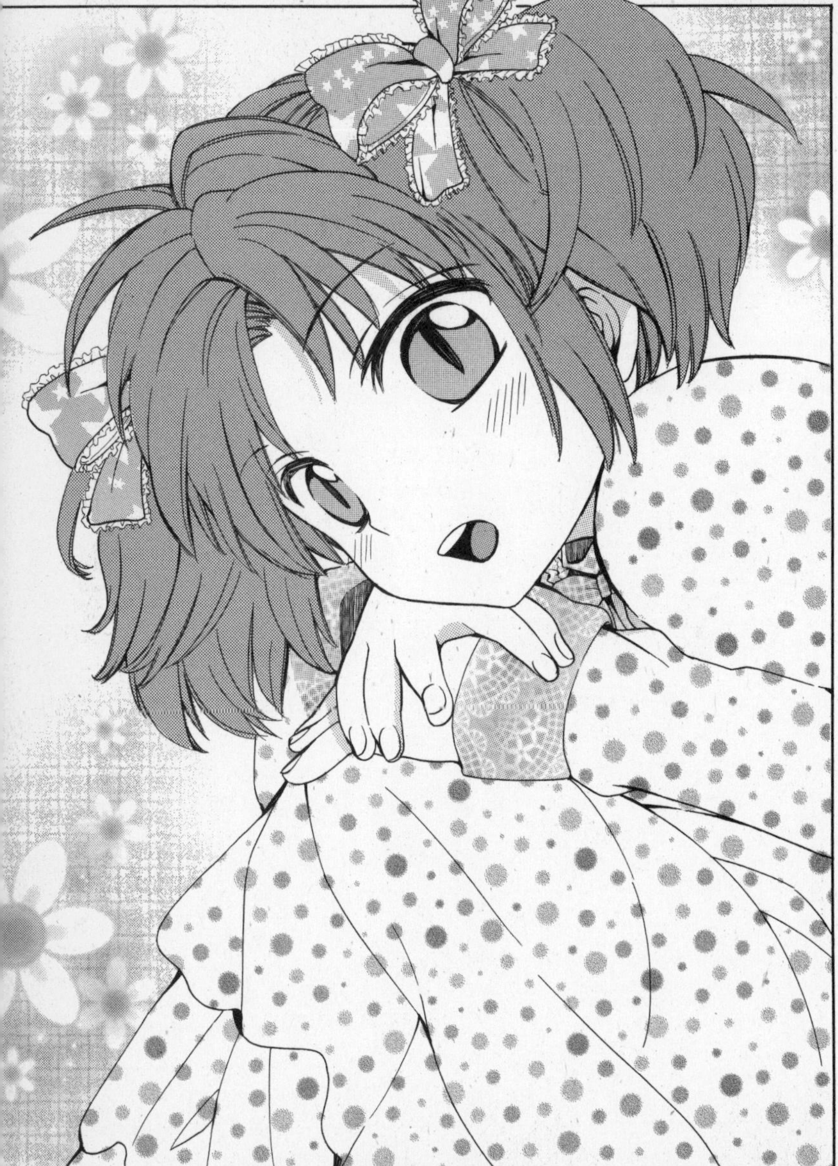

Chapter 74

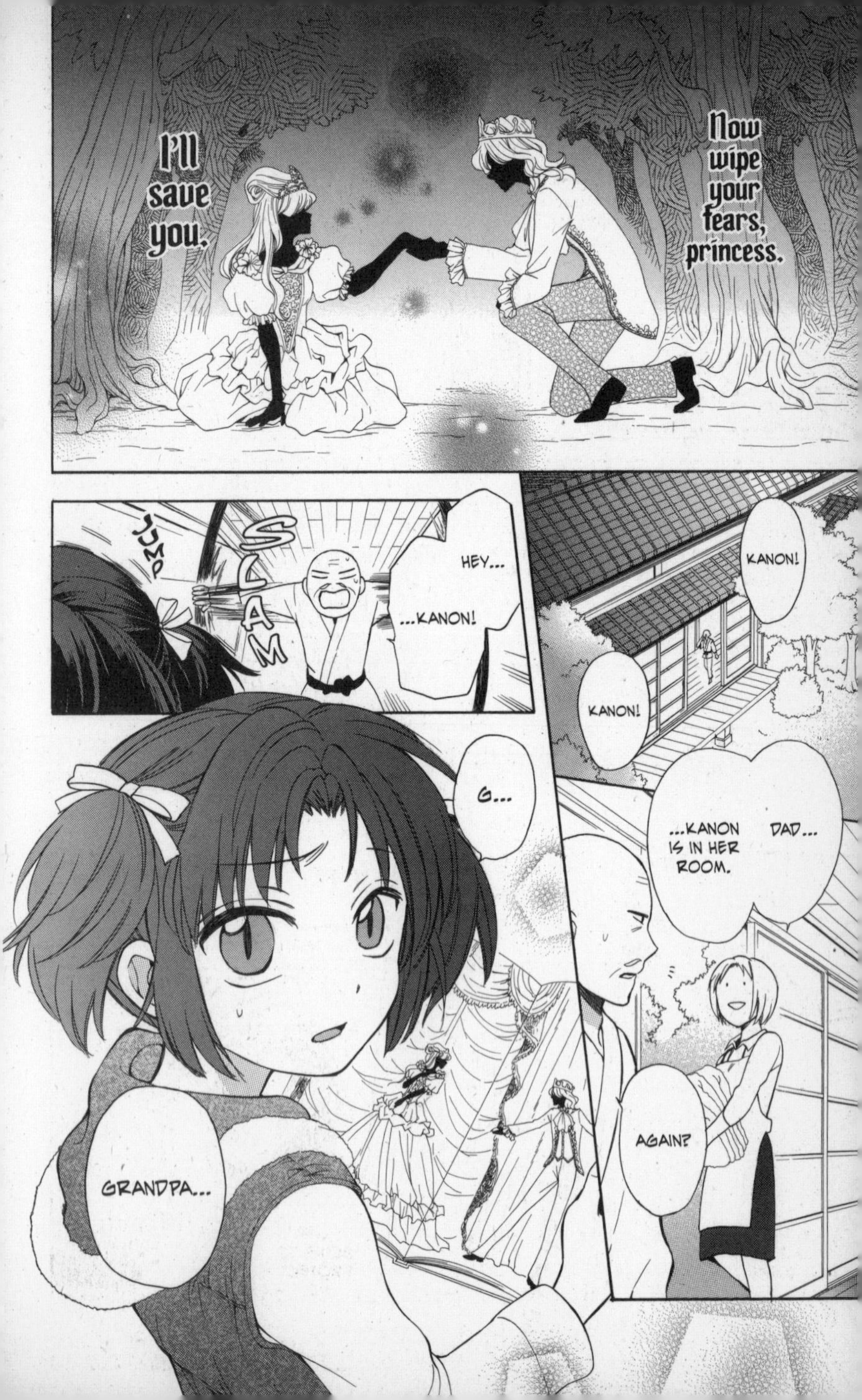
Now wipe your fears, princess.
I'll save you.
KANON!
KANON!
HEY...
...KANON!
SLAM
JUMP
DAD...
...KANON IS IN HER ROOM.
AGAIN?
G...
GRANDPA...

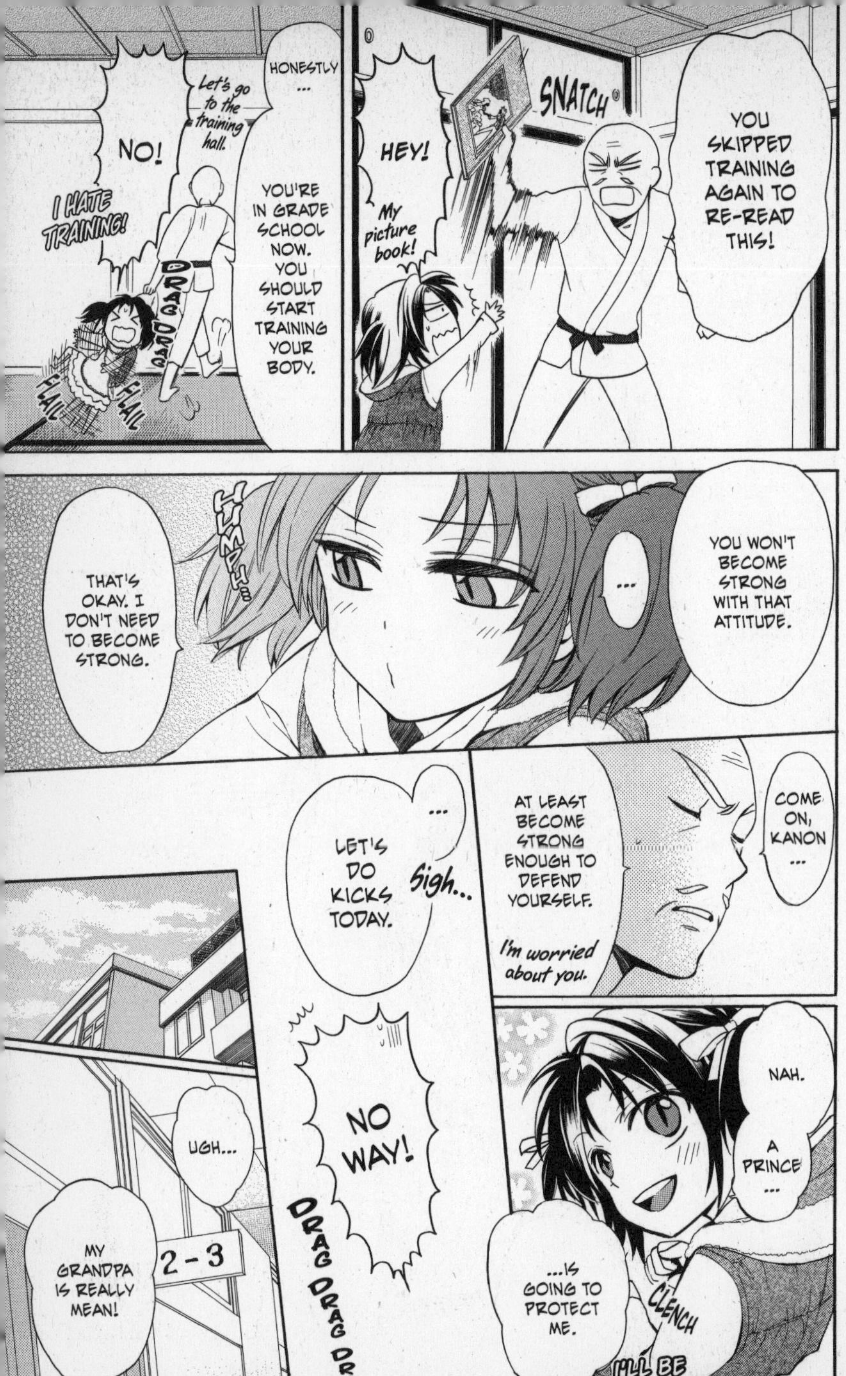
YOU SKIPPED TRAINING AGAIN TO RE-READ THIS!
SNATCH
HEY!
My picture book!
HONESTLY...
YOU'RE IN GRADE SCHOOL NOW. YOU SHOULD START TRAINING YOUR BODY.
Let's go to the training hall.
NO!
I HATE TRAINING!
DRAG DRAG
FLAIL FLAIL
YOU WON'T BECOME STRONG WITH THAT ATTITUDE.
...
HUMPH...
THAT'S OKAY. I DON'T NEED TO BECOME STRONG.
COME ON, KANON...
AT LEAST BECOME STRONG ENOUGH TO DEFEND YOURSELF.
I'm worried about you.
...
Sigh...
LET'S DO KICKS TODAY.
NAH.
A PRINCE...
...IS GOING TO PROTECT ME.
CLENCH
I'LL BE ALL RIGHT!
NO WAY!
DRAG DRAG DRAG DRAG
UGH...
2-3
MY GRANDPA IS REALLY MEAN!

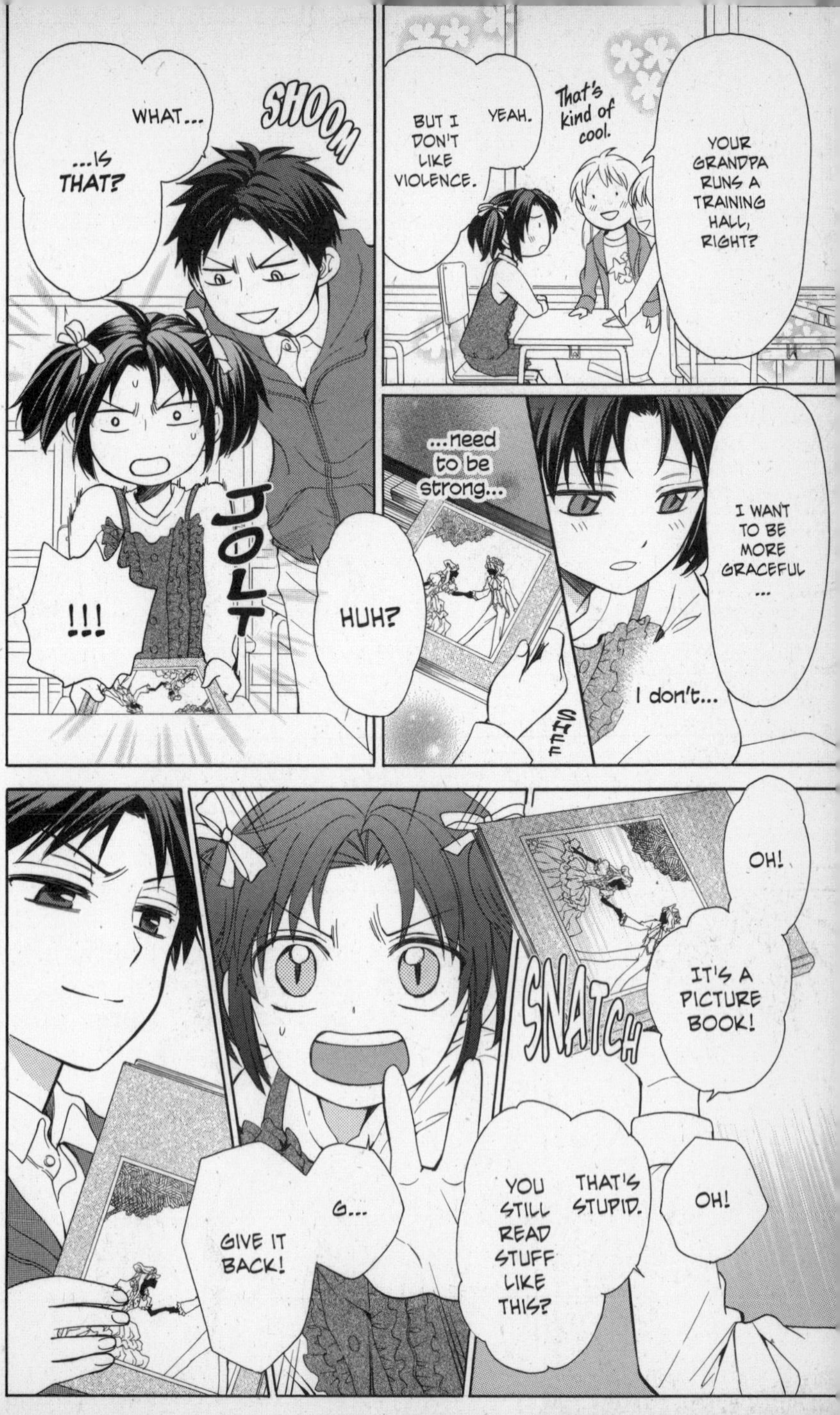
YOUR GRANDPA RUNS A TRAINING HALL, RIGHT?
That's kind of cool.
YEAH.
BUT I DON'T LIKE VIOLENCE.
I WANT TO BE MORE GRACEFUL ...
I don't...
...need to be strong...
SHFF
SHOOM
WHAT...
...IS THAT?
HUH?
JOLT
!!!
OH!
IT'S A PICTURE BOOK!
SNATCH
OH!
THAT'S STUPID.
YOU STILL READ STUFF LIKE THIS?
G...
GIVE IT BACK!

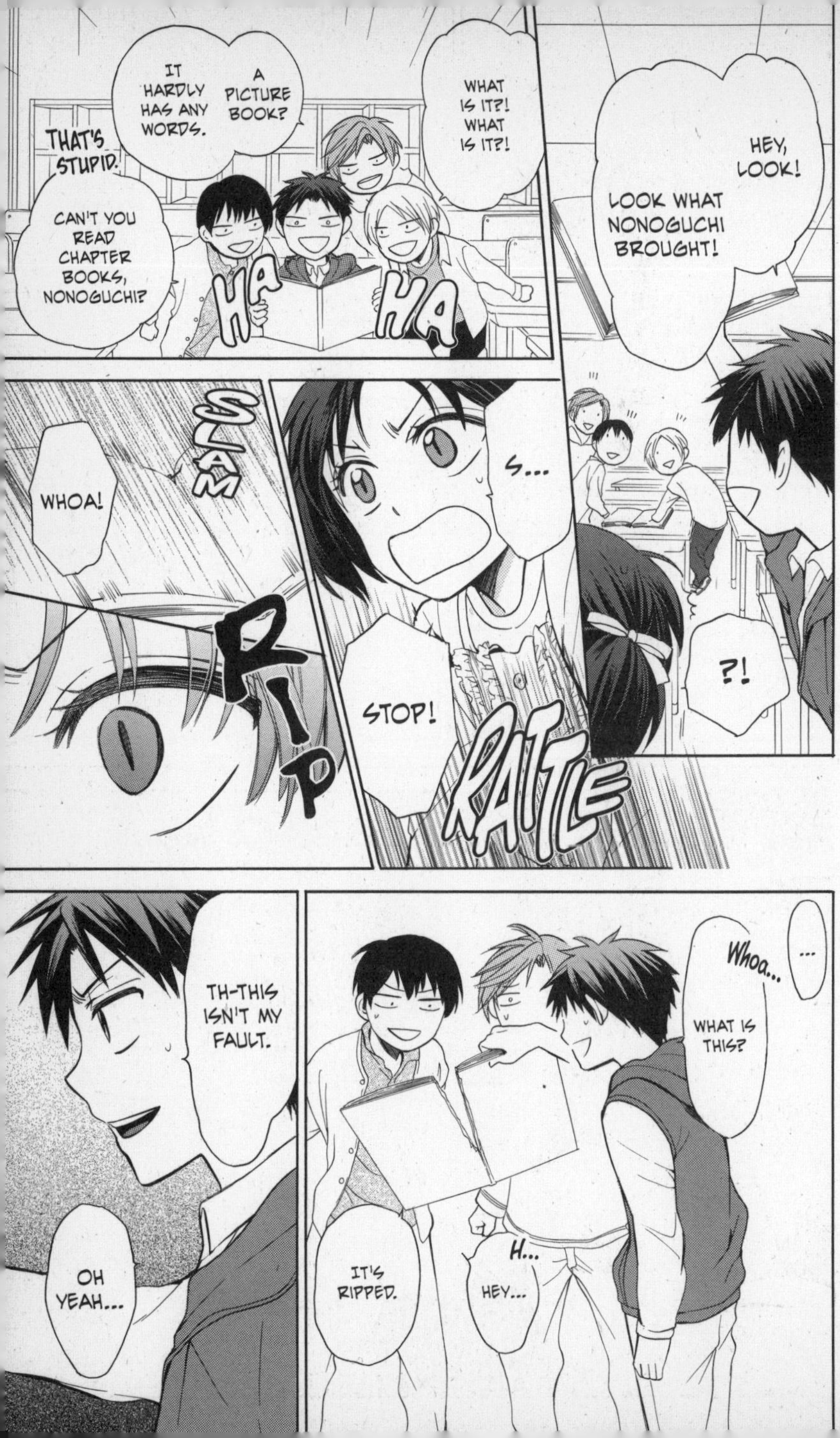
HEY, LOOK!
LOOK WHAT NONOGUCHI BROUGHT!
WHAT IS IT?! WHAT IS IT?!
A PICTURE BOOK?
IT HARDLY HAS ANY WORDS.
THAT'S STUPID.
CAN'T YOU READ CHAPTER BOOKS, NONOGUCHI?
HA
HA
?!
S...
STOP!
RATTLE
SLAM
WHOA!
RIP
...
Whoa...
WHAT IS THIS?
H...
HEY...
IT'S RIPPED.
TH-THIS ISN'T MY FAULT.
OH YEAH...

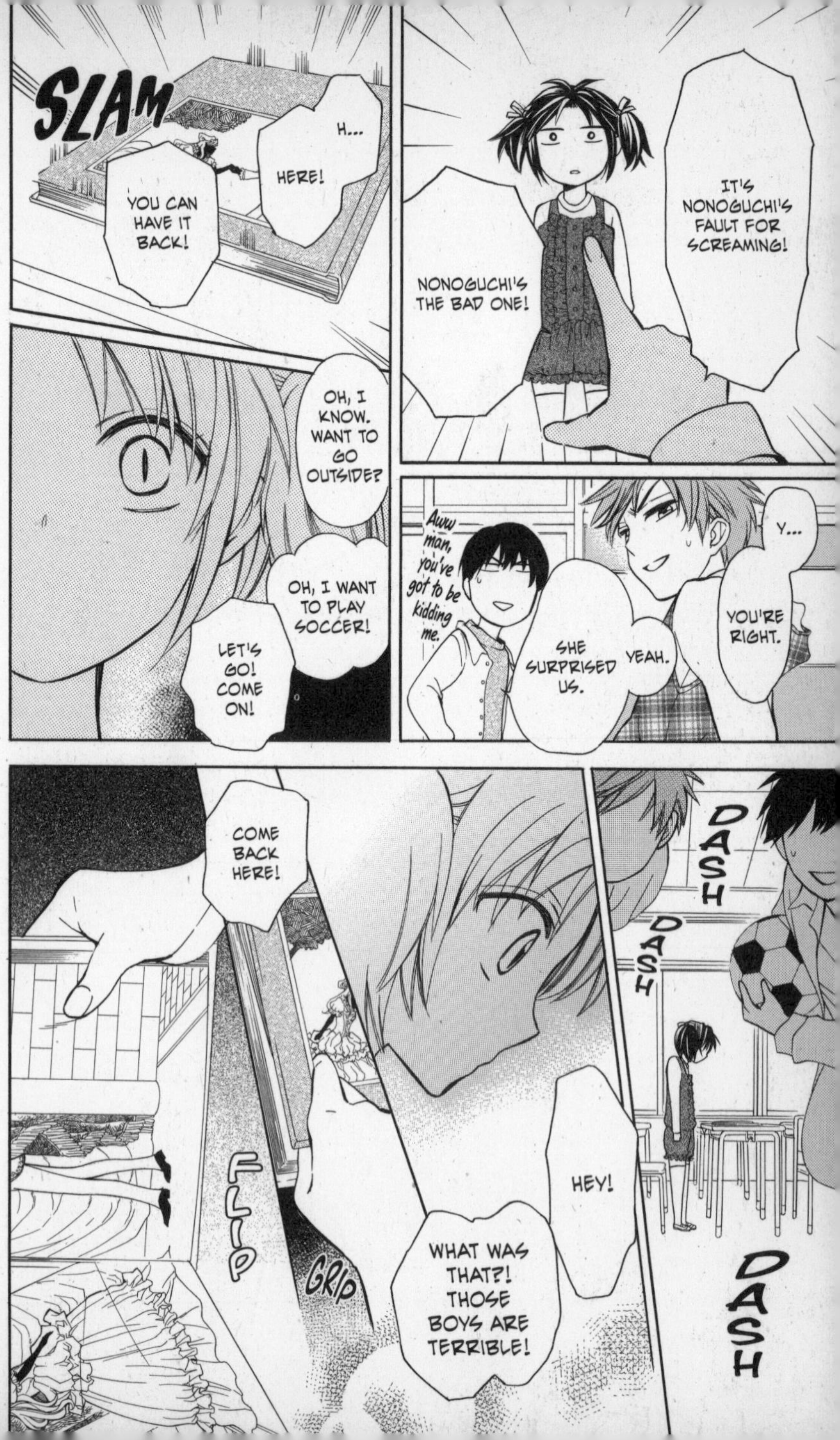
IT'S NONOGUCHI'S FAULT FOR SCREAMING!
NONOGUCHI'S THE BAD ONE!
SLAM
H...
HERE!
YOU CAN HAVE IT BACK!
Y...
YOU'RE RIGHT.
YEAH.
SHE SURPRISED US.
Aww man, you've got to be kidding me.
OH, I KNOW. WANT TO GO OUTSIDE?
OH, I WANT TO PLAY SOCCER!
LET'S GO! COME ON!
DASH
DASH
DASH
HEY!
WHAT WAS THAT?! THOSE BOYS ARE TERRIBLE!
GRIP
COME BACK HERE!
FLIP

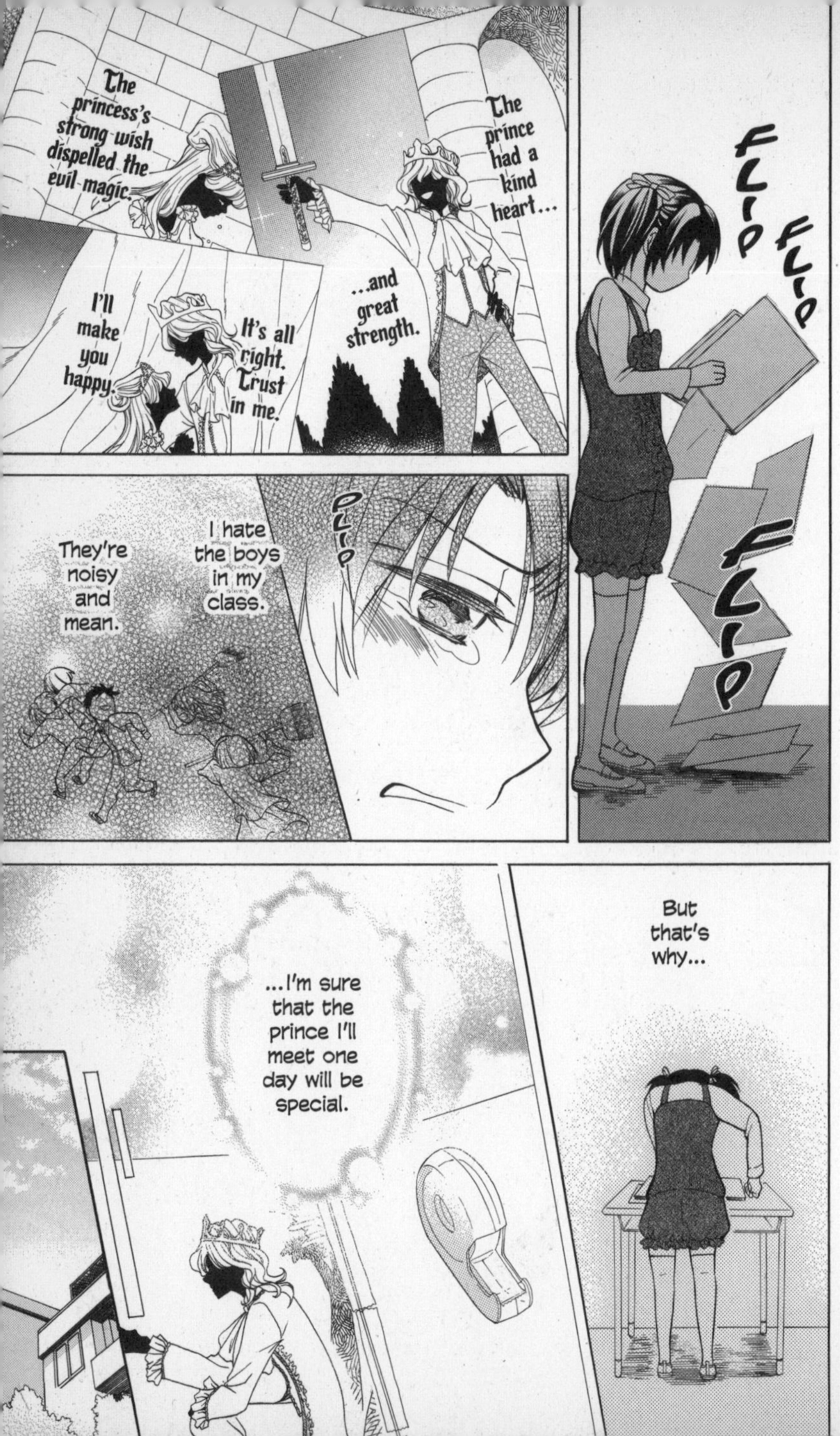
FLIP
FLIP
FLIP
The prince had a kind heart...
...and great strength.
The princess's strong wish dispelled the evil magic.
It's all right. Trust in me.
I'll make you happy.
FLIP
I hate the boys in my class.
They're noisy and mean.
But that's why...
...I'm sure that the prince I'll meet one day will be special.

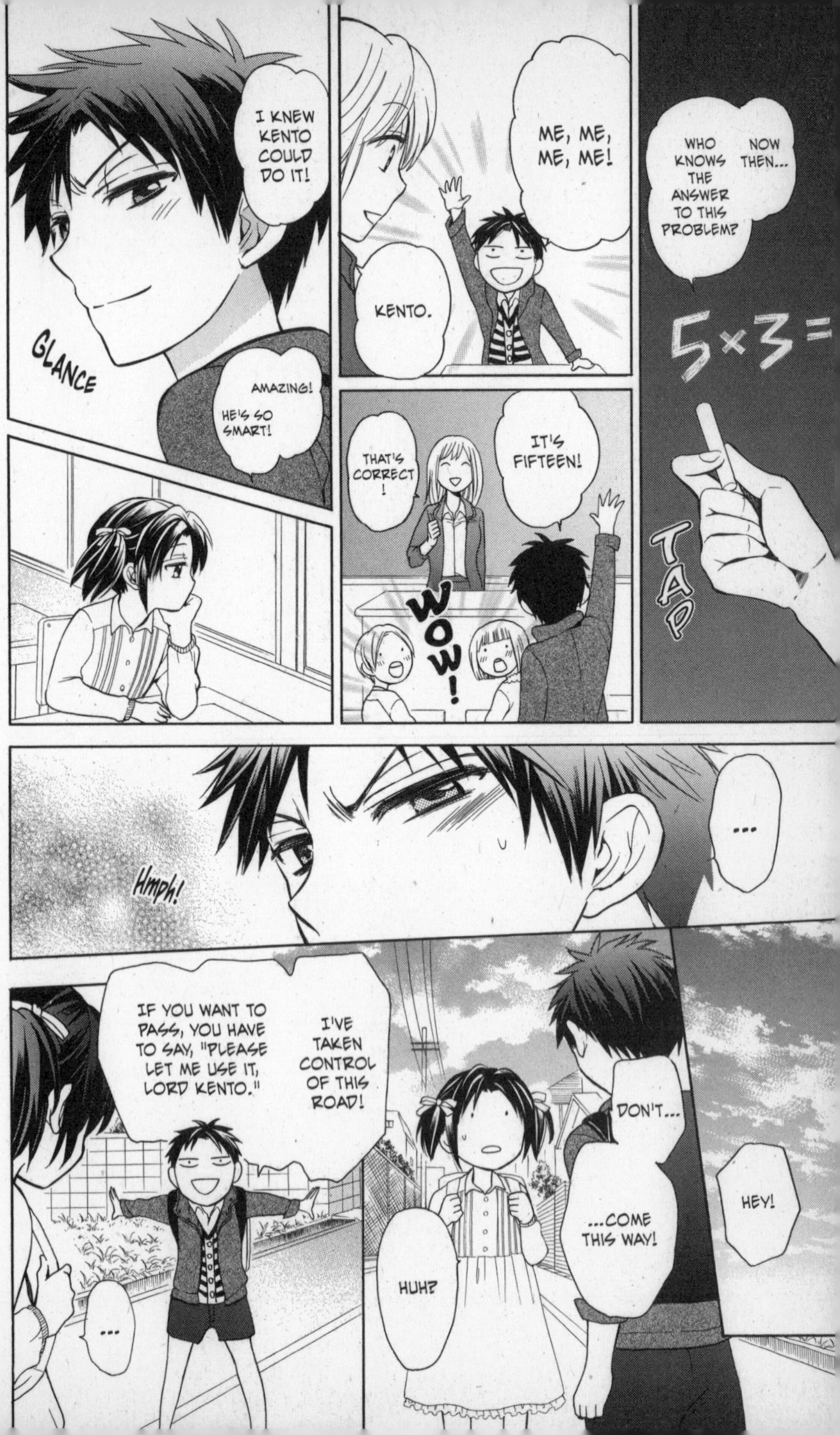
NOW THEN...
WHO KNOWS THE ANSWER TO THIS PROBLEM?
5×3=
TAP
ME, ME, ME, ME!
KENTO.
IT'S FIFTEEN!
THAT'S CORRECT!
WOW!
I KNEW KENTO COULD DO IT!
GLANCE
AMAZING!
HE'S SO SMART!
...
Hmph!
HEY!
DON'T...
...COME THIS WAY!
HUH?
I'VE TAKEN CONTROL OF THIS ROAD!
IF YOU WANT TO PASS, YOU HAVE TO SAY, "PLEASE LET ME USE IT, LORD KENTO."
...

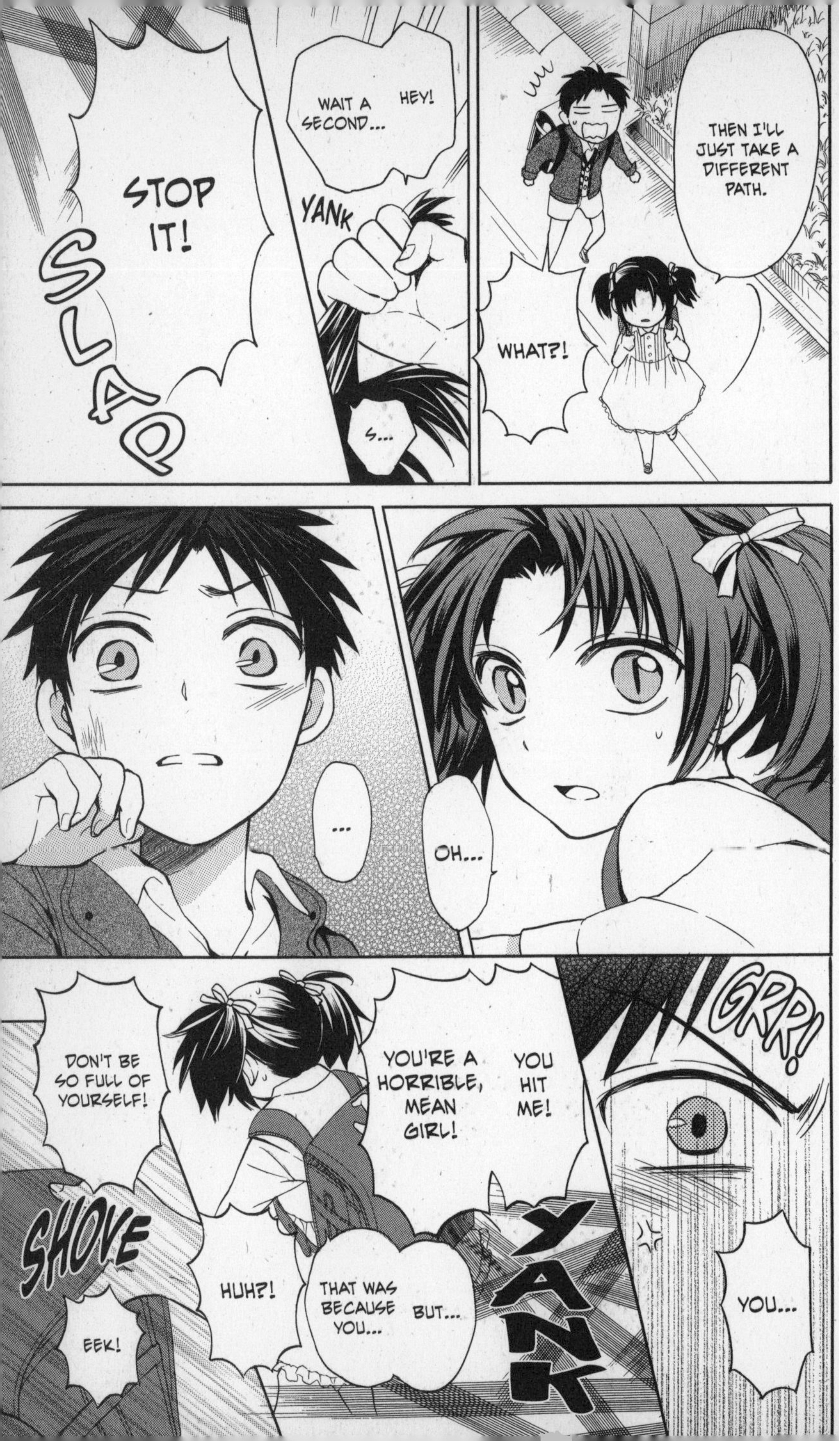
THEN I'LL JUST TAKE A DIFFERENT PATH.
WHAT?!
HEY!
WAIT A SECOND...
YANK
S...
STOP IT!
SLAP
OH...
...
GRR!
YOU...
YOU HIT ME!
YOU'RE A HORRIBLE, MEAN GIRL!
BUT...
THAT WAS BECAUSE YOU...
YANK
DON'T BE SO FULL OF YOURSELF!
HUH?!
SHOVE
EEK!

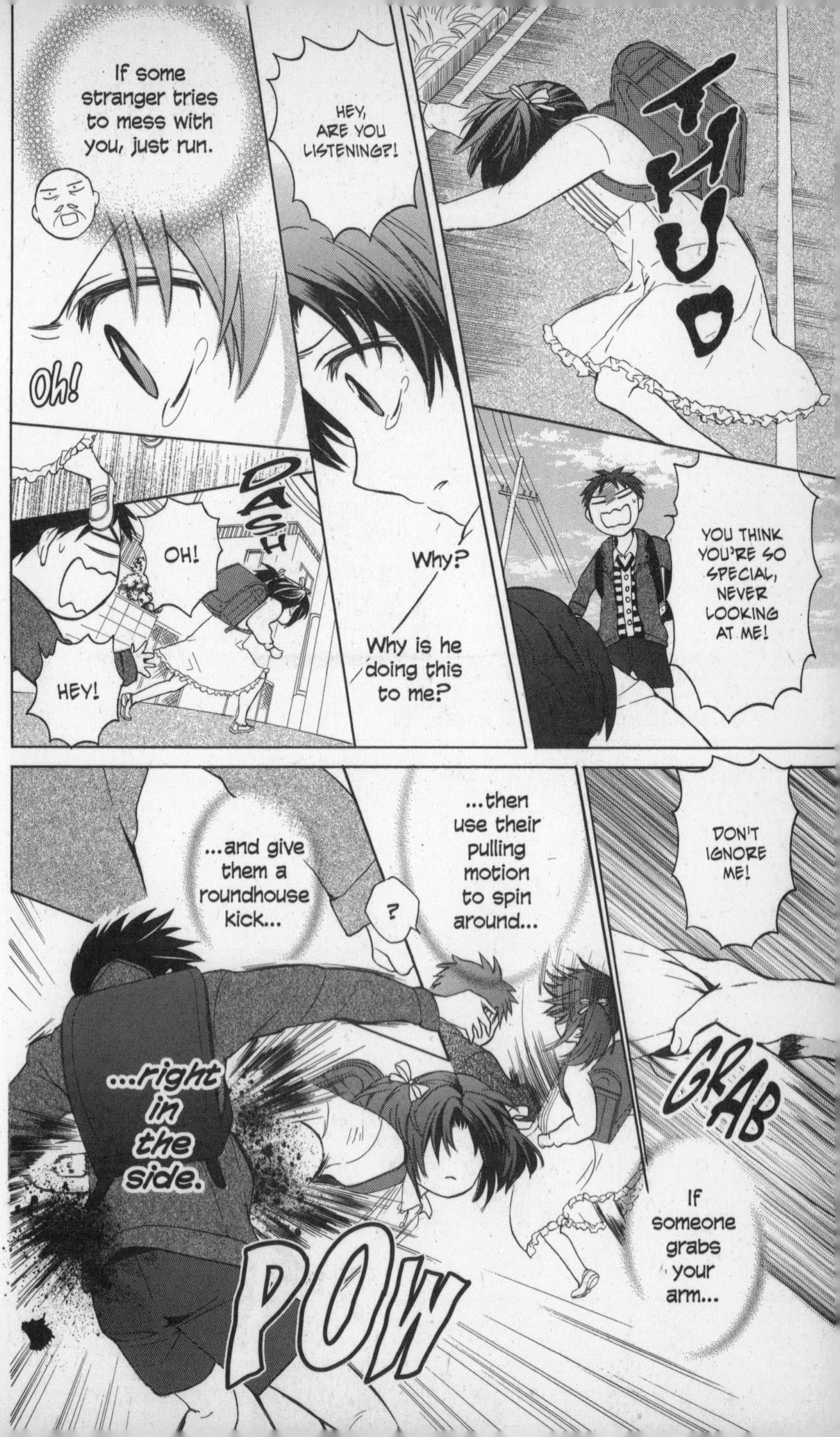
THUD
HEY, ARE YOU LISTENING?!
If some stranger tries to mess with you, just run.
Oh!
YOU THINK YOU'RE SO SPECIAL, NEVER LOOKING AT ME!
Why?
Why is he doing this to me?
DASH
OH!
HEY!
DON'T IGNORE ME!
GRAB
If someone grabs your arm...
...then use their pulling motion to spin around...
?
...and give them a roundhouse kick...
...right in the side.
POW

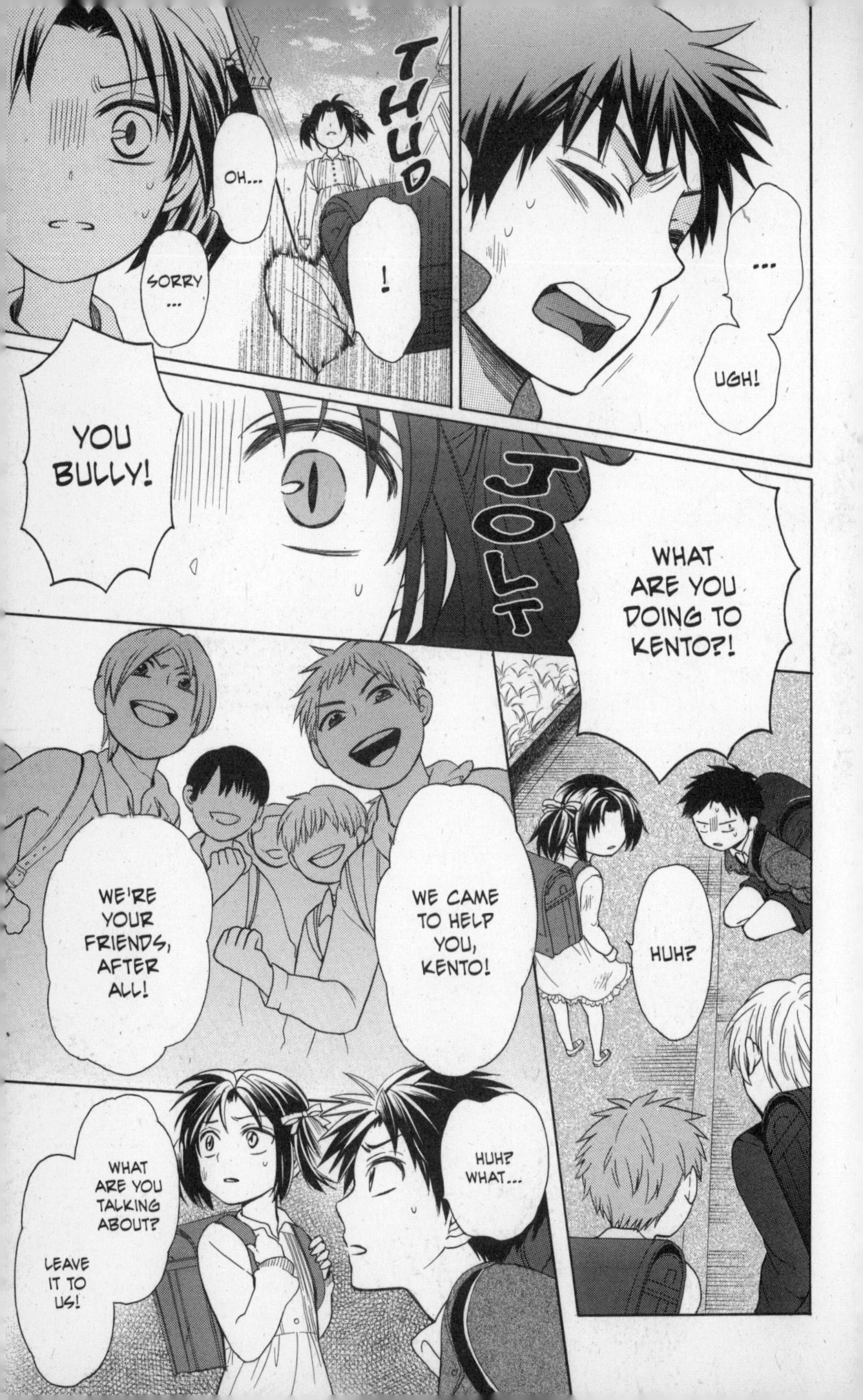
...
UGH!
THUD
!
OH...
SORRY ...
YOU BULLY!
JOLT
WHAT ARE YOU DOING TO KENTO?!
HUH?
WE CAME TO HELP YOU, KENTO!
WE'RE YOUR FRIENDS, AFTER ALL!
HUH? WHAT...
WHAT ARE YOU TALKING ABOUT?
LEAVE IT TO US!

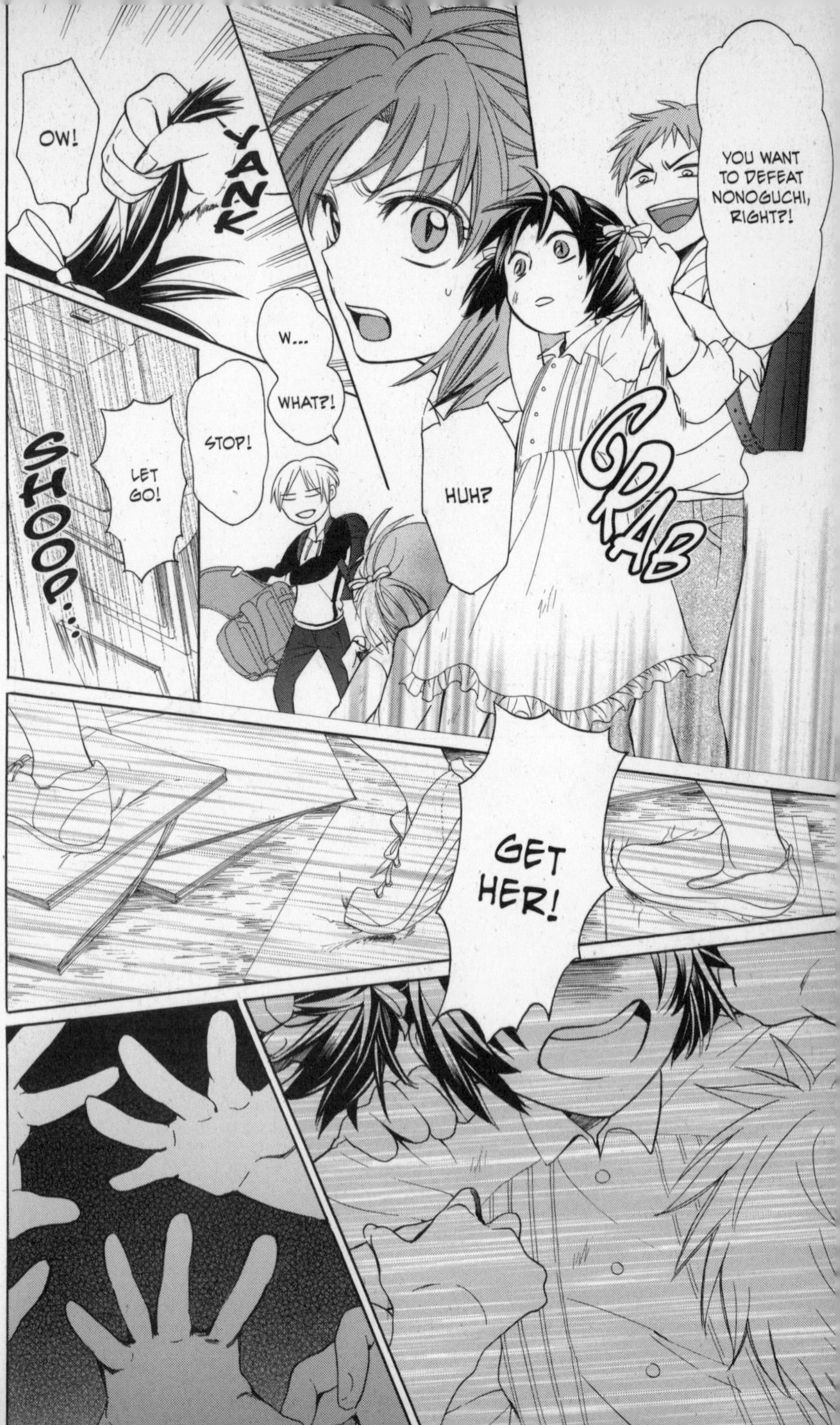
YOU WANT TO DEFEAT NONOGUCHI, RIGHT?!
GRAB
HUH?
W...
WHAT?!
YANK
OW!
STOP!
LET GO!
SHOOO...
GET HER!

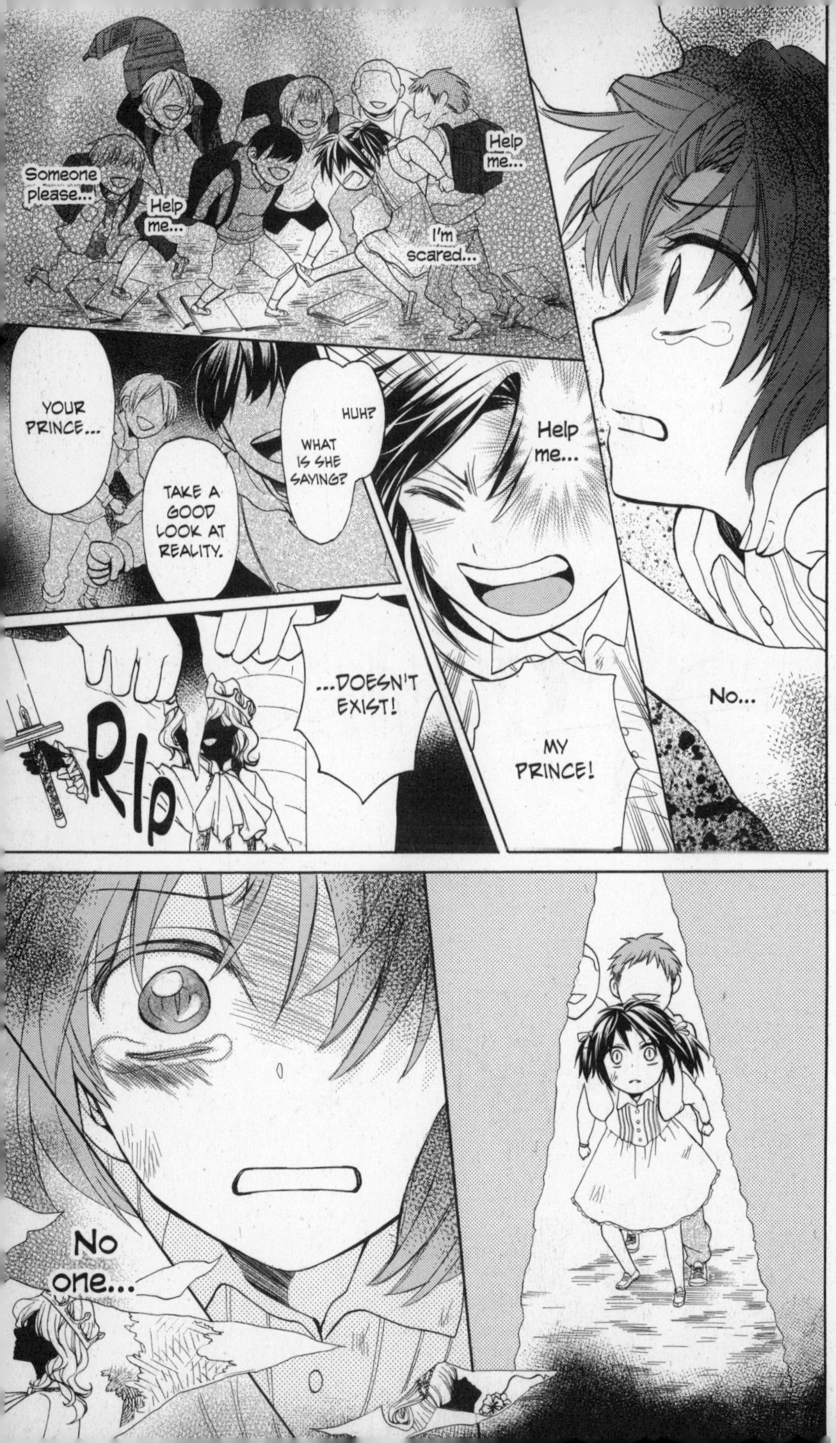

Help me...
No...
MY PRINCE!
Help me...
I'm scared...
Help me...
Someone please...
HUH? WHAT IS SHE SAYING?
YOUR PRINCE...
TAKE A GOOD LOOK AT REALITY.
...DOESN'T EXIST!
RIP
No one...

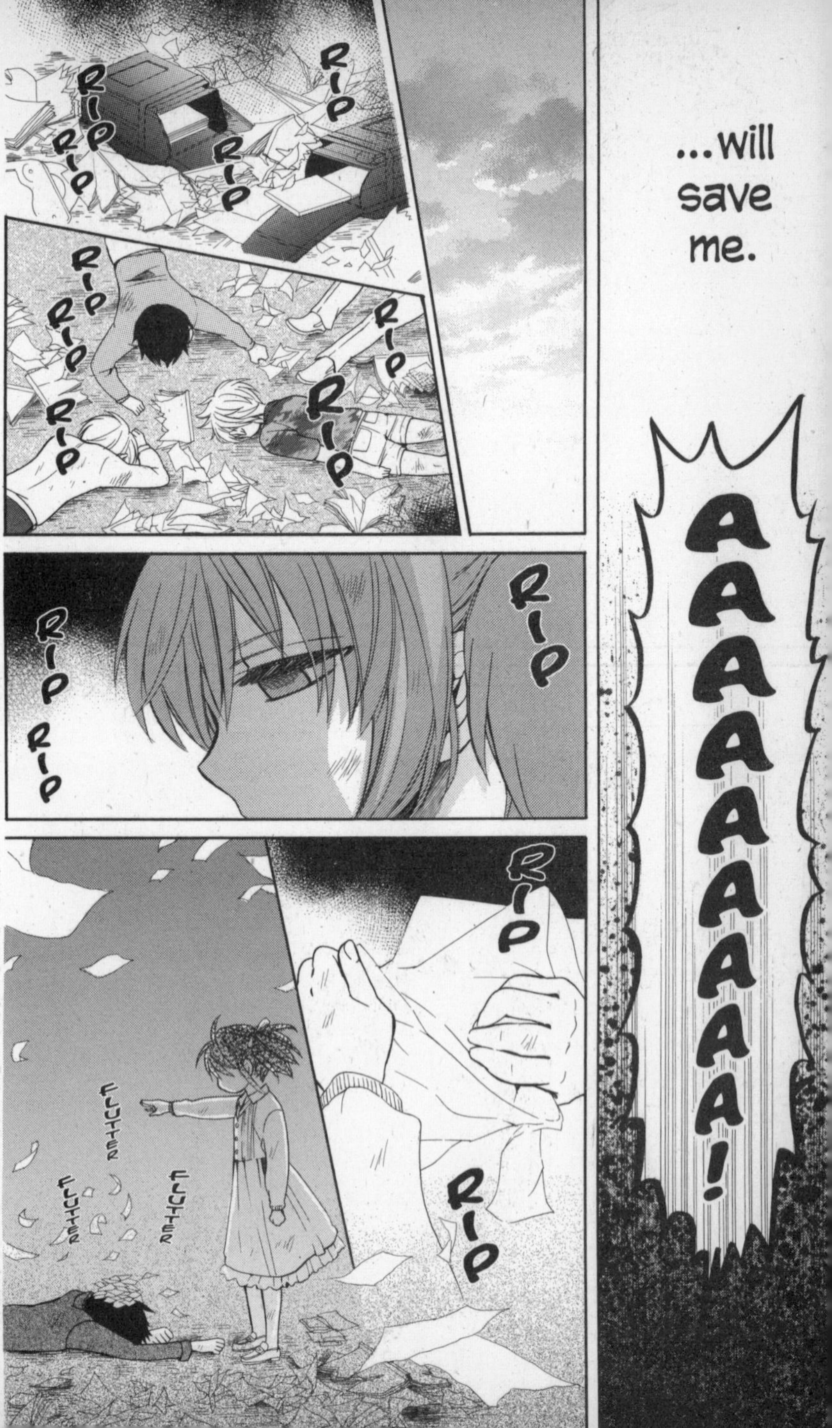
...will save me.
AAAAAAAAA!
RIP
RIP
RIP
RIP
RIP
RIP
RIP
RIP
RIP
RIP
RIP
RIP
RIP
RIP
RIP
RIP
FLUTTER
FLUTTER
FLUTTER

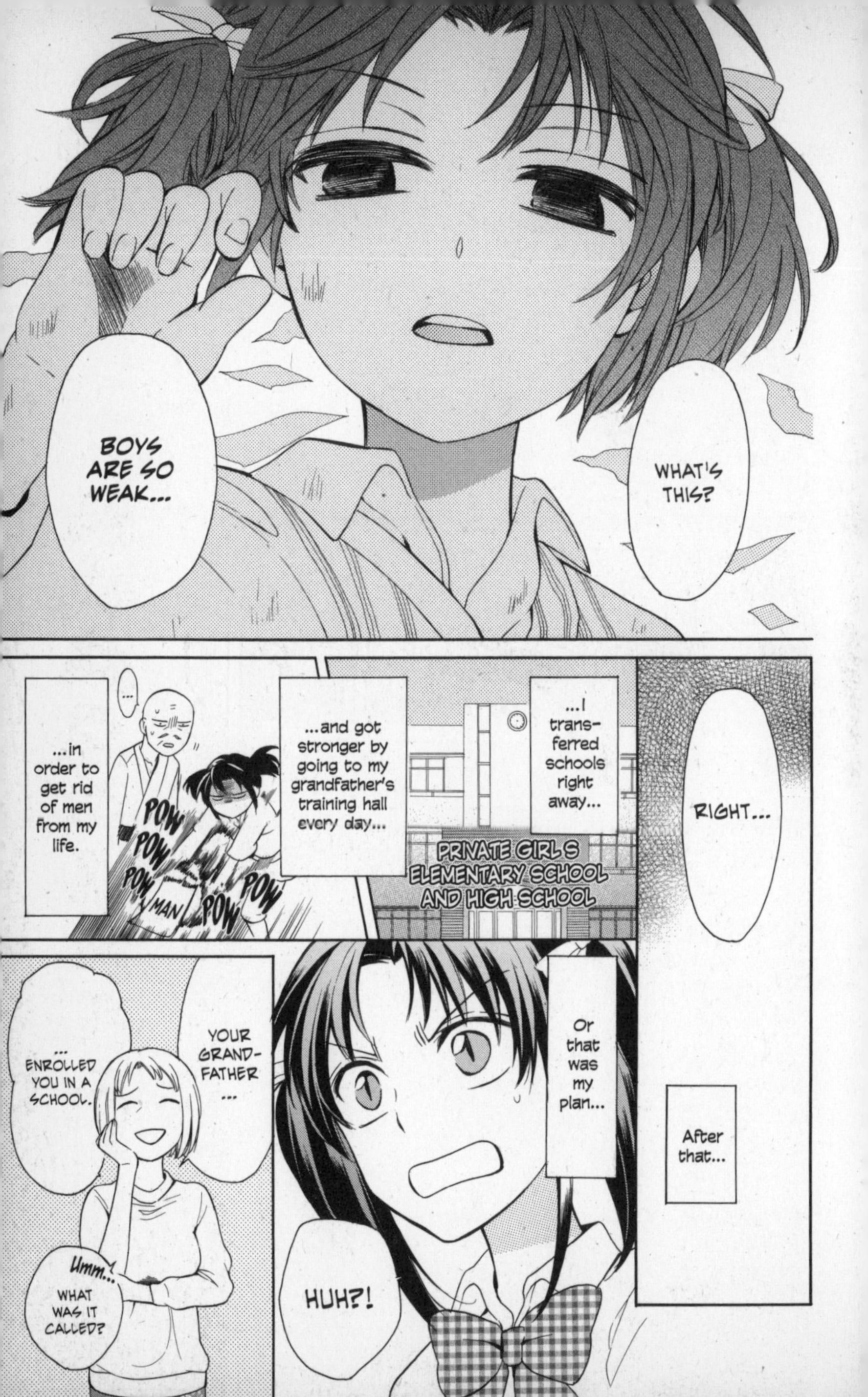
WHAT'S THIS?
BOYS ARE SO WEAK...
RIGHT...
...I transferred schools right away...
PRIVATE GIRL S ELEMENTARY SCHOOL AND HIGH SCHOOL
...and got stronger by going to my grandfather's training hall every day...
...
...in order to get rid of men from my life.
POW POW POW MAN POW POW
After that...
Or that was my plan...
HUH?!
YOUR GRANDFATHER ...
... ENROLLED YOU IN A SCHOOL.
Umm...
WHAT WAS IT CALLED?

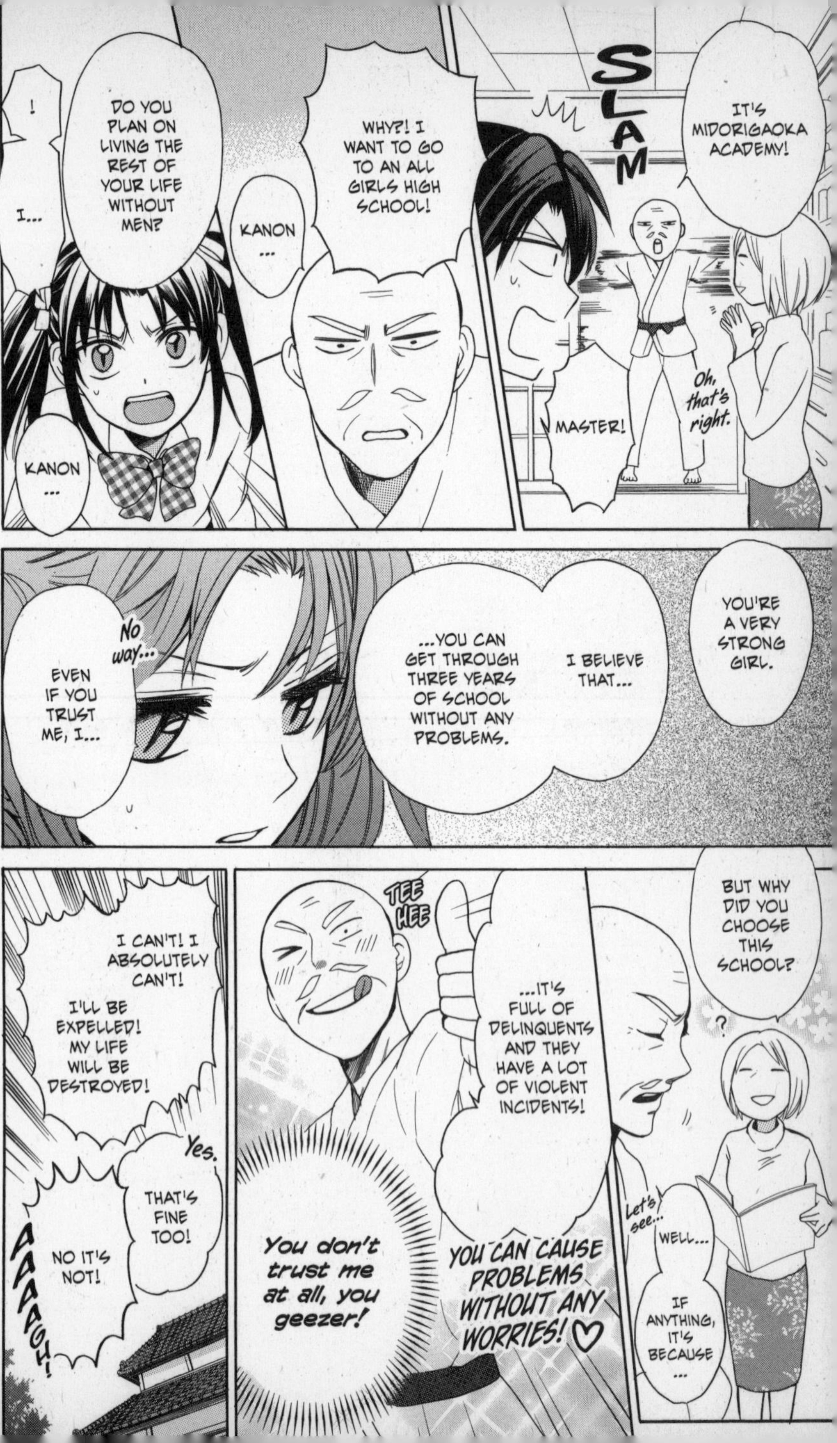
IT'S MIDORIGAOKA ACADEMY!
SLAM
Oh, that's right.
MASTER!
WHY?! I WANT TO GO TO AN ALL GIRLS HIGH SCHOOL!
KANON ...
DO YOU PLAN ON LIVING THE REST OF YOUR LIFE WITHOUT MEN?
!
I...
KANON ...
YOU'RE A VERY STRONG GIRL.
I BELIEVE THAT...
...YOU CAN GET THROUGH THREE YEARS OF SCHOOL WITHOUT ANY PROBLEMS.
No way...
EVEN IF YOU TRUST ME, I...
BUT WHY DID YOU CHOOSE THIS SCHOOL?
?
Let's see...
WELL...
IF ANYTHING, IT'S BECAUSE ...
...IT'S FULL OF DELINQUENTS AND THEY HAVE A LOT OF VIOLENT INCIDENTS!
TEE HEE
YOU CAN CAUSE PROBLEMS WITHOUT ANY WORRIES! ♡
You don't trust me at all, you geezer!
I CAN'T! I ABSOLUTELY CAN'T!
I'LL BE EXPELLED! MY LIFE WILL BE DESTROYED!
Yes.
THAT'S FINE TOO!
NO IT'S NOT!
AAAAGH!

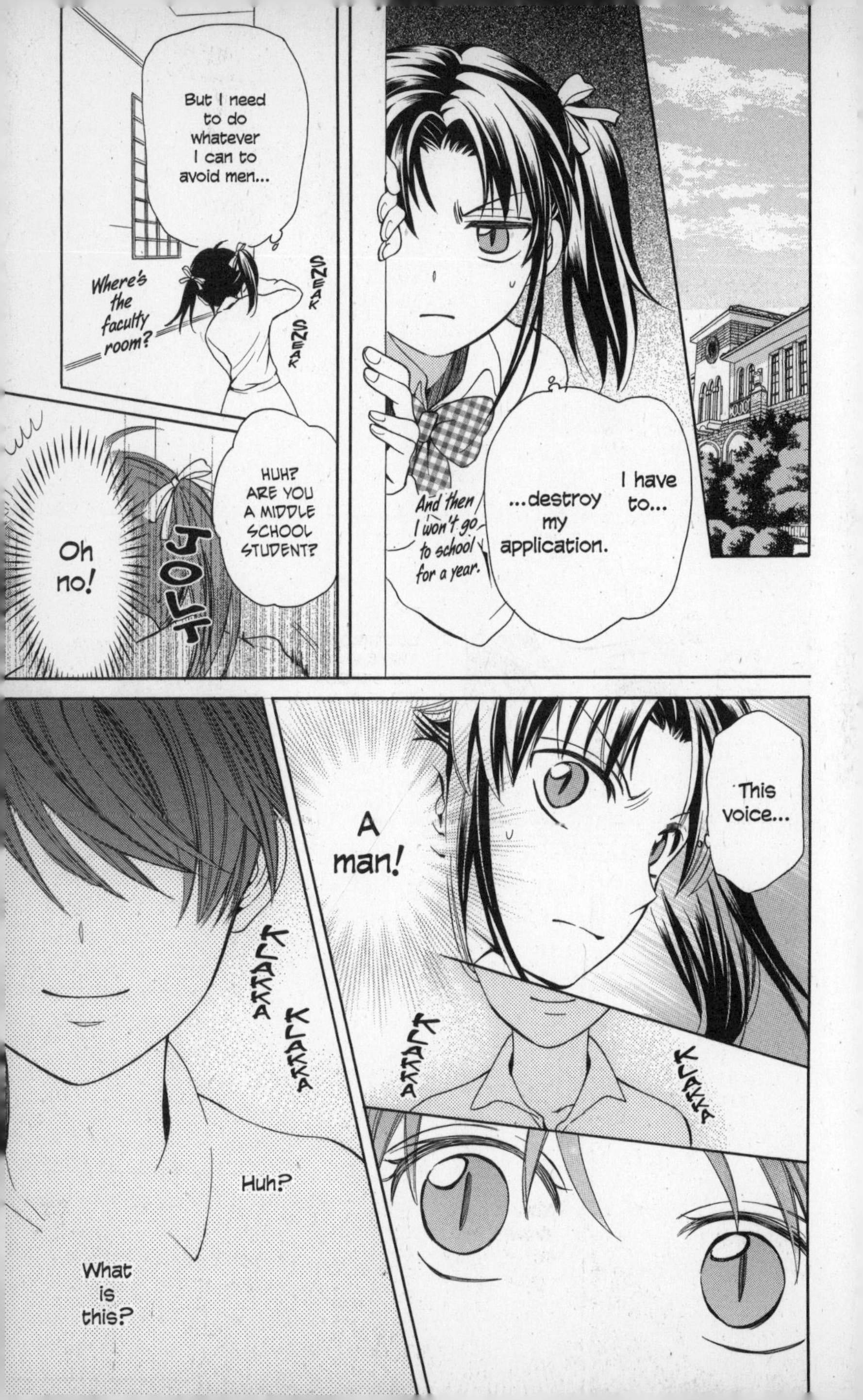
I have to...
...destroy my application.
And then I won't go to school for a year.
But I need to do whatever I can to avoid men...
SNEAK SNEAK
Where's the faculty room?
HUH? ARE YOU A MIDDLE SCHOOL STUDENT?
JOLT
Oh no!
This voice...
KLAKKA
A man!
KLAKKA
KLAKKA
KLAKKA
Huh?
What is this?

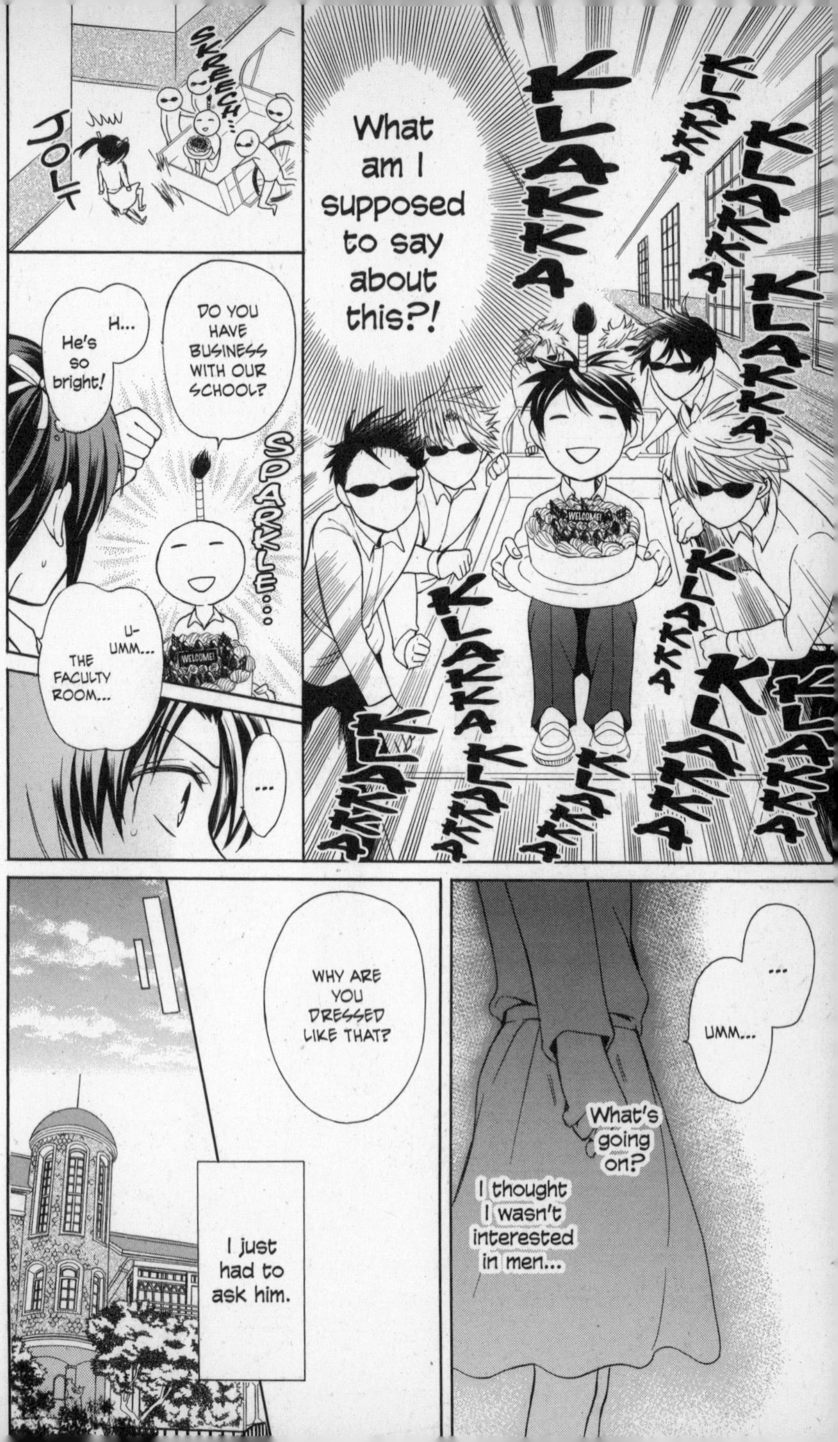
KLAKKA KLAKKA KLAKKA KLAKKA
What am I supposed to say about this?!
KLAKKA KLAKKA KLAKKA KLAKKA KLAKKA KLAKKA
WELCOME!
SKREECH...
JOLT
DO YOU HAVE BUSINESS WITH OUR SCHOOL?
H... He's so bright!
SPARKLE...
WELCOME!
U-UMM... THE FACULTY ROOM...
...
...
UMM...
What's going on?
I thought I wasn't interested in men...
WHY ARE YOU DRESSED LIKE THAT?
I just had to ask him.

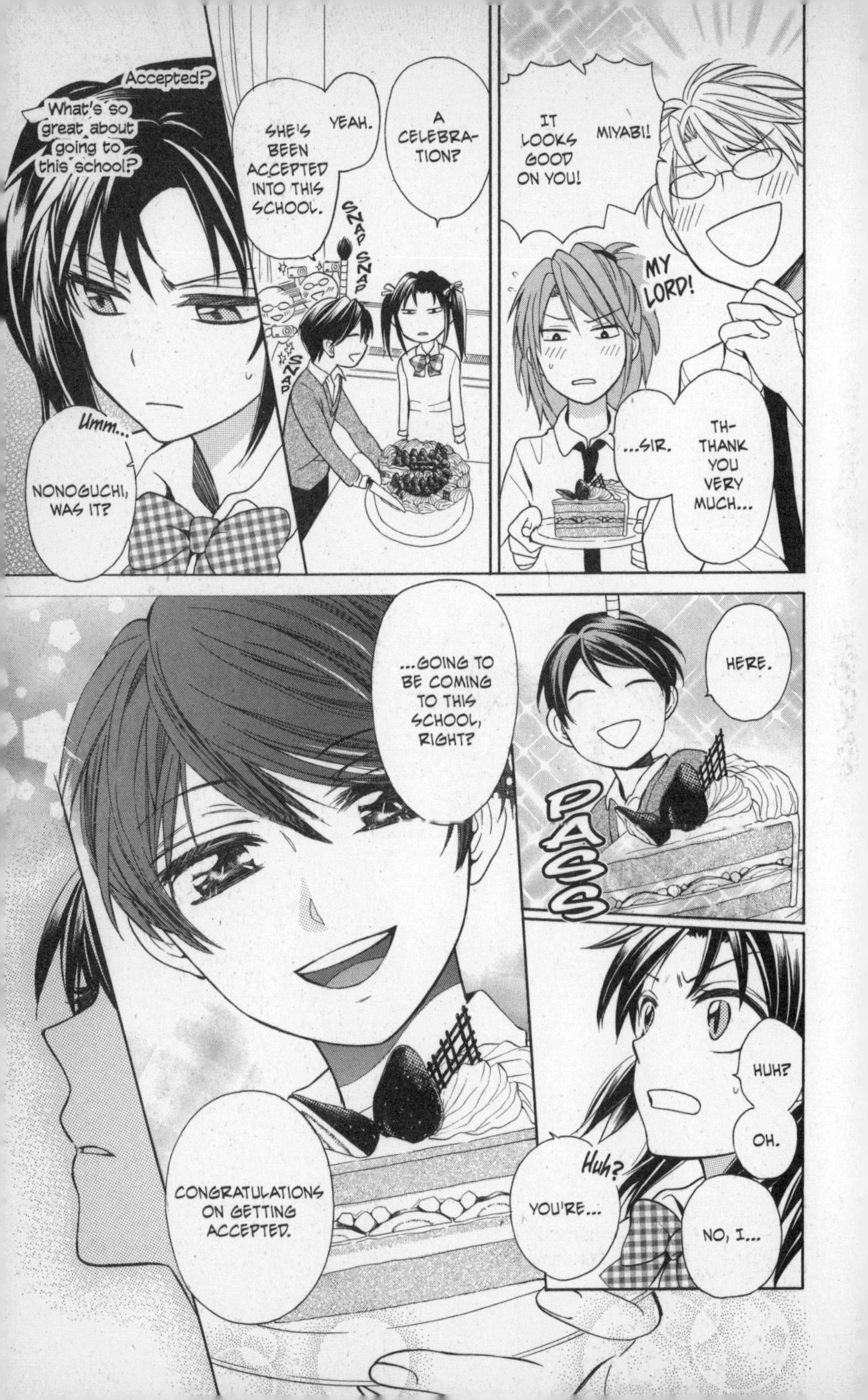
MIYABI!
IT LOOKS GOOD ON YOU!
MY LORD!
TH-THANK YOU VERY MUCH...
...SIR.
A CELEBRATION?
YEAH.
SHE'S BEEN ACCEPTED INTO THIS SCHOOL.
SNAP SNAP
SNAP
Accepted?
What's so great about going to this school?
Umm...
NONOGUCHI, WAS IT?
HERE.
PASS
HUH?
OH.
NO, I...
Huh?
YOU'RE...
...GOING TO BE COMING TO THIS SCHOOL, RIGHT?
CONGRATULATIONS ON GETTING ACCEPTED.

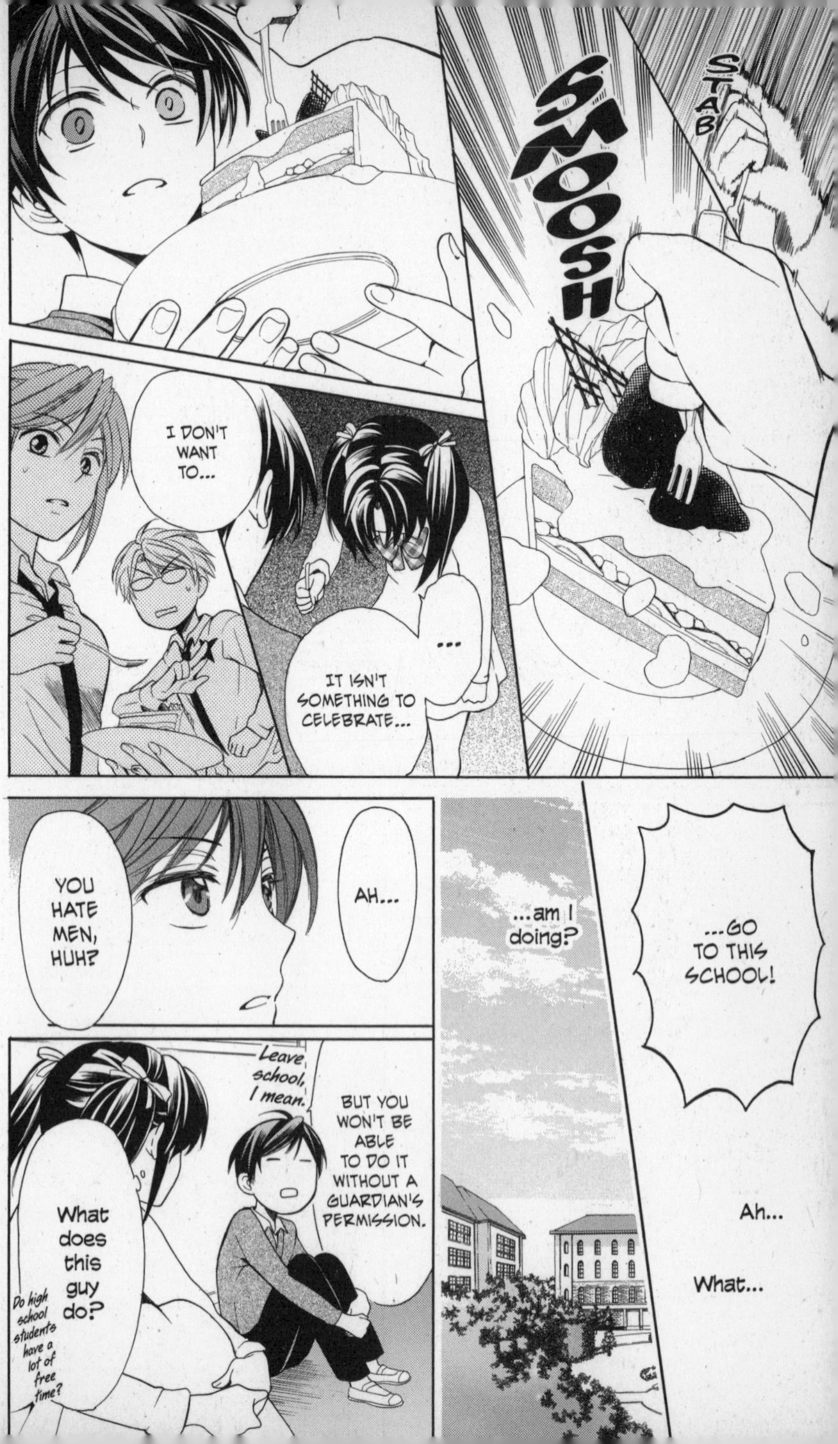
STAB
SMOOSH
I DON'T WANT TO...
...
IT ISN'T SOMETHING TO CELEBRATE...
...GO TO THIS SCHOOL!
Ah...
What...
...am I doing?
AH...
YOU HATE MEN, HUH?
BUT YOU WON'T BE ABLE TO DO IT WITHOUT A GUARDIAN'S PERMISSION.
Leave school, I mean.
What does this guy do?
Do high school students have a lot of free time?

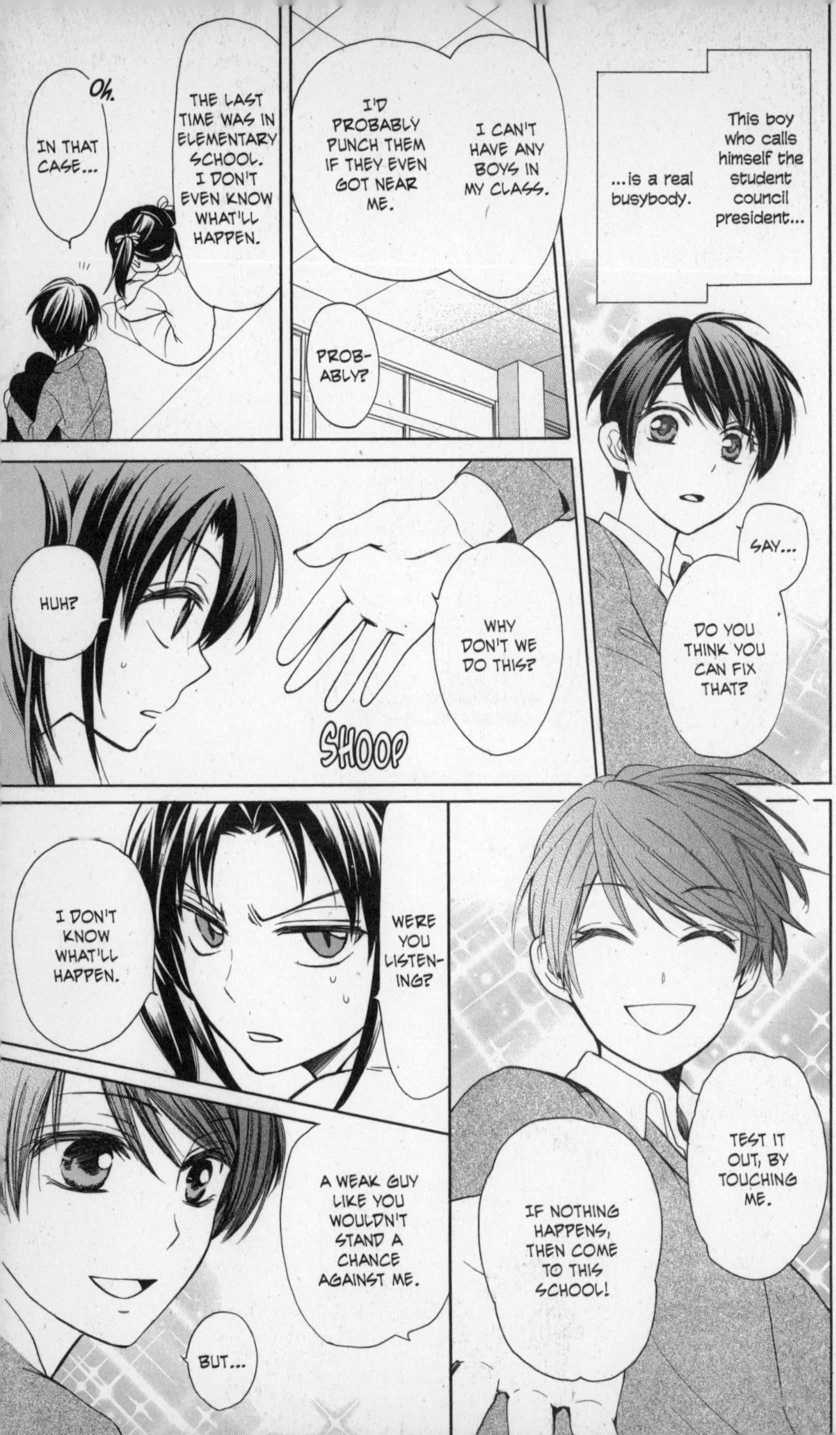
This boy who calls himself the student council president...
...is a real busybody.
SAY...
DO YOU THINK YOU CAN FIX THAT?
I CAN'T HAVE ANY BOYS IN MY CLASS.
I'D PROBABLY PUNCH THEM IF THEY EVEN GOT NEAR ME.
PROBABLY?
THE LAST TIME WAS IN ELEMENTARY SCHOOL. I DON'T EVEN KNOW WHAT'LL HAPPEN.
Oh.
IN THAT CASE...
WHY DON'T WE DO THIS?
SHOOP
HUH?
TEST IT OUT, BY TOUCHING ME.
IF NOTHING HAPPENS, THEN COME TO THIS SCHOOL!
WERE YOU LISTENING?
I DON'T KNOW WHAT'LL HAPPEN.
A WEAK GUY LIKE YOU WOULDN'T STAND A CHANCE AGAINST ME.
BUT...

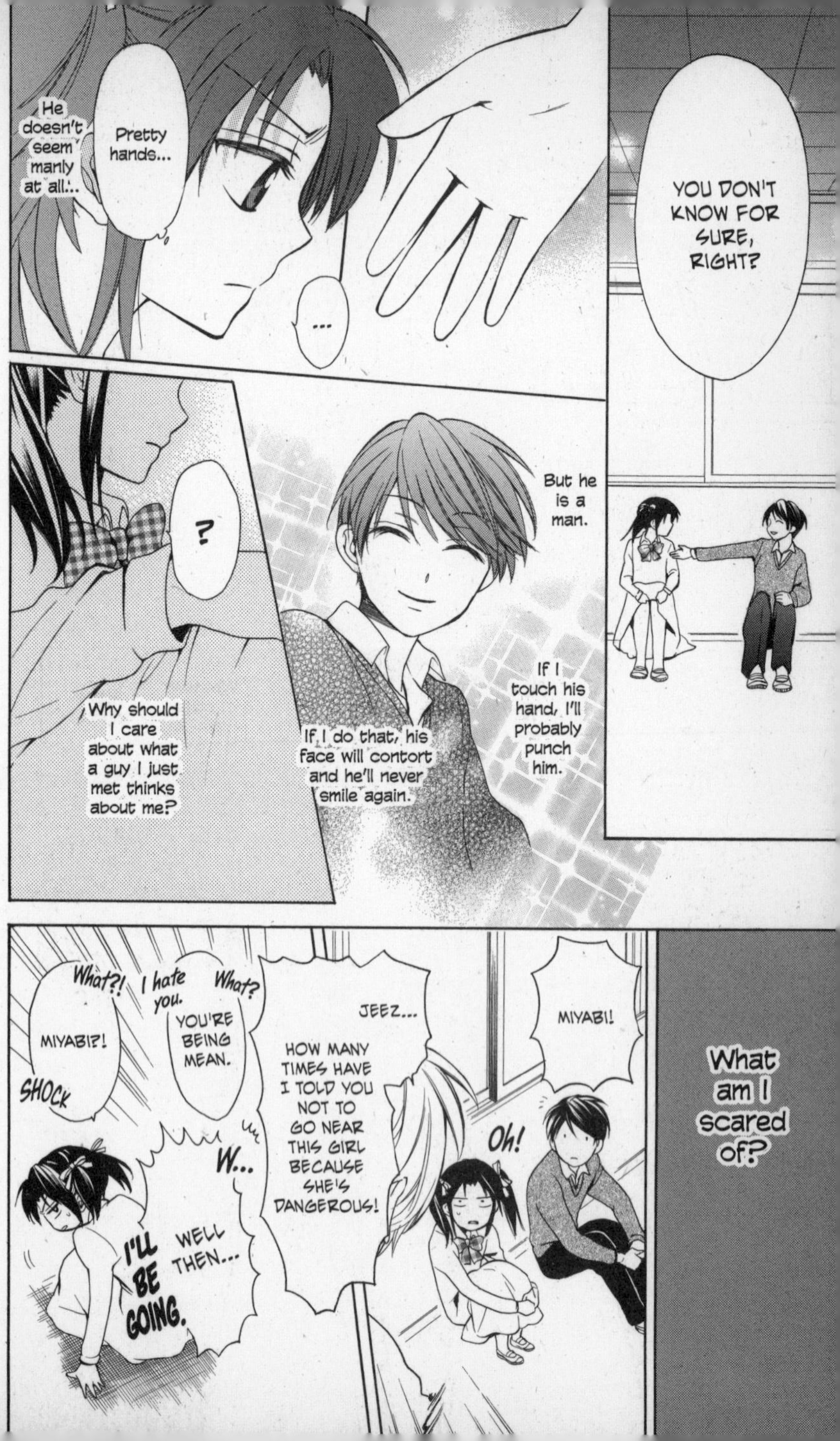
YOU DON'T KNOW FOR SURE, RIGHT?
Pretty hands...
He doesn't seem manly at all...
...
But he is a man.
If I touch his hand, I'll probably punch him.
?
If I do that, his face will contort and he'll never smile again.
Why should I care about what a guy I just met thinks about me?
What am I scared of?
MIYABI!
Oh!
JEEZ...
HOW MANY TIMES HAVE I TOLD YOU NOT TO GO NEAR THIS GIRL BECAUSE SHE'S DANGEROUS!
What?
YOU'RE BEING MEAN.
I hate you.
What?!
MIYABI?!
SHOCK
W...
WELL THEN...
I'LL BE GOING.

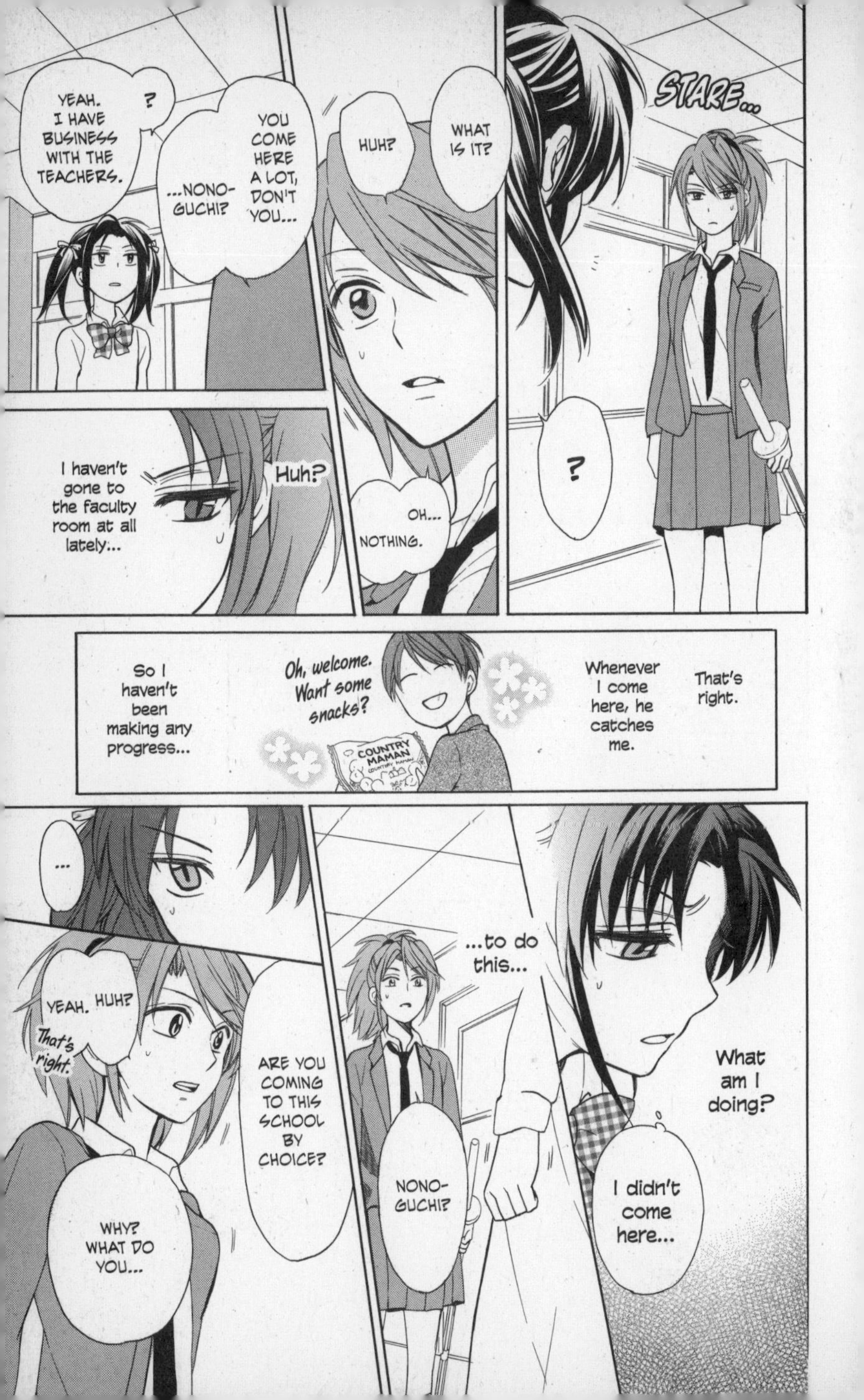
STARE...
?
WHAT IS IT?
HUH?
OH... NOTHING.
YOU COME HERE A LOT, DON'T YOU...
...NONOGUCHI?
?
YEAH. I HAVE BUSINESS WITH THE TEACHERS.
Huh?
I haven't gone to the faculty room at all lately...
That's right.
Whenever I come here, he catches me.
Oh, welcome. Want some snacks?
COUNTRY MAMAN
So I haven't been making any progress...
What am I doing?
I didn't come here...
...to do this...
NONOGUCHI?
...
ARE YOU COMING TO THIS SCHOOL BY CHOICE?
HUH?
YEAH.
That's right.
WHY? WHAT DO YOU...

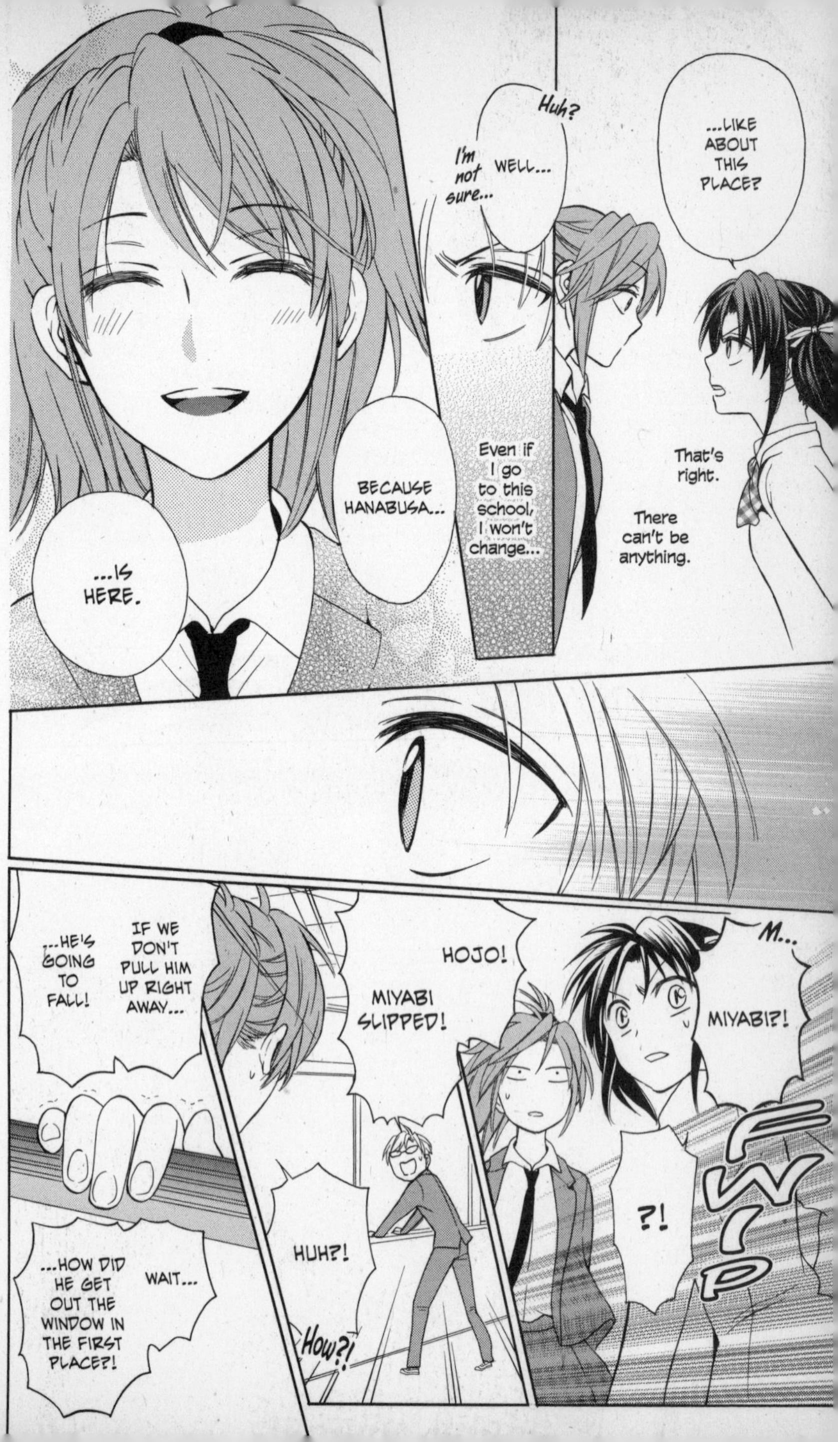
...LIKE ABOUT THIS PLACE?
That's right.
There can't be anything.
Huh?
WELL...
I'm not sure...
Even if I go to this school, I won't change...
BECAUSE HANABUSA...
...IS HERE.
M...
MIYABI?!
FWIP
?!
HOJO!
MIYABI SLIPPED!
HUH?!
How?!
IF WE DON'T PULL HIM UP RIGHT AWAY...
...HE'S GOING TO FALL!
WAIT...
...HOW DID HE GET OUT THE WINDOW IN THE FIRST PLACE?!

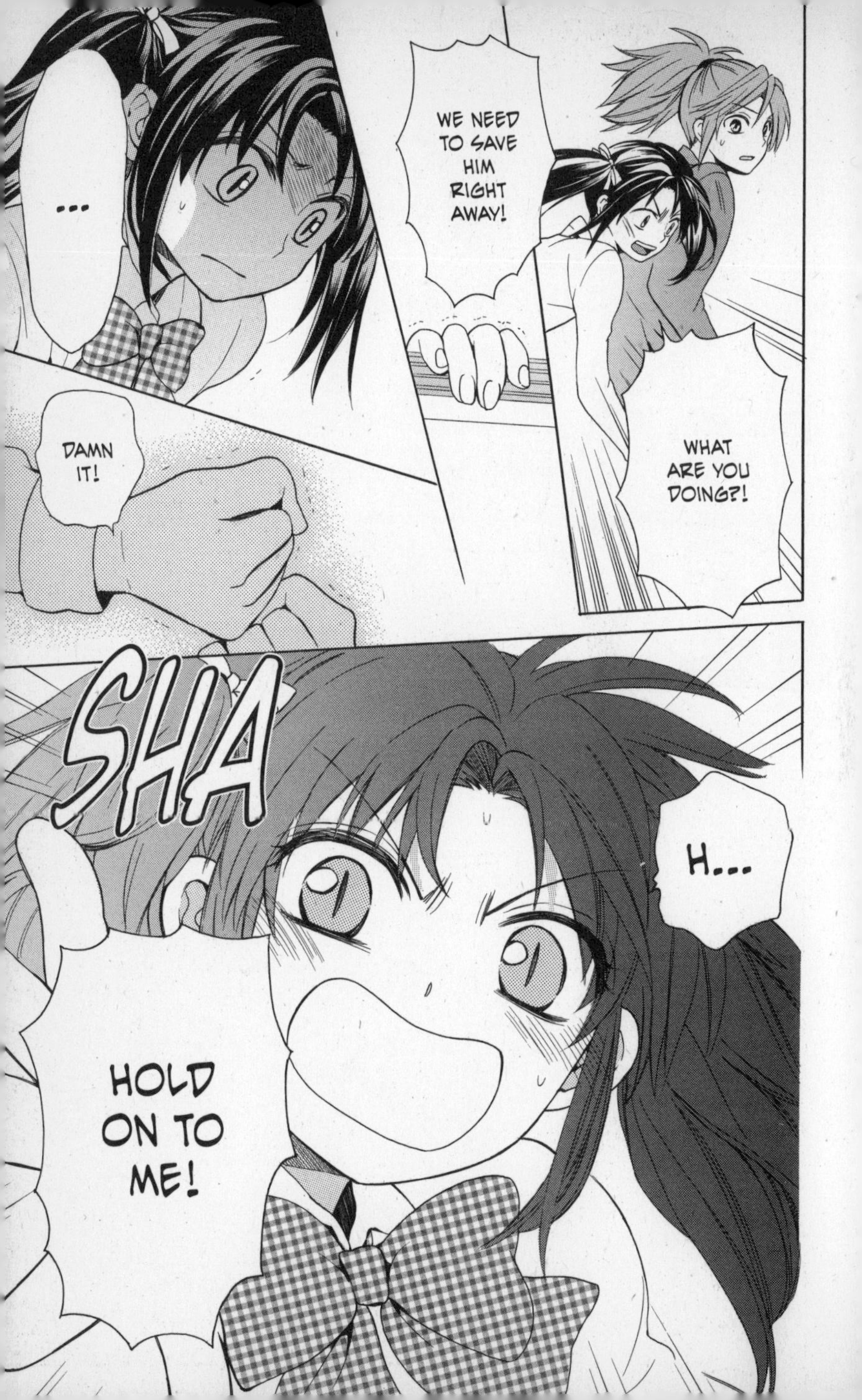
WHAT ARE YOU DOING?!
WE NEED TO SAVE HIM RIGHT AWAY!
...
DAMN IT!
SHA
H...
HOLD ON TO ME!

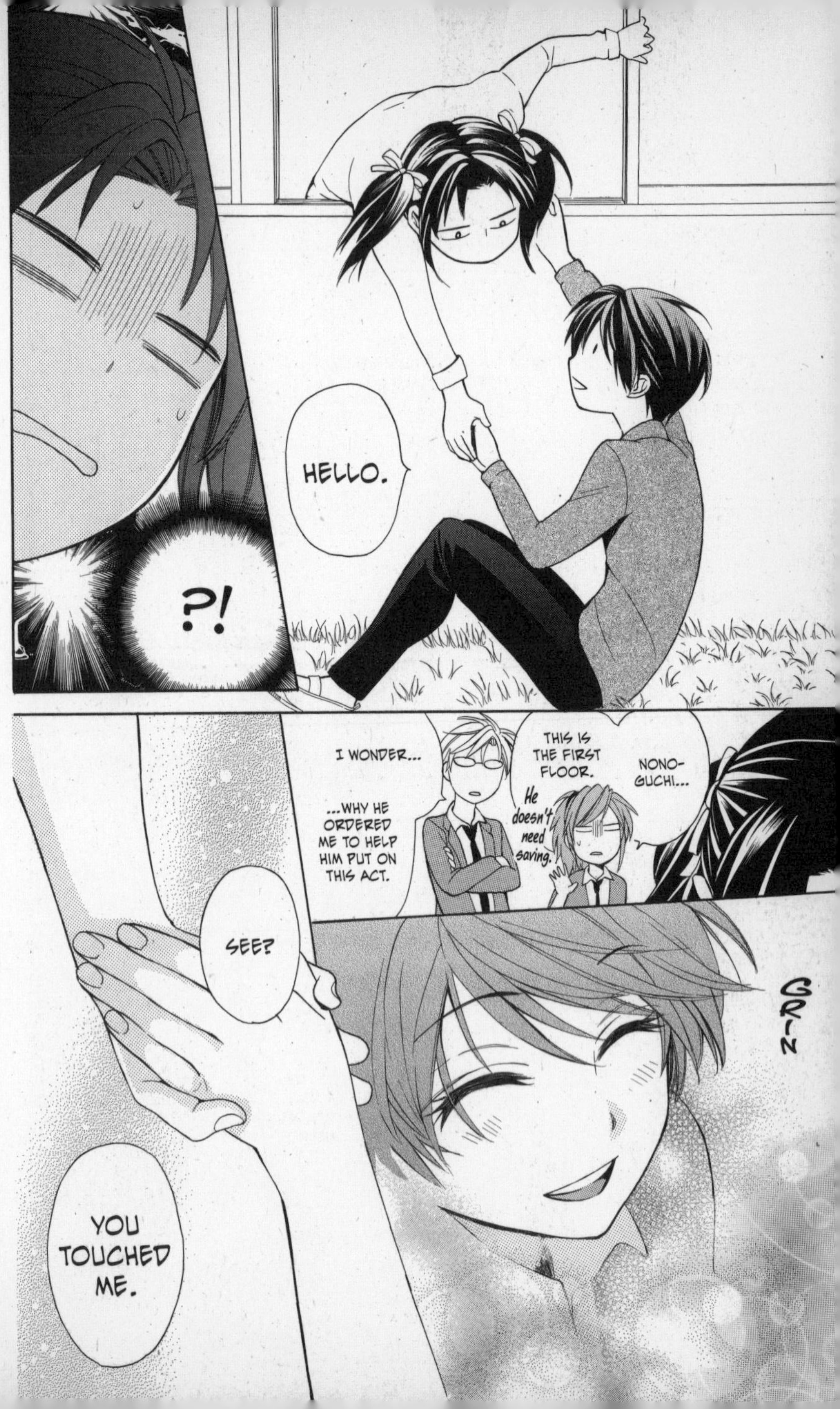
HELLO.
?!
NONO-GUCHI...
THIS IS THE FIRST FLOOR.
He doesn't need saving.
I WONDER...
...WHY HE ORDERED ME TO HELP HIM PUT ON THIS ACT.
GRIN
SEE?
YOU TOUCHED ME.

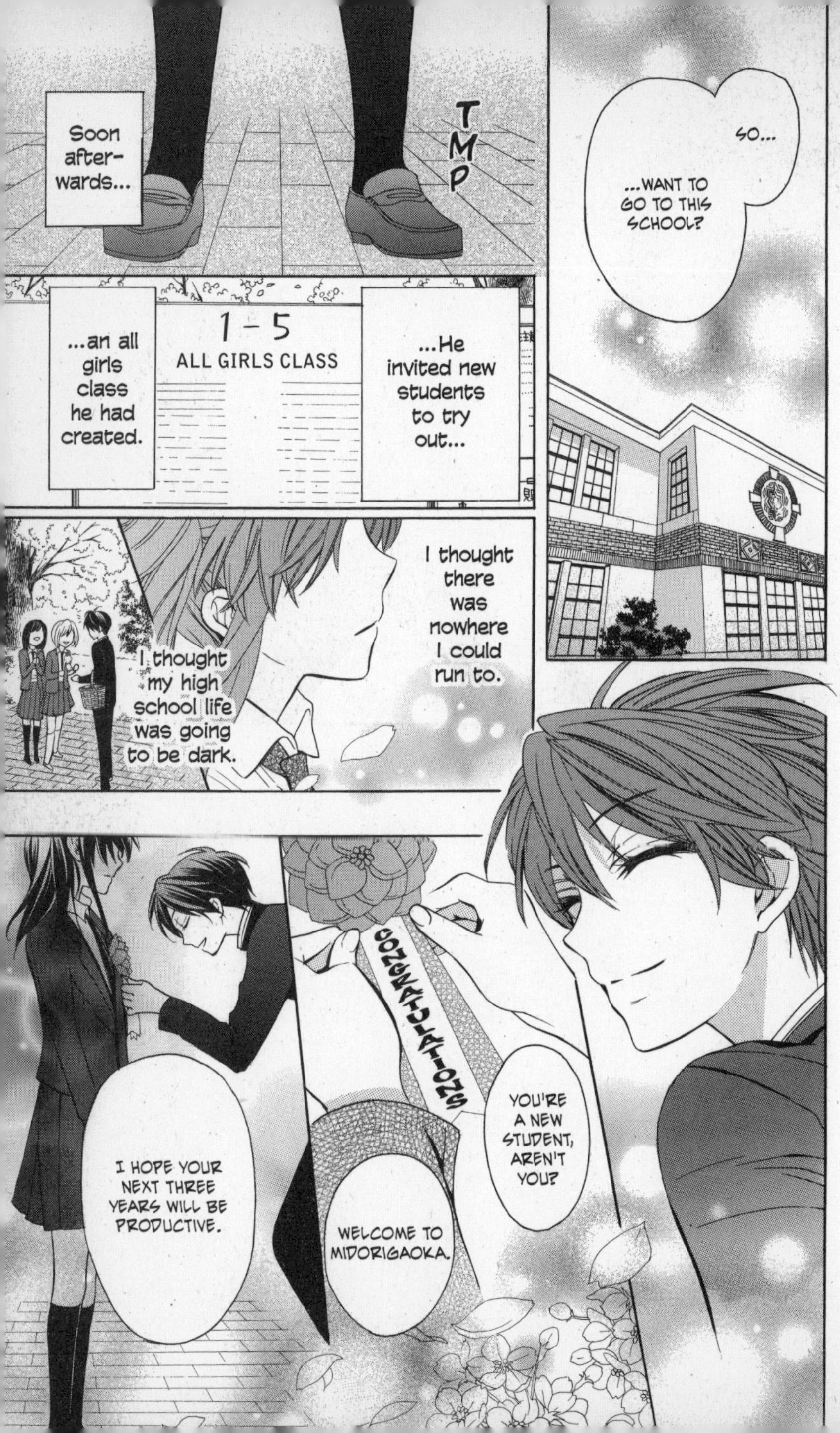
SO...
...WANT TO GO TO THIS SCHOOL?
Soon afterwards...
TMP
...He invited new students to try out...
1-5
ALL GIRLS CLASS
...an all girls class he had created.
I thought there was nowhere I could run to.
I thought my high school life was going to be dark.
CONGRATULATIONS
YOU'RE A NEW STUDENT, AREN'T YOU?
WELCOME TO MIDORIGAOKA.
I HOPE YOUR NEXT THREE YEARS WILL BE PRODUCTIVE.

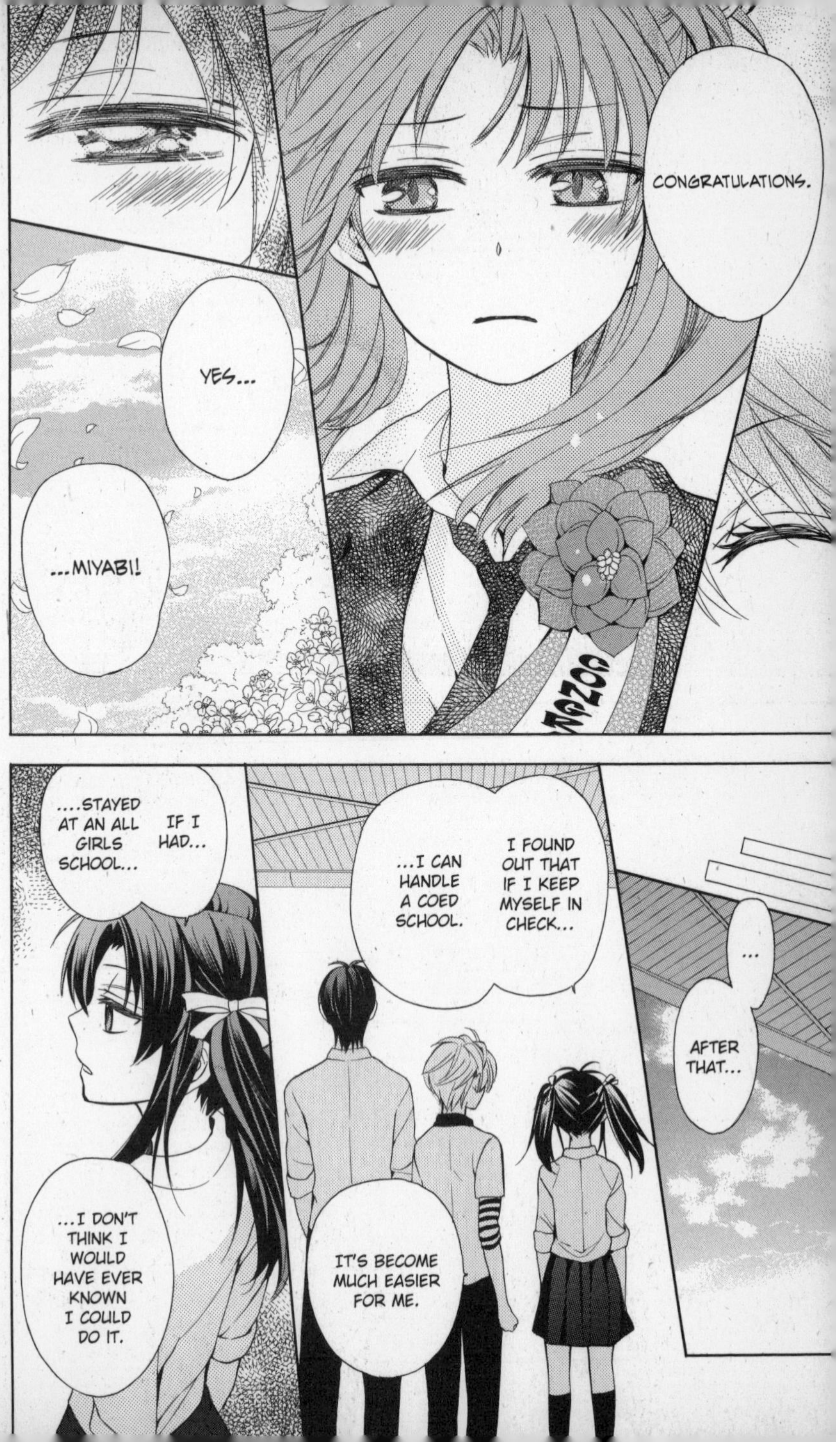
CONGRATULATIONS.
YES...
...MIYABI!
...
AFTER THAT...
I FOUND OUT THAT IF I KEEP MYSELF IN CHECK...
...I CAN HANDLE A COED SCHOOL.
IT'S BECOME MUCH EASIER FOR ME.
IF I HAD...
....STAYED AT AN ALL GIRLS SCHOOL...
...I DON'T THINK I WOULD HAVE EVER KNOWN I COULD DO IT.

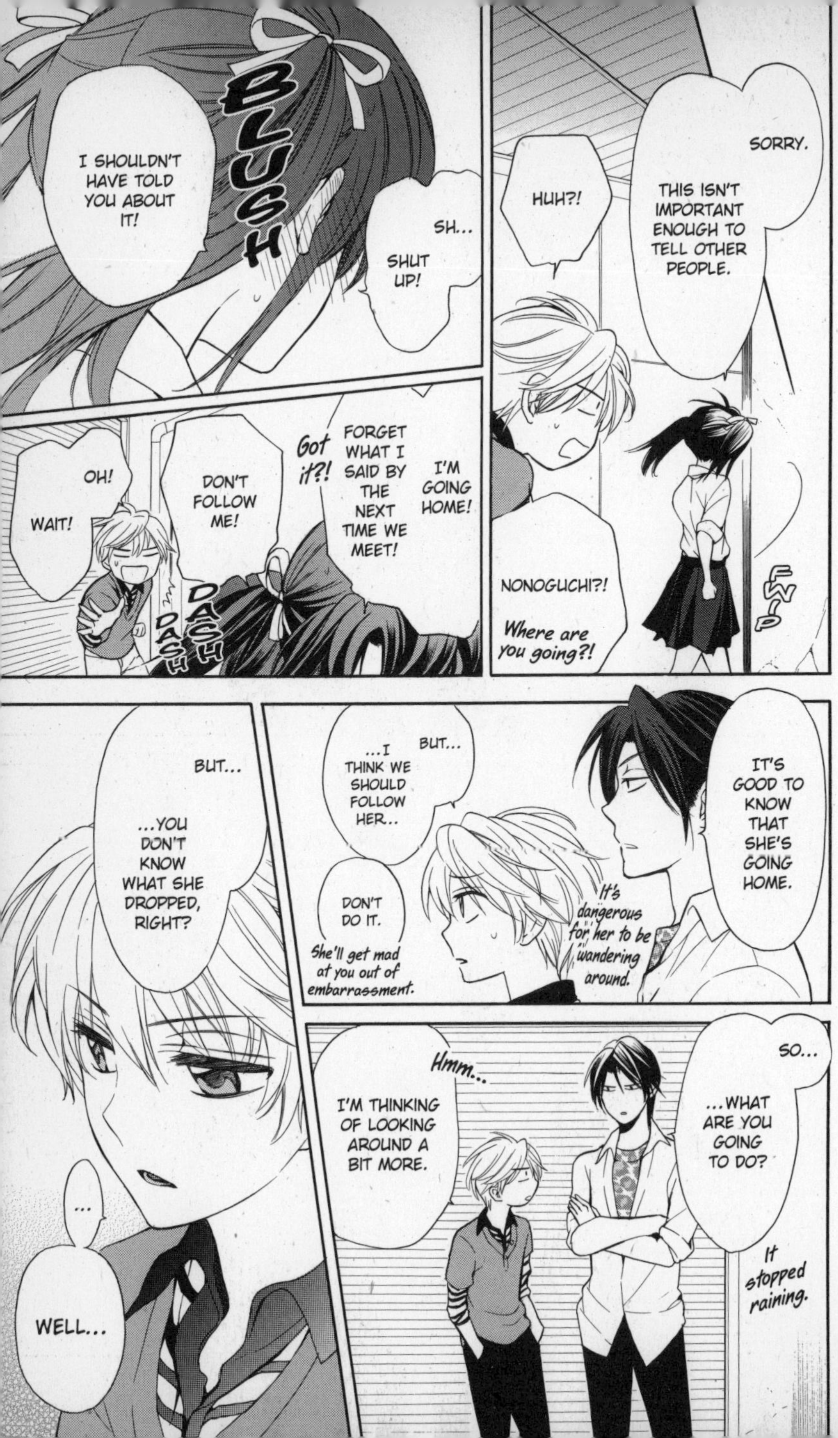
SORRY.
THIS ISN'T IMPORTANT ENOUGH TO TELL OTHER PEOPLE.
HUH?!
NONOGUCHI?!
Where are you going?!
FWIP
BLUSH
SH... SHUT UP!
I SHOULDN'T HAVE TOLD YOU ABOUT IT!
I'M GOING HOME!
FORGET WHAT I SAID BY THE NEXT TIME WE MEET!
Got it?!
DASH DASH
DON'T FOLLOW ME!
OH! WAIT!
IT'S GOOD TO KNOW THAT SHE'S GOING HOME.
It's dangerous for her to be wandering around.
BUT... ...I THINK WE SHOULD FOLLOW HER...
DON'T DO IT.
She'll get mad at you out of embarrassment.
SO... ...WHAT ARE YOU GOING TO DO?
It stopped raining.
Hmm...
I'M THINKING OF LOOKING AROUND A BIT MORE.
BUT... ...YOU DON'T KNOW WHAT SHE DROPPED, RIGHT?
...
WELL...

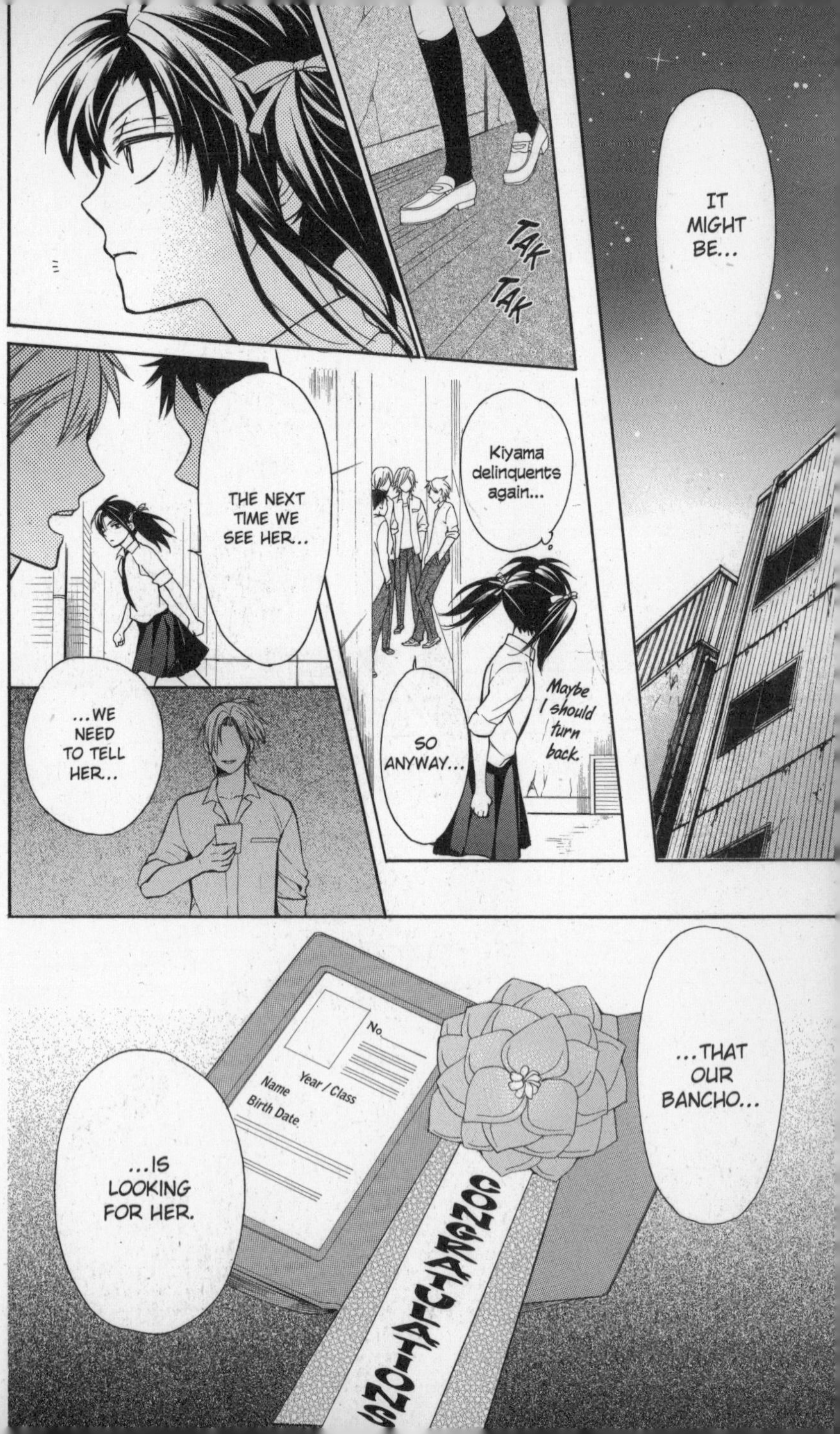
IT MIGHT BE...
TAK TAK
Kiyama delinquents again...
Maybe I should turn back.
SO ANYWAY...
THE NEXT TIME WE SEE HER...
...WE NEED TO TELL HER...
...THAT OUR BANCHO...
No.
Year / Class
Name
Birth Date
CONGRATULATIONS
...IS LOOKING FOR HER.

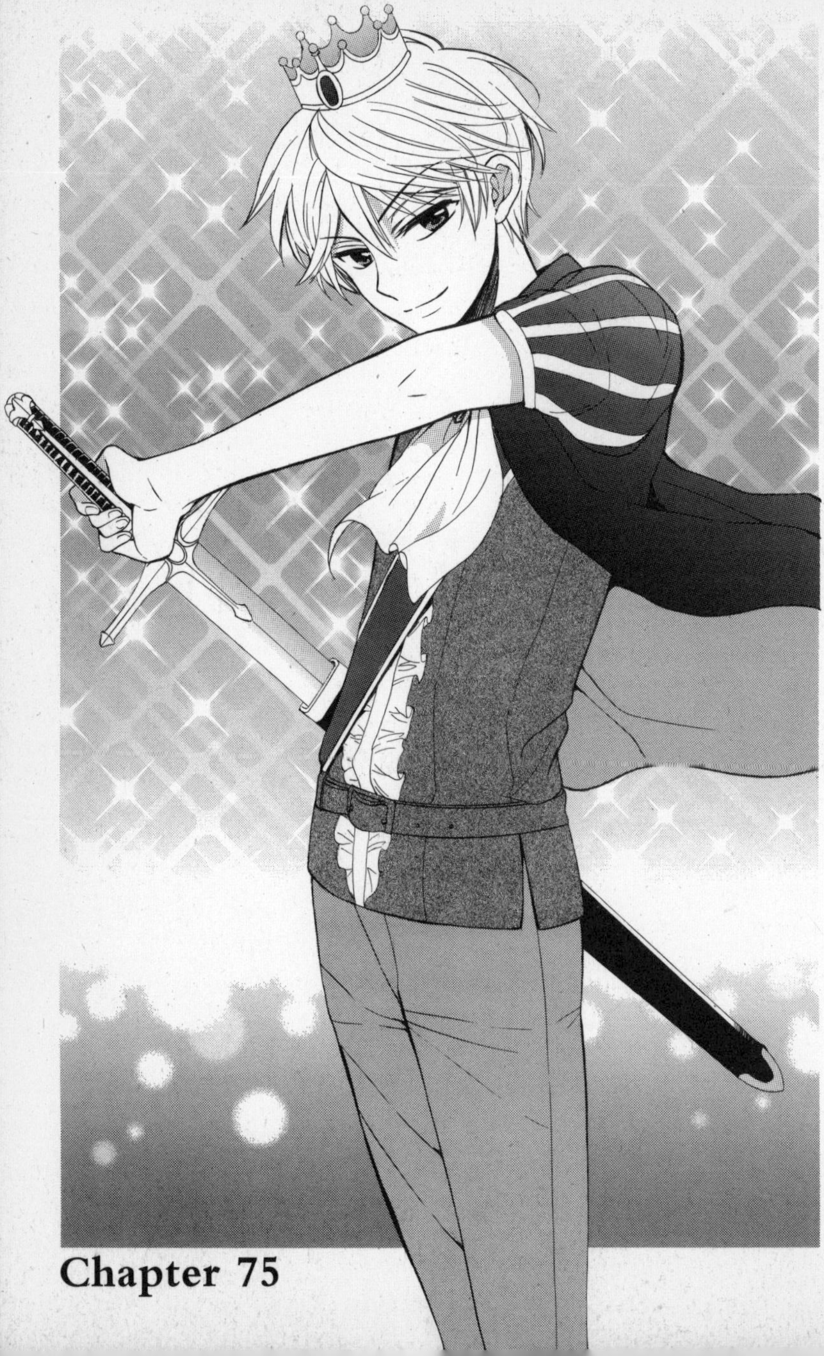

Chapter 75

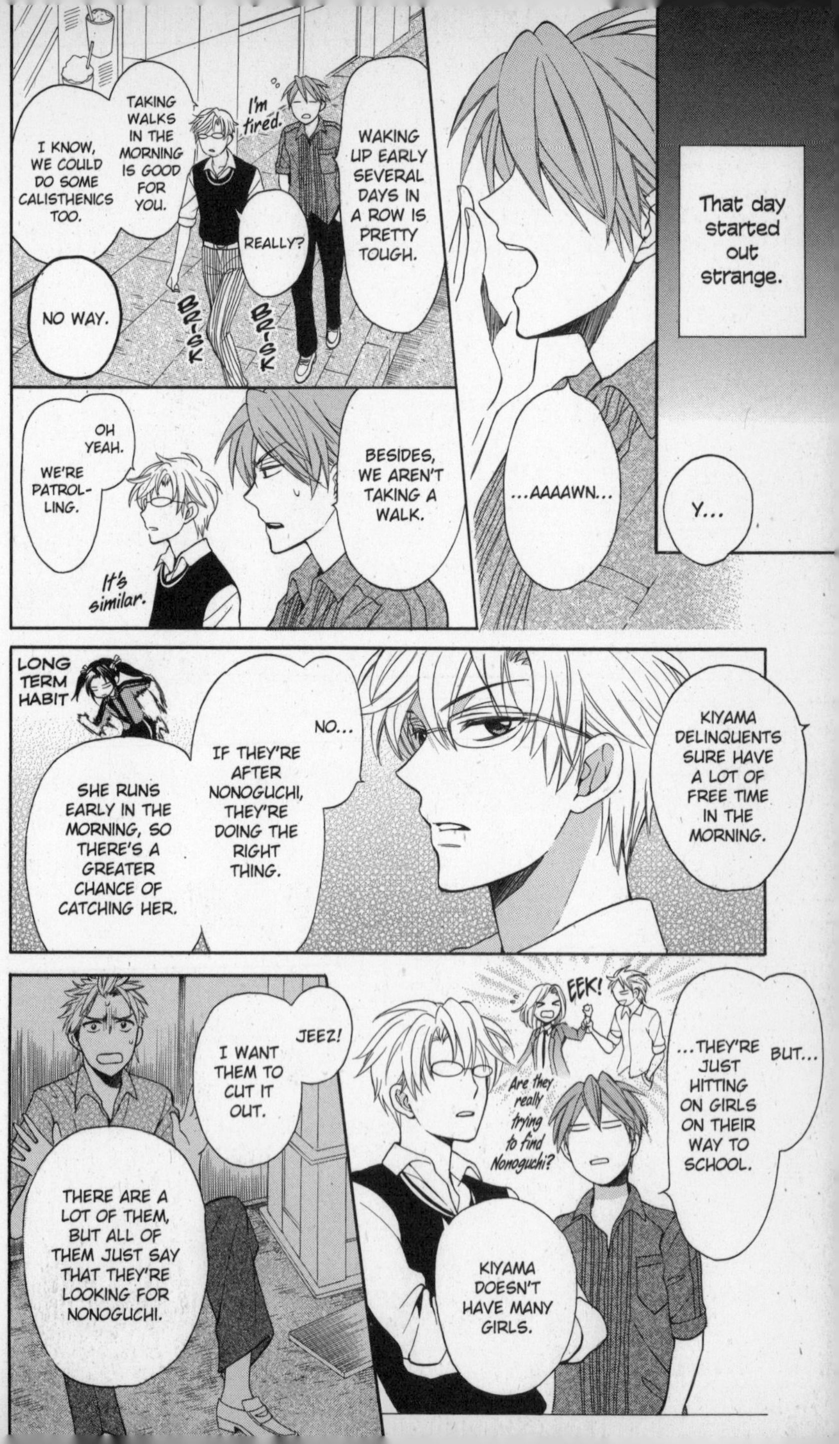
That day started out strange.
Y...
...AAAAWN...
WAKING UP EARLY SEVERAL DAYS IN A ROW IS PRETTY TOUGH.
I'm tired.
REALLY?
TAKING WALKS IN THE MORNING IS GOOD FOR YOU.
I KNOW, WE COULD DO SOME CALISTHENICS TOO.
NO WAY.
BRISK
BRISK
BESIDES, WE AREN'T TAKING A WALK.
OH YEAH. WE'RE PATROL-LING.
It's similar.
KIYAMA DELINQUENTS SURE HAVE A LOT OF FREE TIME IN THE MORNING.
NO...
IF THEY'RE AFTER NONOGUCHI, THEY'RE DOING THE RIGHT THING.
SHE RUNS EARLY IN THE MORNING, SO THERE'S A GREATER CHANCE OF CATCHING HER.
LONG TERM HABIT
BUT...
...THEY'RE JUST HITTING ON GIRLS ON THEIR WAY TO SCHOOL.
EEK!
Are they really trying to find Nonoguchi?
KIYAMA DOESN'T HAVE MANY GIRLS.
JEEZ!
I WANT THEM TO CUT IT OUT.
THERE ARE A LOT OF THEM, BUT ALL OF THEM JUST SAY THAT THEY'RE LOOKING FOR NONOGUCHI.

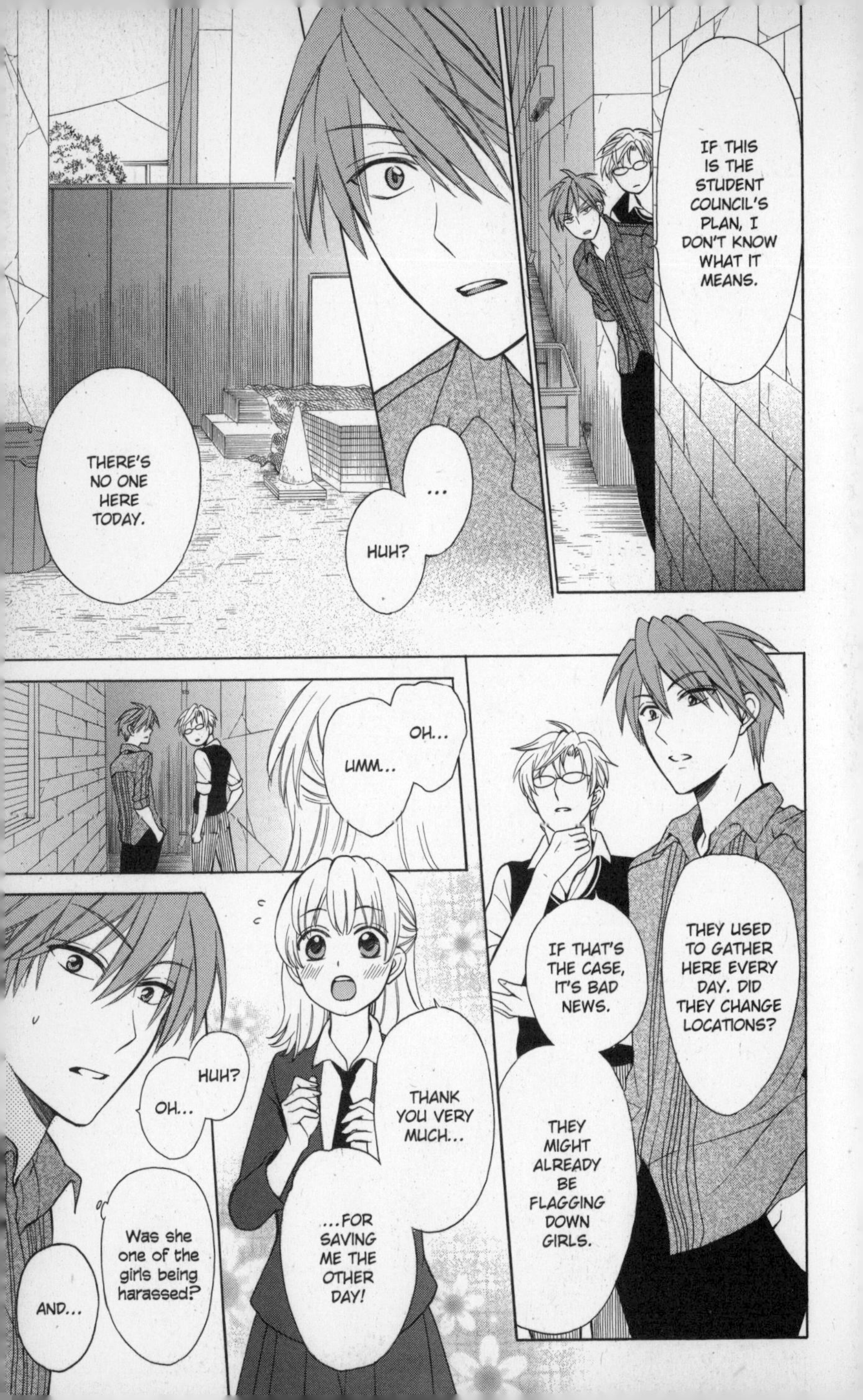
IF THIS IS THE STUDENT COUNCIL'S PLAN, I DON'T KNOW WHAT IT MEANS.
...
HUH?
THERE'S NO ONE HERE TODAY.
THEY USED TO GATHER HERE EVERY DAY. DID THEY CHANGE LOCATIONS?
IF THAT'S THE CASE, IT'S BAD NEWS.
THEY MIGHT ALREADY BE FLAGGING DOWN GIRLS.
OH...
UMM...
THANK YOU VERY MUCH...
...FOR SAVING ME THE OTHER DAY!
HUH?
OH...
Was she one of the girls being harassed?
AND...

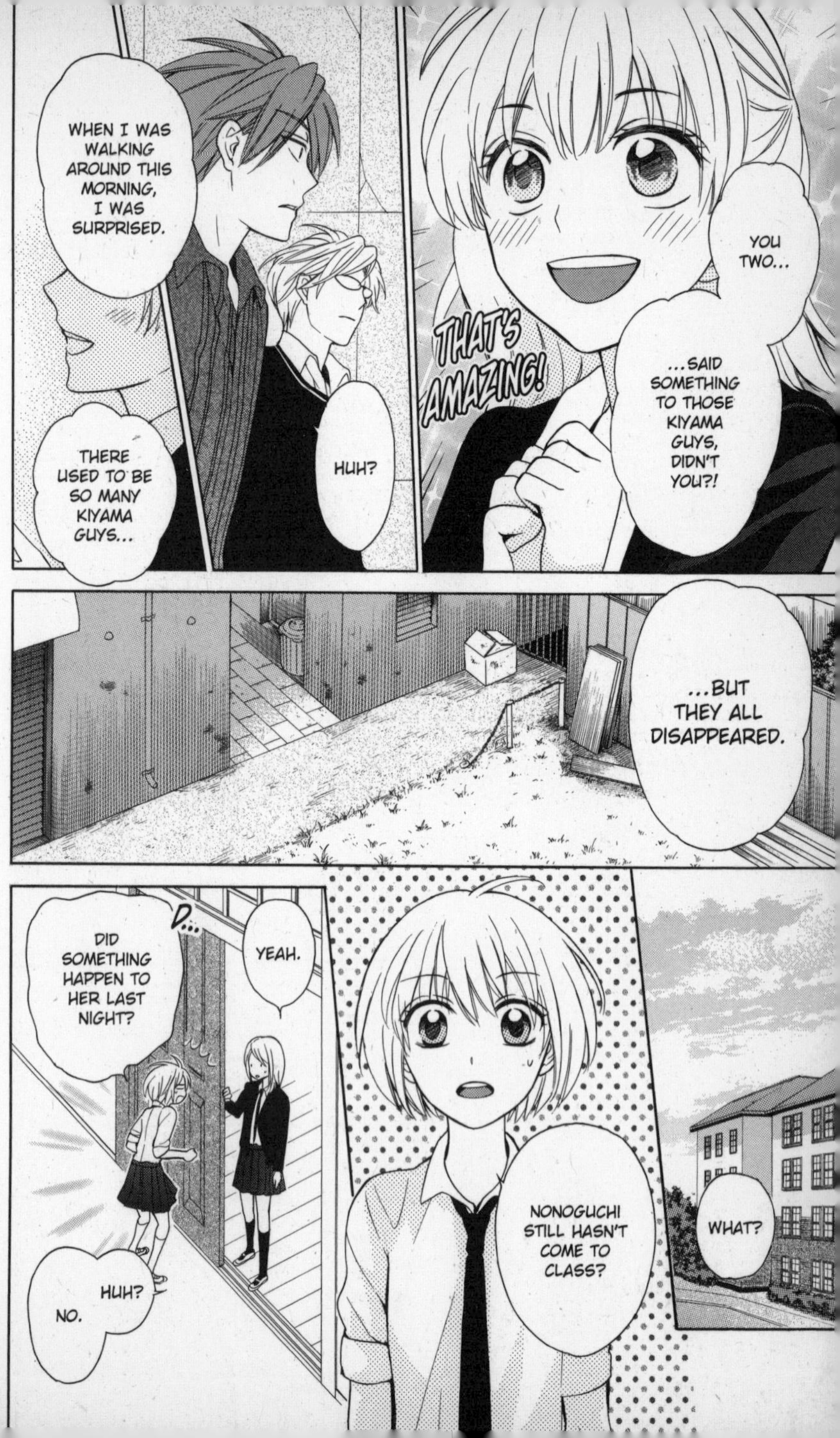
YOU TWO...
...SAID SOMETHING TO THOSE KIYAMA GUYS, DIDN'T YOU?!
THAT'S AMAZING!
HUH?
WHEN I WAS WALKING AROUND THIS MORNING, I WAS SURPRISED.
THERE USED TO BE SO MANY KIYAMA GUYS...
...BUT THEY ALL DISAPPEARED.
WHAT?
NONOGUCHI STILL HASN'T COME TO CLASS?
YEAH.
D...
DID SOMETHING HAPPEN TO HER LAST NIGHT?
HUH?
NO.

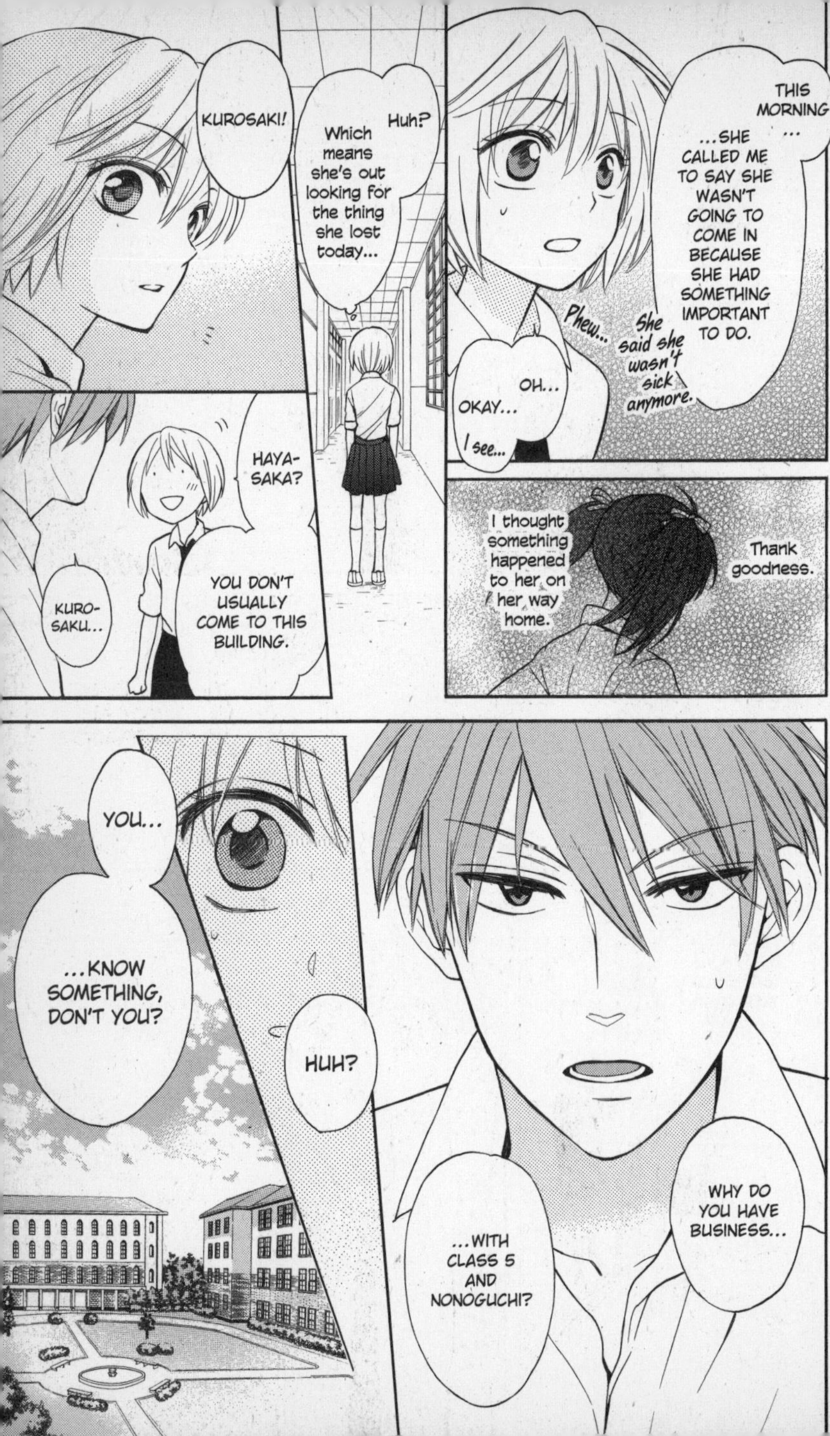
THIS MORNING ...
...SHE CALLED ME TO SAY SHE WASN'T GOING TO COME IN BECAUSE SHE HAD SOMETHING IMPORTANT TO DO.
She said she wasn't sick anymore.
Phew...
OH... OKAY...
I see...
Thank goodness.
I thought something happened to her on her way home.
Huh?
Which means she's out looking for the thing she lost today...
KUROSAKI!
HAYA-SAKA?
YOU DON'T USUALLY COME TO THIS BUILDING.
KURO-SAKU...
WHY DO YOU HAVE BUSINESS...
...WITH CLASS 5 AND NONOGUCHI?
HUH?
YOU...
...KNOW SOMETHING, DON'T YOU?

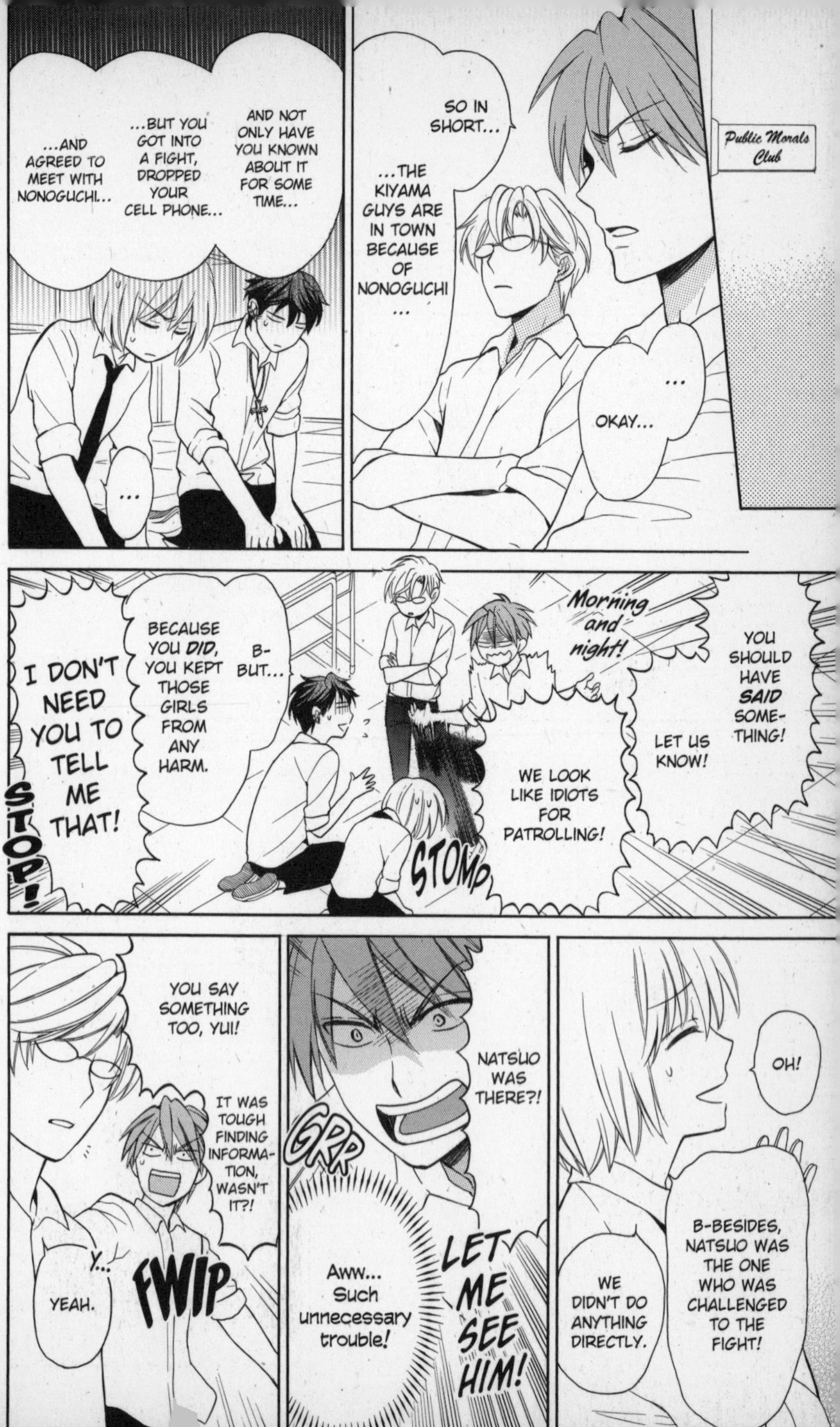
Public Morals Club
SO IN SHORT...
...THE KIYAMA GUYS ARE IN TOWN BECAUSE OF NONOGUCHI...
...
OKAY...
AND NOT ONLY HAVE YOU KNOWN ABOUT IT FOR SOME TIME...
...BUT YOU GOT INTO A FIGHT, DROPPED YOUR CELL PHONE...
...AND AGREED TO MEET WITH NONOGUCHI...
...
YOU SHOULD HAVE SAID SOMETHING!
LET US KNOW!
Morning and night!
WE LOOK LIKE IDIOTS FOR PATROLLING!
STOMP
B-BUT...
BECAUSE YOU DID, YOU KEPT THOSE GIRLS FROM ANY HARM.
I DON'T NEED YOU TO TELL ME THAT!
STOP!
OH!
B-BESIDES, NATSUO WAS THE ONE WHO WAS CHALLENGED TO THE FIGHT!
WE DIDN'T DO ANYTHING DIRECTLY.
NATSUO WAS THERE?!
GRR
LET ME SEE HIM!
Aww... Such unnecessary trouble!
YOU SAY SOMETHING TOO, YUI!
IT WAS TOUGH FINDING INFORMATION, WASN'T IT?!
FWIP
Y... YEAH.

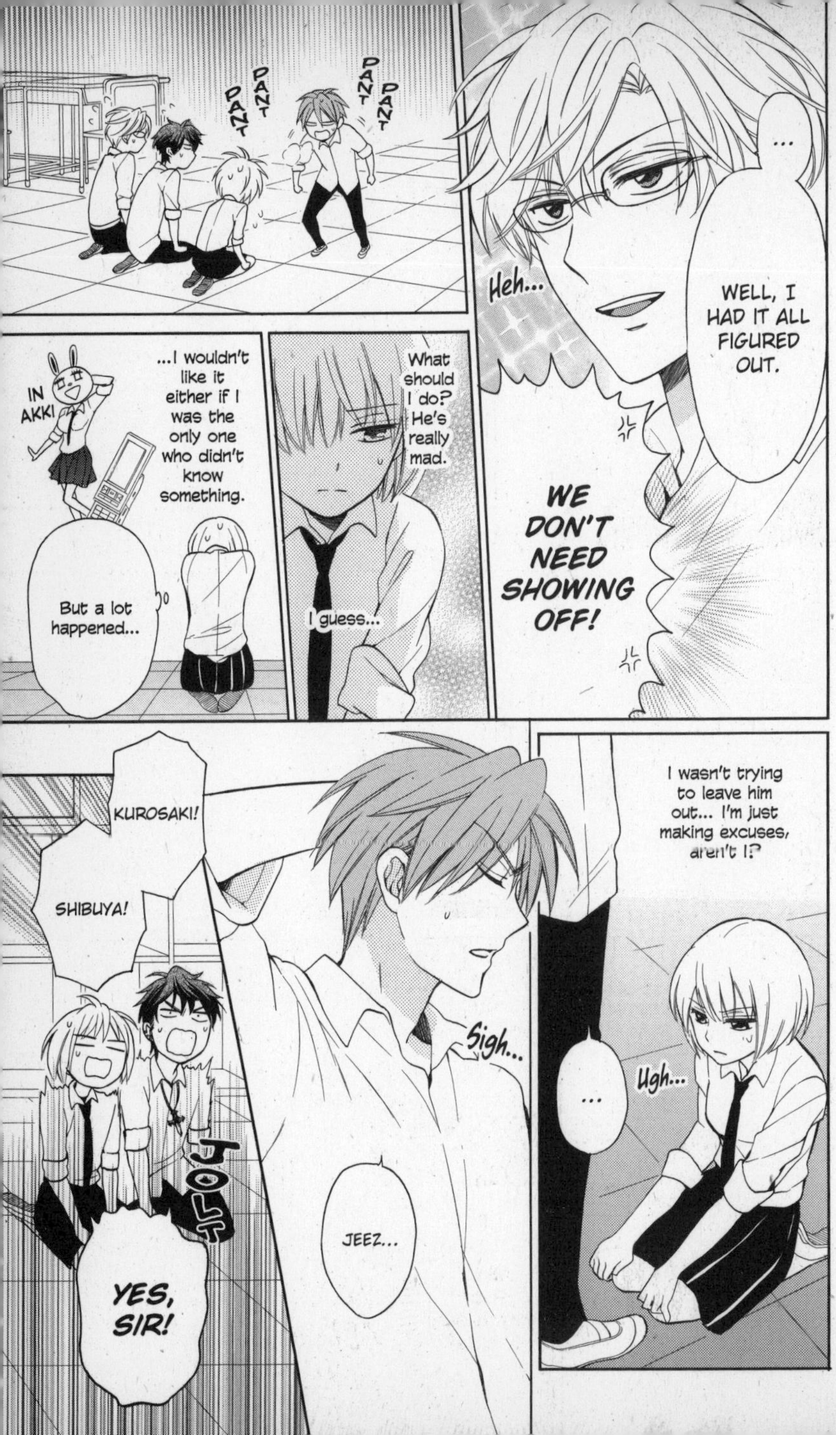
...
Heh...
WELL, I HAD IT ALL FIGURED OUT.
WE DON'T NEED SHOWING OFF!
PANT PANT
PANT PANT
What should I do? He's really mad.
I guess...
...I wouldn't like it either if I was the only one who didn't know something.
IN AKKI
But a lot happened...
I wasn't trying to leave him out... I'm just making excuses, aren't I!?
...
Ugh...
Sigh...
JEEZ...
KUROSAKI!
SHIBUYA!
JOLT
YES, SIR!

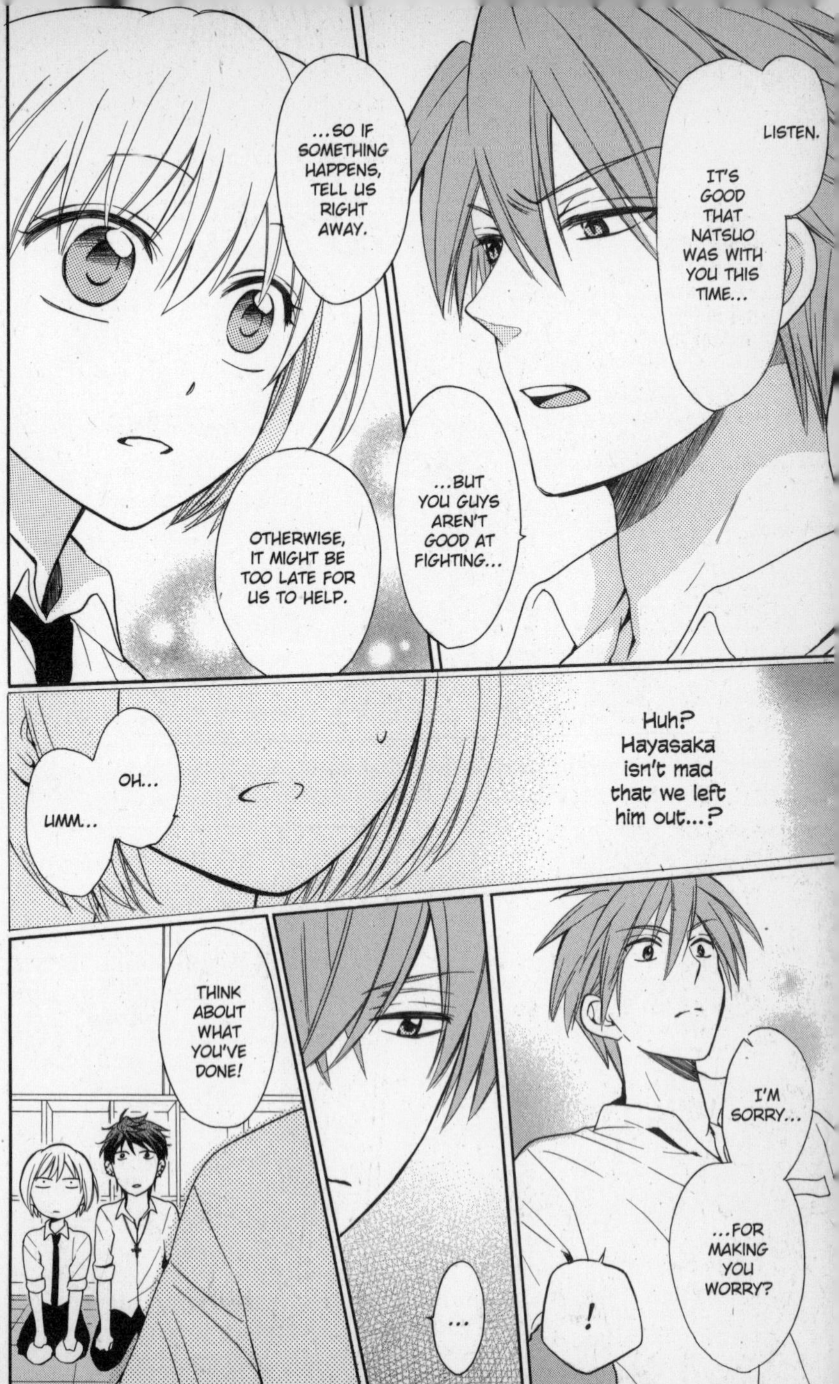
LISTEN.
IT'S GOOD THAT NATSUO WAS WITH YOU THIS TIME...
...BUT YOU GUYS AREN'T GOOD AT FIGHTING...
...SO IF SOMETHING HAPPENS, TELL US RIGHT AWAY.
OTHERWISE, IT MIGHT BE TOO LATE FOR US TO HELP.
Huh? Hayasaka isn't mad that we left him out...?
OH...
UMM...
I'M SORRY...
...FOR MAKING YOU WORRY?
!
...
THINK ABOUT WHAT YOU'VE DONE!

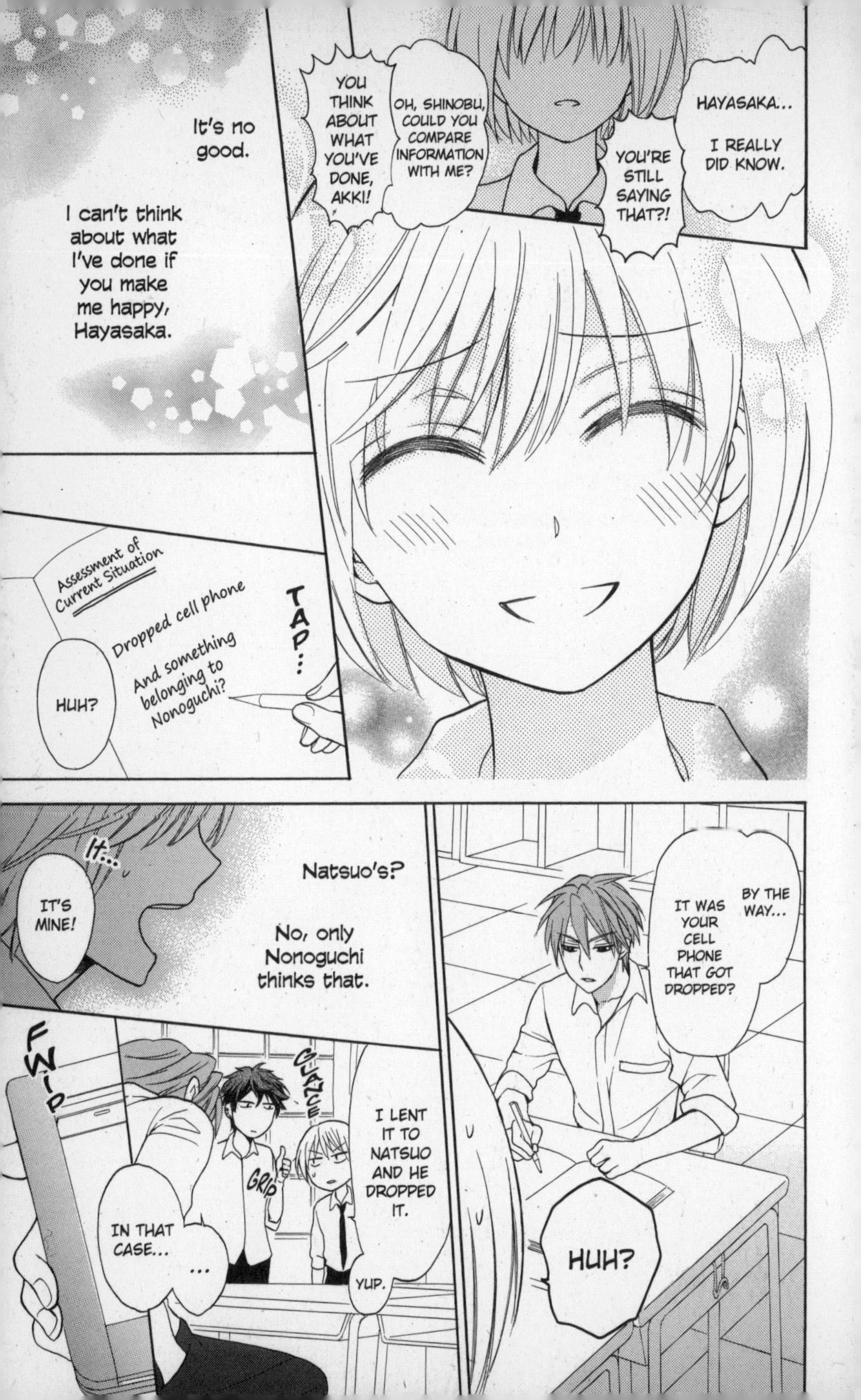
HAYASAKA...
I REALLY DID KNOW.
YOU'RE STILL SAYING THAT?!
OH, SHINOBU, COULD YOU COMPARE INFORMATION WITH ME?
YOU THINK ABOUT WHAT YOU'VE DONE, AKKI!
It's no good.
I can't think about what I've done if you make me happy, Hayasaka.
TAP...
Assessment of Current Situation
Dropped cell phone
And something belonging to Nonoguchi?
HUH?
BY THE WAY...
IT WAS YOUR CELL PHONE THAT GOT DROPPED?
HUH?
It...
IT'S MINE!
Natsuo's?
No, only Nonoguchi thinks that.
GLANCE
I LENT IT TO NATSUO AND HE DROPPED IT.
YUP.
GRIP
IN THAT CASE...
...
FWIP

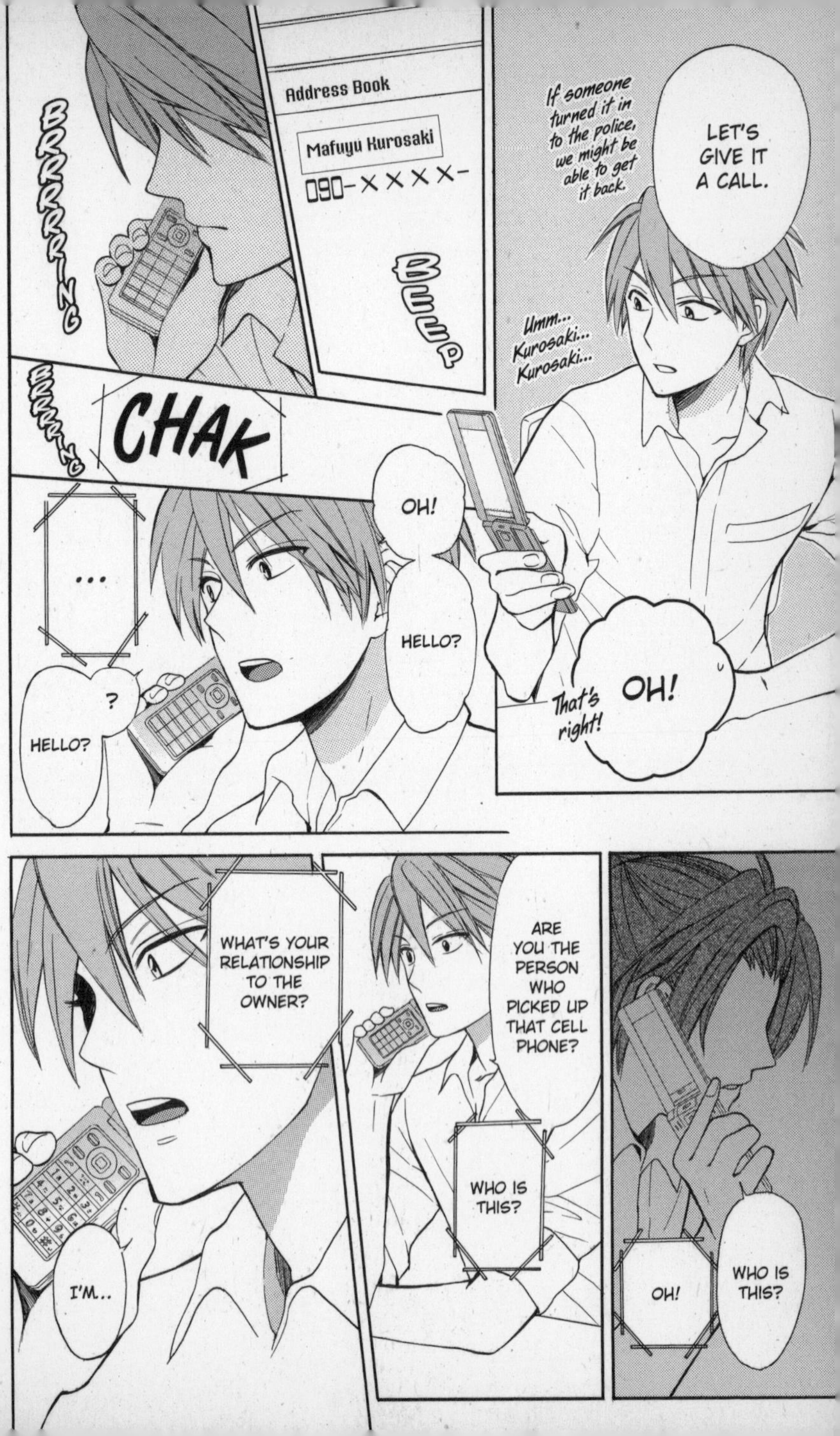
LET'S GIVE IT A CALL.
If someone turned it in to the police, we might be able to get it back.
Umm... Kurosaki... Kurosaki...
OH!
That's right!
Address Book
Mafuyu Kurosaki
090-XXXX-
BEEP
BRRRRRING
BRRRING
CHAK
OH!
HELLO?
...
?
HELLO?
WHO IS THIS?
OH!
ARE YOU THE PERSON WHO PICKED UP THAT CELL PHONE?
WHO IS THIS?
WHAT'S YOUR RELATIONSHIP TO THE OWNER?
I'M...

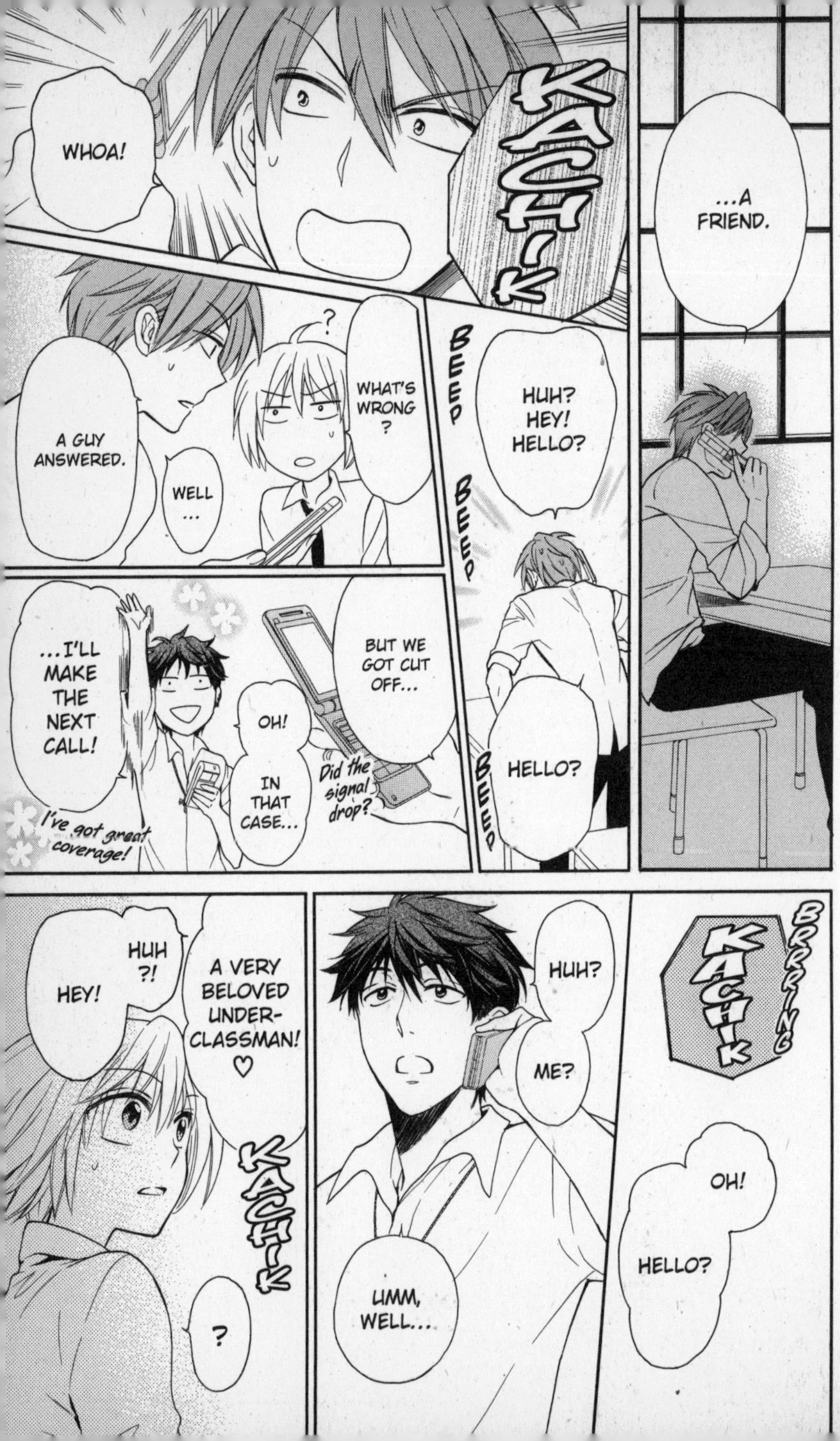
...A FRIEND.
KACHIK
WHOA!
BEEP BEEP
HUH? HEY! HELLO?
BEEP
HELLO?
WHAT'S WRONG?
A GUY ANSWERED.
WELL...
BUT WE GOT CUT OFF...
Did the signal drop?
OH!
IN THAT CASE...
...I'LL MAKE THE NEXT CALL!
I've got great coverage!
BRRRING
KACHIK
OH!
HELLO?
HUH?
ME?
UMM, WELL...
A VERY BELOVED UNDER-CLASSMAN! ♡
HUH?!
HEY!
KACHIK
?

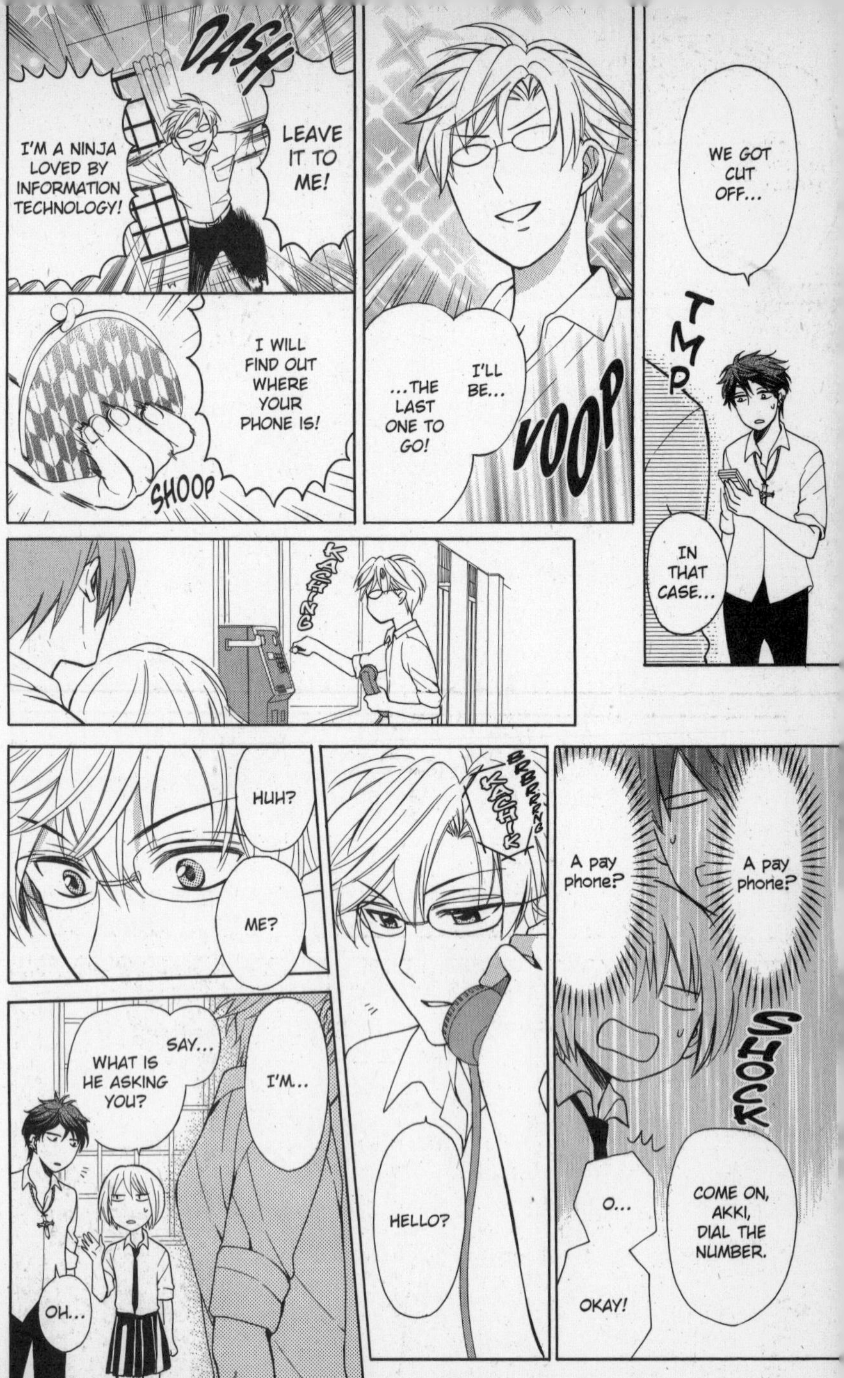

WE GOT CUT OFF...
TMP
IN THAT CASE...
I'LL BE...
...THE LAST ONE TO GO!
VOOP
DASH
LEAVE IT TO ME!
I'M A NINJA LOVED BY INFORMATION TECHNOLOGY!
I WILL FIND OUT WHERE YOUR PHONE IS!
SHOOP
KACHING
A pay phone?
A pay phone?
SHOCK
COME ON, AKKI, DIAL THE NUMBER.
O...
OKAY!
BRRRRING
KACHIK
HELLO?
HUH?
ME?
I'M...
SAY... WHAT IS HE ASKING YOU?
OH...

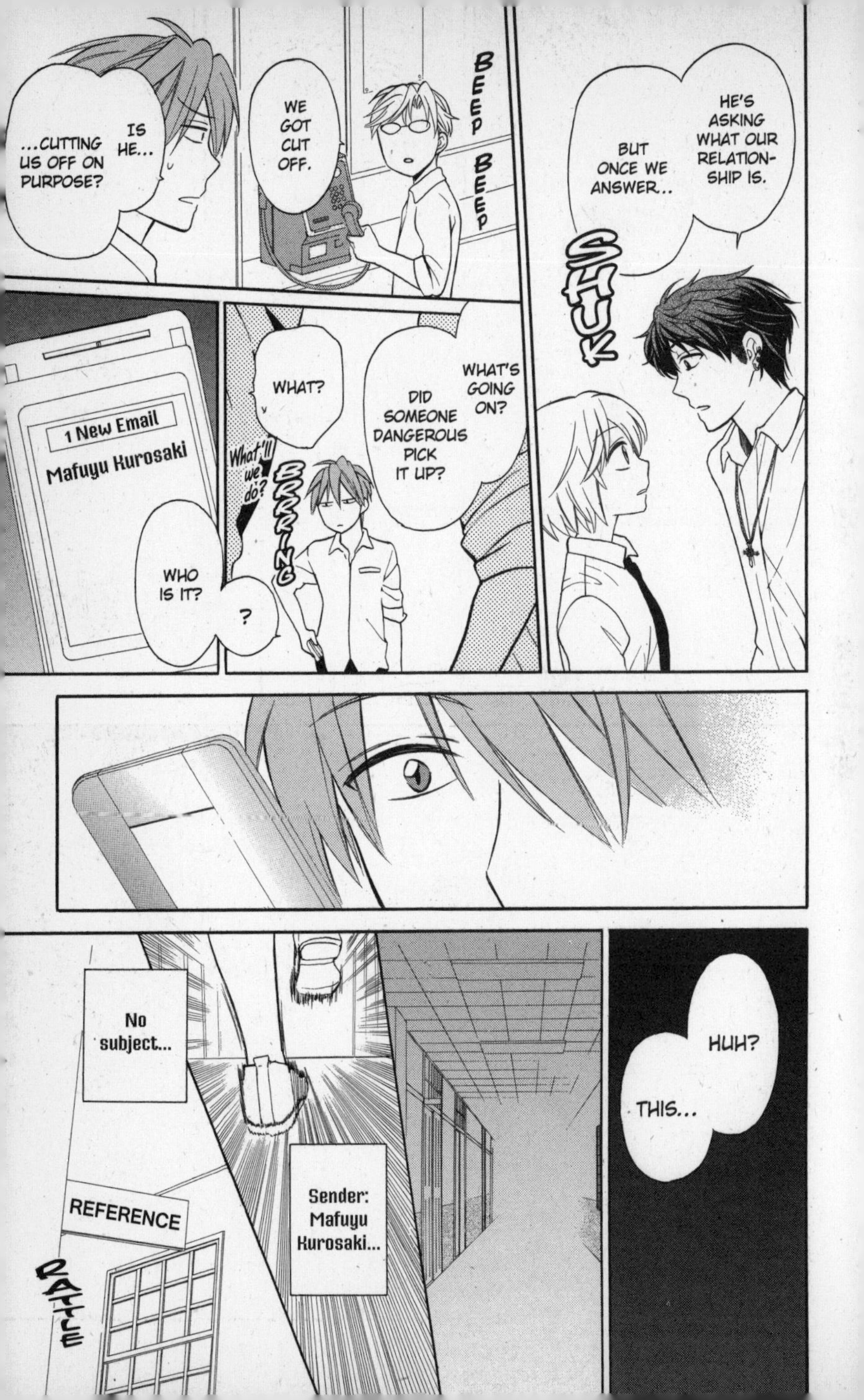
HE'S ASKING WHAT OUR RELATIONSHIP IS.
BUT ONCE WE ANSWER...
SHUK
BEEP BEEP
WE GOT CUT OFF.
IS HE...
...CUTTING US OFF ON PURPOSE?
WHAT'S GOING ON?
DID SOMEONE DANGEROUS PICK IT UP?
WHAT?
What'll we do?
BRRRING
1 New Email
Mafuyu Kurosaki
?
WHO IS IT?
HUH?
THIS...
Sender: Mafuyu Kurosaki...
No subject...
REFERENCE
RATTLE

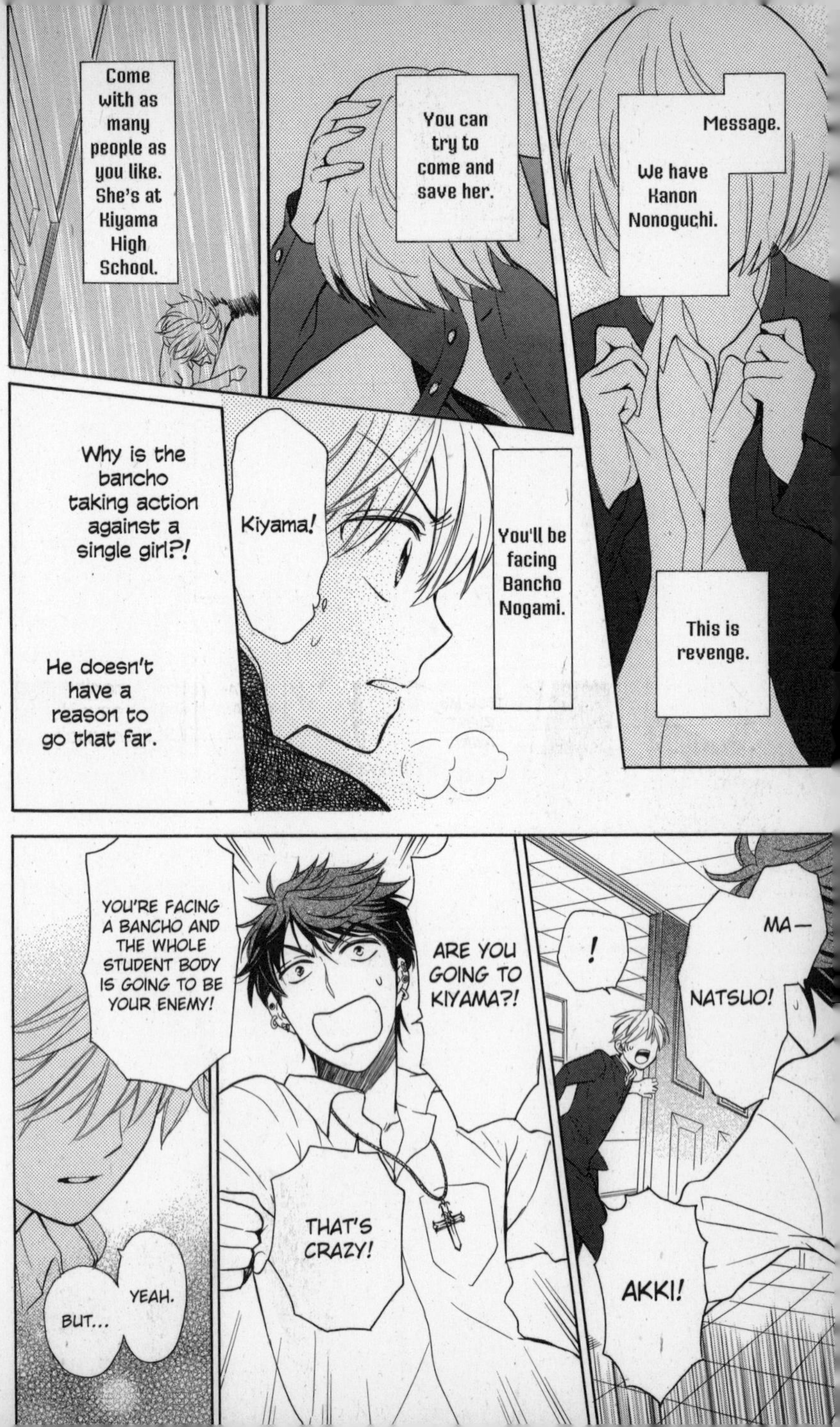

Message.
We have Kanon Nonoguchi.
This is revenge.
You can try to come and save her.
Come with as many people as you like. She's at Kiyama High School.
You'll be facing Bancho Nogami.
Kiyama!
Why is the bancho taking action against a single girl?!
He doesn't have a reason to go that far.
MA—
NATSUO!
!
AKKI!
ARE YOU GOING TO KIYAMA?!
YOU'RE FACING A BANCHO AND THE WHOLE STUDENT BODY IS GOING TO BE YOUR ENEMY!
THAT'S CRAZY!
YEAH.
BUT...

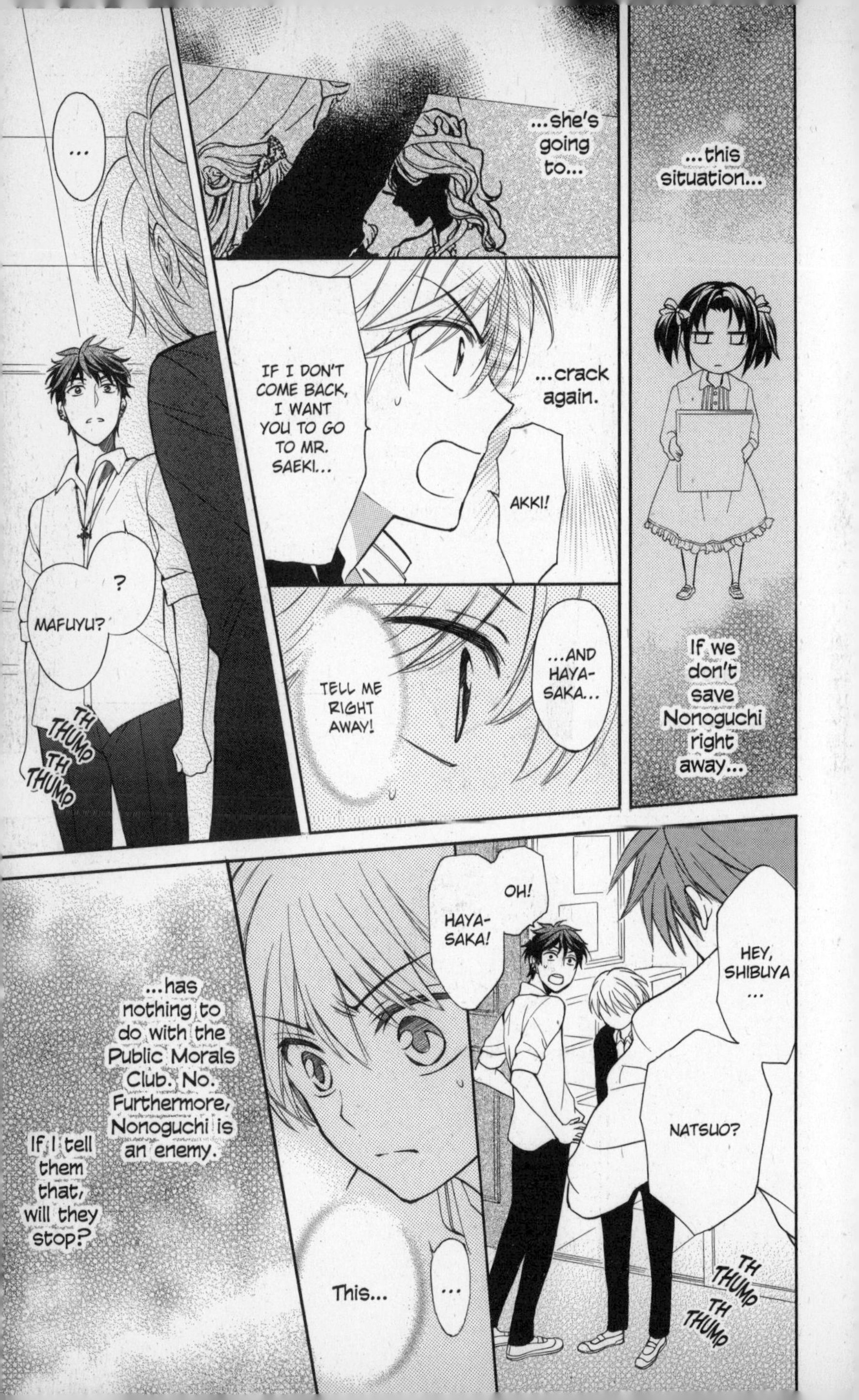

...this situation...
If we don't save Nonoguchi right away...
...she's going to...
...crack again.
AKKI!
IF I DON'T COME BACK, I WANT YOU TO GO TO MR. SAEKI...
...AND HAYA-SAKA...
TELL ME RIGHT AWAY!
...
?
MAFUYU?
TH THUMP TH THUMP
HEY, SHIBUYA ...
OH!
HAYA-SAKA!
NATSUO?
TH THUMP TH THUMP
...
This...
...has nothing to do with the Public Morals Club. No. Furthermore, Nonoguchi is an enemy.
If I tell them that, will they stop?

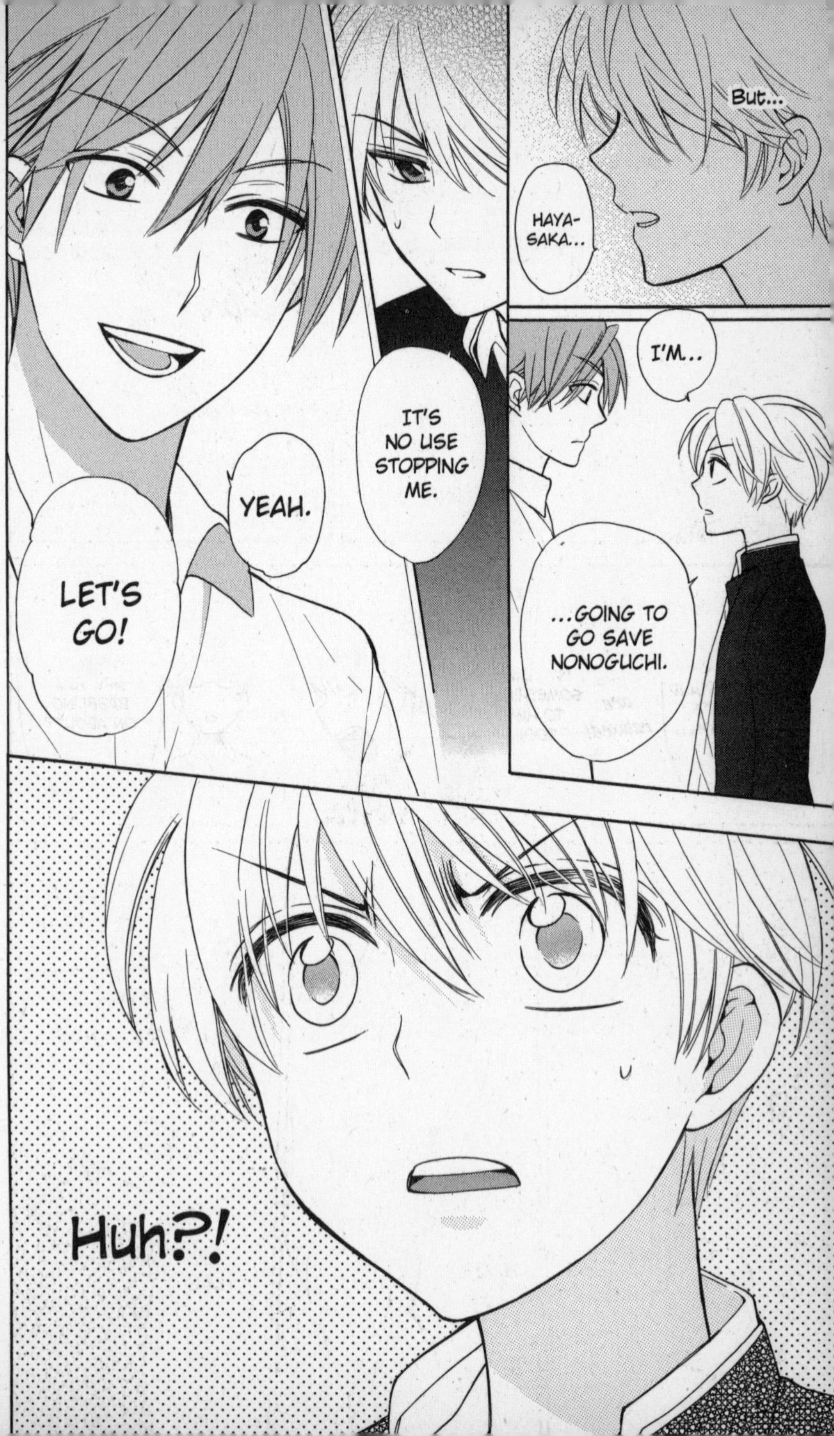
But...
HAYA-SAKA...
I'M...
...GOING TO GO SAVE NONOGUCHI.
IT'S NO USE STOPPING ME.
YEAH.
LET'S GO!
Huh?!

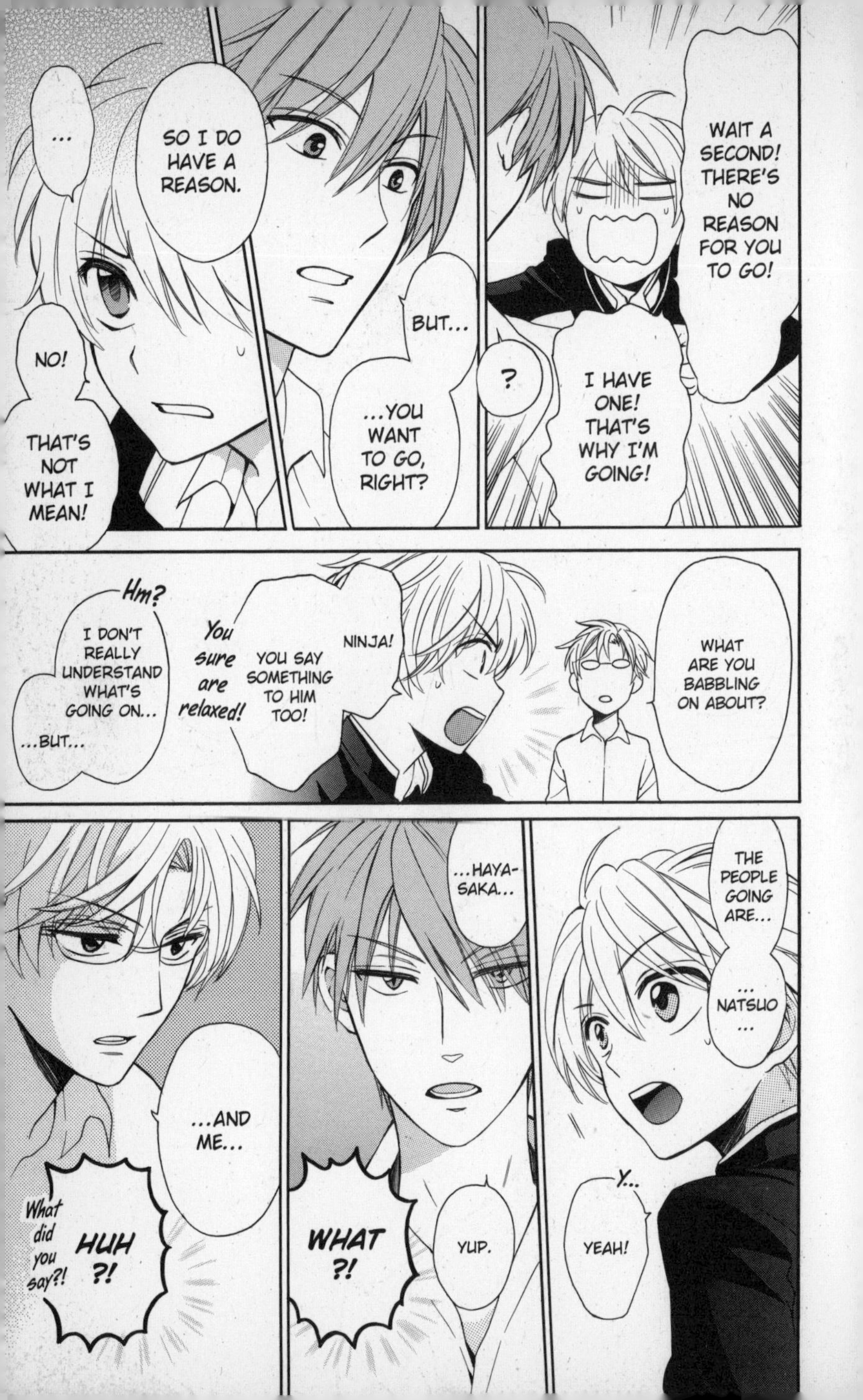
WAIT A SECOND! THERE'S NO REASON FOR YOU TO GO!
I HAVE ONE! THAT'S WHY I'M GOING!
?
SO I DO HAVE A REASON.
BUT...
...YOU WANT TO GO, RIGHT?
...
NO!
THAT'S NOT WHAT I MEAN!
WHAT ARE YOU BABBLING ON ABOUT?
NINJA!
YOU SAY SOMETHING TO HIM TOO!
You sure are relaxed!
Hm?
I DON'T REALLY UNDERSTAND WHAT'S GOING ON...
...BUT...
THE PEOPLE GOING ARE...
...NATSUO...
Y...
YEAH!
...HAYA-SAKA...
YUP.
WHAT?!
...AND ME...
HUH?!
What did you say?!

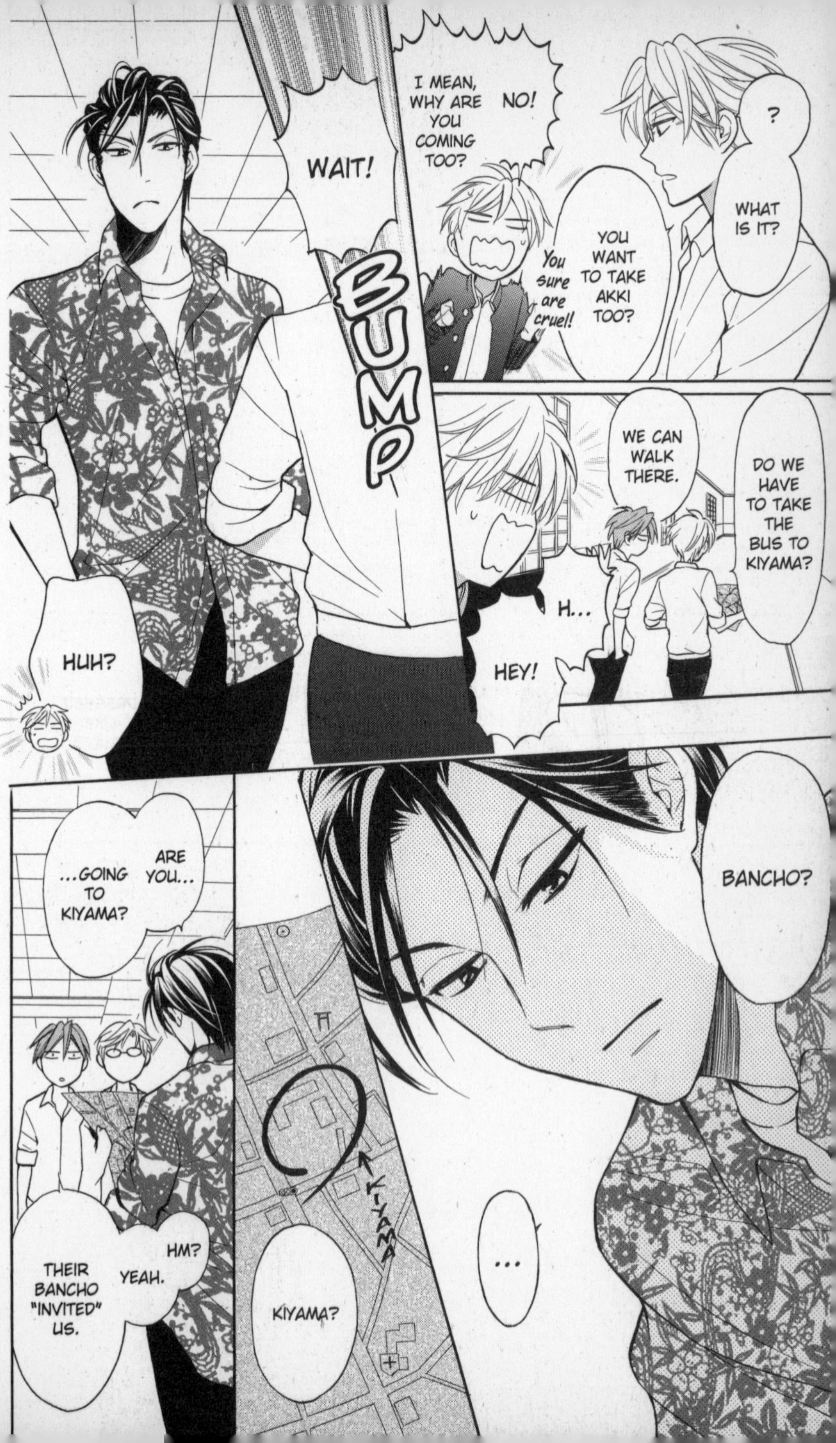
?
WHAT IS IT?
YOU WANT TO TAKE AKKI TOO?
You sure are cruel!
NO!
I MEAN, WHY ARE YOU COMING TOO?
DO WE HAVE TO TAKE THE BUS TO KIYAMA?
WE CAN WALK THERE.
H...
HEY!
WAIT!
BUMP
HUH?
BANCHO?
...
KIYAMA
KIYAMA?
ARE YOU...
...GOING TO KIYAMA?
HM?
YEAH.
THEIR BANCHO "INVITED" US.

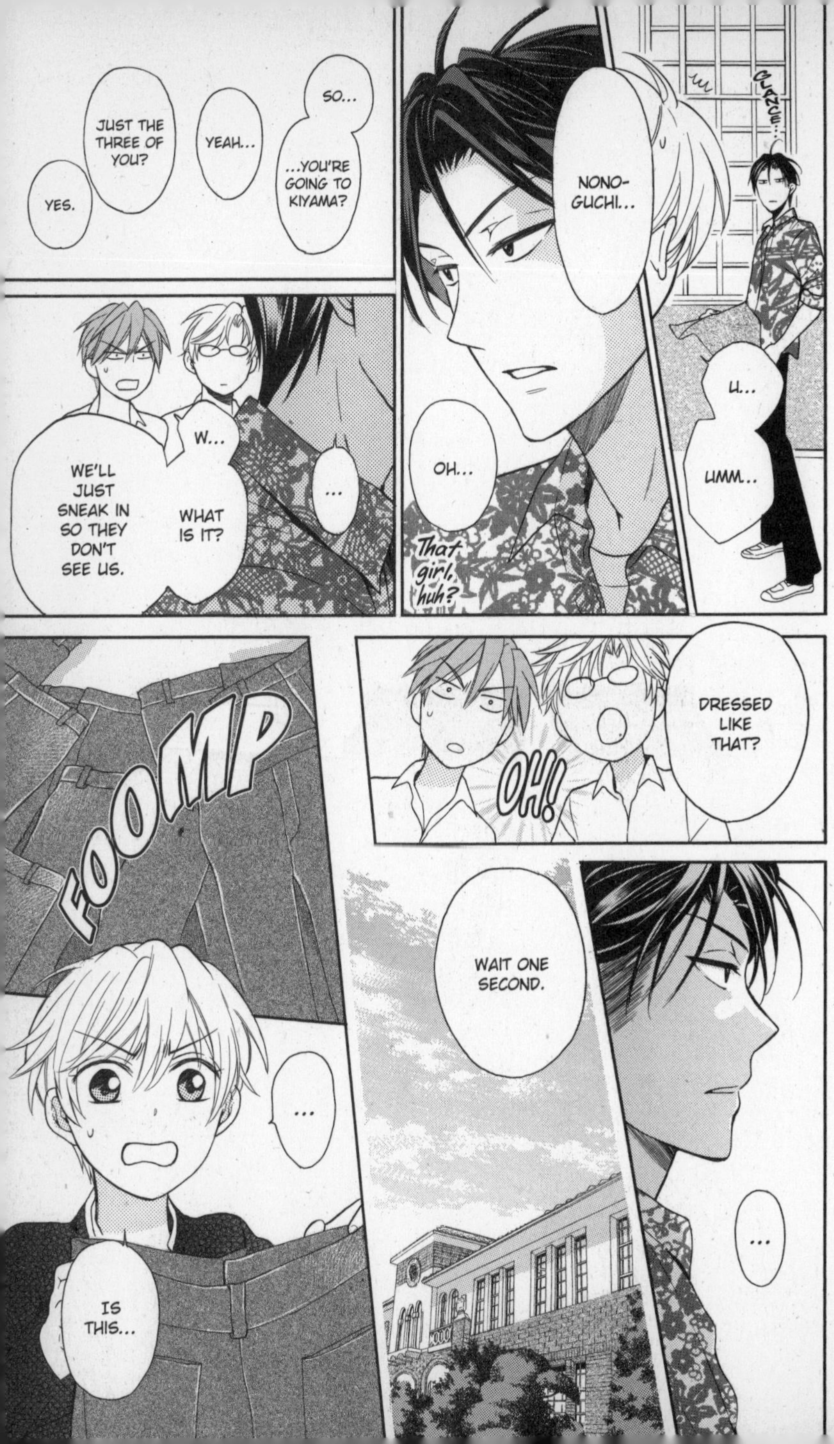
GLANCE...
U...
UMM...
NONO-GUCHI...
OH...
That girl, huh?
SO...
...YOU'RE GOING TO KIYAMA?
YEAH...
JUST THE THREE OF YOU?
YES.
...
W...
WHAT IS IT?
WE'LL JUST SNEAK IN SO THEY DON'T SEE US.
DRESSED LIKE THAT?
OH!
WAIT ONE SECOND.
...
FOOMP
...
IS THIS...

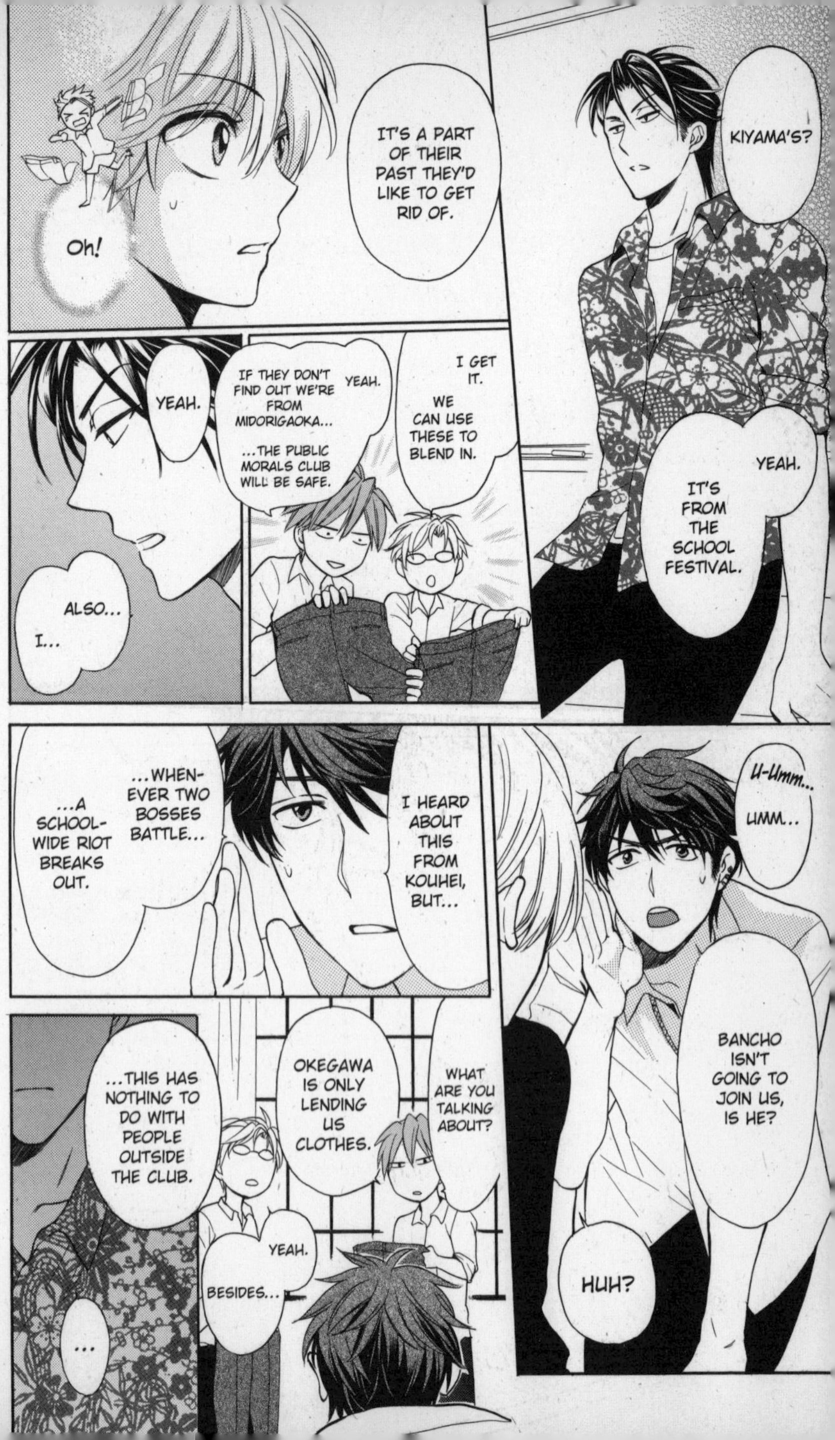
KIYAMA'S?
YEAH.
IT'S FROM THE SCHOOL FESTIVAL.
IT'S A PART OF THEIR PAST THEY'D LIKE TO GET RID OF.
Oh!
I GET IT.
WE CAN USE THESE TO BLEND IN.
YEAH.
IF THEY DON'T FIND OUT WE'RE FROM MIDORIGAOKA...
...THE PUBLIC MORALS CLUB WILL BE SAFE.
YEAH.
ALSO...
I...
U-Umm...
UMM...
BANCHO ISN'T GOING TO JOIN US, IS HE?
HUH?
I HEARD ABOUT THIS FROM KOUHEI, BUT...
...WHEN-EVER TWO BOSSES BATTLE...
...A SCHOOL-WIDE RIOT BREAKS OUT.
WHAT ARE YOU TALKING ABOUT?
OKEGAWA IS ONLY LENDING US CLOTHES.
YEAH.
BESIDES...
...THIS HAS NOTHING TO DO WITH PEOPLE OUTSIDE THE CLUB.
...

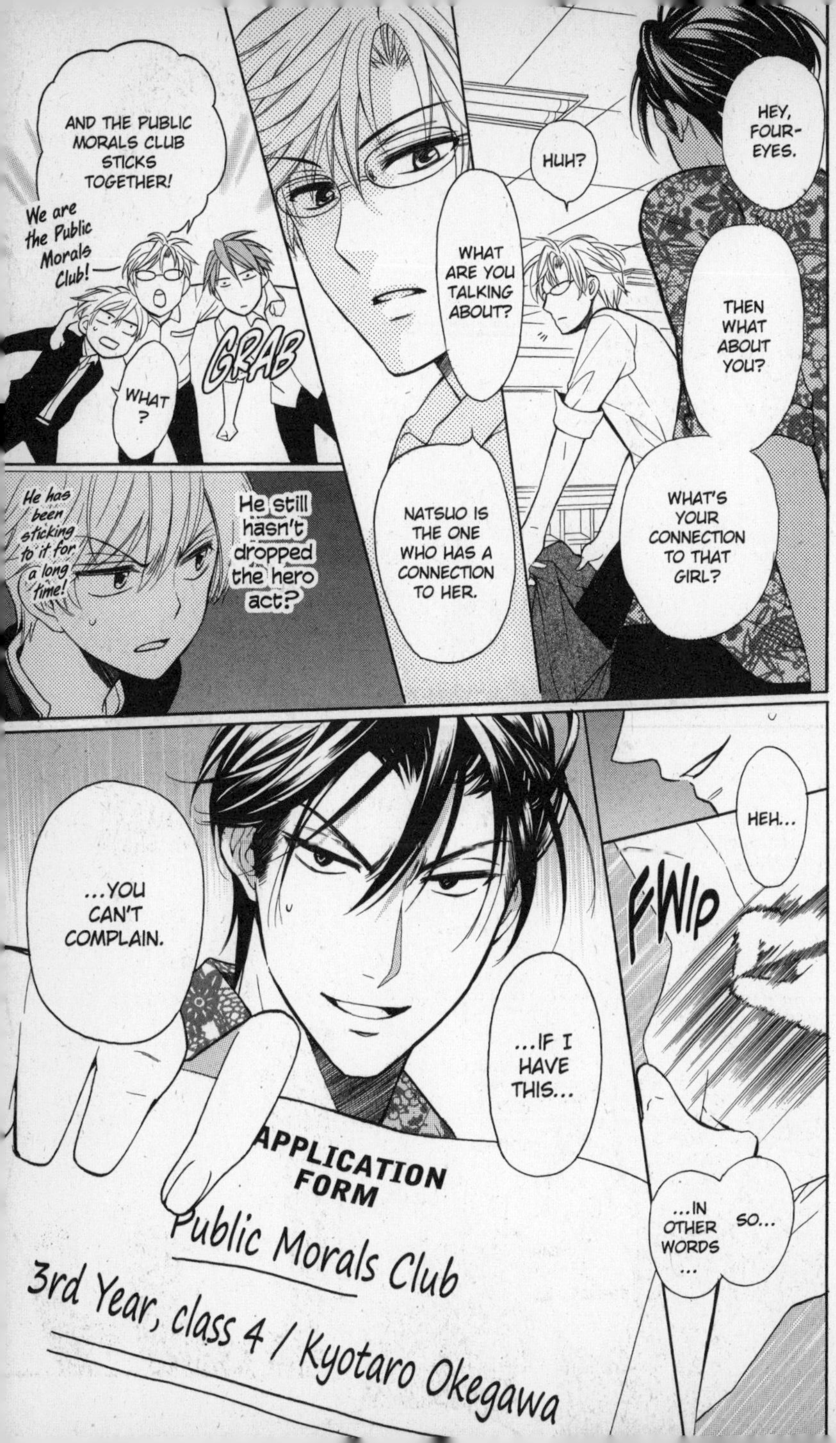
HEY, FOUR-EYES.
HUH?
WHAT ARE YOU TALKING ABOUT?
THEN WHAT ABOUT YOU?
WHAT'S YOUR CONNECTION TO THAT GIRL?
NATSUO IS THE ONE WHO HAS A CONNECTION TO HER.
AND THE PUBLIC MORALS CLUB STICKS TOGETHER!
We are the Public Morals Club!
GRAB
WHAT?
He still hasn't dropped the hero act?
He has been sticking to it for a long time!
HEH...
FWIP
...SO...
...IN OTHER WORDS...
...IF I HAVE THIS...
...YOU CAN'T COMPLAIN.
APPLICATION FORM
Public Morals Club
3rd Year, class 4 / Kyotaro Okegawa

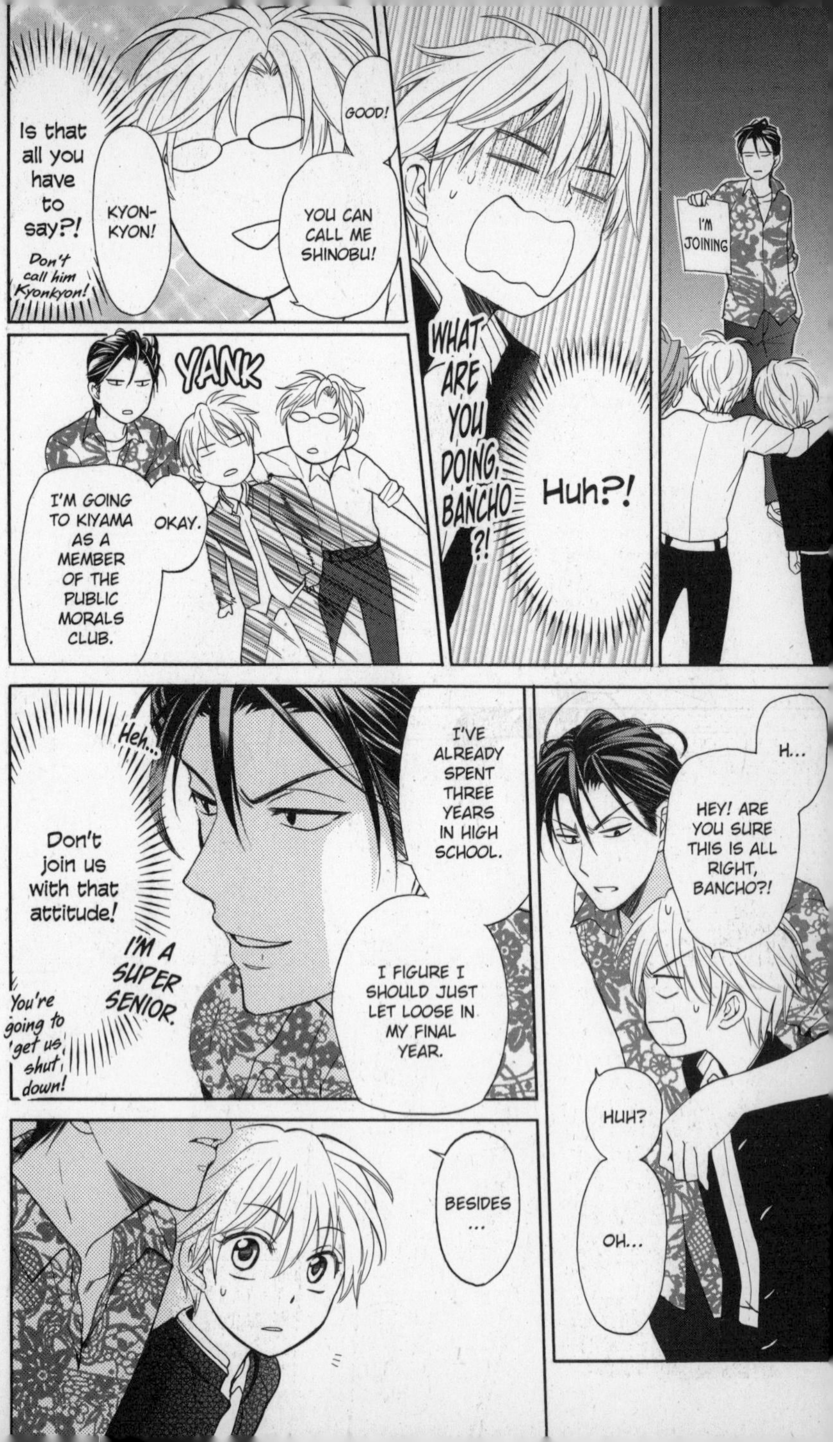
I'M JOINING
Huh?!
WHAT ARE YOU DOING, BANCHO?!
GOOD!
YOU CAN CALL ME SHINOBU!
KYON-KYON!
Is that all you have to say?!
Don't call him Kyonkyon!
YANK
OKAY.
I'M GOING TO KIYAMA AS A MEMBER OF THE PUBLIC MORALS CLUB.
H...
HEY! ARE YOU SURE THIS IS ALL RIGHT, BANCHO?!
HUH?
OH...
I'VE ALREADY SPENT THREE YEARS IN HIGH SCHOOL.
I FIGURE I SHOULD JUST LET LOOSE IN MY FINAL YEAR.
Heh...
Don't join us with that attitude!
I'M A SUPER SENIOR.
You're going to get us shut down!
BESIDES...

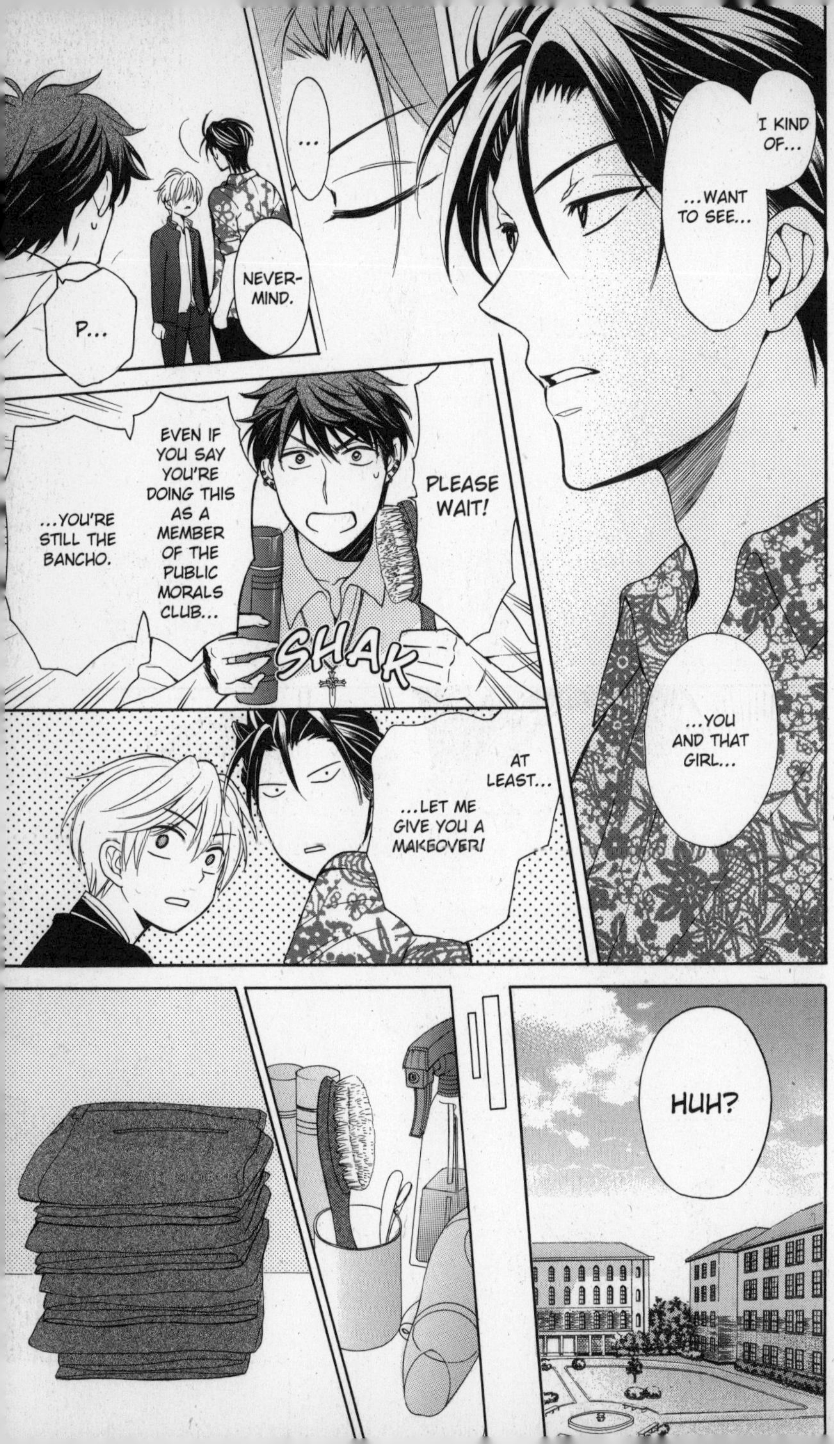
I KIND OF...
...WANT TO SEE...
...YOU AND THAT GIRL...
...
NEVER-MIND.
P...
PLEASE WAIT!
EVEN IF YOU SAY YOU'RE DOING THIS AS A MEMBER OF THE PUBLIC MORALS CLUB...
...YOU'RE STILL THE BANCHO.
SHAK
AT LEAST...
...LET ME GIVE YOU A MAKEOVER!
HUH?

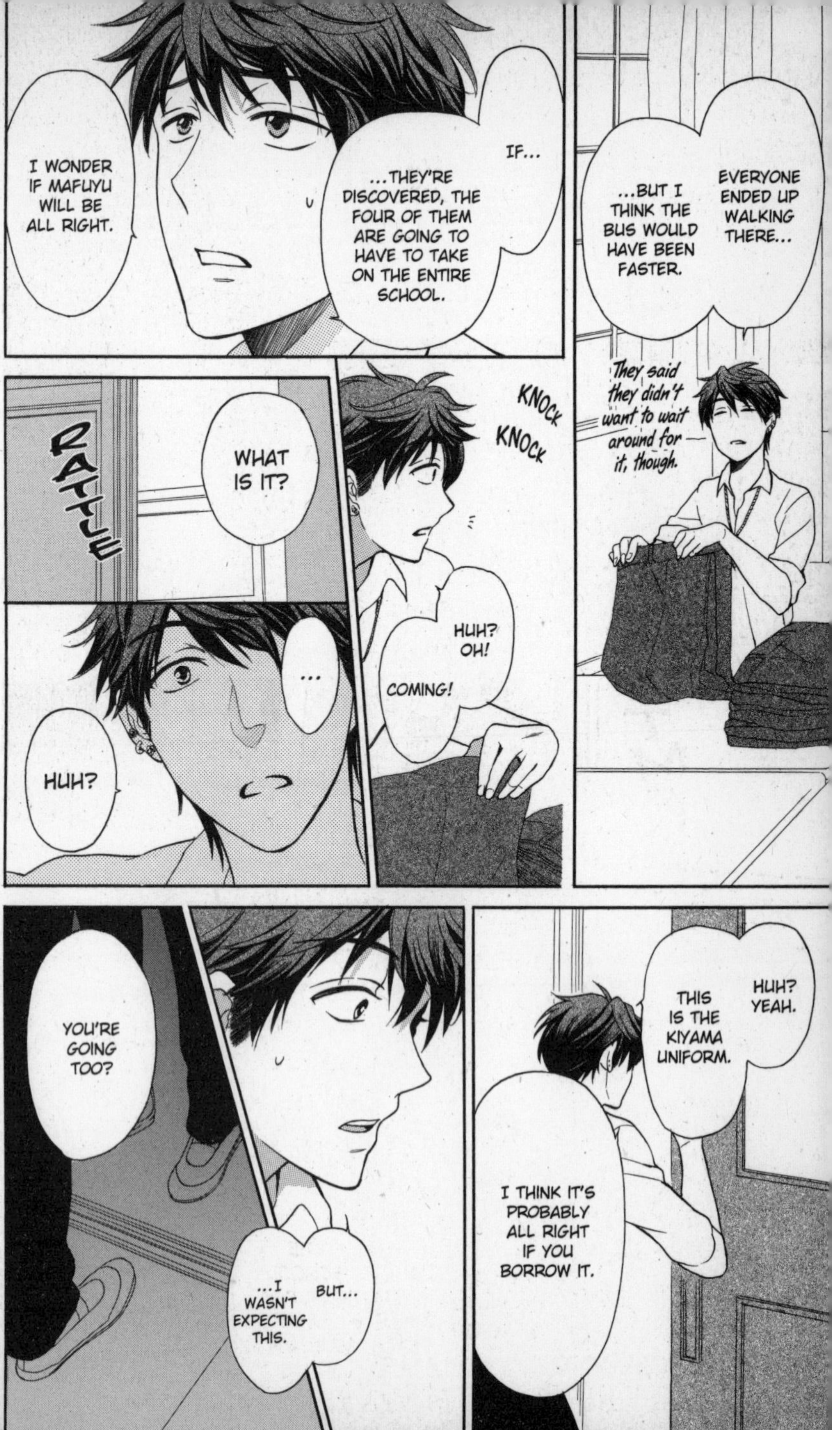
EVERYONE ENDED UP WALKING THERE...
...BUT I THINK THE BUS WOULD HAVE BEEN FASTER.
They said they didn't want to wait around for it, though.
IF...
...THEY'RE DISCOVERED, THE FOUR OF THEM ARE GOING TO HAVE TO TAKE ON THE ENTIRE SCHOOL.
I WONDER IF MAFUYU WILL BE ALL RIGHT.
KNOCK
KNOCK
HUH? OH!
COMING!
RATTLE
WHAT IS IT?
...
HUH?
HUH? YEAH.
THIS IS THE KIYAMA UNIFORM.
I THINK IT'S PROBABLY ALL RIGHT IF YOU BORROW IT.
YOU'RE GOING TOO?
BUT...
...I WASN'T EXPECTING THIS.

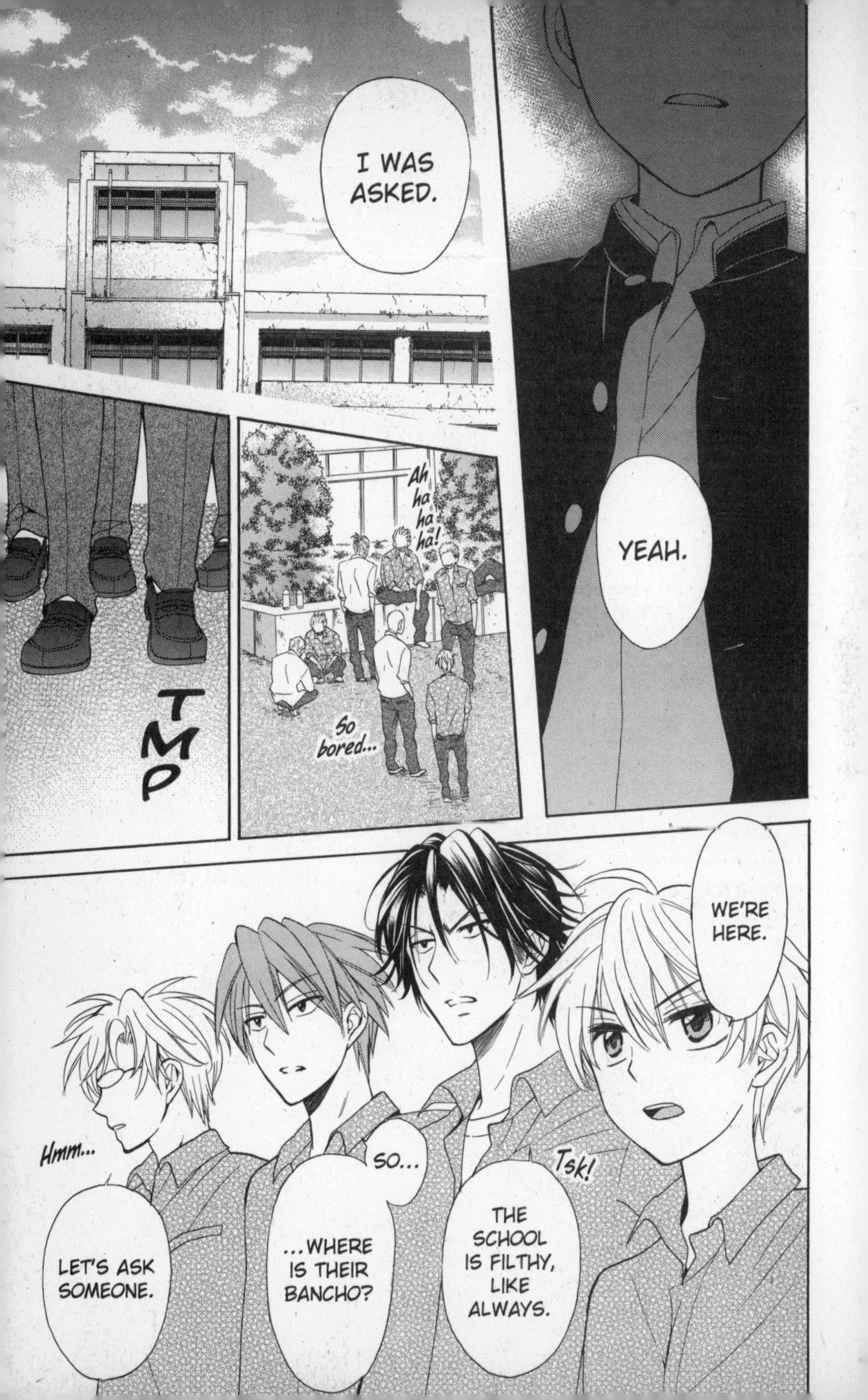
YEAH.
I WAS ASKED.
Ah ha ha ha!
So bored...
TMP
WE'RE HERE.
Tsk!
THE SCHOOL IS FILTHY, LIKE ALWAYS.
SO...
...WHERE IS THEIR BANCHO?
Hmm...
LET'S ASK SOMEONE.

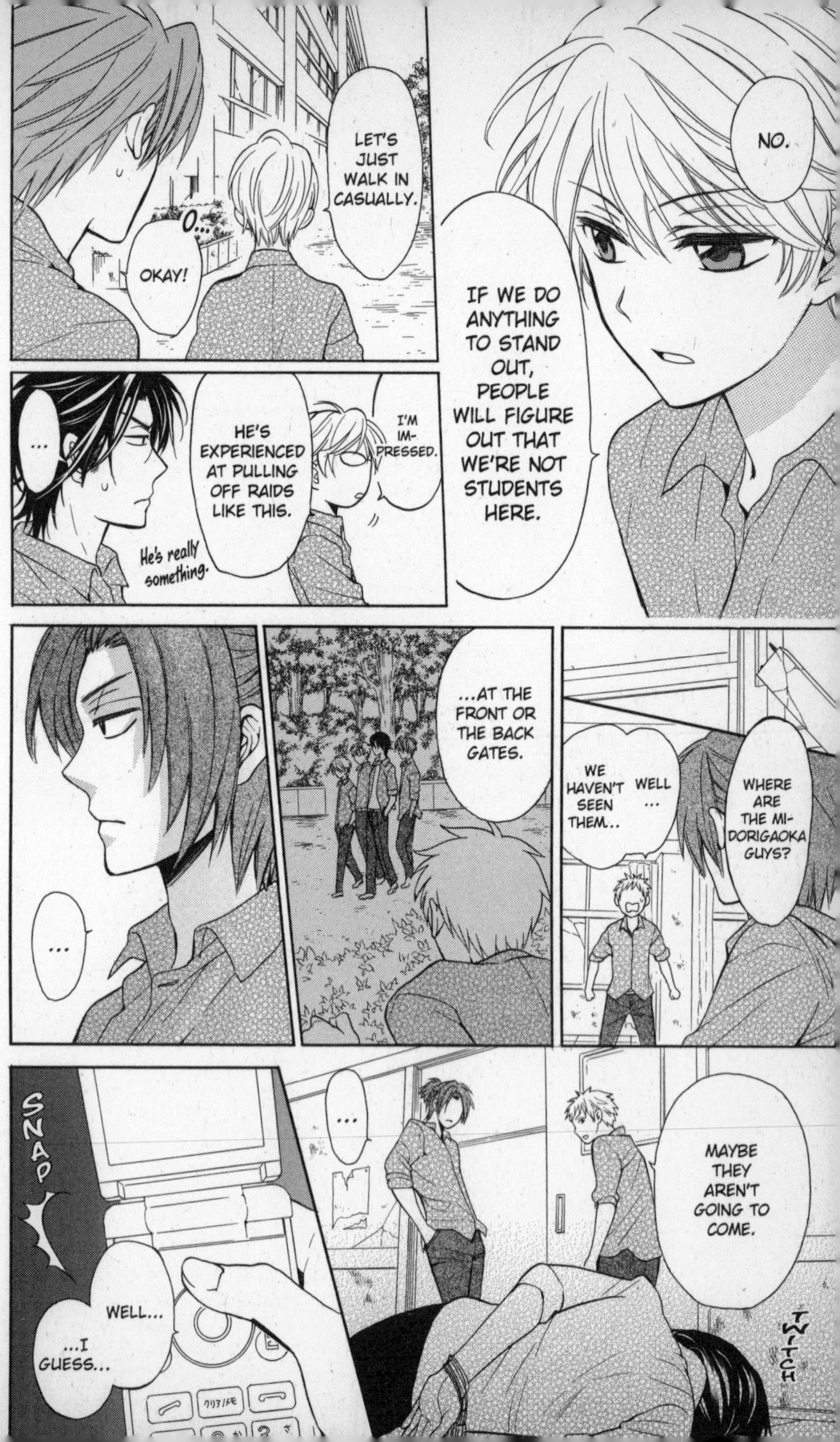
NO.
IF WE DO ANYTHING TO STAND OUT, PEOPLE WILL FIGURE OUT THAT WE'RE NOT STUDENTS HERE.
LET'S JUST WALK IN CASUALLY.
O... OKAY!
I'M IM-PRESSED.
HE'S EXPERIENCED AT PULLING OFF RAIDS LIKE THIS.
He's really something.
...
WHERE ARE THE MI-DORIGAOKA GUYS?
WELL...
WE HAVEN'T SEEN THEM...
...AT THE FRONT OR THE BACK GATES.
...
...
MAYBE THEY AREN'T GOING TO COME.
TWITCH
...
SNAP
WELL...
...I GUESS...

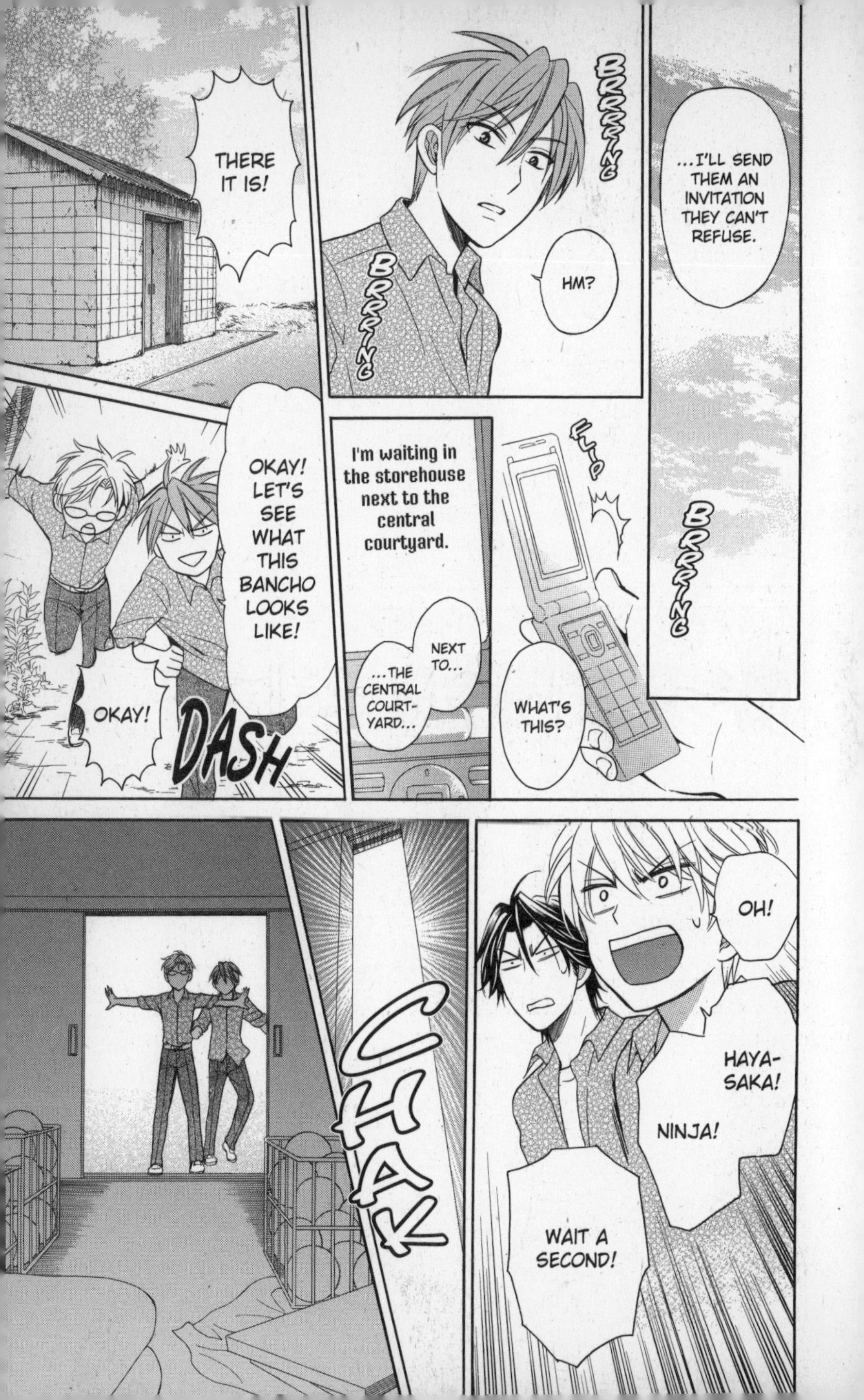

...I'LL SEND THEM AN INVITATION THEY CAN'T REFUSE.
BRRRING
HM?
BRRRING
THERE IT IS!
FLIP
BRRRING
WHAT'S THIS?
I'm waiting in the storehouse next to the central courtyard.
NEXT TO...
...THE CENTRAL COURT-YARD...
OKAY! LET'S SEE WHAT THIS BANCHO LOOKS LIKE!
OKAY!
DASH
OH!
HAYA-SAKA!
NINJA!
WAIT A SECOND!
CHAK

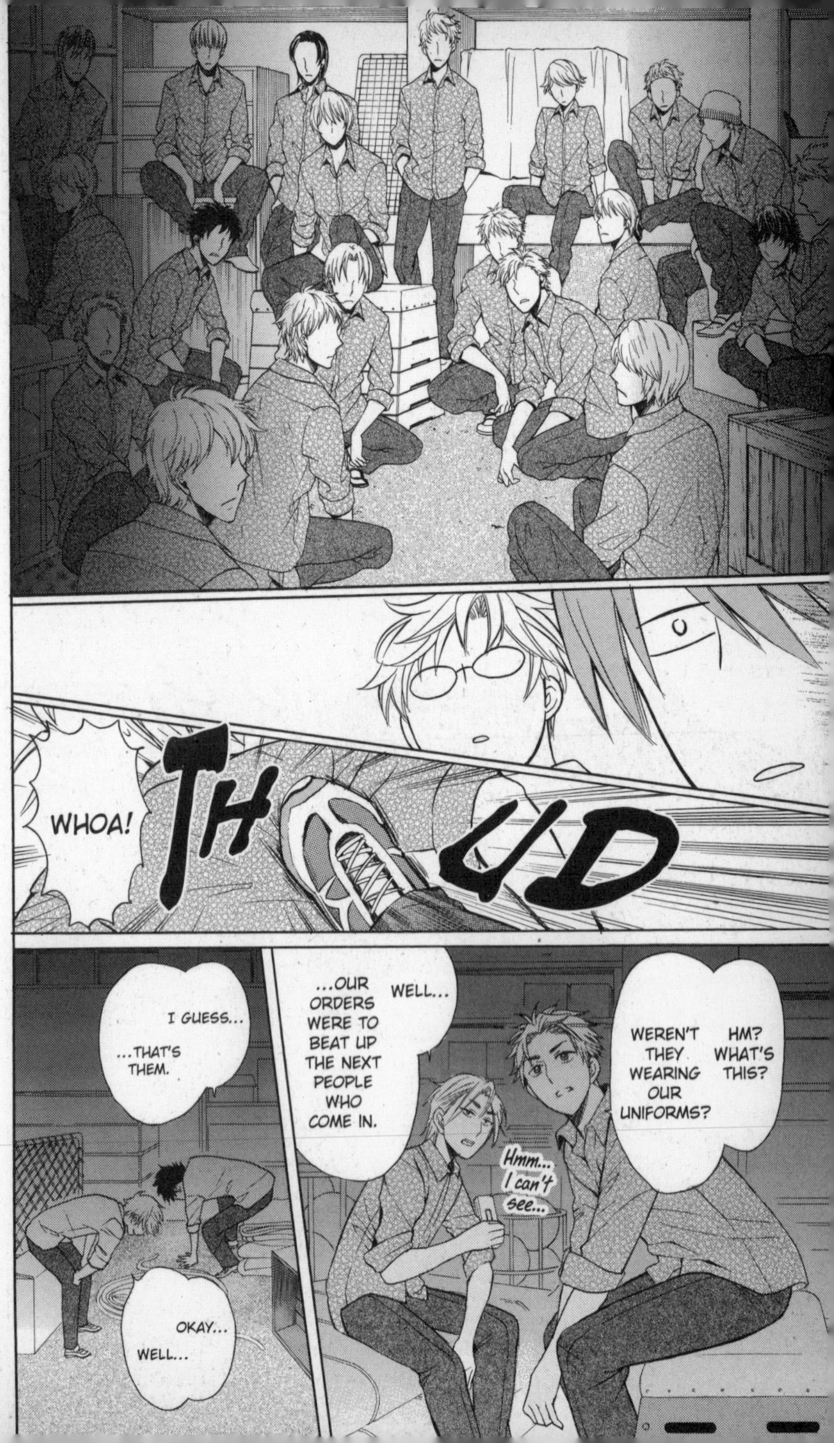
THUD
WHOA!
HM? WHAT'S THIS?
WEREN'T THEY WEARING OUR UNIFORMS?
Hmm... I can't see...
WELL...
...OUR ORDERS WERE TO BEAT UP THE NEXT PEOPLE WHO COME IN.
I GUESS...
...THAT'S THEM.
OKAY...
WELL...

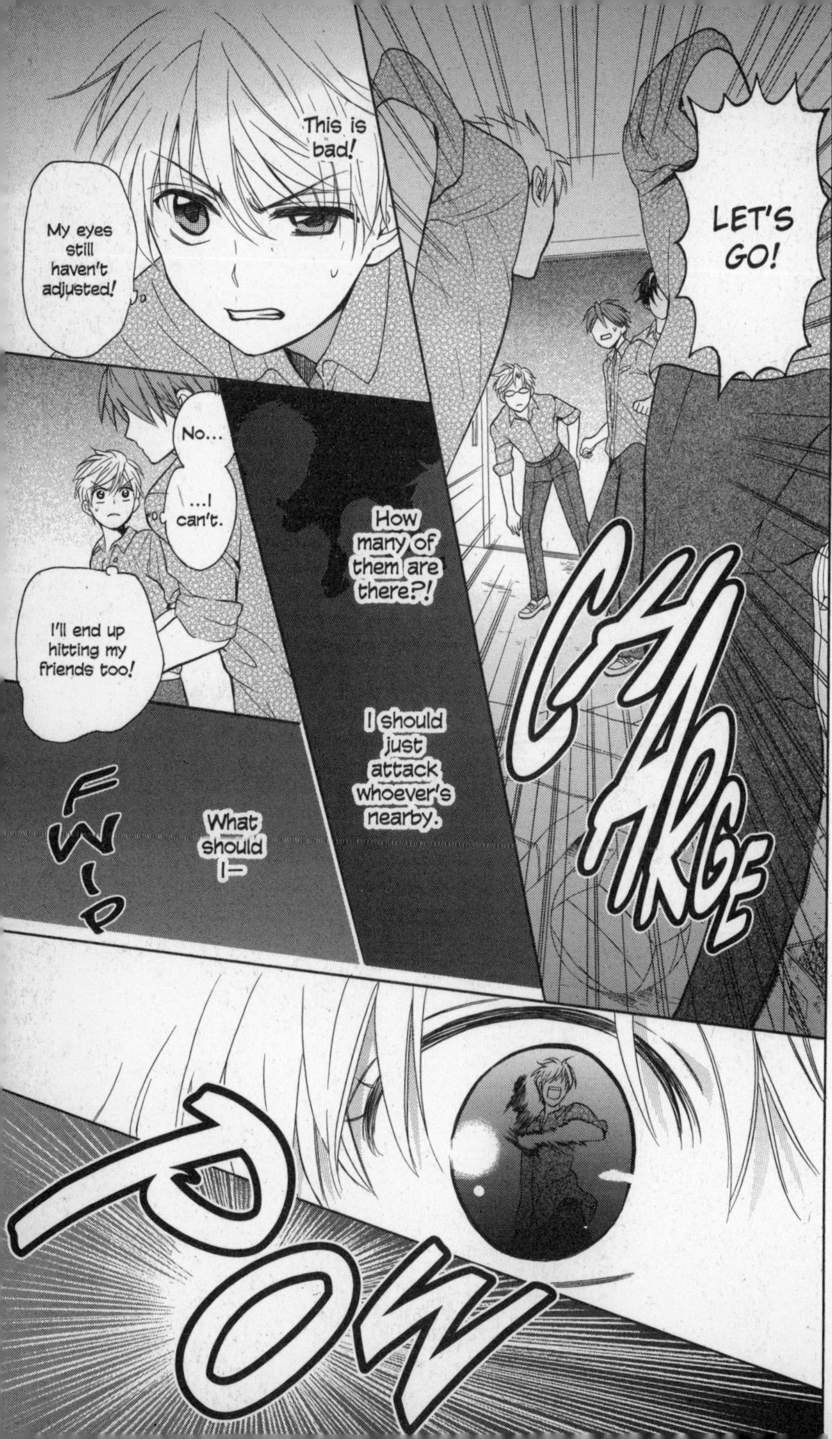
LET'S GO!
CHARGE
This is bad!
My eyes still haven't adjusted!
How many of them are there?!
I should just attack whoever's nearby.
No...
...I can't.
I'll end up hitting my friends too!
FWIP
What should I—
POW

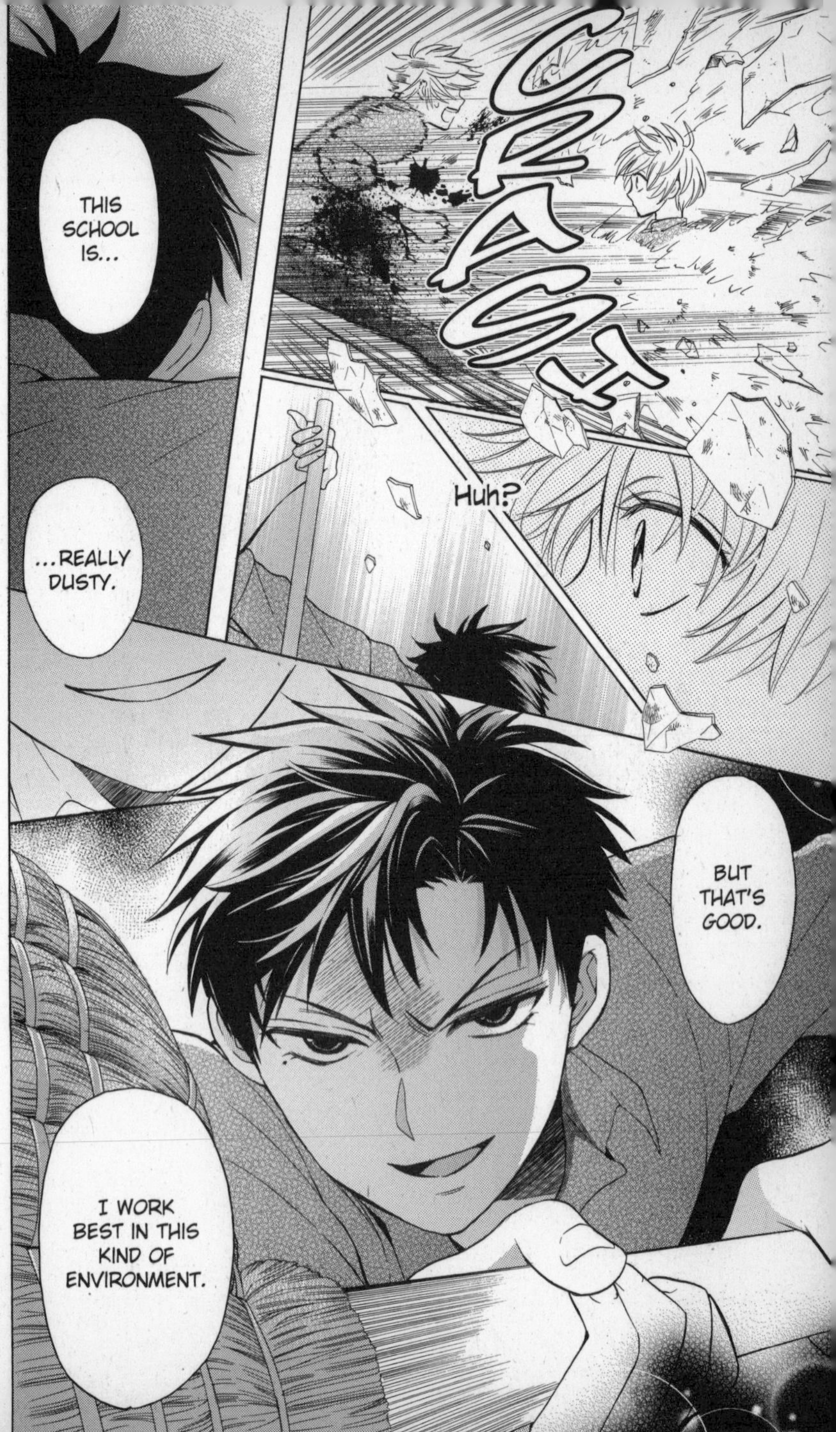
CRASH
Huh?
THIS SCHOOL IS...
...REALLY DUSTY.
BUT THAT'S GOOD.
I WORK BEST IN THIS KIND OF ENVIRONMENT.

North South East West

SOUTH EAST ARC

THE DESIRED CAST

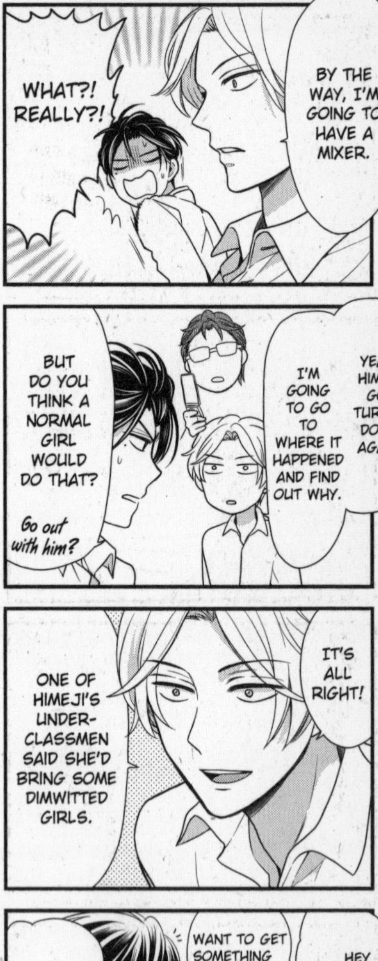
BY THE WAY, I'M GOING TO HAVE A MIXER.
WHAT?! REALLY?!
YEAH. HIMEJI GOT TURNED DOWN AGAIN.
I'M GOING TO GO TO WHERE IT HAPPENED AND FIND OUT WHY.
BUT DO YOU THINK A NORMAL GIRL WOULD DO THAT?
Go out with him?
IT'S ALL RIGHT!
ONE OF HIMEJI'S UNDER-CLASSMEN SAID SHE'D BRING SOME DIMWITTED GIRLS.
HEY THERE, FRIEND. LONG TIME NO SEE.
WANT TO GET SOMETHING TO EAT?
It's my treat.
WHAT?!
SURE, WE'D LOVE TO!

THE MALE CAST

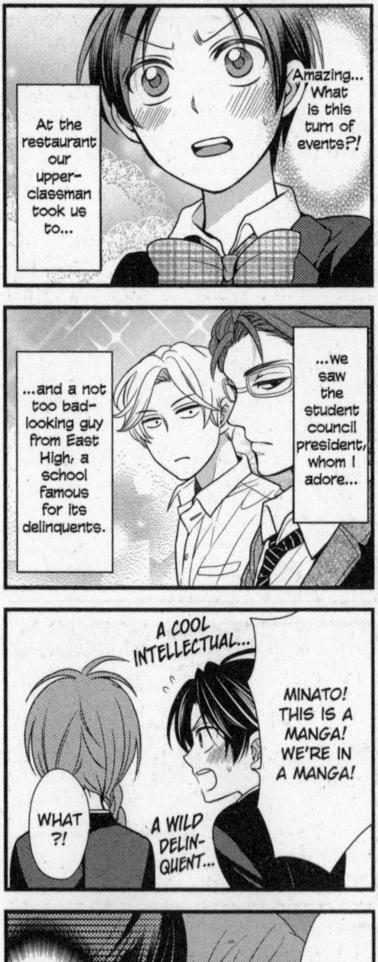
Amazing... What is this turn of events?!
At the restaurant our upper-classman took us to...
...we saw the student council president, whom I adore...
...and a not too bad-looking guy from East High, a school famous for its delinquents.
A COOL INTELLECTUAL...
MINATO! THIS IS A MANGA! WE'RE IN A MANGA!
A WILD DELIN-QUENT...
WHAT?!
IT'S A GAG MANGA!
What?!

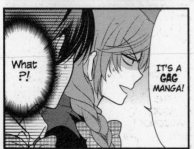

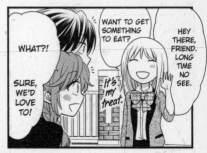

THE EXPERIENCE OF THE PARTICIPANTS

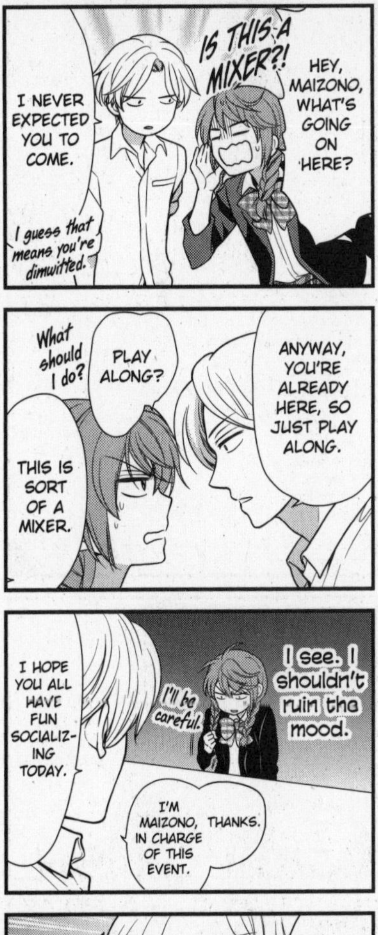
IS THIS A MIXER?!
HEY, MAIZONO, WHAT'S GOING ON HERE?
I NEVER EXPECTED YOU TO COME.
I guess that means you're dimwitted.
ANYWAY, YOU'RE ALREADY HERE, SO JUST PLAY ALONG.
PLAY ALONG?
What should I do?
THIS IS SORT OF A MIXER.
I see. I shouldn't ruin the mood.
I'll be careful.
I HOPE YOU ALL HAVE FUN SOCIALIZING TODAY.
THANKS.
I'M MAIZONO, IN CHARGE OF THIS EVENT.
THE THREE OF YOU AREN'T REALLY MY TYPE, THOUGH.
YOU'RE RUINING THE MOOD, MAIZONO!

CELL-PHONE CONVERSATION

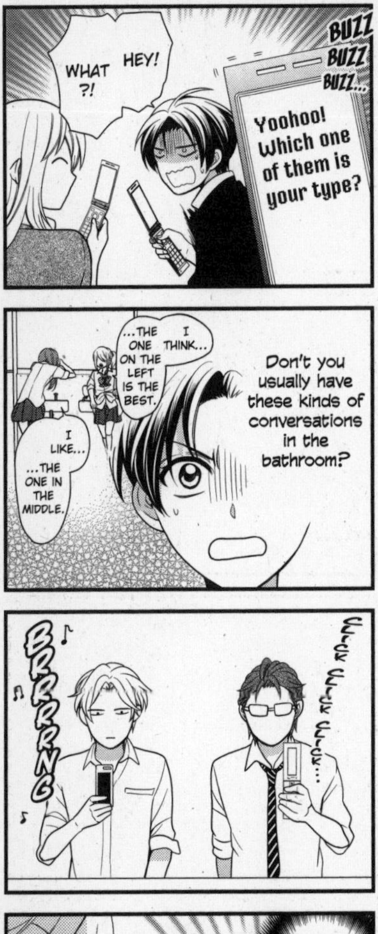
BUZZ BUZZ BUZZ...
Yoohoo! Which one of them is your type?
HEY!
WHAT ?!
Don't you usually have these kinds of conversations in the bathroom?
I THINK... ...THE ONE ON THE LEFT IS THE BEST.
I LIKE... ...THE ONE IN THE MIDDLE.
Click click click...
BRRRRNG
They're doing it too?!
EEP!
Himeji
I'm so nervous, I can't talk.

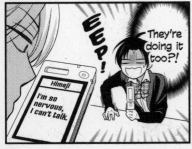

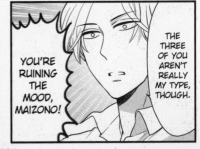

DISTRIBUTION OF AFFECTION AND HOSTILITY

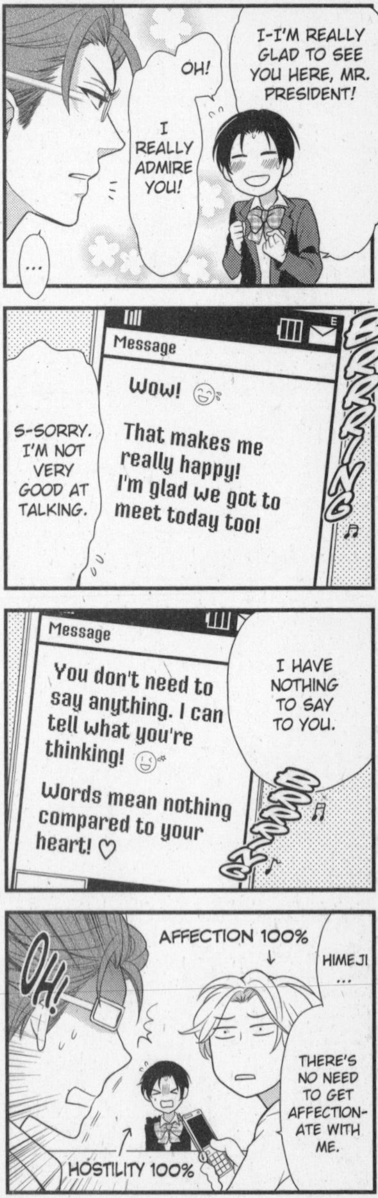
I-I'M REALLY GLAD TO SEE YOU HERE, MR. PRESIDENT!
OH!
I REALLY ADMIRE YOU!
...
BRRRING
Message
Wow!
That makes me really happy! I'm glad we got to meet today too!
S-SORRY. I'M NOT VERY GOOD AT TALKING.
I HAVE NOTHING TO SAY TO YOU.
BRRRING
Message
You don't need to say anything. I can tell what you're thinking!
Words mean nothing compared to your heart! ♡
HIMEJI ...
THERE'S NO NEED TO GET AFFECTION-ATE WITH ME.
AFFECTION 100%
OH!
HOSTILITY 100%

ALL WORKED UP

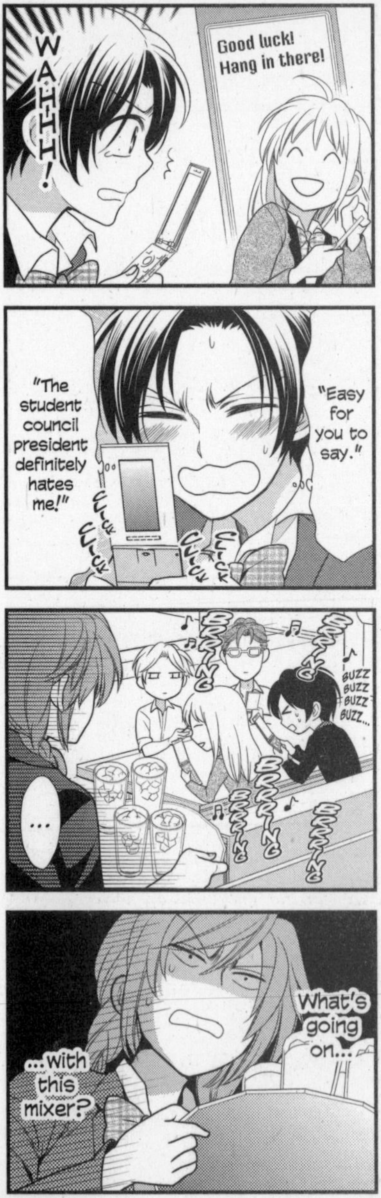
Good luck! Hang in there!
WAHHH!
"Easy for you to say."
"The student council president definitely hates me!"
CLICK CLICK CLICK CLICK
BRRRING
BRRRING
BUZZ BUZZ BUZZ BUZZ...
BRRRING
BRRRING
BRRRING
...
What's going on...
...with this mixer?

THAT KIND OF FETISH

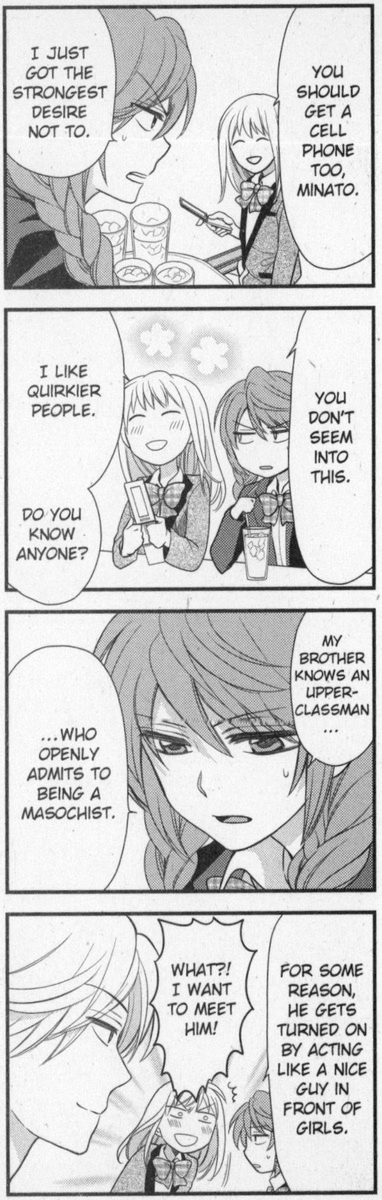
YOU SHOULD GET A CELL PHONE TOO, MINATO.
I JUST GOT THE STRONGEST DESIRE NOT TO.
YOU DON'T SEEM INTO THIS.
I LIKE QUIRKIER PEOPLE.
DO YOU KNOW ANYONE?
MY BROTHER KNOWS AN UPPER-CLASSMAN...
...WHO OPENLY ADMITS TO BEING A MASOCHIST.
FOR SOME REASON, HE GETS TURNED ON BY ACTING LIKE A NICE GUY IN FRONT OF GIRLS.
WHAT?! I WANT TO MEET HIM!

FORMER KNOWLEDGE

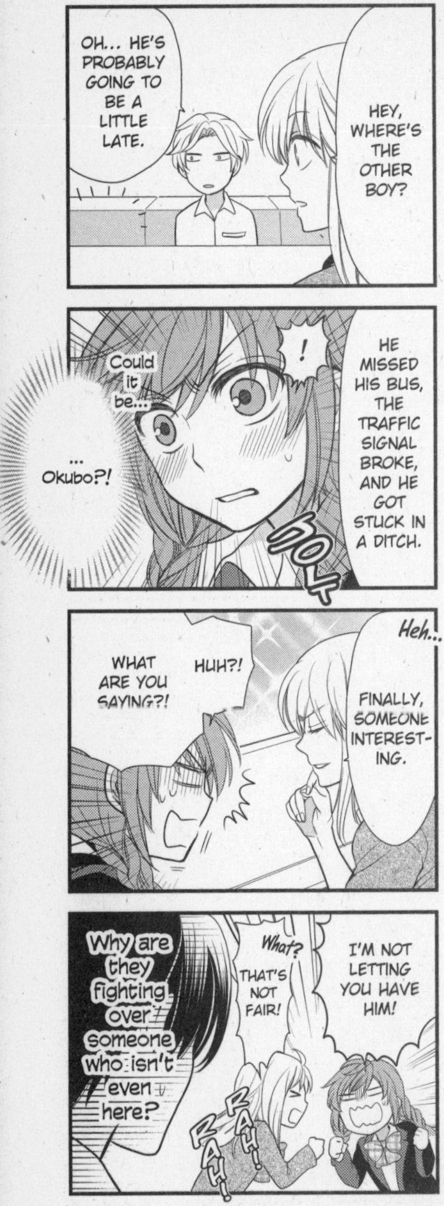
HEY, WHERE'S THE OTHER BOY?
OH... HE'S PROBABLY GOING TO BE A LITTLE LATE.
HE MISSED HIS BUS, THE TRAFFIC SIGNAL BROKE, AND HE GOT STUCK IN A DITCH.
!
GOK
Could it be...
...Okubo?!
Heh...
FINALLY, SOMEONE INTERESTING.
HUH?!
WHAT ARE YOU SAYING?!
I'M NOT LETTING YOU HAVE HIM!
What?
THAT'S NOT FAIR!
Why are they fighting over someone who isn't even here?
RAH! RAH!

SURGING DEVELOPMENT

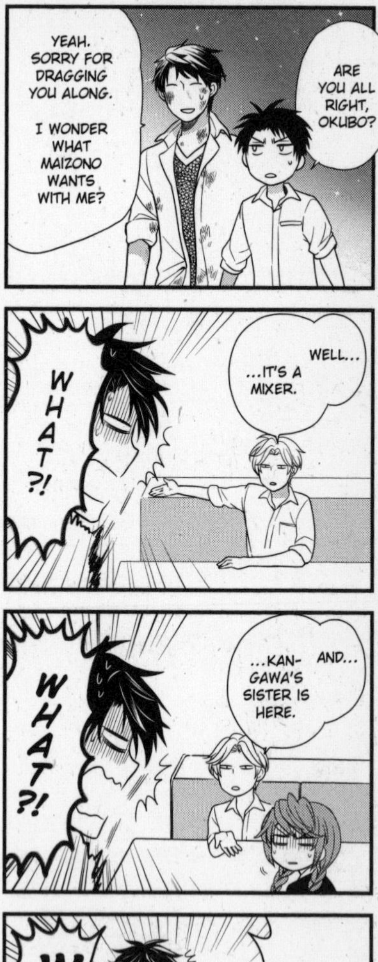
ARE YOU ALL RIGHT, OKUBO?
YEAH. SORRY FOR DRAGGING YOU ALONG. I WONDER WHAT MAIZONO WANTS WITH ME?
WELL...
...IT'S A MIXER.
WHAT?!
AND...
...KAN-GAWA'S SISTER IS HERE.
WHAT?!
I'M TAKING OKUBO WITH ME!
WHAT?!
IT REACHED ITS CLIMAX IN 10 SECONDS

SAVIOR

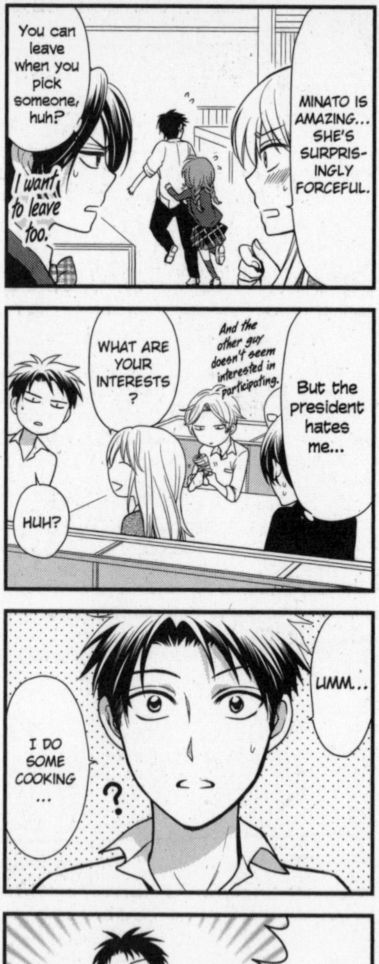
MINATO IS AMAZING... SHE'S SURPRIS-INGLY FORCEFUL.
You can leave when you pick someone, huh?
I want to leave too.
But the president hates me...
And the other guy doesn't seem interested in participating.
WHAT ARE YOUR INTERESTS?
HUH?
UMM...
I DO SOME COOKING...
?
WE'LL TAKE HIM!
GRAB

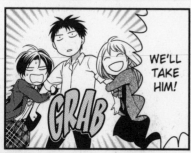

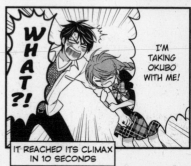

50% CHALLENGE

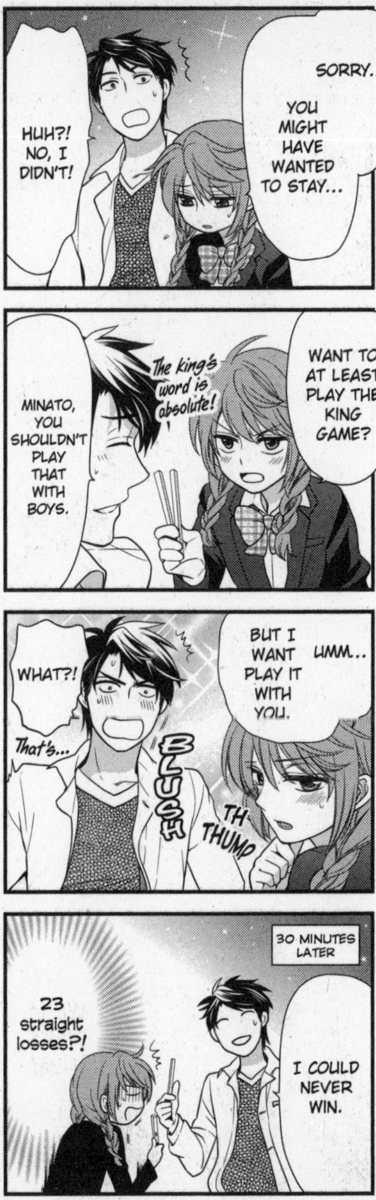
SORRY...
YOU MIGHT HAVE WANTED TO STAY...
HUH?! NO, I DIDN'T!
WANT TO AT LEAST PLAY THE KING GAME?
The king's word is absolute!
MINATO, YOU SHOULDN'T PLAY THAT WITH BOYS.
UMM...
BUT I WANT PLAY IT WITH YOU.
WHAT?!
That's...
BLUSH
TH THUMP
30 MINUTES LATER
I COULD NEVER WIN.
23 straight losses?!

HIMEJI'S ANGUISH

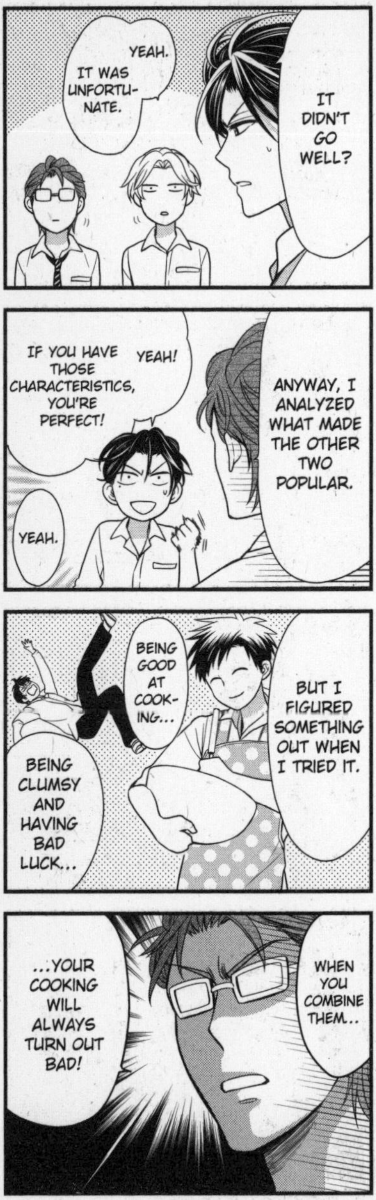
IT DIDN'T GO WELL?
YEAH.
IT WAS UNFORTUNATE.
ANYWAY, I ANALYZED WHAT MADE THE OTHER TWO POPULAR.
YEAH!
IF YOU HAVE THOSE CHARACTERISTICS, YOU'RE PERFECT!
YEAH.
BUT I FIGURED SOMETHING OUT WHEN I TRIED IT.
BEING GOOD AT COOKING...
BEING CLUMSY AND HAVING BAD LUCK...
WHEN YOU COMBINE THEM...
...YOUR COOKING WILL ALWAYS TURN OUT BAD!

TIMING OF A MATURE MAN

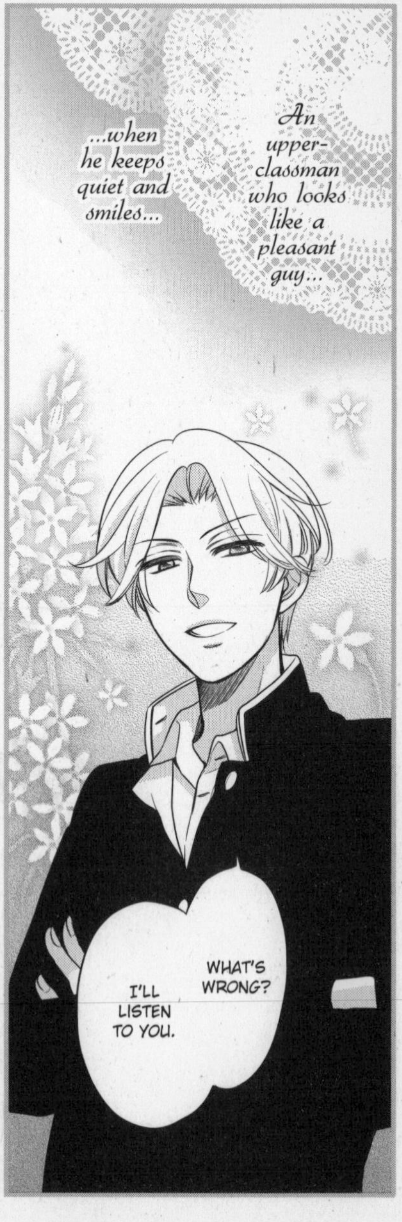
An upper-classman who looks like a pleasant guy...
...when he keeps quiet and smiles...
WHAT'S WRONG?
I'LL LISTEN TO YOU.

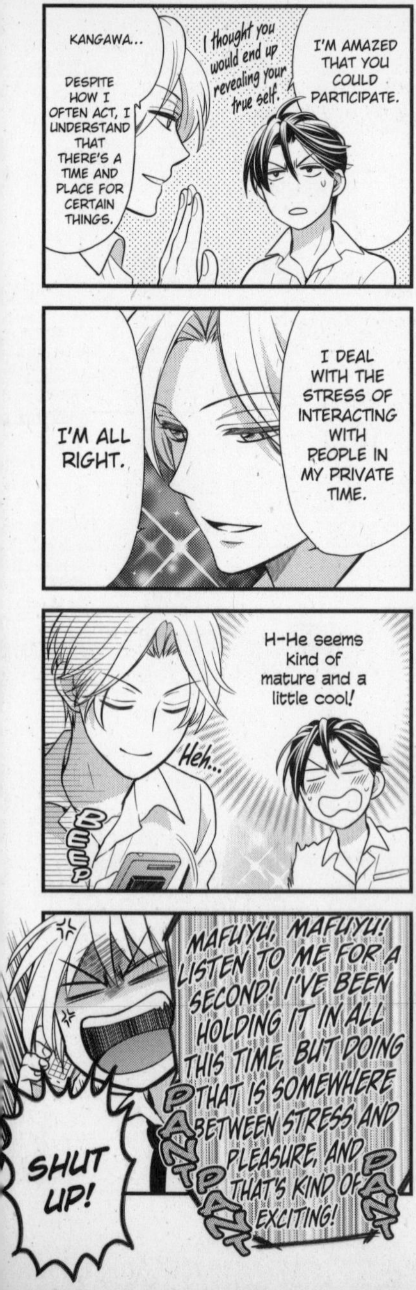
I'M AMAZED THAT YOU COULD PARTICIPATE.
I thought you would end up revealing your true self.
KANGAWA...
DESPITE HOW I OFTEN ACT, I UNDERSTAND THAT THERE'S A TIME AND PLACE FOR CERTAIN THINGS.
I DEAL WITH THE STRESS OF INTERACTING WITH PEOPLE IN MY PRIVATE TIME.
I'M ALL RIGHT.
H-He seems kind of mature and a little cool!
Heh...
BEEP
MAFUYU, MAFUYU! LISTEN TO ME FOR A SECOND! I'VE BEEN HOLDING IT IN ALL THIS TIME, BUT DOING THAT IS SOMEWHERE BETWEEN STRESS AND PLEASURE, AND THAT'S KIND OF EXCITING!
PANT
PANT
PANT
SHUT UP!